Explore the World

NELLES

CANADA

ONTARIO, QUÉBEC, ATLANTIC PROVINCES

Authors:
Eva Ambros, Mary Kelly, Eleanor Morris,
Valentin P. Nadezhnikov, David Ravvin,
J.-Martina Schneider, Jonathan D. Siskin,
Carla Straessle-Compton, Deborah Williams

An Up-to-date travel guide with 149 color photos
and 14 maps

Second Revised Edition
1998

IMPRINT / LEGEND

Dear Reader,

Being up-to-date is the main goal of the Nelles series. To achieve it, we have a network of far-flung correspondents who keep us abreast of the latest developments in the travel scene, and our cartographers always make sure that maps and texts are adjusted to each other.

Each travel chapter ends with its own list of useful tips, accommodations, restaurants, tourist offices, sights. At the end of the book you will find practical information from A to Z. But the travel world is fast moving, and we cannot guarantee that all the contents are always valid. Should you come across a discrepancy, please write us at: Nelles Verlag GmbH, Schleissheimer Str. 371 b, D-80935 München, Germany, Tel: (089) 3571940, Fax: (089) 35719430.

LEGEND

	Public or Significant Building
	Hotel
	Shopping Center
O	Market
✝	Church
•	Underground Station
➘	International Airport
➘	National Airport
	National Border
	Provincial Border
Kapuskasing	Place mentioned in Text
✱	Place of Interest
♣	National Park, Provincial Park
\ 25 /	Distance in Kilometers
Mt. Otish 1135	Mountain Summit (Height in Meters)
90	Interstate
	Toll Expressway
	Expressway
	Principal Highway
	Main Road
	Other Road
	Railway
7	Trans-Canada Highway
20	U.S. Highway
14	Route Number

CANADA
Ontario, Québec, Atlantic Provinces
© Nelles Verlag GmbH, D-80935 München
All rights reserved

Second Revised Edition 1998
ISBN 3-88618-089-1
Printed in Slovenia

Publisher:	Günter Nelles
Editor in Chief:	Berthold Schwarz
Project Editors:	Eva Ambros, Valentin P. Nadezhnikov
Editor:	Marton Radkai, Margarete Batt
Photo Editor:	Heinz Vestner
Translation:	Anne Midgette
Cartography:	Nelles Verlag GmbH, München
Color Separation:	Priegnitz, München
Printed by:	Gorenjski Tisk

No part of this book, not even excerpts, may be reproduced without prior permission of Nelles Verlag
- X04 -

TABLE OF CONTENTS

Imprint / Legend 2
Maplist 6

GEOGRAPHY, HISTORY AND PEOPLE

Geography 13
History and People 17
European Colonizers 20
New France 22
British North America 26
The long way to confederation 27
Unity through diversity 31
Who are the Canadians? 35
The "French Fact" 38

TRAVELING IN EASTERN CANADA

TORONTO 49
On the waterfront 50
Downtown Toronto 52
Neighborhoods 57
Excursions 60
INFO: Hotels, Restaurants, Sights 62

OTTAWA 65
Washington of the North 66
Festivals 71
INFO: Hotels, Restaurants, Sights 72

ONTARIO 75
Grey and Bruce Counties 75
Niagara Peninsula 82
Huronia 85
Muskoka 88
Central and Eastern Ontario 93
Northern Ontario 96
INFO: Hotels, Restaurants, Sights 98

MONTRÉAL 103
Vieux Montréal 104
Downtown Montréal 107
Arts and Entertainment 109
The Square Mile 110
Parks 112
INFO: Hotels, Restaurants, Sights 114

TABLE OF CONTENTS

QUÉBEC CITY 119
Haute Ville 121
Basse Ville 126
Québec City Entertains 127
Winter activities / Excursions 128
INFOS: Hotels, Restaurants, Sights 129

QUÉBEC PROVINCE 131
L'Estrie 133
Les Laurentides 141
Along the St. Lawrence 150
INFOS: Hotels, Restaurants, Sights 154

NEW BRUNSWICK 159
Saint John River Valley 159
Fundy Tidal Coast 162
Miramichi Basin 164
The Acadian Coast 164
Restigouche Uplands 166
INFOS: Hotels, Restaurants, Sights 167

NOVA SCOTIA 171
Lighthouse and Evangeline Trails 171
Glooscap Trail 173
Sunrise Trail 174
Cabot Trail 175
Three Cape Breton Trails 177
Marine Drive 178
INFOS: Hotels, Restaurants, Sights 179

HALIFAX 181
INFOS: Hotels, Restaurants, Sights 189

PRINCE EDWARD ISLAND 193
Prince County 194
Queens County 196
Kings Byway Drive 198
INFOS: Hotels, Restaurants, Sights 199

NEWFOUNDLAND AND LABRADOR 203
St. John's 206
Traveling Newfoundland 208
In the Wilderness of Labrador 213
INFOS: Hotels, Restaurants, Sights 215

FEATURES

National Parks 220
Economy 226
Environment 229
Ice Hockey 232
Baffin Island 234
The Cree Way of Life 236

GUIDELINES

Preparations 240
   Climate and Travel Times 240
   Clothing 240
   Customs 240
   Border crossings 241
   Currency 241
   Embassies and Consulates of Canada 241
   Health 241
   Tourist Information 242

Traveling to Canada 242

Traveling in Eastern Canada 243
   Ferries 244

Practical Informations 244
   Accommodations 244
   Automobile club 244
   Auto rentals 245
   Banks 245
   Business hours 245
   Electricity 245
   Embassies and Consulates 245
   Emergencies 246
   Post Offices 246
   Public Holidays 246
   Telecommunications 246
   Time Zones 247
   Tipping 247
   Weights and Measures 247

Québec Special 247
Authors 248
Photographers 249
Index 250

MAPLIST

MAPLIST

Canada 6/7	Estrie / Laurentides 132/133
Toronto. 52/53	Southeastern Québec. 151
Ottawa 67	New Brunswick. 160
Southern Ontario 76/77	Nova Scotia. 172/173
Ontario 96	Halifax. 185
Montréal. 102	Prince Edward Island 195
Québec City 121	Newfoundland / Labrador. . . . 204/205

CANADA

CANADA	0 — 500 km

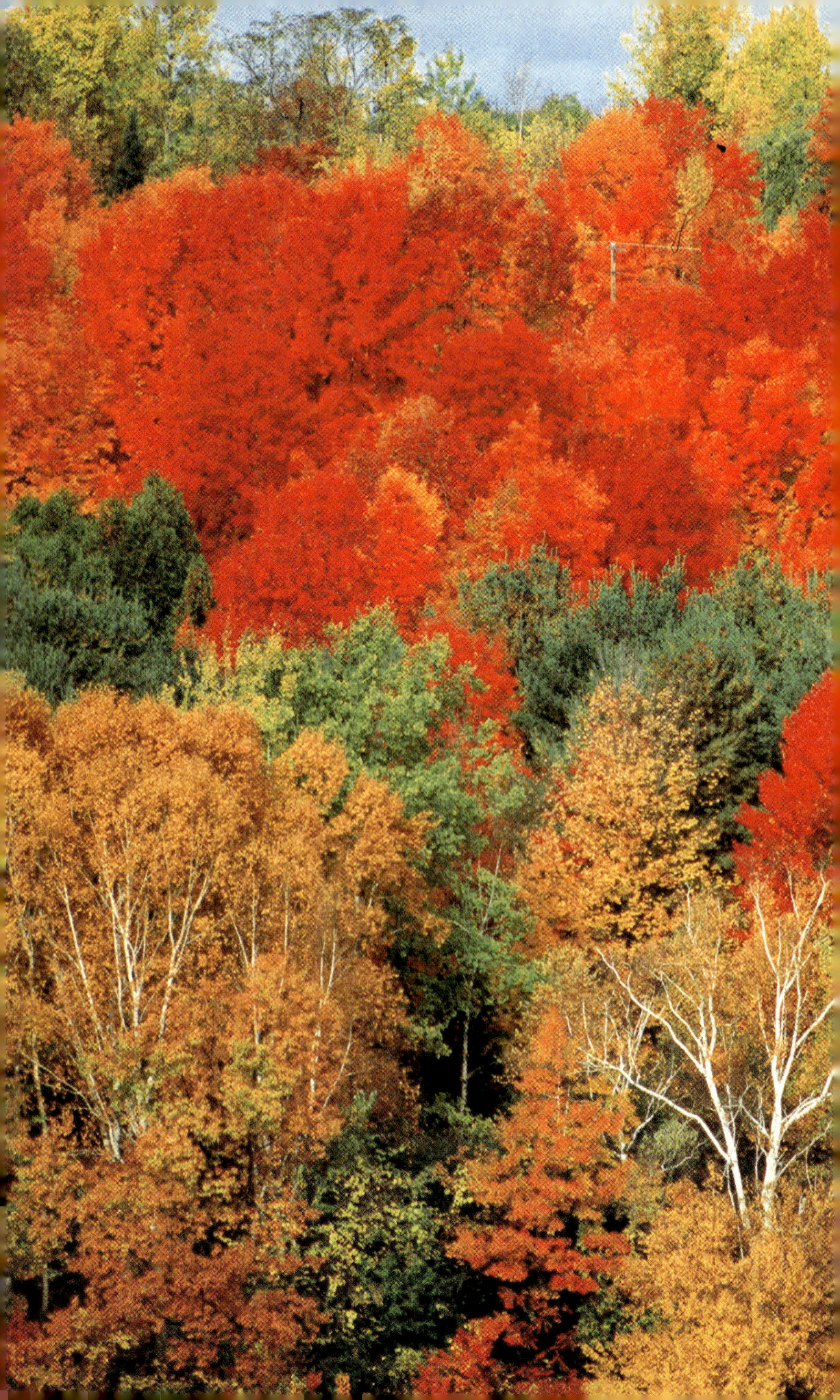

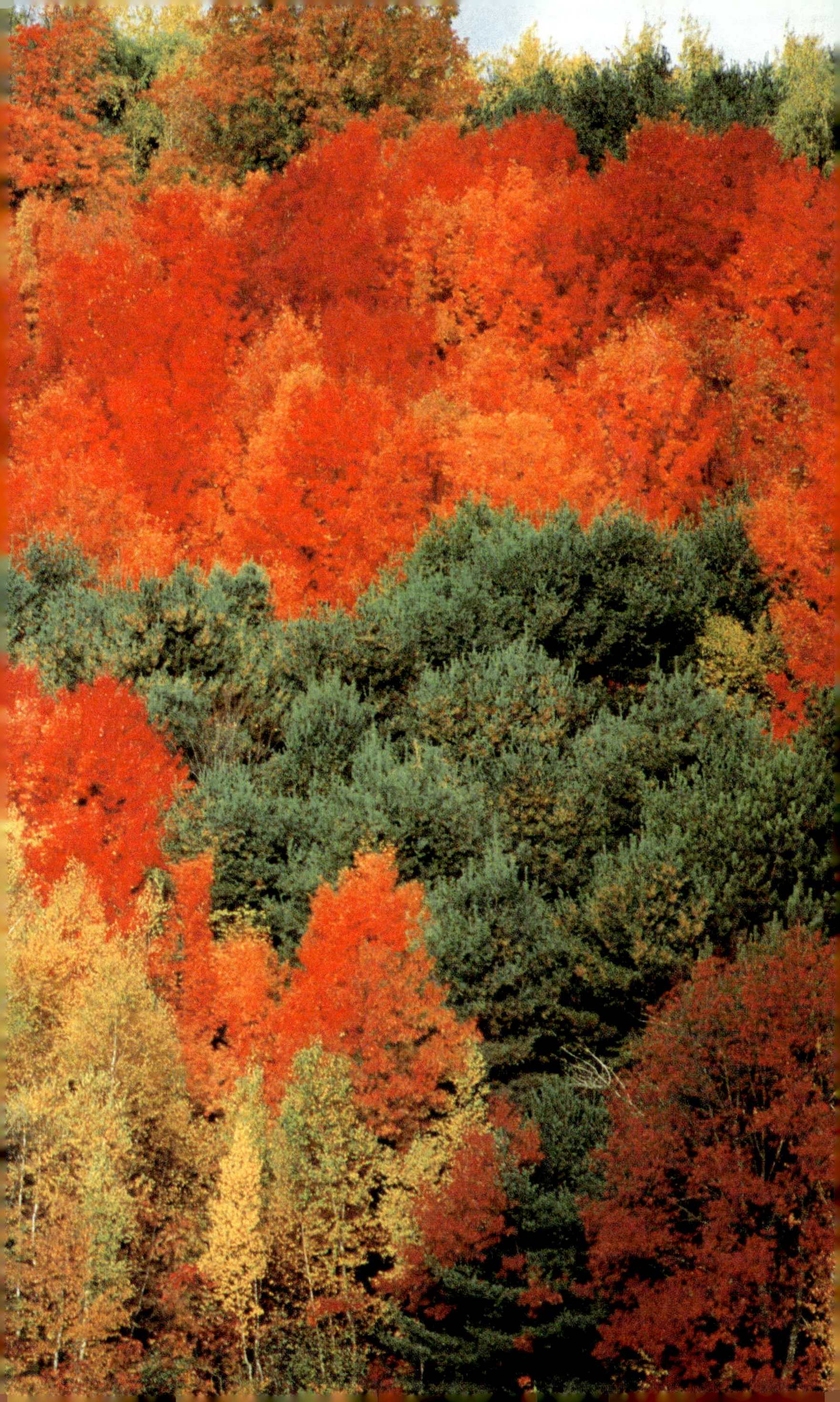

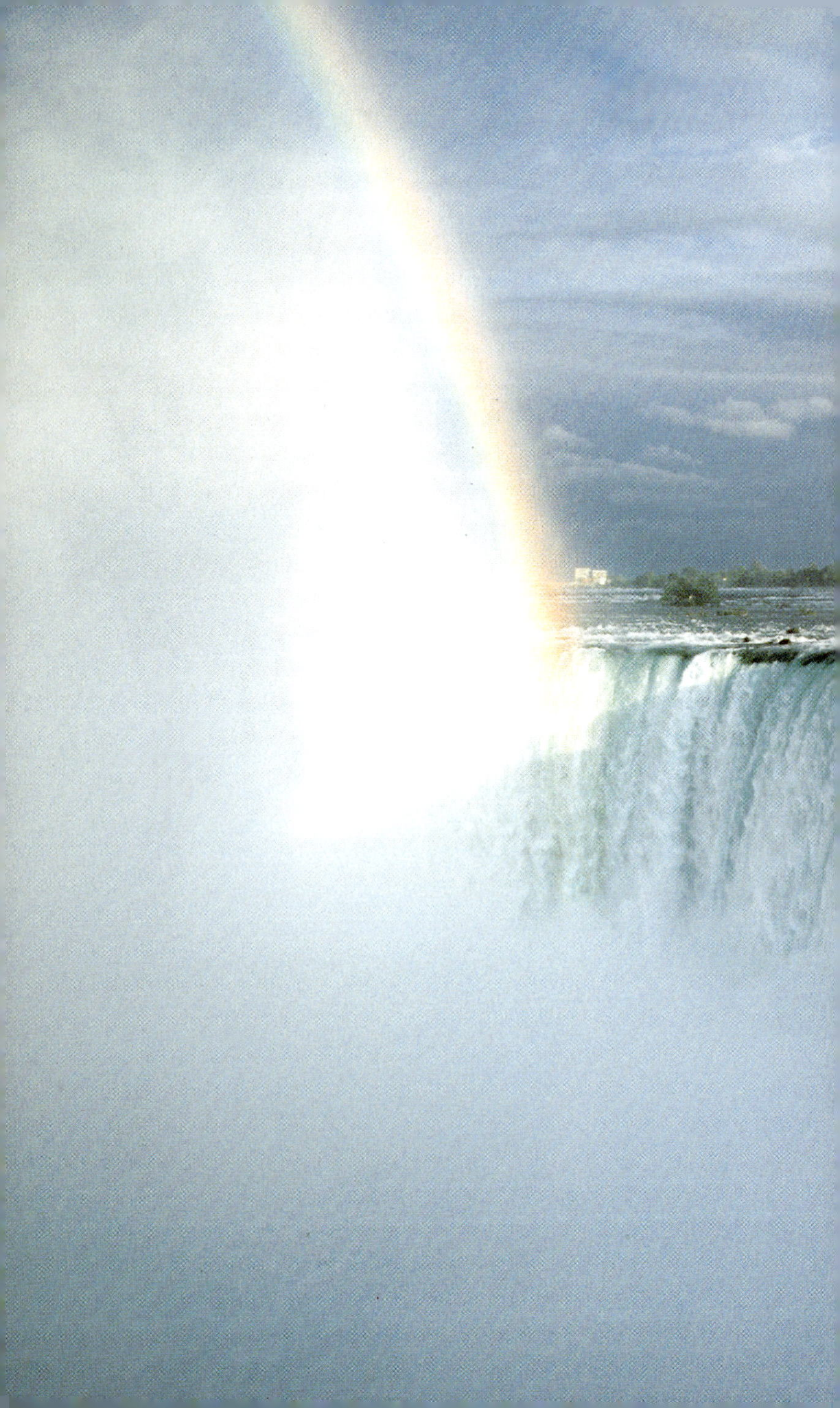

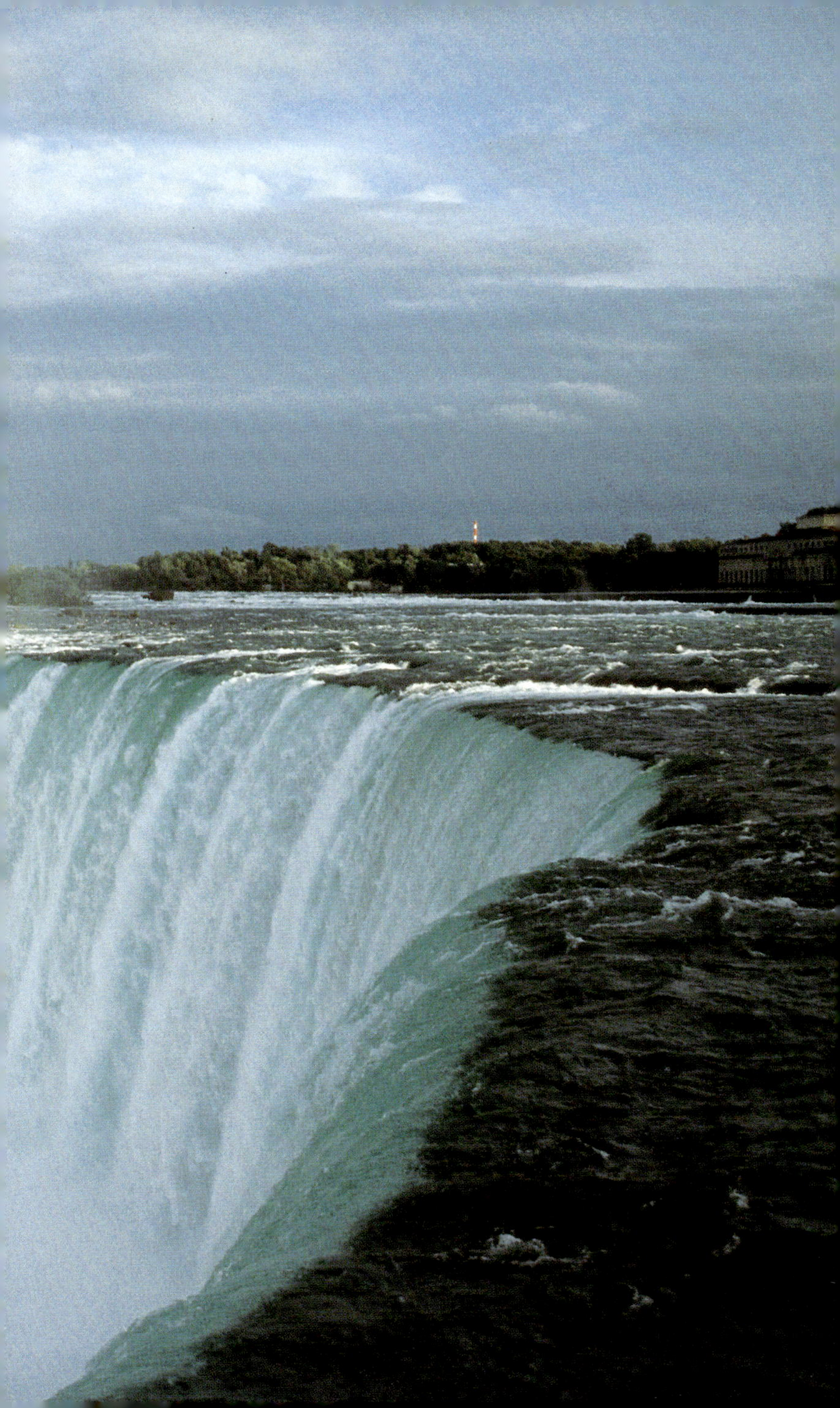

GEOGRAPHY

GEOGRAPHY

Geography is often said to be central to the Canadian imagination. It is perhaps more important to it than to any other country's in at least the Western world. The European pioneers and their Canadian progeny who founded Canada suffered great hardships developing a civilization because of the harshness of the natural environment. Stories of these times have endured as cultural myths, and some Canadians, such as writer Robertson Davies, have suggested that Canada retains today a "loser's" mentality because of its historical memory of brutal struggles waged against an indomitable, unforgiving northern landscape and climate. Canadian novelist Margaret Atwood has pointed out that, while the American Frontier was perceived enthusiastically as a site of spiritual renewal by its new settlers, Canadians saw their challenge as something simply to be survived – hushed endurance, surely not self-laudatory triumph, was the only thing.

But this picture of the self-pitying Canadian staving off hypothermia in a storm-beaten old shack in-the-middle-of-nowhere- warm is too one-sided. Canadians did conquer and civilize this northern landscape, or at least the bottom southernmost quarter of it. And there is a feeling of national pride which accompanies this accomplishment (and hopefully a feeling of deep regret over the destruction this accomplishment brought to the human cultures already here). Another, more positive, tendency exists in the Canadian imagination: one which sees itself as somehow morally strong be-cause of its undeniable affinity with the wilderness, and because of its ongoing, honest struggle with at least the harsh climate which early settlers faced.

Most of eastern Canada (and all of Western Canada) lies north of the 49th parallel, where the northernmost states of America extend to. The greatest majority of Eastern Canada's, and over half of Canada's population, however, lives south of the 49th in the industrialized Great Lakes/St. Lawrence River area of Ontario and Québec which borders, from west to east, the states of Michigan, New York and Maine. To the north Canada's arctic islands extend almost all the way to the north pole. This area divides up into four major physiographic regions which are based on the distinct features of the land, air, water and vegetation of a given area. The four are the Canadian Shield, the Great Lakes-St. Lawrence Lowlands, the Atlantic or Appalachian region, and the Arctic.

The Canadian Shield covers almost half of mainland Canada. In eastern Canada it extends as a semi-circle through virtually all of Ontario, Québec, and Labrador, with the exceptions of the southernmost Great Lakes and St. Lawrence Lowlands area in Ontario and Québec and of the Hudson Bay Lowlands, a slice of land south of the Hudson Bay. The Shield consists of very old, hard, exposed, crystalline Pre-Cambrian rock, which developed between 3.5 and 1 billion years ago. The semi-circular shape of the Shield is often called saucer-shaped because its south, east, and northeast sides are all raised, either as fold mountains or as plateaus. The Shield rises highest in the Laurentides and Laurentian hills north of the St. Lawrence River in Québec or in the imposing mountains of Northern Labrador.

The land itself is quite beautiful. The region is covered by thousands of diverse lakes which are surrounded by rocky, wooded hills. Protrusions of bare granite

Preceding pages: A burst of color: Canada's Indian Summer. Niagara Falls. Left: Landscape in Québec.

GEOGRAPHY

are everywhere, whether on top of cliffs or jutting out of river beds. There are also great stretches of forest, covering thousands of square miles of area with tall cedar, spruce, jack pine, and aspen trees.

The climate in the Canadian Shield is predominately continental but varies greatly depending on location. The farther north you are, of course, the colder it can get. But more than bearable temperatures can certainly be found in the region. Sudbury, for instance, which is on the southern tip of the Shield, enjoys pleasant summer highs of 24°C. The farther east you are the more precipitation falls, while in general precipitation is relatively uniform. Sudbury receives eight inches of rain in both summer and winter.

The Great Lakes-St. Lawrence Lowlands region marks the southern termination of the Canadian Shield. This region is often called the "heartland" of Canada because its hospitable agricultural landscape has created the country's largest urban centers (Toronto and Montréal), and its most productive manufacturing industries. It is generally divided into the two halves of Southern Ontario and Southern Québec.

Southern Ontario, which borders Great Lakes Huron, Erie, and Ontario, is dominated by rolling agricultural landscape. Good soil and a warm, moderate climate have made this excellent farming territory. The landscape, when it isn't urban, is dominated by large, well-maintained farmhouses, barns, rectangular crop fields, and, of course, the farm animals which reside on these farms. The countryside tends to be flattest in the southern portion of the region and becomes hillier the farther north you travel. The most striking feature of Southern Ontario is the Niagara Escarpment, a broad limestone ridge extending from the tip of the Bruce Peninsula in the Georgian Bay all the way

Above: Lonely bay on Cape Bon Ami on the Gaspé. Right: Taureau Reservoir, north of Montréal.

GEOGRAPHY

down to the Niagara Falls on the border of the State of New York.

If Southern Ontario is rolling countryside, Southern Québec, when it isn't urban, is flat but angular land. A description of idyllic farmland applies to southern Québec as much as to southern Ontario, but marine waters and glaciers have cut sharply defined terraces into this landscape. Steep hills are common, as are ravines and river valleys. Many areas are in fact to steep for cultivation while others are to flat for proper drainage.

The climate in the Great Lakes-St. Lawrence Lowlands, being hundreds of miles from the ocean, is continental. The entire area receives, in a relatively uniform pattern, 30-40 inches per year. Temperatures in the Ontario area are generally warmer than those in Québec. Summers highs in Toronto are 27°C and slightly cooler in Montréal. Summers in this region can be very humid especially in cities.

Appalachia consists of the Atlantic provinces of New Brunswick, Newfoundland, Prince Edward Island, and Nova Scotia. To this is added the Gaspé Peninsula of southeastern Québec, which, bordering New Brunswick, has much in common with the landscape of the Atlantic provinces. Of the four maritime provinces New Brunswick is the only one which is in its entirety part of the Canadian mainland. (Nova Scotia is attached to the mainland by only a narrow land-lock at the Bay of Fundy and the separate Labrador region of Newfoundland directly borders Québec.) The Atlantic provinces tend to suffer from high unemployment, and depend on transfer payments from the wealthier provinces.

Appalachia possesses a diversity of physical environments and a noticeable absence of large liveable areas. As a result, there are no large centers and only a few mid-sized centers. In general the landscape is a jumble of rugged uplands and lowlands, created by tectonic movement millions of years ago. The Appalachians reach up to 4100 feet (1399 m) but highlands drop to beneath 3000 feet (950 m) in New Brunswick and Newfoundland.

New Brunswick terrain is rugged in the north and south, but blessed with lovely terraces and hillsides in the middle of the province. Prince Edward Island is relatively flat, built out of flat red shale rather than folded rock. As with Nova Scotia rivers have cut valleys through its terrain. Nova Scotia, however is dominated by rocky, tree covered hills. Newfoundland is covered by rugged hills with a few lakes, swamps or pastures between.

The Atlantic provinces are famous for their coastal fog. This is caused, throughout the year, by the meeting of the cold Labrador current with warm air over the Gulf Stream. Temperatures never get to cold or too warm here, with summer highs in Halifax of 23°C and winter lows of -7°C. Precipitation on the east coast is exceeded in Canada only on its west coast. The Maritimes receive approximately 39 (1 m) inches of rain a year.

HISTORY AND PEOPLE

HISTORY AND PEOPLE

For decades now, scientists from a variety of schools have sought to solve the mystery of who were the first inhabitants of the American continent, where did they come from and above all at what point in time did they arrive. Their research spawned a great number of controversial theories that frequently had to be rejected in the light of new evidence. Dates were shifted about in increments of millenia, new races were created to explain the unknowns, in short, it constituted the daily bread of the researcher, and rather than enlighten the layperson, it only brought about more confusion. In the meantime the newest finds at excavation sites have given the great puzzle new contours and a relatively consistent picture has begun to emerge. Establishing a time frame is still a divisive issue among archeologists. The differences of opinion vary by 35,000 years, and there is some doubt regarding the reliability of the carbon 14 tests. If the latter are accurate, however, then the history of the settlement of the American continent looks as follows:

The entire continent was a natural paradise about 50,000 years ago, without the slightest trace of *homo sapiens*, who at that time lived beyond the seas, in Asia, Europe and Africa. During the last Ice Age the sea level dropped so low that a natural bridge almost 1000 miles wide in part appeared between Siberia and Alaska, where the Bering Strait is today. It gave giant herds access to the American continent, and in their wake came the hunters, the ancestors of the Indians. They originated in Central and Eastern Asia, but were not members of the Mongolide tribes, as these only developed later in that area. These nomadic groups known as "Indianides" gradually spread throughout the entire American continent, while new tribes kept pouring – or maybe only seeping – in through the Alaskan bridgehead. Only little can be determined about the size and make-up of these groups. Little is known, too, about the way of life of these early hunters. One thing is sure, however, and that is, that some time between 13,000 and 20,000 years ago, the freezing of the great continental glacier in inexorable southward direction blocked the road for the new "immigrants," leaving them stranded in the northwestern part of the continent.

Besides the Indianides, the ancestors of the Eskimos also appeared. They reached the Alaskan peninsula around 15,000-10,000 years ago, and penetrated the entire area of modern Canada as far as Greenland. Some 10,000 years ago the Ice Age thawed, flooding the Bering Strait and cutting off any retreat.

The Inuit

While the Indians were expanding throughout the continent, reaching the southern tip of the Tierra del Fuego about 11,000 years ago, the Eskimos were making the Arctic their domain. Their life rhythm followed the Arctic seasons and animal life, for they survived from cariboo and seal hunting and fishing. Nowadays the Eskimos call themselves *Inuit*, which means "people," a term that is accepted and used throughout Canada. The word Eskimo comes from the Indian and means "eaters of raw meat," which many consider something of an insult.

The Inuit are classic Mongols, a fact that is obvious from the characteristic epicanthic fold of their eyelids. The oldest known Inuit culture is the so-called Pre-Dorset culture (approximately AD 2000-1000), a collective term referring to

Left: The high altar in the basilica Notre-Dame of Montréal.

HISTORY AND PEOPLE

a group of regional related cultures that left finely decorated stone tools and other smaller artifacts to posterity (hence the oft-used denomination: Small Tool Culture). Another known fact now is that the Inuit of that period used canoes of leather and bone to go hunting seals. The Dorset Culture, named after Dorset Cape on Baffin Island, began around AD 1000. Traces of this culture have been found as far south as Newfoundland. The Dorset Inuit developed entirely new methods of hunting from the edge of the ice, and they probably built small sleds. Their houses were of stone and turf and sunken into the ground. They were heated with large oil lamps that also served as cookers. Of particular interest were the stone, walrus-tooth or bone statuettes representing people or animals that along with drums and masks demonstrate the practice of advanced shamanistic rituals.

Above: The Inuit, caught between tradition and modern times. Right: You can buy Algonquin clothing in souvenir shops.

Thule Culture spread from Alaska over all of northern Canada all the way to Thule in Greenland from about AD 1000 onward. The igloo, a domicile built of snow, and the dog sleds, which we consider so typical of Inuit culture, date to this period. Whereby the igloo was hardly known to all Inuit. Only those of Labrador and west of Hudson Bay built them as winter housing. In other areas they were used as hunting "lodges."

The appearance of Europeans in the Canadian Arctic and the discovery of Hudson Bay in 1610 portended the end of the Thule Culture. Contact with European civilization, often lethal for the Inuit, brought about a profound change in the independent cultures of North America, especially after about 1750.

The Indians

As opposed to the Inuit, the Indians of North America represented a veritable kaleidoscope of peoples whom scientists categorized according to their linguistic

HISTORY AND PEOPLE

characteristics. This method, however, did not do justice to the cultural spectrum within one linguistic family, nor to the sheer variety of Indian languages. There are in fact no less than 19 linguistic roots with over 100 separate languages and numerous dialects. Furthermore, the members of some of the linguistic groups lived quite far from one another and had reached differing levels of civilization. Thus while some still carried on as nomadic gatherers and hunters, others had already settled down and were going about the business of farming. Ordering these tribes according to racial or purely geographical aspects proved futile after a while. Nowadays they are categorized into large cultural areas that cover the entire North American continent without regard for the political borders of more recent times. These cultural domains consist of areas where comparable civilizations developed under similar living conditions.

The northernmost of these cultural regions is the Arctic, the realm of the (non-Indian) Inuit and their related Aleuts. The next area is the neighboring sub-Arctic to the south, a gigantic belt that runs all the way to Newfoundland and lies almost exclusively in Canada. This huge land of forests was (and to a certain extent still is) the home of the Athabaska- and Algonquin-speaking Indians. They lived from hunting (caribou, bison, bears) and fishing, and from seal-hunting, when living by the sea. Besides skins and pelts, their most important all-purpose material was birch bark, which they used to build tents, canoes, sleds and even vessels in which they cooked using hot stones.

The Beothuk of Newfoundland, who also belonged to the Algonquin family, are thought to be the first Indians to make contact with the white man. Presumably the first were the Vikings, who arrived around the end of the 10th century and settled there for a short period. In the 15th century, Giovanni Caboto landed on Newfoundland shortly after Columbus' discovery of America. His report describing how the Beothuks painted their bodies red, which gave rise to the term "redskin" for the Indians in general. By the beginning of the 19th century the Beothuks no longer existed. Slave traders, inimical merchants from any number of European nations, Christian Micmac Indians, whom the French had settled in Newfoundland and last but not least smallpox had gotten the better of them.

The eastern forest land, an area in southeastern Canada extending from the Great Lakes to the Atlantic Ocean and divided in the middle by the Appalachians, was mainly settled by members of the Iroquois and the Algonquin, who had moved southward from Hudson Bay. The erstwhile densely forested area whose lakes were well supplied in fish, was ideal for settlement, and provided the basis for an organized tribal structure and agriculture. The Iroquois, who are remembered nowadays for their unusual hair-dos, came from the southern part of

HISTORY AND PEOPLE

the American continent to establish themselves around Lakes Erie and Ontario and in the lowlands around the St. Lawrence. They were by no means an isolated, homogenous tribe, but rather members of a much larger Iroquois-speaking community that numbered a host of tribes with many names. Since the creation of the still extant Iroquois Federation in the 15th or 16th century, only the founding tribes were referred to as Iroquois. The so-called Five Nations, consisting of the Onondaga, Mohawk, Oneida, Seneca and Cayuga, invited a sixth tribe, the Tuscarora to join in 1715. Their most implacable enemies were also Iroquois-speaking, the neighboring Hurons. In order to pursue their continuous feuds and wars, the Hurons sought alliances with other poeples, but they never achieved the size and power of the Iroquois federation.

Above: "Death of Hiawatha, the last chief of the Iroquois." Right: The first Vikings landed in Newfoundland in the 10th century.

The Iroquois lived in villages that had up to 100 long houses, in which several families lived, something typical for Southeast Asia, by the way. They were built of wood and bark. The Indians hunted and fished, but their main livelihood came from rather advanced agriculture. They cultivated corn, beans, squashes and sunflowers, and kept large apple, peach and pear orchards. In other fields they grew tobacco for their religious ceremonies. Land and the harvest belonged to the women. The tribes were organized in a matrilinear system, where women had the last word – even indirectly in the Great Council of the Federation whose chiefs were chosen by the Iroquois women.

Iroquois men cleared the fields, went hunting and cared for the defense of the villages, and they were known for their gruesome torture methods that many a white settler became acquainted with. But in the end it was the Europeans who signalled the end of the Iroquois.

EUROPEAN COLONIZERS

The first explorers from Europe are believed to have been the Vikings, Norsemen who as early as the 10th century sailed across the Atlantic Ocean to sight the American coast. They even established a small settlement named *Vinland* near L'Anse-aux-Meadows (Newfoundland), but they were soon chased away by the local Beothuks. Yet even though they never succeeded in getting a firm foothold, the Vikings kept returning to Labrador, Newfoundland, and probably even Nova Scotia right up until the 14th century to trade in covetted wood. The next European to land on Canadian soil was the Genovese Giovanni Caboto (John Cabot), who was working for the British Crown. In 1497 he discovered the eastern coast of Newfoundland, and later landed on Cape Breton Island, the northern tip of what is now Nova Scotia. Cabot also ran across the fishing banks off Newfoundland, and Portuguese fishermen were wintering in Ingonish, Nova Scotia, as early as the 1520s.

Other Europeans also began coming to Canada in the 16th century. The shores of the Bay of Fundy were explored in the 1520s, and in 1534 Jacques Cartier, landing on the coast of the Gaspé Peninsula, claimed the land for Francis I of France. The following year he explored the region along the St. Lawrence all the way to where Montréal is today. The name *Canada* was first used in 1556 in Cartier's account of his voyage, and several myths attempt to account for its origin. However, the most plausible etymology of the name is in the Iroquois word *kannata*, pronounced Cannada and meaning "settlement" or "group of villages."

Both the Algonquin and the Huron-Iroquois had extensive contact with the Europeans arriving in the early 16th century and were influenced by European culture. They were eager for European metal knives and hatchets and Europeans were eager for furs; beaver hats became all the rage in the Old World. France offered fur monopolies to traders on condition that they began colonies, but most failed to honor the agreement. Consequently, it was not until the 17th century that European settlements began.

In 1603 Samuel de Champlain, known as the Father of Canada, sailed up the St. Lawrence River in the interests of fur-trading monopolies. He returned in 1604 with two ships led by the Sieur de Monts, who set sail from France with 79 people aboard under orders to form a trading company and a settlement to be called Acadia. To escape the cold winters in the St. Lawrence Valley, they settled for the winter on a small island further south, located in the Bay of Fundy (which they named La Baie Française). It proved a disaster. There was no fresh water on the island, they could plant no crops in the sandy topsoil, and the men became ill and died from scurvy, a then-unknown disease but which they correctly suspected was caused by their diet of salted meat,

HISTORY AND PEOPLE

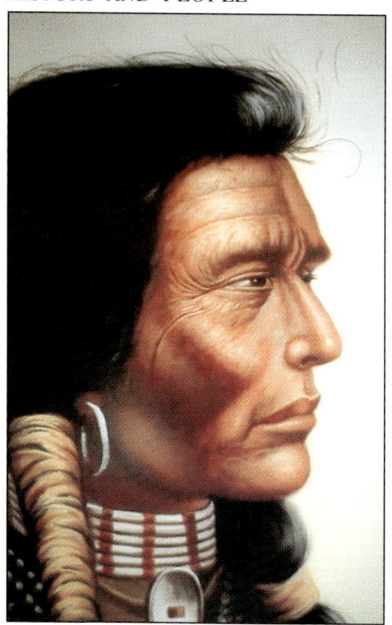

fish, oatmeal and biscuits. When winter came early, trees needed for a windbreak were cut for fuel, huge chunks of ice made the surrounding water dangerous and they were trapped on the island until the spring thaw. But tempting as it was to return to France, the survivors decided to load everything on their ships and moved across the bay to a place they named Port Royal. It was the first permanent French colony in America. Soon fur traders and merchants set up trading posts in Acadia, by that time composed of half of what is now Nova Scotia plus a small section in New Brunswick directly across the bay from Port Royal. These trading posts, sending as many as 3000 beaver, moose and otter skins home to France, kept the settlement in Acadia growing.

Champlain, however, was mainly interested in exploring the land. In 1608 he once again sailed up the St. Lawrence and established a post on the spot where Québec is today. From there he took off on two further expeditions inland in 1613 and 1615, still entertaining the dim hope of finding the coast of the Chinese Sea. France's great dream was to discover a northwest passage to the Pacific. After all, the Spaniard Vasco Nuñez de Balboa had already explored Panama in 1513, and Fernâo de Magelhâes, better known as Magellan, had already reached the Philippines in 1520 through the straits (later named after him) in the southern part of the continent.

NEW FRANCE

Champlain did his best to fulfill the wishes of his superiors and colonize the country. Jesuit and Franciscan missionaries came to spread Christianity among the Indians in Acadia and Québec as early as 1615. They sent glowing reports of the plentiful land in Acadia back to France and farmers were encouraged to emigrate. With hard work, they were told, they could make a better life for

Above left: Mohawk Indian. Above right: Samuel de Champlain, the "Father of Canada."

themselves in the new land than in France. But the only people eager to leave France were the Huguenots, and as Protestants they were excluded from New France.

But despite the efforts to develop Canada as a colony, the population, even with the addition of new arrivals during the 17th century, grew too slowly to insure the solidity of this foothold in the New World. Cardinal Richelieu, chief minister of France, founded the Company of New France in 1627. As an incentive, large plots of land were offered by the crown, but only for the purpose of clearing fields for planting and bringing settlers to cultivate the land. Land thus granted was called a *seigneurie* and the landowner was known as a *seigneur*. A total of 34 of them were granted in what is now New Brunswick.

Not too many Frenchmen were attracted to Acadia, however, until the seigneurs began to permit their *habitants*, as they were called, to combine fur trading and fishing with farming. Even so, the *habitants* were held subject to the seigneurs, who ruled the land like lords. In 1681, one Richard Denys, writing about his father's *habitants* at his seigneurie on the Miramichi River, reported that there were 72 French residents living on the land. Because his father treated them well, allowing them to marry, most of them had no desire to leave, and 14 or 15 more men were expected to arrive in the new year. But other seigneurs were not so liberal and there were many men who defected. Life in the wilderness gave French peasants who crossed the Atlantic a sense of freedom totally alien at that time to France, and with liberty beckoning through the forest and along the waterways, not many were content to continue to be ruled by feudal lords. Many a man chose to take to the woods and lead the free life of a *coureur des bois* (in English "woods runners"), or a *voyageur*, literally "traveller." As trappers and fur traders, they explored the forests and streams of North America. They sometimes even married Indian woman and became members of a tribal community.

Indian Wars

In 1535, while at the mouth of the Saguenay near Tadoussac, Jacques Cartier had already come across Indians of the Algonquin linguistic family that Champlain later named the *Montagnais*. Their tribal territories consisted of a richly endowed landscape of forests and rivers, and Tadoussac was an important trading center for all local tribes. The Montagnais of Tadoussac, however, were intent on being the only ones to do business with the white traders, and to achieve this, they established a kind of wholesale monopoly that excluded all direct trade between the French and the other tribes. Pelts and hides were exchanged for weapons, knives, cauldrons, cloth and pearls. The Montagnais made substantial profits, and Tadoussac soon developed into one of the most important trading centers of sub-Arctic Canada.

During one of the tribal conflicts brought about by the lucrative fur business, the French decided to ally themselves with their Indian partners. In 1609 Champlain joined the Algonkians on the warpath against the Mohawks, who were from the powerful Iroquois group. This formed the basis of the New France alliance first with the Algonkians and later with the Hurons.

In Champlain's days, the Hurons lived in along Lake Erie and Lake Huron, an area known for its beavers and other pelt animals. During his second inland trip in 1615, Champlain spent a winter with them and besides establishing good trade relations, he also helped in the war against the Onondaga Iroquois. Enmities between the Iroquois on the one hand and the Huron and Algonkian tribes on the other were not caused by the arrival of the European fur dealers, but the increased demand for pelts did exacerbate the Indian tensions over hunting grounds to the point of all out war. The Iroquois' first white allies were the Dutch, who had settled in what is today New York State in the early 17th century. They traded with the Iroquois from their Fort Orange post on the upper Hudson, and delivered a substantial number of weapons. The closer the alliance between the French and the Hurons, the more violent the assaults by the Iroquois. They repeatedly attacked the Jesuit outposts that had especially proliferated between 1632 and 1662. Montréal alone withstood no less than 20 Iroquois assaults. Under extreme pressure, the French finally appealed for additional help from King Louis XIV. In 1663 he declared New France (which to date was still ruled by the French trading company of the "Hundred Partners") a royal province and sent a military force which defeated the Iroquois and reestablished peace. 3000 settlers followed in its wake, and New France experienced an economic upswing. The most lethal enemy, however, had already appeared on the scene.

War with England

Since 1664, when the English had taken the colony of New Netherlands from the Dutch, New York traders had supported the Iroquois. In the meantime little had happened to change the status quo. The British, who were far better at the colonization game than their French rivals, coveted Acadia with its fishing grounds, which they had captured in 1613 and again in 1654, only to cede them them back to France most unwillingly after the Peace of Breda in 1667.

Right: Port Royal Habitation from 1605, the oldest European settlement north of Florida.

The Anglo-French rivalry over territorial claims in the New World intensified with the creation of the Hudson Bay Company in 1670. This English trading company, which was soon to grow into the most powerful mercantile enterprise in the world of that time, arrogated exclusive rights to the gigantic area along the rivers that flowed into the Hudson Bay. French settlers in the lowlands of the St. Lawrence were caught between the Hudson Bay Company in the north and the Iroquois in the south. It was a volatile situation that ultimately broke out into open war between the two colonial powers supported by their respective native allies in 1689.

The war ended in 1697 with the Treaty of Ryswick, which gave to France Hudson Bay as well as its former possessions, with the exception of Newfoundland. In 1700 peace was made between the Iroquois and New France and its Indian allies. New France seemed finally well on its way to achieving stability and fortune. But this was not destined to last. In 1701 the War of Spanish Succession broke out in Europe, and it was the English and their American colonists, not New France, who profited at the end of that conflict. The treaty of Utrecht enabled them to recover the much-coveted Hudson Bay, to limit French rights in Newfoundland, to force the cession of Acadia from New France (except Cape Breton Island) and to get a better foothold on the lucrative fur trade.

Nevertheless, 30 years of peace followed, which the French used to build the great fortress of Louisbourg on Cape Breton to protect the entrance of the St. Lawrence. The colony again prospered, with the population growing to 42,000 in 1744. In Europe, in 1741, the War of Austrian Succession broke out, with France and England on opposing sides of the battlefield. New Englanders felt free to attack Louisbourg on Cape Breton Island, capturing and holding it until the

HISTORY AND PEOPLE

treaty of Aix-la-Chapelle ostensibly brought peace once more in 1748. But to the New Englanders it was not peace, merely a truce. The two colonial powers once again fell out over territorial claims, this time over the Ohio Valley, which offered excellent prospects for the fur trade. An English force, under the leadership of George Washington clashed with a french force in 1754 and lost. It fired up what came to be known as the French and Indian War, which would ultimately kindle the Seven Years' War between France and England in Europe. In Nova Scotia, Acadians who refused to swear allegiance to the British crown were deported, beginning one of the saddest chapters in Canadian history immortialized in the poem *Evangeline* by the American poet Henry Wadsworth Longfellow. Charged with inciting the Indians against the British and being dangerous to the peace and safety of British Acadia, 6000 were exiled, some to Louisiana (still a French possession at the time), some to French possessions in the Caribbean, others to France, and for all intents and purposes they disappeared from the life of the Atlantic region.

But there were some who, loathe to leave the land they had worked so hard for and loved, went into hiding in New Brunswick; others went up the river to Québec or ran away into the woods. The Seven Years' War influenced developments in the New World and settled once and for all the fate of New France. For two years French troops and Canadian militia managed to be victorious, but British and American strength, fortified by British sea power, turned the tide. In 1758 Louisbourg fell; in 1759 Wolfe captured Québec; and in 1760 Montréal and all New France surrendered. With the treaty of Paris in 1763 ending the European war, all of New France east of the Mississippi was ceded to Great Britain. Nothing was left to New France except two little islands, St. Pierre and Miquelon near Newfoundland, and the fishing rights there. All French Canadians now became British subjects.

HISTORY AND PEOPLE

BRITISH NORTH AMERICA

An influx of New Englanders was expected in Québec as a result of the treaty of Paris, and the proclamation of 1763 promised them a government comparable to the rest of the British colonies. But instead, the New Englanders went to Nova Scotia, eager to take over lands confiscated from the Acadians when they were deported in 1755. As a result, British policy in Québec changed. The "Québec Act" passed in 1774 restored French civil law and allowed it to exist alongside English criminal law. French became the second official language, Catholicism was legally recognized and Catholics were allowed to hold public office.

While the act of 1774 placated the French Canadians, it angered the American colonies to the south because it included as part of the province of Québec the entire territory France had claimed south to the Ohio River and west to the Mississippi. This added oil to the fire of the American movement for independence. In 1775 an unsuccessful invasion of Québec was begun. After the American Revolution of 1776, the treaty of Versailles gave Nova Scotia, Newfoundland and Canada (without the Ohio Valley and the land east of the Mississippi, which would become Michigan) to what was now to be called British North America.

New Englanders loyal to the British Crown, refugees from the American Revolution of 1776, now swarmed into British North America. Opposing the Revolution had cost them their homes and their land as the 13 British colonies to the south became the United States of America. The immigration swelled the population by more than 40,000. This wave of refugees brought about a reorganization of the British colonies, with Nova Scotia divided into two provinces, and the area on the mainland across the peninsula be-

Above: A 300-year-old cannon in Fort Henry, near Kingston. Right: Fort Louisbourg, Nova Scotia.

coming New Brunswick. Then the entire area was divided into Upper Canada (almost entirely English, the present Ontario) and Lower Canada (almost wholly French, the present Québec).

Annexation by the USA?

Europe's wars had created a demand for lumber from the New World and the colonies prospered in peace until the next European wars: the French Revolution and the Napoleonic Wars. The French blockade of Great Britain during these conflicts, suggested to the Americans an opportunity to "liberate" Canada from Britain as they had been liberated. What could be more desirable for Canada than being annexed to the United States? But the Canadians viewed this with alarm. To them it became a war of defense against what they regarded as a threatened invasion by the United States. They, in turn, were quick to seize upon it as an opportunity to try to regain the lost lands of the west.

Both sides claimed victory in this War of 1812 but in truth the war ended with a stalemate. In 1814, the Treaty of Ghent put things back where they were at the beginning. It took the Convention of 1818 to peacefully partition the continent. The Canadian-American boundary was extended from the Lake of the Woods to the Rocky Mountains, and the Oregon territory west of the mountains was to be occupied jointly for ten years.

On the Way to the Confederation

The long years of war, combined with the problems of survival in small communities in the wilderness, had precluded any sort of political life in French Canada. It was not until the first newspaper in French, *Le Canadien*, begun in 1806, that some controversy arose in Lower Canada. But it was not until 1820, when large immigration from the British Isles began, that political agitation to change governments began in the two Canadas and the other colonies. Unrest in Upper and Lower Canada finally convinced the government in England of the necessity of introducing reforms. None were successful, but an English statesman, Lord Durham, was sent out as governor general to investigate the cause of the rebellions and to make recommendations. Guided by the false impression that the French Canadians, once swamped by English immigration, could be quickly and quietly assimilated into the English population, he recommended that the two Canadas be reunited. He also suggested that the colonies have responsible self-government in local matters. The British government acted upon the first part of Durham's advice and by an act of parliament in 1840 united Lower Canada and Upper Canada into Canada East and Canada West.

In 1848 British North American legislatures began to remodel their laws and institutions. Seigneurial tenure was abolished, church and state separated, the French Code Civil, a Napoleonic institution, was codified, primogeniture was stricken from the inheritance laws, public education was instituted, the legislative council of Canada was made elective, and French became the official language in Québec.

For several years a proposal had been before the Canadian parliament to merge all of British North America, including the northwest, into a confederation. The huge continent developing west of the Maritime provinces was agitating for just such a union of the two. But Nova Scotia, New Brunswick, Prince Edward Isle and Newfoundland wanted their own Atlantic Union, not a union with the northwest. By the 1860s they had become prosperous as never before, thanks to fisheries, lumber, farm produce and shipping. It was the heyday of the clipper ship, the Golden Age of the Maritime provinces and they refused to budge for fear of losing their property.

Since the four colonies of the Maritime Provinces, often called today by the newer term of Atlantic Provinces, had such a long history of separate and satisfactory development before coming into union with Canada, the deadlock over the confederation issue was not resolved until the Québec Conference in 1867, when the two colonies of Nova Scotia and New Brunswick united federally with Québec and Ontario under the name of Canada.

What caused Nova Scotia and New Brunswick to change their minds? Until recent times the focus of the Atlantic region was the sea, with fishing, timber, shipbuilding and trade as the principal sources of economic growth. But eventually it occurred to the Maritimes that union with Canada would offer the advantages of a railway link with the attendant opportunity of combining the economy of the Maritimes with the wealth of central Canada. The Intercolonial Railway, completed in 1876, joined railways in Nova Scotia and New Brunswick at Rivière du Loup with the Grand Trunk Railway in the St. Lawrence Valley, spurring the development of Canada's winter ports on the Atlantic and funneling Maritime products to central Canada.

Consequently, on July 1, 1867, the provinces of Québec, Ontario, New Brunswick and Nova Scotia, with the blessings of England, joined together to form the Dominion of Canada as essentially a self-governing country. By 1873, the huge territory of the erstwhile Hudson Bay Company, which stretched from Labrador all the way to the Rocky mountains, British Columbia, Manitoba and Prince Edward Island joined up with the four founding provinces. Newfoundland only joined the Canadian union in 1949, and July 1 became Canada's national holiday number one.

Right: The pioneer days of railway travel. Photo in Huronian Museum.

Canada in two World Wars

Between 1885, when the Canadian Pacific Railroad physically joined the Canadian provinces into one nation and 1914, when Canada entered World War I, seemingly endless new resources were discovered. A great gold rush began in 1896 when deposits were found in Klondike in the northwest of the country. Even more significant, however, were the copper, lead, zinc and silver deposites and coal veins in British Columbia and the gold and nickel deposits of Québec and Ontario. Large-scale farming in the prairies also gave agriculture a boost.

In 1914, Britain's declaration of war automatically included, as one of her colonies, Canada, but at war's end in 1918 Canada signed the Armistice on her own. Canada's troups had proven that their country had to be taken seriously as a political partner – the war had cost 60,000 deaths and 170,000 wounded.

Another by-product of the war was a considerable population increase and an economic upswing. The promise of land and work attracting many Europeans from all over the continent. The strong financial community of Montréal, where the majority of Canadian banks, insurance companies and trading firms were headquartered, was augmented by capital from Great Britain and the United States. War's end in 1918 brought a burst of American capital investment across the border which engendered a certain amount of anti-American feeling on the part of many Canadians who resented what was considered excessive American domination of Canada's economic life. As well, high inflation was blamed on the government in Ottawa, which was accused of regulating the economy to the advantage of the east at the expense of the west. By 1929 the Great Depression was threatening Canada. The country was very vulnerable to the severe worldwide economic woes: Canada had always been dependent, however unwillingly, upon foreign capital and the exporting of raw materials to industrial nations. By

HISTORY AND PEOPLE

1933 approximately one-fourth of the country's labor force was unemployed, with bankruptcies, evictions, and farm foreclosures. Canadian economic life remained depressed all through the 1930s.

When Nazi Germany invaded Poland in September 1939, and Great Britain declared war on Germany, Canada was once again caught up in the European conflict. There had been a great deal of anti-conscription feeling in Québec during World War One, and it rose again during the second conflict. Canada had pursued a basically isolationist foreign policy during the previous decades, involving itself very little in matters concerning the League of Nations or for that matter, Great Britain. It had done very little to build up the size and quality of its armed forces and in 1939 was quite unprepared for war. Most Canadians felt that their country's contribution would be

Above: Canadian soldiers in World War I, Bordeaux. Right: Citadel of Québec, built in 1832.

mainly economic since Canada was indeed a crucial source of supplies for Britain, especially in the months prior to the United States' entry in the war. The fighting forces were composed almost entirely of volunteers and almost a million Canadians served valorously. Conscription for overseas duty began in April of 1942 after a controversial plebiscite asked Canadians to vote on the issue. Results showed how divided the country was: in English Canada 80 percent voted yes; in Québec 72 percent said "no." But many Québecois either joined Québec units or the United States army (once the US entered the conflict) and fought courageously. And although the Canadian people as a whole had resisted the idea of a Canadian navy, the Canadian armed forces, including the famous eleven squadrons of the Royal Canadian Air Force, went to war, joined by many Americans eager to fight the common enemy before the United States entered the war. The deepwater ports of Halifax, Nova Scotia, and St. John's in Newfoundland were used to form convoys which carried desperately needed supplies at first to England and later to Russia, convoys which had the hazardous duty of avoiding Nazi U-boats that prowled about the waters of the North Atlantic.

At the end of World War Two Canada became one of the founding nations of the United Nations, as well as an important member of NATO. There was strong feeling that the country, having lost almost 42,000 troups, had paid its dues as a member of the League of Nations and could no longer be considered a minor cog in the wheel of the British colonial system. In 1952 the first native Canadian was appointed governor-general of the country when the Right Honorable Vincent Massey took office. Canada was instrumental in effecting the change from the British Commonwealth to the multiracial Commonwealth of Nations and in implementing the Colombo Plan of 1950 to provide aid to underdeveloped nations in South and Southeast Asia. Government social systems were expanded, especially in the field of health care. In 1959 the St. Lawrence Seaway, a joint Canadian-American project, opened the way for shipping from the Great Lakes to the Atlantic Ocean.

UNITY THROUGH DIVERSITY

The end of the war also opened up a floodgate of immigration on a record scale. Most of the newcomers came from Europe, with Italy, Portugal and Greece at the top of the list of countries of origin. Many were skilled workers and educated people who settled in cities in and around the industrial centers of eastern Canada, joining the masses of native-born Canadians who were beginning to leave the land in favor of a more urban lifestyle. The immigrants socially transformed many cities, in particular Toronto, which today is an exciting multiracial, multicultural community.

Since barely a third of the new immigrants were of British extraction, citizens of British heritage no longer constituted an absolute majority of the population. However, this did nothing to make the French-Canadian population feel more secure; the effect was quite the opposite. Although the immigrants continued to speak a wide variety of languages in their homes and churches, they almost invariably chose English, rather than French, as their new language. This was perceived as threatening by the French-speaking Canadians, already struggling with the fact that their birth rate had been dropping dramatically since 1945. This anxiety came to ahead in the province of Québec especially.

It would take until the 1960s for a movement to gather momentum on the way to political, social, educational, economic and religious reforms. The so-called *révolution tranquille*, the quiet revolution began with the election of the liberal politician Jean Lesage as prime minister of Québec. The principal thrust

HISTORY AND PEOPLE

of this movement was autonomy for French Canadians, first and foremost in promotion of French language and culture. Equality with Anglo-Canadians, who seemed to have a monopoly on all important economic and public posts, and the introduction of French as Canada's second official language were also demended. The revolution was not always quiet, and was not only promoted by the government. Acts of terrorism were committed subsequent to the founding of the *Front de Libération du Québec* (FLQ) in 1967, the National Liberation Front of Québec.

By 1967, the nation's 100th anniversary, Canada had adopted a policy of bilingualism, with federal business legally required to be conducted in both French and English. Bilingualism in all sectors was encouraged, with product labels being printed in both languages. A new flag was designed and a new slogan, "unity through diversity," was adopted in hopes of promoting a sense of national unity for the entire country. Canadian industry was booming and the people were enjoying one of the highest standards of living in the world. The nation celebrated its coming of age as a union by staging centennial celebrations around the country, capped by the worldwide success of Montréal's EXPO '67.

In this same year of happy self-congratulation, French president Charles De Gaulle came to visit Québec and gave a speech at the end of which he cried "long live free Québec!" De Gaulle's bombshell acted as a rallying cry. By the end of the decade a survey revealed that 40 percent of Québecois decided that the province could indeed survive on its own. As a result of frustration over more than 200 years of British "superiority," violence also erupted. The Front de Liberation du Québec (FLQ) began bombing wealthy English sections of the city.

The most visible effect of this conflict was the flight from Québec of many Eng-

Above: Hot blood, cold feet – Carnival in Québec.

lish business and other commercial enterprises such as the majority of Canadian banks, insurance companies and trading firms. Many resettled in Toronto, with the result that the traditional competition between Montréal and Toronto as to which would be the most economically important city in Canada was ultimately won by Toronto.

The French Canadian Pierre Trudeau, who headed the government until 1984, was undoubtedly the politician best suited to prevent the country from disintegrating. On the one hand he was thoroughly French, on the other hand he was a passionate federalist. During his tenure the Official Language Act was passed, making French the second official language from 1968 onward, and preparations were gotten underway to introduce bilingualism in all federal matters. By the same token he vigorously opposed Québec independence, which the separatist Bloc Québecois hoped to reach by a referendum in 1980. It failed by a solid margin of 60 to 40.

What the French-English conflict did for Canada as a whole was to force it to redefine itself as a nation. Canadians began to be aware that they were not entirely sovereign after all. Although Québec did not endorse it, a new constitution was signed in 1982 by Queen Elizabeth II and the Canadian prime minister, a constitution that at long last made the Canadians masters in their own house. The only link with the mother country today is the symbolic recognition of the British monarch as the formal head of state.

Five years later, after a long and bitter dispute, the Meech Lake Accord resulted in a new constitution, spelling out provincial rights and containing a bill of rights that could be evoked by anyone who perceived language discrimination anywhere in the country.

Québec was the first province to ratify the accord but those Canadians who had fought for a single Canada, bilingual and multicultural were outraged. Although the decentralizing clauses were good for all provinces, women and native peoples found no protection of their particular rights and Anglophones and minority language groups throughout all of Canada were incensed. In June of 1990 two provinces, Manitoba and Newfoundland, representing only six percent of the population, ended the Accord.

In 1992 a second attempt was made to introduce profound changes in the constitution which were to include not only the Québecois but Canada's Indians and Inuit as well. The resulting Charlottetown Accord, however, did not find much popular support. The French-Canadians also pronounced a resounding "no," as they felt that the accord held to few guarantees for greater autonomy for Québec. The fact that that is the holiest concern of French Canadians was illustrated by the parliamentary elections of autumn 1993, when 54 Bloc Québecois MPs took seats in Ottawa, making that party the strongest opposition party. It was closely followed by the populistic Reform Party, an anglophone counterpart to the Québecois from the western provinces. The federalists still managed to garner the absolute majority, even though the Progressive Conservative Party will be replaced by the Liberal Party after a stunning defeat.

The new Prime Minister Jean Chrétien has been having a rough ride, however. Unemployment is still around 11 percent, the budget deficit is high, and NAFTA, the North American Free Trade Agreement is putting the economy under competitive pressure. The tensions between the French and English Canadians have not subsided, especially after the referendum in 1995 on French Canadian independence was very narrowly defeated. Under the circumstances, Chrétien's promises of jobs, improved social security, and budget cuts are not being fulfilled, and new elections are already looming.

HISTORY AND PEOPLE

WHO ARE THE CANADIANS ?

Because of the enormous differences in the language and cultural heritage of Canada, a heritage originally both strongly English and tenaciously French, it is difficult to define Canada as a "nation." Yet this group of diverse peoples have shaped a democratic, prosperous and peaceful country against those great odds. And against other odds as well, such as the strong influence exerted by that boisterous country sharing the entire length of Canada's southern border: the populous United States of America. Having appropriated the name "Americans," these neighbors tend to see Canadians as "just like us," to which the Canadians do not necessarily subscribe. On the contrary, they prefer to dwell on the differences between the two countries, not the similarities Americans focus on. Canadians have always had a great respect for authority, using the Mountie, a policeman, as a national symbol. They prefer not to call attention to themselves, not to cause a fuss, particularly in public.

Yet visitors traveling in Canada are assailed in all five senses by what seems to be Americana. They meet with people who are dressed pretty much like Americans, in jeans and jogging shoes, jackets emblazoned with sports team logos, T-shirts with messages on them. They talk with people who seem to talk just like Americans, with the exception of their pronunciation of the letter O. They hear American music, see American films and television shows. Except for the fact that Canadians are less inclined to trash their environment, their cities have an American look, with American-style fast-food chains and convenience stores, gas stations and billboards.

Yet unlike Americans, Canadians are not necessarily intensely patriotic. Al-

Left: Salmon fisherman on the Rivière Ste-Marguerite, Québec.

though Canada has a flag, a red maple leaf on a white ground flanked on each side by wide red bars, there is no formal pledging of allegience to that flag. Victoria Day in May is a school holiday honoring Queen Victoria who never once set foot on Canadian territory in all her long reign.

Two reasons may account for the fact that there seems to be no such thing as Canadian patriotism. One is that the diversity of ethnic identity precludes the formation of a homogenous Canadian nation. In addition to English and French-speaking Canadians, there are many other population groups all speaking different languages and who are ethnically different as well, and who themselves resist total assimilation with other Canadians. The other is that although its neighbor to the south has a similar history of many ethnic groups immigrating to America to form a new nation, Canada has eschewed the American concept of a "melting pot." Instead, the country has a tradition of encouraging each ethnic group to keep to its own customs and traditions first and foremost, thus discouraging total assimilation into a homogenous nation.

Although in the past the French Canadians have considered themselves to be the largest and consequently the most important minority in the country, studies made during the French-Canadian/English-Canadian conflict of the 1960s revealed that in spite of the claims of the French Canadians, Canada had no ethnic majority.

Except for the French and British, Canadians were descended from Germans, Italians, Ukranians, Japanese, Chinese, Inuit and native Indians, among others. Consequently, since Canadians from infancy on are conditioned to think of themselves as citizens of a country without a strong national identity, the dominating influence on a Canadian of any origin is more a sense of regional rather than national identity. Canadians seem to be loyal to the area from which they come: Eastern Canada is separated from Western Canada by more than miles. The province of Ontario considers itself to be the heart of the country, while any Québecois worth his or her salt knows that their province is unique and special. As for the Maritimers, their history of dependency on the sea has certainly given them a different perspective from that of Ontario, the power base of the country today. They often still refer to those regions as Upper Canada in reference to the historic division of the country into Upper Canada and Lower Canada.

Language Differences

Given the dual languages of the country right from the beginnings of its modern-day history, the struggle for the country to achieve some accord is admirable. The fact that today, with 96 percent of the population speaking English, both English and French are the official languages of Canada is a triumph for the French Canadians. In 1969 Canada officially became bilingual; all government services were made available in both French and English; all products had to be labeled in both languages. However, like the Québec Act of 1774, this policy was a result more of necessity than desire. Back in the 18th and 19th centuries the British Canadians never dreamed that the French Canadians would struggle so long and so successfully against assimilation.

Yet the 24 percent who speak French as their mother tongue also speak English, if perhaps with a French accent, and nowadays Anglophone children flock to French immersion schools to reap the advantages of being bilingual. It must be noted that the French spoken by most French Canadians is viewed by the European French as an archaic version of their language and they have a propensity to ridicule it. They call it *joual*, a dialect they consider vulgar. Interesting to note is the current tendency to create a mixture between the two languages, forming a newer language often derisively referred to as "Franglais": French sprinkled liberally with English words. But derision has not lessened the impact of such expressions on either French as spoken in French Canada or on Parisian French in Europe. However, as a result of the province of Québec's legislation insisting on the use of French on both Radio Canada and television, a more international French is currently being broadcast.

Multiculturalism

The stirrings of Québec nationalism, which brought about the official recognition of the multiculturalism by the Canadian government, has benefitted other minorities as well. At first many French Canadians were uneasy about this inclusion of other minorities because it seemed to them to undermine their view of Canada as a union of two peoples, French and English, rather than a collection of ethnic minorities of which the French would be merely another one.

Not to be discounted is the fact that a Canadian's origin, language and ethnic background are still socially relevant in the Canada of today. The largest and most privileged group of Canadians historically has been the British: a decade ago 76 percent of all Canadians claimed at least one British ancestor. This group, which also includes Scots, Irish and Welsh, makes up slightly more than 40 percent of the total population and is steadily decreasing. The second largest group, the French Canadians, which makes up about 24 percent of the total population, is also declining. The third

Right: Summer, sun, sidewalk cafés – in Toronto, the long winter is forgotten.

HISTORY AND PEOPLE

largest group, only five percent and perhaps the most assimilated, consists of Canadians of German ancestry. Canadians with Italian origin make up a little more than three percent. Although Canada has always been a land of immigrants, today the increasing percentage of immigrants of non-European heritage has ellicited a certain amount of negative response. The rise of Asian, Caribbean, South and Central American immigration has caused some resentment among the country's European population. Many Canadians now believe that the government should discontinue its policy of encouraging these immigrants to preserve their separate heritage. Rather, the majority of Canadians believe they should integrate with Canadian culture. Another minority, that of the native Inuit and Indian population, is a growing concern to the Canadians and their government. In spite of various forms of state assistance they are among Canada's poorest citizens, disadvantaged by lack of education and employment and plagued by alcoholism.

The Future

Canada faces many challenges, with cultural aspects inextricably intertwined with governmental and economic (see the NAFTA issue) concerns. Canadians are beginning to ask themselves: "Shall we keep the country together or let it fall apart?" More and more Canadians of all ethnic backgrounds, and especially those of the two primary language-speaking groups, are beginning to realize what they have to lose if they are not willing to recognize that real changes in both attitude and institutions must be effected. There is a serious desire to explore at length such long-term concerns as parliamentary reform, Québec's distinct society, clarification of federal and provincial powers, economic union and aboriginal rights. Canada never has been a nation based on a specific philosophy of government and society, and ideally its citizens will come to graciously accept whatever is necessary to live together peacefully and prosperously.

THE "FRENCH FACT"

From the moment you arrive on Québec soil, you realize that Canada's largest province is also its most distinct. Throughout its near 400-year history, Québec's French majority or "French Fact" has determined the province's language, culture, social and religious systems. Unlike the rest of Canada, with its predominantly British Anglo-Protestant heritage, past and present Québec is deeply rooted in the political, social and religious customs and traditions of its mother country, Roman-Catholic France. But while Québec is intensely French, it is uniquely so. Québec's "French Fact," in all its manifestations, is not the French of France, just as the English of Canada and the United States is not the English of Britain. Language, culture and politics are very much of this place – born of it, shaped by it and defined in reaction to its political marriage with the rest of Canada, as well as its proximity to the cultural leviathan (and perennial bugaboo) of the United States in the south.

Québec's status as an entity unto itself is most evident in the development of the Québecois language that so clearly reveals the soul and mindset of its majority Francophone population. When Oxford Dons smile indulgently at Canadian English, we smile ironically back. The French or Québecois of Canada are equally unimpressed by patronizing Parisians. They are proud of their French, which is pronounced in bold tones and is alive, fluid, constantly evolving from absorbing many words and concepts unknown in Europe. At the same time, Francophone Québecois are not the same as other Canadians or Americans. They are not descended from the British traditions which have so stamped the rest of Canada; nor do they wish to have their language or culture drowned by the ocean of English that surrounds them. At times, this has made for what seems like overly zealous and reactionary measures on the part of those whose business it is to "caretake" the French language and culture in Québec. But a careful reading of Québec's history demonstrates that overall, tolerance, warmth and generosity towards *les autres* has prevailed here for over 400 years.

Despite headlines and the constitutional tango that seems to have gone on for at least as long as it has been part of the Canadian confederation, and indeed, for at least 100 years before that, Québec is a stable society politically, socially and culturally. Nevertheless, it is a province seemingly eternally in transition, still defining its national identity and place within or without the Canadian federation, as world headlines confirmed in 1992.

To a considerable degree, the two solitudes (French and English) which the late great Canadian novelist and essayist Hugh MacLennan portrayed in his seminal novels, *Two Solitudes* (1945) and *Return of the Sphinx* (1967), co-exist in relative isolation and harmony in the Québec of today, just as they did at the end of World War Two. Indeed, as they have since the British "conquest" of New France in 1759.

The outcome of that final 20-minute battle on the Plains of Abraham outside Québec City, in which General James Wolfe's forces defeated the French forces led by General Louis-Joseph Montcalm, is still the subject of bitter debate here. It has also led at times to historical accounts and attitudes reflecting a French nationalist and highly subjective or revisionist view of Canadian history. The French separatist or pro-sovereignty political and social movements that first gained widespread acceptance during Québec's Quiet Revolution of the 1960s and still exist today stem from this his-

Right: The fall of Fort Louisbourg is still a sore subject for many French Canadians.

torical grievance and the wrenching changes it meant for Québec society at that time and subsequently. Québec under an English flag was, indeed, to be a very different society than Québec under a French flag. The worst humiliation of all was that France chose Caribbean spoils over French Québec in the 1763 "trade" with England that could have restored this colony to France but instead turned it loose forever, at the mercy of its English "conquerers." Therein lie the seeds of the conflict which continues to this day and likely will until the end of time, judging by contemporary Québec's position on this historical about-face occasioned by military defeat two centuries ago.

Equally important in assessing contemporary Québec's mood and mores is the fact that the English, for better or worse, chose not to impose assimilation on the French or *Les Canadiens*. Though the subject of much debate, what is indisputable is that whatever limitations this relatively peaceful and humanitarian solution imposed on *Les Canadiens* at the time, it ultimately preserved the French culture in Québec.

First discovered by French sea captain Jacques Cartier in 1534, while he was looking for the Northwest Passage to China around the North American continent, and first settled by the "Father of New France," French explorer Samuel de Champlain, who arrived in 1608, Québec officially became a crown colony of France in 1663. For almost a century, this vast region remained under French rule, in which the Roman Catholic Church, and specifically, the Franciscan, Jesuit and Sulpician religious orders, dominated all aspects of colonial life. Along with tending to the souls of their flocks, priests and nuns were largely in charge of the social welfare, education and physical wellbeing of Québec's first French settlers and their descendants. They also oversaw business arrangements between the *habitants*, as they were called, as well as between French-speaking traders and English-speaking merchants.

La Survivance

Their "dominion" over French Québec was further amplified by the Québec Act of 1774, passed by the British Parliament. It gave full "governing" authority to the Roman Catholic Church, maintained the 100-year-old seigneurial landlord system instituted by Québec's first intendant Jean Talon and provided for civil justice under the existing French law. As a result, the survival of the traditional Québecois way of life was maintained more or less intact until this century. Up until the 1950s, one doctrine of the Roman Catholic Church in Québec was still strictly practiced by French Québecois: *la survivance*, ensuring the survival of the French and their culture by having large families.

It was a god-given duty for Francophone couples to have as many children as possible: 10 to 12 children per family was the norm, not the exception. While this is no longer prevalent – indeed the overall birth rate in Québec is now one of the lowest in Canada – the doctrine of *la survivance* dominates the political, social and cultural reality of contemporary Québec. Almost all government policies are now determined by this, but not without controversy.

"Collective Versus Individual Rights"

During all of this time, relations between French and English inhabitants of Québec ranged from indifferent to warm, with intermarriage between the French and the Irish, Scottish or English becoming more common in the 19th and 20th centuries. Governed by different civil codes, raised with different moral values, customs and traditions, speaking different languages, educated under separate school systems, and earning their livelihoods in very different occupations, Québec's two major cultural groups re-

Above: Humor affords some protection against the cold. Right: Bilingualism remains a highly controversial subject.

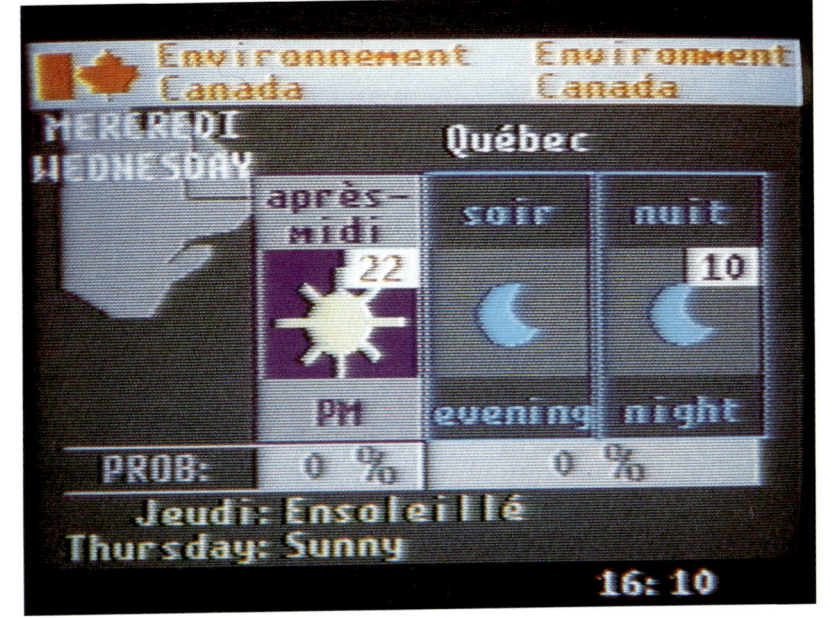

ally co-existed in separate worlds, while sharing the same geographical "homeland." This is still the case today, with major social and political flashpoints of their common history illuminating the very different view of Québec held by Francophones and Anglophones.

In very general terms, Francophone Québecois view Québec as their country and themselves as a nation first and foremost, and as Canadians second. Anglophones, by and large, considers themselves Canadians first, who live in Québec and have, nonetheless, a fierce attachment to their native province. Allophones (any ethnic group not originally native to France, Ireland, Scotland, Wales or England) are more likely to view themselves as Canadians whose ancestors or themselves have chosen to live in the province of Québec for largely economic or social reasons, as well as because of the relatively high policial stability and civil liberties they are guaranteed by law, regardless of where they live in the Canadian federation.

Historically the case, this was once more proven by the voting patterns in Québec during the October 1992 national referendum on the Charlottetown Accord. The majority of Francophones voted "No;" while the majority of Anglophones and Allophones voted "Yes." Québec was one of six provinces that voted against the Accord, which effectively brought to a standstill multilateral government efforts to formally recognize Québec as an "official" partner in the Canadian Constitution. Québec is a de facto partner under the British North America Act of 1867. As such, it is governed by the Canadian Constitution and its Charter of Rights and Freedoms enacted by Québec native and former prime minister Pierre Elliot Trudeau in 1982.

However, since the mid-1970s, the Québec government has acted unilaterally in passing laws that promote the preservation and growth of the French language and culture in all aspects of daily business, education, civil, and social welfare throughout the province. The

HISTORY AND PEOPLE

Parti Québecois has provided the government for Québec since 1976, and since 1993, the *Bloc Québecois* has been the official opposition party in Ottawa. In 1977, the Bloc Québecois, whose primary raison d'être is formal separation from the Canadian confederation, or at the very least, sovereignty association (envisioned as largely maintaining economic ties), instituted the now infamous Bill l0l Charter of the French Language, which laid out deadlines and fines to enforce compliance in using French as the chief language of the workplace and all other areas of Québec life.

This, along with a growing number of terrorist acts by the *Front de Libération du Québec* against Anglophones brought about serious repercussions: Many English companies that were considered pillars of the Canadian establishment, and which had been founded in Québec and headquartered here for at least a century, relocated their operations outside the province, primarily in Toronto, Ontario. Consistent with all of this, and still ongoing, more than 200,000 Anglophone Québecois, many of whose families have been in Québec since the "conquest," have moved away.

In 1980, the Bloc Québecois held its first referendum on separation from, or sovereignty association with, the rest of Canada. Pro-sovereignty sentiment continuerd growing, however. The 1992 Charlottetown Accord was intended as a compromise solution. It was engineered by former prime minister Brian Mulroney, his special constitutional minister Joe Clark (a former leader of the Conservative Party and a former prime minister), 10 provincial premiers, (including former Québec hold-out Robert Bourassa), two territory leaders and the elected Grand Chief of the Native Band Councils, Ovide Mercredi.

The Phoenix risen out of the ashes of the failed 1990 Meech Lake Accord, like-

Above: Instructions on Québec schoolbuses are written in French. Right: Toronto leans toward British usages.

wise engineered by Brian Mulroney and his then provincial counterparts, the Charlottetown Accord was the most complex constitutional compromise put together since the British North America Act of 1867, which created the original confederation of Canada. Enormously ambitious, it was a revolutionary attempt to address not only Québec's concerns, which had dominated the Meech Lake Accord agenda, but to take into account perceived and actual historical grievances, and imbalances of power, about financial and natural resources, standards of living and civil liberties across Canada. Significantly, the Accord was intended to redress the de facto exclusion of Canada's aboriginal peoples from almost every sphere of social, economic and political power for more than two centuries.

Ironically, among other key changes to the Canadian constitution, a "Yes" vote for the Charlottetown Accord would have entrenched the concept of Québec as a distinct society in the Canadian Charter of Rights, with special powers to ensure that the French language, culture and civil law would be preserved, protected and promoted in perpetuity within Québec. This was considered necessary to prevent the further "incursion" of North American influences (read English) and the further "erosion" or feared assimilation of Francophones into North American society.

It may seem surprising then, that the Francophone majority in Québec would have voted "No" but to explain that would require an intricate understanding of Canadian politics, the "Two Nation" concept, the promotion and interplay of bilingualism versus multiculturalism as official federal and provincial government policies and the impact of these on the daily lives of "ordinary" Canadians. Suffice it to say that the Accord was not accepted, either in its parts or in sum, by the citizens of Canada as being in their best interests, either in the short or long-term. Interestingly, their reasons for rejecting it are as divergent as the reasons given for accepting it. And while it was not perceived either in Québec or in the rest of Canada, as the feared rejection of French-Canadians, as was the Meech Lake Accord, the "No" votes reiterated an historical paradox: The commonly held view among French Québecois was that the Charlottetown Accord didn't give enough benefits to Québec to ensure the survival and flourishing of its French constituency in perpetuity within the Federation. The next referendum on secession, held in 1995, came very close indeed 49 per cent for, 51 per cent against.

Outside of Québec, lumped together as the "Rest of Canada (ROC)" by the news media and political pundits, the commonly held view among Canadians of all ethnic backgrounds (excepting French), social and political classes, was that, for all intents and purposes, Québec was once again getting the lion's share of benefits in this deal, from here to eternity.

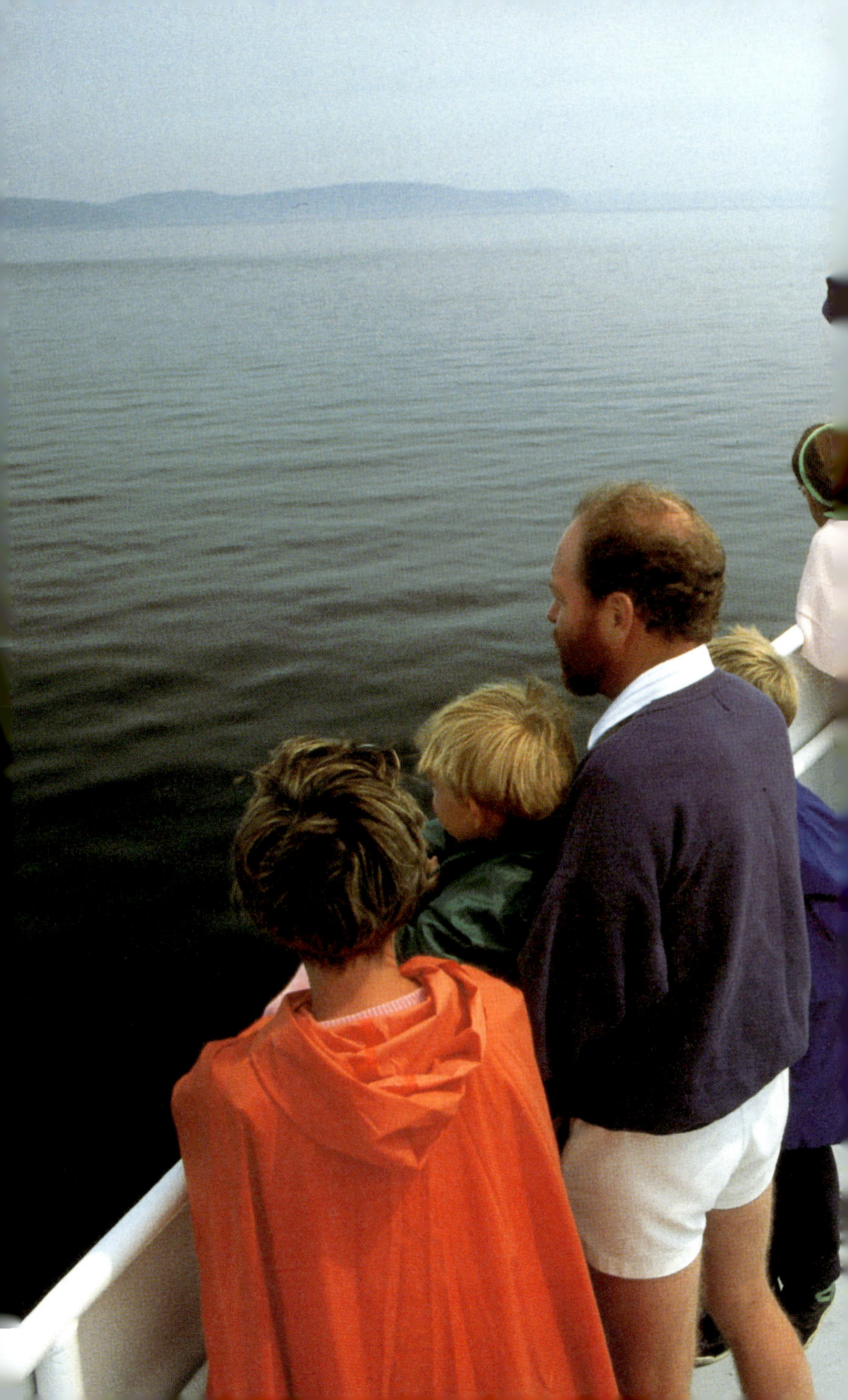

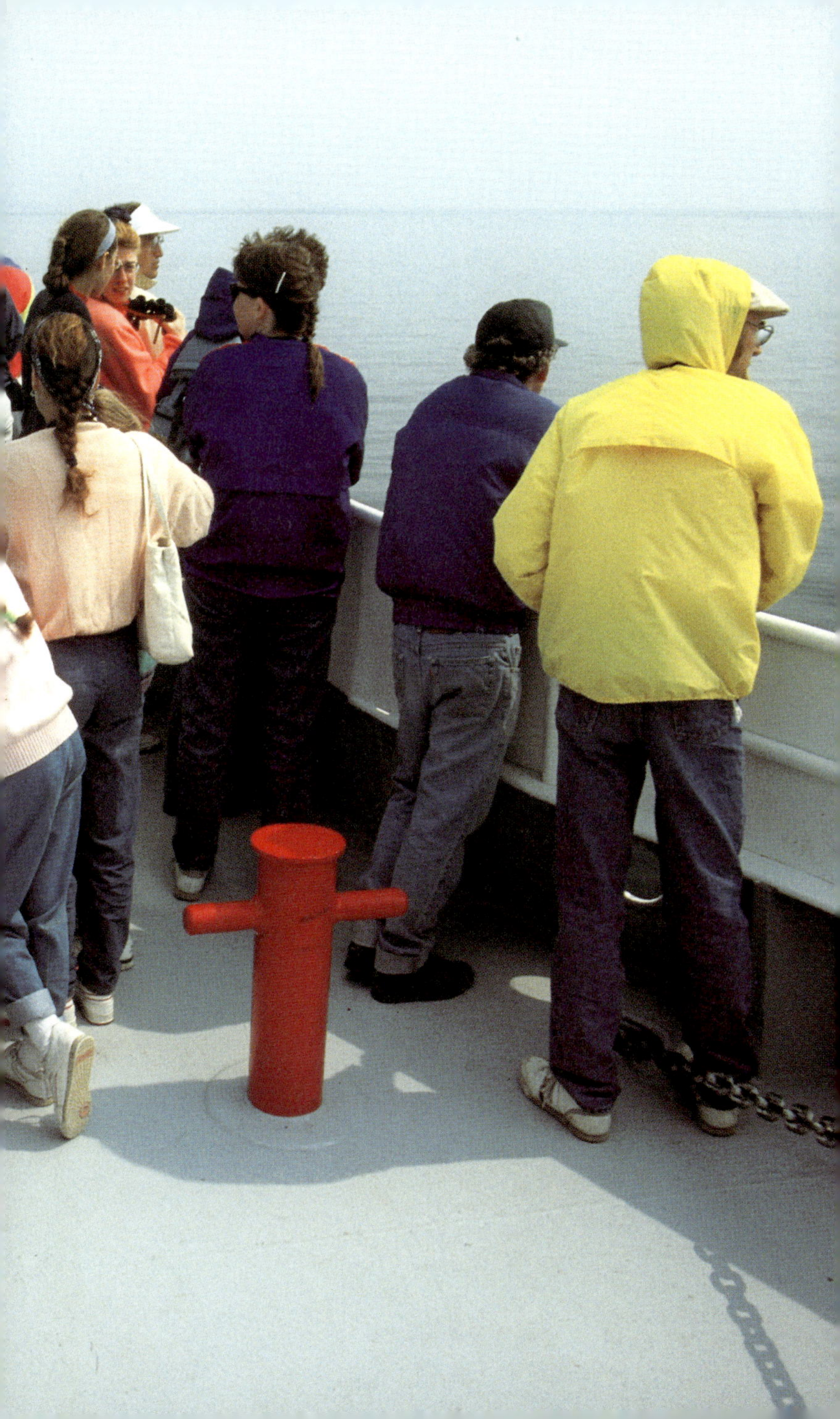

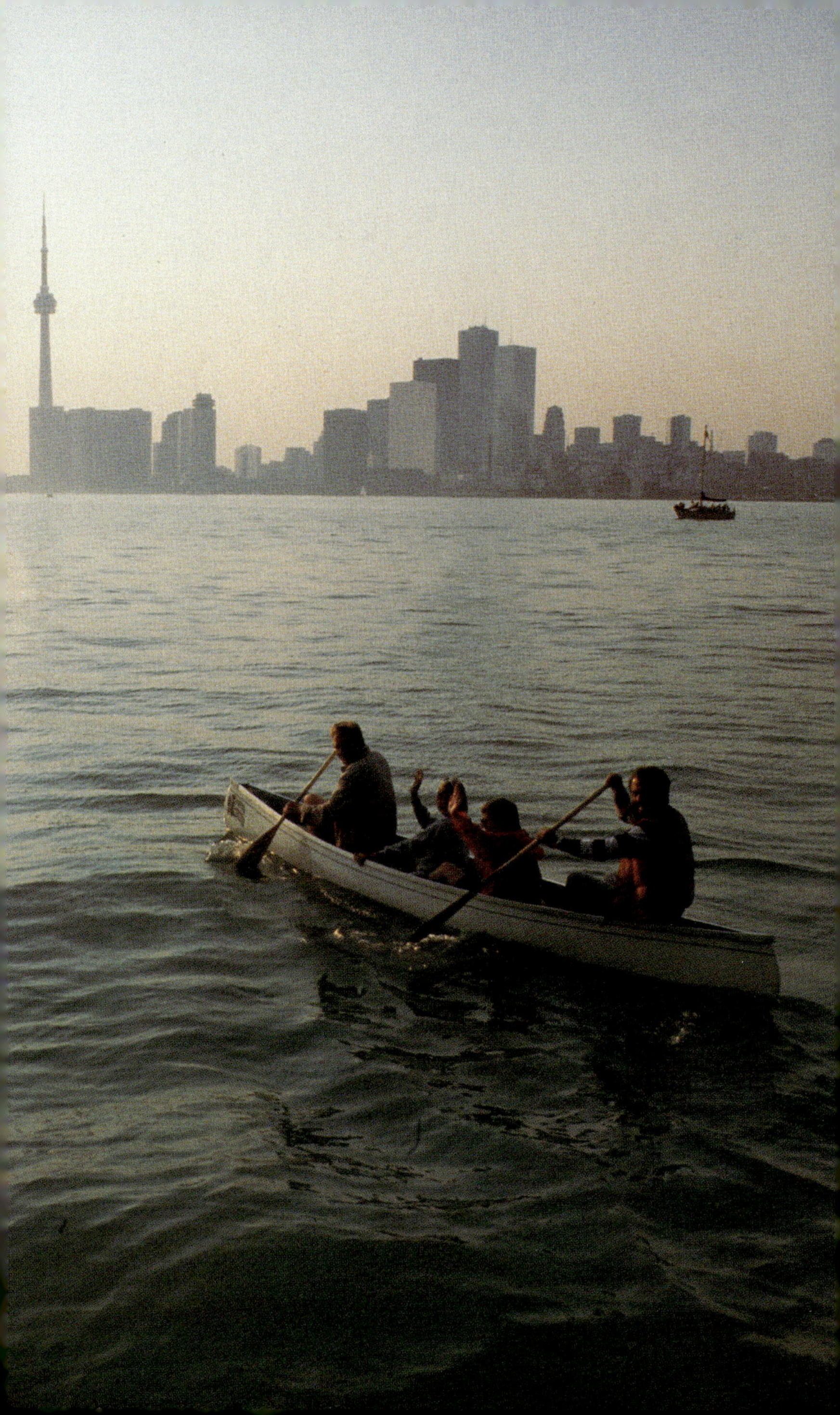

TORONTO

TORONTO

ON THE WATERFRONT
DOWNTOWN
NEIGHBORHOODS
EXCURSIONS

A picturesque, remarkably clean metropolis encircled by fast-growing suburbs, Toronto is Ontario's main Great Lakes port and industrial center as well as the commercial and financial hub of Eastern Canada. And, despite its sprawling layout and imposing downtown cityscape, it is refreshingly green. For example, High Park in the city's west end sprawls over 400 acres (160 hectares) and is made up of trails, ponds, gardens, an outdoor swimming pool, picnic areas and even a small zoo.

Toronto was once lampooned as a dull, stodgy city. Torontonians purportedly retreated behind closed doors at suppertime for lack of anything better to do. In the words of the late, outspoken radio and TV broadcaster Gordon Sinclair: "Everyday life was dreary enough, but Sundays were murder."

Toronto is now internationally regarded as an attractive and exciting tourist destination. The city's relatively recent transformation is largely due to a massive influx of different cultures since World War II. Of the 3.9 million residents now in Metropolitan Toronto, more than one million have roots in non-English-speaking countries. These groups have brought with them their customs, cultures and cuisines, sharply changing – and improving – the city's character. No longer a predominantly White Anglo-Saxon Protestant (WASP) city, Toronto is now a cosmopolitan melting pot with dwellers speaking more than 100 different languages.

Torontonian origins

The city's history actually started with the Huron Indians who set up camp in the area. French fur traders built a fort here in 1749 in a section the British later bought from the Indians in 1787. In 1793, Toronto – a native Indian word for "meeting place" – was proclaimed the capital of Upper Canada (now the province of Ontario). The British had named the settlement York, after the Duke of York, a major opponent of the American Revolution. It was also settled in part by United Empire Loyalists from the United States who fled to the north in the wake of the American Revolution. The new town got its start on the shore plain at the eastern end of the harbor. Back in those days Toronto consisted of a mere eight square blocks with a garrison protecting the western entrance of the harbor.

Preceding Pages: Whale-watching on the St. Lawrence River near Tadoussac. Canoe tour on Lake Ontario near Toronto. Left: Canada Day on Nathan Phillips Square.

TORONTO / WATERFRONT

Although the area drew all sorts of new residents, tradesmen and officials once it was named Upper Canada's capital, growth remained slow at first. In 1812, the town still had only 700 residents. That year, war broke out between the British and the Americans, and York was completely destroyed by American troops. They burned the Parliament buildings and archives and stole the mace, the symbol of British sovereignty. In retaliation, the British marched on Washington, D.C., and burned all the public buildings, including the home of the President.

By 1834, however, when the city was officially rebuilt and incorporated and its name reverted from York to the original Toronto, it boasted 9254 citizens and 100 shops. In 1867, upon the Confederation of Canada, Toronto became Ontario's capital.

Above: View of the city from Queen's Quay. Right: Front Street – which window is real?

In subsequent years the most remarkable thing about it was its steady growth. Writers who visited what was sometimes called "Muddy York" – because of the marshy wetlands next to the shoreline – were less than flattering in their descriptions. In 1862, British novelist and travel writer Anthony Trollope said "the country around it is flat and although it stands on a lake, the lake has no attributes of beauty." Today, the city has the dubious distinction of being the Western Hemisphere's most expensive. That doesn't seem to hinder visitors. For some, the low Canadian dollar in recent years has even made it a bargain.

ON THE WATERFRONT

The thousands of tons of rubble that resulted from excavating the subway and from other massive construction projects have generally been put to good use in Toronto. In 1971, **Ontario Place**, an outdoor entertainment complex with its striking geodesic dome, opened on Toronto's western waterfront. This world-renowned complex was built on islands reclaimed through the dumping of this rubble. It is part playground, part exposition and cultural center and mostly lush green park. **Children's Village** is two acres of imaginative play areas for kids. The **Cinesphere** was one of the first IMAX installations in the world, and the Forum is the scene of live entertainment. The **Pavilion**, a series of interconnected pods built on stilts right in Lake Ontario, houses restaurants and exhibits about Ontario.

Adjacent to Ontario Place, near the lake, is the site of the world's largest annual exhibition, which began as an agricultural fair in 1879. The **Canadian National Exhibition** (CNE), or "Ex" as it is fondly known by Torontonians, attracts more than two million visitors each year during its three-week summer season. There are scores of frightening rides at the midway (including bungee jumping), concerts at the Grandstand, miles of display booths, an international air show, foreign pavilions, agricultural exhibits, a casino and more. It is open from mid-August to early September. A large agricultural fair still takes place on the Exhibition grounds every November. The highlight of the Royal Winter Fair is without a doubt the equestrian events.

The **Marine Museum of Upper Canada**, located at Exhibition Place just off Lakeshore Road West, is an excellent spot to learn all about Toronto's extensive maritime history. It's open daily.

Also at Exhibition Place, the **Hockey Hall of Fame** pays homage to Canada's favorite sport, and visitor's can catch a glimpse of the National Hockey League's coveted trophy, the Stanley Cup. The **Canadian Sports Hall of Fame** documents Canada's sporting history and star players.

Fort York played a crucial role in the War of 1812/14 with the United States and boasts the largest collection of rebuilt War of 1812 buildings in Canada – eight brick, log and stone relics brightened by the brilliant red coats of guides dressed as British soldiers. There are musket drills, music and interpretative exhibits including a 32-man barracks bristling with period military regalia.

Just east of Ontario Place and the Exhibition grounds, an area known as **Harbourfront** spans the scenic shore of Lake Ontario from the foot of Bathurst Street in the west to York Street in the east. A transformation of 10 acres of former industrial properties along the lakefront into a recreational and cultural complex, Harbourfront is probably one of the cleanest and most attractive big-city harbors anywhere. Although the area is at its busiest during the summer, activities continue on a year-round basis with shopping, restaurants, concerts, films, art galleries, and an antique and flea market.

Queen's Quay Terminal is a dramatically renovated 1920s warehouse reopened in 1983 as a major point of interest in the heart of Harbourfront. The green-

TORONTO

trimmed concrete-and-glass structure houses a variety of boutiques, restaurants, some with lakefront patios, and the **Premiere Dance Theatre**.

For the highly energetic sightseer, **Skate Toronto**, in the west side of Queen's Quay Terminal, rents inline skates as well as all the padding (knee, wrist and elbow) necessary, by the hour, half-day or entire day.

From Harbourfront, visitors can board a ferry for a quick trip to the **Toronto Islands**. Made up mostly of tranquil parkland and sandy beaches, the islands include **Hanlan's Point**, **Ward's**, **Centre**, and **Algonquin Islands**. Centre Island, the busiest, has 612 acres of park, picnic grounds, restaurants, boating, a barnyard zoo and Centreville, a child-sized replica of a 19th-century Ontario village with lots of rides. There are also boats and bicycles for rent. The islands offer a very pleasant escape from city heat and bustle during the summer.

DOWNTOWN TORONTO

Visually, Toronto is an eclectic mixture of ethnic neighborhoods and well-preserved historical buildings. As a city, it has gained a reputation for preserving the best of the past while looking to the future.

Without a doubt, Toronto's most noteworthy – and noticeable – landmark is the **CN Tower**. It is built with one foot in

DOWNTOWN TORONTO

A more recent addition to the high-tech image of Toronto is the grand stadium known as the **SkyDome** – home to the 1992 World Series champion Toronto Blue Jays American League Baseball Team, and the Canadian Football League's Argonauts. It is a technological marvel with its four-panel, fully convertible eight-acre retractable roof that can transform the place from an open stadium to a closed, domed stadium in about 15 minutes. As well as sports, a variety of cultural events take place at the "Dome," including opera and rock concerts.

Almost as amazing is the integrated Skydome Hotel with hotel rooms that offer a bird's eye view of the action on the field. The story of a couple who put on an unscheduled amorous performance to the fascination of thousands of onlookers is a true one. Hotel rooms now have discreet signs warning the occupants to keep the drapes drawn unless they are fully clothed.

Nearby is the city's main train terminal **Union Station**, another downtown landmark. Construction began in 1914, but the station was officially opened on Aug. 6, 1927, when the Prince of Wales and his brother, Prince George, cut the ribbons for what his Highness said resembled a palace. During this visit they also dedicated the gates at the CNE on the east end of the grounds. The gates have ever since been known as the **Princes' Gates**.

Two years later, almost on the eve of the Great Depression, Canadian Pacific Railways officially opened the Empire's largest hotel across from Union Station, the **Royal York**. The $16-million, 1,200-room hotel opened on June 11, 1929, and marked the beginning of a new period of growth and development for Toronto that transformed it from a small town into a booming metropolis.

Over the years, the Royal York has housed royalty, dignitaries, politicians and celebrities. A number of movies have been filmed at the hotel over the years,

---

1 George M. Gardiner Mus.
2 Osgoode Hall
3 Old City Hall
4 Pantages Theatre
5 Metro Convention Centre
6 O'Keefe Centre, St. Lawrence Centre for the Arts
7 **Windsor Arms**
8 **T. Marriott Eaton Ctr.**
9 **The Sheraton Centre**
10 T. Dominion Ctr.
11 Commerce Court
12 Royal Bank Plaza

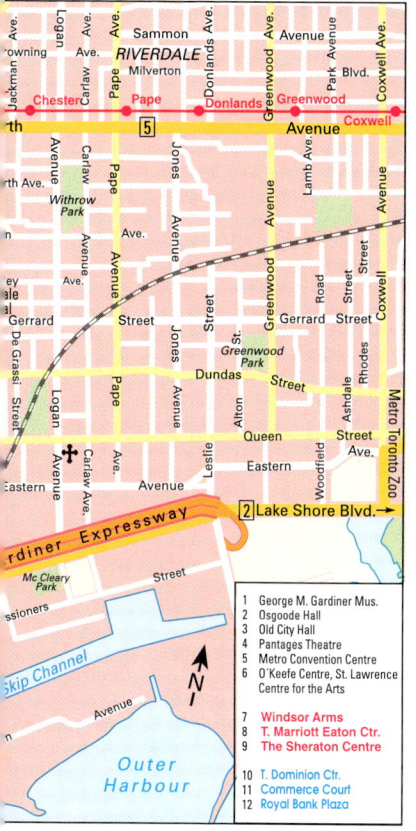

what was the site of Toronto's first swimming hole (when the water's edge was just south of Front Street). When it opened in 1976, it became the world's tallest free-standing structure at 1705 feet (553 m). It is a communications tower complete with observation decks and the world's largest revolving restaurant. Visitors can zoom via high-speed elevator to the main observation deck in 58 seconds and enjoy an outstanding view of Lake Ontario on one side and the city on the other.

From a still higher level, 1430 feet (447 m), called the **Space Deck** – the highest public observation gallery on earth – the mist of Niagara Falls, about 50 miles away, is visible on clear days.

53

and Arthur Hailey lived here to research his novel *Hotel*.

A stone's throw away are the imposing modern concrete office towers of the Central Business District, housing the headquarters of Canada's five major banks. When the **Bank of Commerce** opened in January, 1931, the 34-story, 426-foot-high (133-m) building was the tallest in the British Commonwealth. Today, the most notable, perhaps, is the **Royal Bank of Canada's** bold triangular building which boasts windows that shimmer with real gold.

Underneath all of these buildings lies a warren of interconnected underground shopping malls. They include the Royal Bank Plaza, Commerce Court, First Canadian Place, the Toronto Dominion Centre, among others. This underground consumer heaven, Underground Toronto, stretches north from Front Street to Queen Street, and between Bay and York streets.

A number of important historical and cultural centers can be found just east of **Yonge Street** – allegedly the world's longest street –, in a district that covers many blocks along Front Street East. Ballet and opera aficionados should check out the **O'Keefe Centre for the Performing Arts** by the National Ballet of Canada and the Canadian Opera Company, as well as by guest performers from all over the world. Built in 1969, it was at that time the largest concert hall of its kind in North America.

For theater buffs, there is the **St. Lawrence Centre for the Arts** nearby, which includes the **Jane Mallett Theatre**, seasonal home to Theatre Plus Toronto; and the **Bluma Appel Theater**, home of the Canadian Stage Company. Once Toronto's City Hall (prior to E.J. Lennox's version) **St. Lawrence Market** stands at the corner of Jarvis. It has a farmers' market on Saturdays and an antique and collectibles market on Sundays.

Above: Unusual means of transportation in Yonge Street. Right: Jogging past the Old City Hall.

Heading east from downtown along the shoreline is a former cottage community known as the **Beaches**. While it is now absorbed into the city, it maintains its small-town atmosphere. In the heat of the summer, a stretch of parkland and beach along the lake with a well-used boardwalk are popular among bicyclists, pedestrians and sun-seekers. In recent years, the strip of Queen Street East which is the Beaches' mainstreet has evolved into a trendy shopping and dining area.

Construction of Toronto's **Old City Hall**, 60 Queen St. West, began in 1889, and by November 21, 1891, work had progressed sufficiently to allow the laying of a cornerstone. When it officially opened for business on September 18, 1899, the imposing sandstone structure was Toronto's largest building and second-largest municipal headquarters in North America. E. J. Lennox, the City Hall's architect, was a man of imagination and wit. When refused permission to have his name placed on a plaque on the building he came up with a special solution. Swearing his workers to secrecy, he had them fashion his name, letter by letter on large stone supports under the eaves below the upper windows. Starting on the west side, following around the building, they spell E. J. LENNOX ARCHITECT A.D. 1898.

The building is covered with intricate carvings, both inside and out. Italian marble pillars support the mezzanine, and their gold-trimmed capitals are carved with grotesque caricatures said to be the judges in office at the time. Old City Hall's original roof of red tile dominated Toronto's skyline and served as a beacon for ships on Lake Ontario. It was replaced in the early 1920s with copper sheeting that weathered and turned green.

Its 300-foot clock tower gracefully surveys Bay Street, its three bells striking the quarter-hour, half-hour and hour. They were heard for the first time at midnight December 31, 1900, when the building superintendent and his sons climbed the 262 steps to the top of the

DOWNTOWN TORONTO

tower and rang in the New Year with sledgehammers. When **New City Hall** was built in 1965, some people felt Old City Hall should be torn down, which caused an uproar. The preservationists once again prevailed.

Across Bay Street are the New City Hall and Nathan Phillips Square. City Hall is a distinctive modern complex designed by Finnish architect Viljo Revell. Two curved towers of unequal height focus on the low-domed Council Chambers. Surrounding the buildings is the square named for long-time mayor Nathan Phillips who initiated plans for the City Hall back in 1957. The square is a popular gathering place and site of special events. The reflecting pool and fountains circulate 12,000 gallons of water a minute. During the winter, this pool becomes an imposing skating rink. The

Above: The New City Hall is formed of two concave skyscrapers. Right: Asian immigrants have had great economic success.

Archer, a bronze work by British sculptor Henry Moore that was bought with public contributions, stands in the Peace Garden.

The **Eaton Centre**, a massive shopping complex that opened in 1977, is almost next door to Old City Hall on Yonge Street between Queen and Dundas streets. It has swallowed up numerous blocks, and is still growing. Hundreds of shops of every description, a multi-screen movie complex, restaurants and more are its claim to fame. It's open during the week from 10 a.m. to 9 p.m., Saturdays, 9:30 a.m. to 6 p.m. and on Sundays from noon. One of the world's largest and most successful shopping malls, the Center generates millions of dollars in business and attracts more than a million shoppers a week (subway station and parking garage are included in the complex). The four-level atrium has a glass roof and is furnished with fountains, trees, plants and even a flock of lifelike Canada geese (by Canadian artist/musician/film-maker Michael Snow) suspended in flight high above the heads of shoppers. Geyser-like fountains shoot up several storeys and there are park benches everywhere.

Cradled by the Center are three of Toronto's oldest landmarks – the 1847 **Holy Trinity Church**, **Scadding House** and the **Old Parsonage**. Preservationists insisted that the sun continue to shine on the church's twin towers, and it does. Across from the Eaton Center on Yonge Street – reputedly the longest street in the world – is the elegant **Pantages Theatre**.

NEIGHBORHOODS

The city has lost much of its British connection, and has truly become a city of neighborhoods, most of them drastically different in ambience. It is interesting to explore a few of these areas. For instance, the city boasts three separate **Chinatowns**, the oldest of which lies along Dundas Street from Bay Street to Spadina Avenue, then continues north on Spadina to College Street. It is North America's largest Chinatown by area – even larger than San Francisco's.

The street signs, as well as everything else, are in Chinese. There are exotic markets, shops and a crush of people, especially on Saturday shopping days. There is also some of the best Chinese food to be had in North America. Chinatown supports several large cinemas that are starting to draw patrons from across the city to movies from Hong Kong, Chinese and Taiwanese studios. Most films are subtitled in English. Art galleries abound and Chinatown also has its own dance company.

Just east of the city center, Danforth Avenue (the continuation of Bloor Street) between Broadview and Pape can be recognized by street signs in the Cyrillic alphabet which identify this as the Greek part of town. This community, known as **Riverdale**, also has its own national restaurants, nightclubs and shops.

To the south clustered around Broadview and Gerrard, one finds another, smaller Chinatown. It, too, has some excellent restaurants and colorful fruit and vegetable stores.

India is east of China in Toronto, tucked away on **Gerrard Street East** between Greenwood and Coxwell avenues. It consists of a little pocket of grocery stores, sari shops and restaurants featuring some of the best – and cheapest – Indian food to be had anywhere.

Heading west over the Don Valley towards downtown is a neighborhood called **Cabbagetown**. It acquired its less than attractive name between the World Wars, when its predominantly working-class residents used their front gardens to grow cabbage. Today, it is a mixed residential area. There are still rich and poor in this neighborhood with the balance tipping in the favor of gentrification. The historic, very pretty brick homes, are worth a side trip.

For a taste of the country, city residents – and visitors – make regular excursions to **Riverdale Farm**, on the eastern border of Cabbagetown. It's a full-scale, immaculately kept farm with weathered barns, several paddocks and a good assortment of farm animals and educational displays geared largely to children. It even sells fresh chicken eggs on Saturdays.

Another, perhaps more popular, place to buy fresh eggs and glimpse some more of Toronto's ethnic soul is **Kensington Market**, just west off Spadina Avenue. It covers an eight-square-block area between College and Dundas streets. Although the shops open at 6 a.m. every day but Sunday, Saturday is the busiest and best time to visit. Kensington Market is one of the most interesting and vibrant sections of the city, with a distinct ethnic mix. While the neighborhood population is predominantly Portuguese, West Indians have also gained a significant place in the market. There are Jamaican bakeries and restaurants where visitors

Right: The Royal Ontario Museum's world-renowned Far East collection.

can savor meat patties, coco bread, hard buns and boiled dumplings. And the shops carry goat meat, exotic spices, and other specialties of the Caribbean.

Every year since 1969, Toronto goes all out for nine days at the end of June to celebrate its cultural diversity. Formally known as **Metro International Caravan**, the citywide festival encourages every ethnic community to set up a pavilion offering its special food, entertainment and cultural activities. Caravan is "a celebration of differences," according to former Toronto Mayor David Crombie. It is now the largest North American ethnocultural festival. From the beginning, Caravan has operated through existing organizations, such as churches and community centers. Most of the pavilions are located in Toronto's central core within walking distance of each other.

Every year in late July the city's West Indian community celebrates its heritage with **Caribana**. The highlight of the 10-day festival is a parade downtown. The costumes are worthy of a Mardi Gras celebration and the West Indian music and rhythms throb throughout the city.

The event that helped the revival of the once-decaying neighborhoods was the election in 1972 of a "reformist" city council. The mood of residents changed and restoration of old neighborhoods began in earnest. Though there has been a dizzying number of skyscapers built in the past 20 years, a number of old buildings have also been preserved.

Along College Street, east and west of University Avenue, is the **University of Toronto**, which dates from 1827. The campus sprawls over several city blocks. The Medical Sciences Building is home to many scientific firsts, including the discovery of insulin in 1921. The first electric heart pacemaker, and Pablum, the first precooked vitamin-enriched cereal, were also developed here. Student guides lead free walking tours Monday through Friday. Immediately north of the

UNIVERSITY / PARLIAMENT / MUSEUMS

intersection of College and University is Ontario's stately pink sandstone **Parliament Building**. And just north of the Legislature lies the **Royal Ontario Museum** (ROM), Canada's largest museum. More specifically, it can be found on the southwest corner of Bloor Street West and Queen's Park. Opened in 1912, the ROM has one of the finest Chinese collections in the world which includes Chinese temple wall paintings. There's also a good Egyptian collection which includes 2000-year-old jewelry, mummies and models. A favorite among children and the young at heart is the fascinating, highly realistic South American bat cave. Giant West Coast totem poles soar on either side of the ROM's central staircase.

Opposite the ROM is the **George M. Gardiner Museum of Ceramic Art** featuring pre-Columbian, Italian Majolica, English Delftware and 18th-century porcelain from Europe and England.

But perhaps the most impressive of Toronto's museums is the **Art Gallery of Ontario** (AGO) on Dundas Street West close to Chinatown. Recently reopened following extensive renovations and expansion, it's more stunning than ever. Sculptor Henry Moore was so impressed with the citizens of Toronto who raised money for his sculpture outside the New City Hall that he gave the city a large collection of his works. The museum now boasts the world's largest public collection of **Henry Moore sculptures**. The AGO also has outstanding collections of Canadian, Western Renaissance, Post-Modern, and Modern works to see. It's truly worth a visit. Open Wednesday to Sunday year-round.

There are also small art galleries scattered throughout downtown, with more modern, avant-garde work generally to be found in the "funky" **Queen Street West** area that starts west of University Avenue. More traditional or representational work tends to show up in the city's most fashionable shopping area centred along Yorkville and Bloor avenues between Avenue Road and Bay Street. There are also several good gal-

MUSEUMS / CASA LOMA / EXCURSIONS

leries on Hazelton Avenue, which runs north off Yorkville.

Just north of the downtown core is a magnificent, rambling 98-room turreted castle, **Casa Loma**, which is open for tours. Built by Sir Henry Pellatt between 1911 and 1914 to house his collection of furniture and art and to provide a home away from home for visiting royalty, no private home in the city is larger or more grandiose. Peacock Alley, running the length of the house, is modeled after no lesser a site than the Peacock Alley in the England's royal residence of Windsor Castle. And the wine cellar has space for 1700 (excellent) bottles.

Pellatt spent $3.5 million to equip his castle. He installed one of the first private elevators and gold-plated bathroom fixtures. There's a long, underground passage to the horse stables and porcelain troughs for the horses. Not surprisingly, the cost of castle-living broke Pellatt in the 1920s and he lost it to back taxes.

EXCURSIONS

The **Ontario Science Centre,** about 6 miles (10 km) northeast of the city center (770 Don Mills Road),is designed for the curious of all ages. It has millions of dollars' worth of educational, experimental, hands-on machines and exhibits. It was built in 1967 as Ontario's contribution to Canada's Centennial.

About a 20-minute drive east of the city, along highway 401, is **Metro Toronto Zoo**, one of the largest zoos in the world. It stretches between two arms of the Rouge River over 750 acres (300 hectares). The six pavilions and many open fields have been designed to simulate the natural habitats of the zoo's over 4000 animal residents. The geographic regions represented include Africa, Australia, Eurasia, Indo-Malaysia, North America and South America. An electric monorail covers the 3 1/2-mile (5 km) path through

Above: Creative subculture enlivens city streets. Right: Casa Loma, once the castle of millionaire Sir Henry Pellatt, today a museum.

EXCURSIONS

the Canadian Domain, where deer, Arctic wolves, moose and antelope play. During the winter, visitors can tour the zoo on cross-country skis.

Canada's Wonderland is just half an hour northwest of downtown Toronto on Highway 400 (exit Rutherford Road). The theme park complex covers 370 acres with games, rides including four roller coasters, shops and restaurants. The park's two theaters feature big-name musical productions, while dolphins and sea lions perform at the 2000-seat **Saltwater Circus Theatre**.

The **McMichael Gallery** on Islington Avenue in the town of Kleinburg is also just a half hour's drive from downtown Toronto. Rustically set in the woods, the McMichael Gallery houses the McMichael Canadian Art Collection which is made up of the haunting landscapes of Canada's famous Group of Seven and a good variety of Native and Inuit art.

Near Kleinburg is the **Kortright Centre for Conservation**, an educational, environmental facility in the middle of the woods, once again. Perfect for hiking or just to observe the interesting exhibits and demonstrations, it's on Pine Valley Drive.

Farther afield but certainly worth the drive is **Stratford**, a very well-known small town 1 1/2 hours from Toronto. Shakespeare buffs flock to Stratford in hordes for five months of the year (May to October) for a wide variety of top-quality Shakespearean theatre.

And last but not least is one of the more awesome and unique sights this part of the country has to offer. Located on the Canada-U.S. border, **Niagara Falls** is the largest waterfall by volume in the world. It is found where the Niagara River drops from Lake Erie to Lake Ontario. **Goat Island** divides the falls into the **American Falls** and Ontario's **Horseshoe Falls**. It can be seen in a variety of ways – by tunnel behind the falls, by boat, by helicopter, or from a safe distance at one of several walkways that border the massive falls. The Falls are illuminated at night.

GUIDEPOST: TORONTO

TORONTO
Area Code 416

How to get there
By air: Many major carriers including KLM, Air France, Alitalia, El Al, American Airlines, USAir and Air Canada land at **Lester B. Pearson International Airport**.

By train: Via Rail link with the United States' Amtrak at Montreal, Windsor and Buffalo, NY.

By bus: Service to all points in Ontario and to other provinces is provided by Eastern Canadian Greyhound Lines Ltd., Gray Coach Lines, Voyageur Colonial and others.

By car: The Queen Elizabeth Highway links Toronto with Hamilton, Niagara Falls, Fort Erie and New York State. The Macdonald Cartier Freeway (Hwy. 401) passes through Toronto from the east and west. Hwys. 11 and 400 are major routes north.

Local transit: Buses, streetcars and subways provide fast, clean and realiable transportation throughout the city. Buses and streetcars will only take exact fares. Subways use tokens. Call 393-INFO for transit information. From the airport limousines provide access to downtown hotels. Airport buses also travel between the airport and the major hotels and subway lines.

Accommodation
In recent years hotel building has kept pace with the demand and some of the city's venerable institutions have undergone major renovations. The result is a wide choice for the visitor.

DELUXE: **Four Seasons**, 21 Avenue Rd. M5R 2G1, Tel: 964-0411. Rock stars and heads of state have visited here. Located in fashionable Yorkville. There's an outdoor and indoor pool. **Harbour Castle Westin**, 1 Harbour Square. M5J 1A6, Tel: 869-1600. Spectacular views of Toronto's harbor with complimentary transportation to the downtown shopping area.

Royal York, 100 Front St. M5J 1E3, Tel: 368-2511. When it opened in 1929, it was the largest hotel in the British Commonwealth. It has recently undergone a total renovation and plays host to royalty, international leaders and celebrities.

The Sheraton Centre, 123 Queen St. W. M5H 2M9, Tel: 361-1000. Across the street from City Hall with almost 1,400 rooms, indoor waterfall, shopping arcade and indoor/outdoor pool. **L'Hotel**, 225 Front St. W. M5V 2X3, Tel: 597-1400. Connected to the Metro Toronto Convention Center. **SkyDome Hotel**, 45 Peter St. West, M5V 1J4, Tel: 360-7100. Part of the city's unique SkyDome with a roof that opens to the sky, this hotel offers some of the world's most unique views. It's possible to watch a major league baseball game from many rooms. **Toronto Marriott Eaton Centre**, 525 Bay St. M5G 2E1, 597-9200. Adjacent to Eaton Centre. Indoor pool and exercise facilities.

LUXURY: **Delta Chelsea Inn**, 33 Gerrard St. W. M5G 1Z4, Tel: 585-4362. More than 1,500 rooms with two indoor pools and children's program. **Park Plaza Hotel**, 4 Avenue Rd. M5R 2E8, Tel: 924-5471. The quiet quality of this hotel attracts celebrities. The rooftop bar is favored by literary types. **Windsor Arms**, 22 St. Thomas M5S 2B9, Tel: 979-2341. A small hotel in the midst of the Bloor St. shopping district. There's no pool but individually decorated rooms. **Radisson Plaza Hotel Admiral**, 249 Queen's Quay W. M5J 2N5, Tel: 364-5444. On Lake Ontario in the heart of Harbourfront. Small elegant hotel within walking distance to SkyDome. **The Bristol Place Hotel**, 950 Dixon Rd. M9W 5N4, Tel: 675-9444. Just down the road from the airport; indoor pool and exercise facilities.

MODERATE: **Best Western Primrose Hotel**, 111 Carlton St. M5B 2G3, Tel: 977-8000. Across from Maple Leaf Gardens. **The Carlton Inn Hotel**, 30 Carlton St. M5B 2E9, Tel: 977-6655. Adjacent to Maple Leaf Gardens. **Bond Place Hotel**, 65 Dundas St. M5B 2G8, Tel: 362-6061. Adjacent to Eaton Centre. **Journey's End Hotel**, 250 Bloor St. West, M5C 2T9, Tel: 968-0010. **Hotel Ibis Toronto Centre**, 240 Jarvis St. M5B 2B8, Tel: 593-9400.

Restaurants
DELUXE: **Nekah**, 32 Wellington St. E., Tel: 867-9067. Wild meats and fish. **Auberge Gavroche**, 90 Avenue Rd., Tel: 920-0956. Elegant, very French. **The Beaujolais**, 165 John St., Tel: 598-4656. Two West Coast chefs dish up California nouvelle cuisine. **Fenton's**, 2 Gloucester St., Tel: 961-8485. Three rooms including one with an open fireplace. Inventive food. **The Palmerston**, 488 College St., Tel: 922-9277. Exotic flavors, owners are quite serious about food. **The Restaurant, Three Small Rooms**, 22 St. Thomas St., Tel: 979-2212. Classic cooking has earned an international reputation for this establishment.

EXPENSIVE: **Babsi's**, 1731 Lakeshore Blvd. W., Tel: 823-3794. Owned by one of Canada's best chefs, this restaurant concentrates on local ingredients. **Gaston's**, 35 Baldwin St., Tel: 920-0956. French cuisine, a backyard patio for warm summer nights. **Noodles**, 1221 Bay St., Tel: 921-3171. This futuristic Italian restaurant serves veal, fowl and ravioli. **Trattoria Giancarlo**, 41 Clinton St., Tel: 533-9619. Specialties: fresh pasta with mushrooms and giant shrimp. **Barberian's**, 7 Elm Ave., Tel: 597-0335. Attractive Toronto steak house. **La Fenice**, 319 King St. W., Tel: 585-2377, exquisite Italian-Mediterranean dishes. Specialties: grilled fresh fish, pasta. Conveniently located in the theater district. **Le

GUIDEPOST: TORONTO

Trou Normand, 90 Yorkville Ave., Tel: 967-5956, cosy, central spot, charming outdoor patio in summer. Delicious fare.
MODERATE: **Ed's Warehouse**, 270 King St. W., Tel: 593 6672. Steak and prime rib - one of a series along King St. owned by discount king and theater lover Ed Mirvish. The Warehouse restaurant is elaborately decorated with antiques and signed photos of stars of stage and screen who have visited the city. **The Keg Mansion,** Jarvis at Wellesley, Tel: 964-6609. The setting in the former mansion of the Massey family outshines the food, ribs and steak are good value. **Ouzeri**, 500A Danforth Ave., Tel: 778-0500, popular Greek restaurant where one can order an assortment of appetizers only (all delicious) or the traditional lamb or pork shish-kababs with rice, potatoes and Greek salad. Children welcome.
INEXPENSIVE: **The Hop and Grape**, 14 College St. English food is a specialty in the Hop. Full dining at the Grape, Tel: 923-2818. Casual pub fare at the Hop. **The Old Fish Market**, 12 Market St., Tel: 363-0334. Big brick rooms accommodate seafood lovers attracted by the reasonable prices. **Byzantium**, 410 Danforth Ave., Tel: 466-2845. Greek specialties are served from the open kitchen. **La Chaumière**, 77 Charles St., Tel: 922-0500. Ample portions, well-prepared with a prix fixe menu. **Switzer's Delicatessen**, 322 Spadina Ave., Tel: 596-6900. Corned beef and baby beef sandwiches are the best in the city. This is an authenic New York style kosher deli. **Ho Yuen**, 105 Elizabeth St., Tel: 977-3449. For serious Chinese food lovers. The setting is far from elegant but the food is worth the visit. **Metropolis**, 838 Yonge Street, Tel: 924-4100, just north of Bloor, serves reasonably priced, delicious Canadiana such as Ontario lamb, salmon, Brome Lake duck, and impressive wines by the glass. **Grano Caffe-Forno**, Yonge Street, just south of Eglinton, offers a lively Italian trattoria-type atmosphere and a good choice of reasonably priced pastas and salads. **Bemelmans Restaurant**, 83 Bloor Street West, Tel: 960-0306, just west of Bay Street, an old-world-style restaurant-bar with a charming outside patio in the back. A variety of fare, from burgers to eggs benedict to chicken stir-fry.

Museums
Royal Ontario Museum (ROM), 100 Queen's Park. Fine Chinese und Egyptian collections, May 15-Oct 15 daily, rest of year daily exc. Mon, Tel: 586-5549. **George M. Gardiner Museum of Ceramic Art**, opposite ROM, daily exc. Mon, Tel: 586-8080. **Art Gallery of Ontario (AGO)**, 317 Dundas Street West, open Wed-Sun, free admission Wed evenings, Tel: 977-0414. **Ontario Science Centre**, 770 Don Mills Rd., open daily, Tel: 696-3127. **McMichael Gallery**, Islington Avenue, Kleinburg, Inuit Art, June-Oct. daily rest of year, Mon closed, Tel: 905/893-1121. **Marine Museum of Upper Canada**, Exhibition Place, off Lakeshore Blvd. West, daily, Tel: 392-1765. **Hockey Hall of Fame**, Exhibition Place, open daily, Tel: 595-1345. **Canadian Sports Hall of Fame**, Exhibition Place, daily, Tel: 595-1046. **Casa Loma**, Austin Terrace, daily, Tel: 923-1171.

Theaters / Dance
Premiere Dance Theatre, in Queen's Quay Terminal, 207 Queen's Quay West, Tel: 363-4411. **O'-Keefe Centre for Performances**, 1 Front Street East, Tel: 872-2262. **St. Lawrence Centre for the Arts** (including the **Jane Mallet Theatre** and the **Bluma Apple Theatre**), Front St. East and Scott St., Tel: 366-7723.

Sightseeing
New City Hall, Nathan Phillips Sq., free tours on weekends by appointment, Tel: 392-6907. **Fort York**, Garrison Rd.,daily, Tel: 392-6827. **Ontario Place**, outdoor entertainment complex, 955 Lakeshore Rd. West, Tel: 965-7711, open May-Sept. **Canadian National Exhibition** (CNE), Lakeshore Blvd., Strachan, Tel: 393-6000 for information. **Harbourfront**, recreational and cultural complex, Queen's Quay West, daily, Tel: 973-3000. **Queen's Quay Terminal**, recreational and cultural complex, 207 Queen's Quay West, daily, Tel 363-4411. **CN-Tower**, 301 Front St. West, Tel: 360-8560.

Seasonal Events
Crowds celebrate *New Year's Eve* by skating on the free skating rink in front of City Hall. On *May 24*, weekend fireworks at Ontario Place celebrate the birthday of Queen Victoria. In *June* it's time for the running of the Queen's Plate, the oldest stakes in North America. Metro International Caravan, a nine-day salute to the food, drink and dance of the city's ethnic communities begins in late *June*.
July 1 is Canada Day which kicks off a long holiday weekend that includes fireworks and parades. Toronto's West Indian population celebrates its heritage with Caribana in *mid-July*. There are parades, music and a real Mardi Gras atmosphere.
August marks the opening of the Canadian National Exhibition, one of the oldest and largest, with exhibition, entertainment and an air show. Autumn is ushered in by the Festival of Festivals, an international film festival, and Dockside '92, a floating boat show held at Ontario Place.In *November*, the Royal Agricultural Winter Fair opens.

Tourist Information
Metropolitan Toronto Convention and Visitors Assn., 207 Queens Quay West, Toronto, Ontario, Canada M5J 1A7 , Tel: 800/363- 1990, 203-25001. **Niagara Falls Visitors Bureau**, 5433 Victoria Ave., Niagara Falls, Tel: 905/356-6061.

OTTAWA

OTTAWA

WASHINGTON OF THE NORTH
FESTIVALS AND CULTURE

Ottawa's status as the nation's capital oozes from every pore of this city of 1 million inhabitants. The choice of this location as the capital was an astounding one to many people in Canada as well as Great Britain when Queen Victoria made the pronouncement in 1867. At the time the town was called Bytown and it was regarded as a remote village with all the atmosphere of a rambunctious wilderness town.

The choice was a compromise between the English Canadians who were championing Toronto and the French Canadians who were championing Montréal or Québec. The story goes that the Queen was fed up with all the petty bickering over which colonial post was more deserving of the honor. Her choice transformed the place from the brawling mill town it was into a dignified city. The choice of the town as the young colony's capital was not only quite surprising but it was unpopular with many.

The town's early history gave no indication of its later national status. The Outauac Indians (from whom the city takes its name) used the area as a regular stopover on their nomadic jaunts. The unwelcoming climate – Ottawa is colder

Left: Invitation to visit the Canadian Parliament.

in winter than Moscow – discouraged permanent settlement. Samuel de Champlain, the French explorer, paused briefly near the site of the present parliament buildings in 1613 to admire the Chaudière Falls, pronounced himself much impressed, then hurried on in search of more rewarding discoveries.

Fur was the mainstay of Canada's early economy. As this commerce grew in importance in the 18th and 19th centuries, freighter canoes by the hundreds appeared on the Ottawa River. The traders, or *voyageurs*, as they were called, portaged three times where Hull now stands before continuing their long annual journey to the Great Lakes.

In 1796, a hardy New Englander, Philemon Wright, brought his family and friends to a spot on the north side of the Ottawa River which is now the city of Hull over the border in the province of Québec. He established a small settlement called Wright's Town and soon recognized the economic potential of the area's huge stands of pine trees. He devised a way to float the timber down the largely unnavigable Ottawa River to market in Québec. His method of tying the logs into rafts was used into the 20th century.

The early settlers were joined in 1826 by Lieutenant-Colonel John By and the Royal Engineers, a band of Irish laborers,

PARLIAMENT HILL

Above: View from Peace Tower over the Ottawa River and Hull (Québec).

army engineers and British veterans of the Napoleonic and American wars who had been assigned the task of constructing a canal from Ottawa to Kingston, Ontario. The nearly 125-mile-long (ca 200 km) system of locks, dams, rivers and lakes was originally intended to serve as a secure military route from Montréal to Kingston in the event of American attack. The **Rideau Canal** was completed in only six years and was one of the great engineering feats of the century. The threat of military attack never materialized and the canal became a commercial venture almost as soon as it was completed in 1832. It's one of the city's major attractions today, especially the "stair" of eight locks at Parliament Hill.

It was Colonel By who surveyed and laid out the new town on the south shore of the Ottawa River. Every spring hundreds of rowdy raftsmen came into town on their way back from winter camps and stopped to celebrate in the streets and taverns of Lower Town.

Immigration was also straining the community's resources. Thousands of poor immigrants who came to Canada in the wake of the Irish potato blight in the 1840s entered Ontario via the Rideau Canal and many of them settled.

WASHINGTON OF THE NORTH

Once the town was chosen as the capital of Canada it did not change overnight. However, a quick decision was made to spend $3750 for the original 29-acre site which became **Parliament Hill**. The decision was made to award an $800,000 contract to architects Thomas Fuller and Chilion Jones, and the Neo-Gothic **Parliament Buildings** were erected on a 150-foot promontory overlooking the Ottawa River by 1700 laborers whose pay ranged from 80 cents to $2.45 a day. In 1860, the young Prince Edward (son of Queen Victoria and Later Edward VII)

OTTAWA

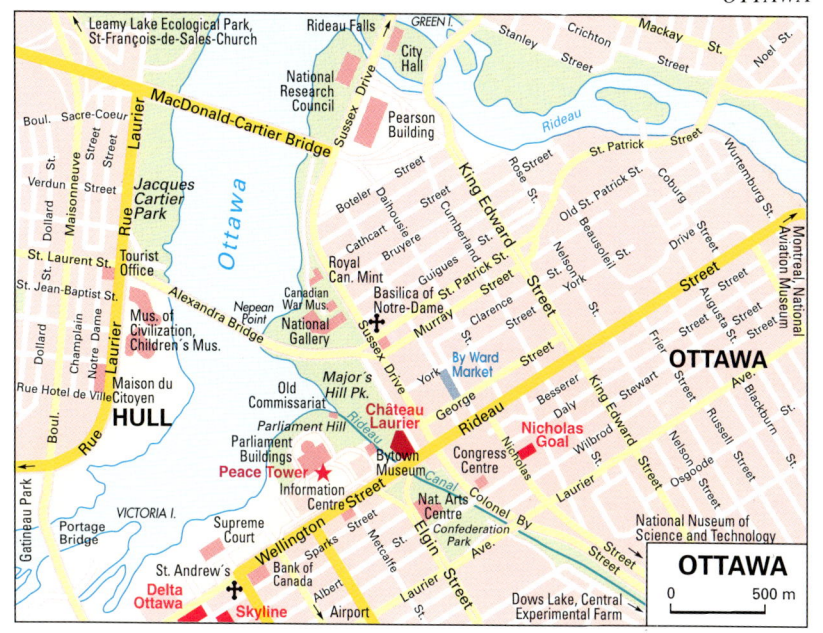

came to Ottawa to lay the cornerstone of the new Parliament Buildings. These grandiose project was ready by 1867 to host the inaugural session of the first Parliament of the new Dominion of Canada. The Centennial Flame, now burning at the south gate of Parliament Hill, was lit in 1967 to mark the century.

The **Houses of Parliament** with the **Peace Tower** are must-see sfor most visitors. The **Center Block** is where the Senate and House of Commons work to create the laws of Canada. The chambers are open to the public. The Senate is housed in an imposing hall with red chairs and carpets, and a throne for Canada's monarch or her representative, the Governor General. The Center Block was almost completely destroyed by fire in the year 1916; only the **Library** of Parliament was saved from the original building.

The Library of Parliament which was completed in 1876, is virtually sandwiched by the Senate and the House of Commons. A white marble statue of the young Queen Victoria stands in the center of this high, many-sided chamber, whose walls are lined with bookshelves and elaborately carved wooden galleries.

The **West Block** was originally built to house the civil service, which numbered only a few hundred people in the mid-1800s. It now contains offices for parliamentarians and is closed to the public. The **East Block**, which was restored between 1976 and 1981, has four historic rooms open to the public: the original Governor General's office, restored to the period of Lord Dufferin (1872-1878); the offices of Sir John A. Macdonald and Sir George-Etienne Cartier (Fathers of Confederation, 1867); and the Privy Council Chamber.

The Parliament Buildings stand on a cliff overlooking the Ottawa River, which is one of Ottawa's prettiest sites. There are many statues on the grounds, including the bell from the original Center Block, behind the Library. This bell crashed to the ground after tolling midnight during the fire of 1916. Same-day

Above: Rideau Canal – the hotel Château Laurier (right), Parliament Hill (left). Right: Changing the Guard before Parliament.

reservations for tours of the Center Block and East Blocks and for "Discover the Hill" walking tours, must be made in the tent located east of the Centre Block on Parliament Hill during the summer.

At 10am during the summer there is a daily pomp-and-circumstance spectacle on the lawns of Parliament Hill – the **Changing of the Guard** performed by Her Majesty's Canadian Guards. It's not Buckingham Palace, but still, no tourist should pass up an opportunity to click off a few exposures. Canada's history unfolds in a dazzling half-hour display of **sound and light** against the dramatic backdrop of the Parliament Buildings. Also not to be missed is the walk along the Ottawa River, where a number of statues stand around idly.

The best place to get an overview of the capital is from the lookout of the **Peace Tower**, a Parliament building on Wellington Street, that was erected in 1927 as a memorial to the Canadians who were killed during World War One. It has a 53-bell glockenspiel. The 300-foot high (91 m) tower opens up a panoramic view extending up to 40 miles (64 km) in all directions. To the north stand the new glass and concrete government buildings rising up from the Québec side of the Ottawa River. Beyond lies Gatineau Park, an 88,000-acre (35,000 ha) wilderness and recreation area popular with locals and visitors alike. To the east is the **Rideau Canal**. In the summer, pleasure boats sail along the calm channel. In the winter, skaters glide along its frozen length. To the south and west is the city itself, graced by lush parkland.

By the turn of the century Sir Wilfrid Laurier, Prime Minister from 1896, began to dream of creating a great capital: a "Washington of the North." His vision and that of a successor – Mackinzie King – followed by a century of planning and work have created the liveable, people oriented capital Ottawa is today.

OTTAWA

Despite its aura of power, Ottawa is very much a city of human proportions. The Metropolitan Area has a population of just over 920,000 including the Québec city of Hull which is on the other bank of the river in Québec but considered part of the capital district and connected by a bridges. Because of Ottawa's national significance, the city has amenities other cities its size might not be able to support. Its international function as a capital has also has imbued the city with a definite international flair and the corresponding crowd. The choice of foods, for example, is astounding. While French and French-Canadian dominate, there are restaurants offering specialties from around the world. The cultural scene is equally cosmopolitan. The **National Arts Center** at Confederation Square features performers from across Canada and from around the world – including the resident National Arts Center Orchestra. The Center features more than 900 performances a year that take place in one of its four auditoriums.

Most of Ottawa's main sights are conveniently located around what has come to be known as the **Mile of History**, which basically runs along Wellington Street and Sussex Drive and forms the oldest part of the city. The number of museums here is quite astonishing. The oldest house of Ottawa, the **Old Commissariat**, stands near the Rideau Canal Locks. Accordingly it displays exhibits relating to the "birth" of Ottawa. Nearby is one of the world's most unusual youth hostels, **Nicholas Goal**, which indeed served as a prison from 1862 to 1972. This stern limestone building can be toured on Tuesdays, and of course, if residing there, you will sleep in a cell.

Colonel By used to live on **Major's Hill Park** on the other side of the Canal. Where his house once stood is a statue of the Colonel. An old cannon from the Crimean War also found a resting place here, but it's not so peaceful, as the Ottawans fire it daily at noon and 10am on Sundays and holidays. If you head toward the river through the park, you will

MUSEUMS

come to **Nepean Point**, which offers a fine view across the river. Champlain is here in effigy, holding his famous astrolabe, a precursor of the sextant, which he lost in the area.

Before running the mile along Sussex, however, take note of the **Byward Market** which is down York Street in the Lower Town. From a basic farmer's market back in 1840 this on-going event has spawned a wide variety of shops and stalls selling everything from scents to fuel, maple syrup to lettuce. Galleries, cafés, discos have also congregated here to partake in the fun. It's truly a place for day and night.

Back to Sussex Drive: **The Canadian Ski Museum** at number 457 reveals the past and present of one of Canada's great outdoor activities. Nearby on the corner of St. Patrick street is a superb collection of cartoons, some dating as far back as the 18th century. The neighboring church

Above: The National Gallery, opened in 1988, also displays the art of gardening.

is the Roman Catholic **Basilica of Notre Dame**, which was built in the mid-19th century, and displays typically neo-Gothic features. The most interesting aspect of the interior is the large statuary around the main altar.

The **National Gallery of Canada** at 380 Sussex is one of the more interesting modern buildings in Ottawa, a tent-like structure built mostly of glass. Its main thrust is Canadian art, but one also finds American, Asian and European works on display. The reconstructed Rideau Convent Chapel, with its unique (for North America) fan-vaulted ceiling, constitutes one of the most important examples of religious art in the country.

Nepean Point, mentioned above, is accessible behind the Gallery, which also has three restaurants where one can take a break before going on to the next set of museums. These include the self-explanatory **Canadian War Museum** (330 Sussex Dr.), which coverss Canada's participation in World Wars One and Two, and the **Royal Canadian Mint**

(320 Sussex Dr.), which still strikes special coins, medals, tokens and the like.

1 Sussex Drive was built by a Scottish stonemason named Thomas McKay in 1836. A humble beginning, perhaps, but the house became the residence of the Governor General of Canada, the direct representative of the King or Queen of England. The house stands in the midst of a beautiful park with well-tended paths. The hourly changing of the guards in summer is one of the spectacles not to be missed.

At the northern and eastern edges of the city are two more museums with considerable technical charm: the **National Aviation Museum**, presenting the history of Canada's air adventures, and the National **Museum of Science and Technology**, with a well-appointed Observatory.

Alexandra Bridge, behind the Gallery, leads across the river to Hull, where the first stop is the **Canadian Museum of Civilization** on Laurier Street. This expansive modern complex has enough exhibits to keep one occupied for several hours. The museum's pride exhibits are the six Indian long houses with totem poles that were transplanted from the northwestern coast, and the giant reconstructions of scenes from Canada's history. There is also a cinema which uses Imax and Omnimax technology for some impressively vivid projections. And the **Children's Museum** provides hands-on activities that certainly make the discovery of Canadian and foreign cultures a great deal more enjoyable.

Most Hull sights are near the river. You can stroll southwards on Laurier Street and drop in to the modern **Maison du Citoyen**, Hull's city hall, where there is a small exhibition of Canadian art. Further the old Sentier de Portage steers a course along the river. This old trail was used by Canadian Indians for millenia and later by Europeans. If you go far enough you will come to **Chaudière Falls**, which still bears many traces from the old logging days. The Mill, a restaurant nowaydays, once served as a saw and grist mill.

Laurier Street northward takes you through **Jacques Cartier Park**, a pleasant place to stroll about or have a picnic. The bicycle path that skirts the river leads ultimately to **Leamy Lake Ecological Park**, which offers further recreational activities including windsurfing. **Saint-François-de-Sales Church** near the Gatineau Exhibition Center is a pretty Neo-Gothic building.

The MacDonald-Cartier Bridge connects Jacques Cartier Park with the riverside greenery of Ottawa. **Green Island**, which stands where Rideau River pours into the Ottawa, is a pleasant patch of nature. **Rideau Falls** on the northern bank is a double cataract that was once the hub of an industrial area, of which nothing at all is left. Ottawa's City Hall is on the island, a somewhat unimaginative modern building dating to the 1950s.

Among the more far-flung attractions of Ottawa is **Dows Lake**, another recreational area on an artificial lake formed from the Rideau Canal. A little to the west, in the city itself, is the remarkable **Experimental Farm**, a 1200-acre (485 ha) site, featuring everything from domestic animals to an arboretum and a tropical greenhouse. It is also an ideal place for a wagon ride, and those interested in the development of farming can also drop into the **Agricultural Museum**. A similar site is even further out in the Greenbelt area (off Rte. 417). **The Log Farm** is a traditional 19th-century Canadian homestead, and the interpreters who mill about are dressed appropriately to give the right atmosphere.

FESTIVALS

There are festivals throughout the year but no single Ottawa celebration is more eagerly awaited or more beautiful than

FESTIVALS

Above: A wet amusement – rafting on the Ottawa River.

the **Canadian Tulip Festival** in May when the city is set ablaze with more than 200 varieties of tulips. Ottawa in fact has the largest collection of tulips in North America. Each year, the royal family of the Netherlands adds new varieties to this already growd collection. This Dutch connection dates from World War Two, when Queen Juliana fled the Nazi occupation of her country and accepted Ottawa's hospitality. The first Dutch tulips were given to the city to celebrate the birth of her daughter, Princess Margriet, at Ottawa Civic Hospital in 1943. To ensure the princess was born a citizen of The Netherlands, the Canadian government proclaimed the Queen's hospital room to be part of Holland. The festival itself is set high on a bluff above the confluence of the Ottawa, Gatineau and Rideau Rivers with the Gatineau Hills as the northern backdrop. The Festival opens on a page out of the Olympics, with a colorful field of runners competing in the National Capital Marathon. It continues with nightly open-air concerts and performances at Major's Hill Park. The Rideau Canal Flotilla attracts fleets of creative boaters from Ontario, Québec and the United States, who deck out their craft and sail their fantasies down the canal past picnicking spectators. At Dows Lake in the center of the city there are wet and wild motorized bathtub races, skillful and daring water ski shows, antique car parades, concerts, classical and modern dancers, hot air balloon rides and historical displays. Just steps from Parliament Hill the Outdoor Craft market displays of work by some of the finest local craftspeople and artists.

Of course, Ottawa citizens hold a winter celebration – to break up the long winter season and to enjoy a good party. It is the 10-day **Winterlude**, held every February. It demonstrates that cold is no detriment to fun and merriment. It includes a parade, ice sculptures, sleigh rides and harness racing on.

OTTAWA

Area code 613

How to Get There

By air: The **Ottawa International Airport** serves Air Canada, Canadian Airlines Int., USAir, Air Alliance, Air Nova, Air Ontario and First Air.

By train: Via Rail provides passenger rail service with daily service to and from Montréal and Toronto. The local transit system serves Ottawa train station.

By car: The Trans-Canada Highway links Ottawa with Montréal from the east and goes west through Sault Ste. Marie, Thunder Bay and into Manitoba. Hwy. 7 is the scenic central route between Ottawa and Toronto.

By bus: Voyageur Colonial Bus Lines provide inter-city bus service from many Canadian and American points.

Local transit: OC Transport serves the metropolitan region of Ottawa-Carleton on the Ontario side of the Ottawa River. It operates buses on city streets and on the Transitway – an extensive system of bus-only roads.

Accommodation

Most of Ottawa's hotels serve a governmental clientale and tend to be a little more expensive. However, there are numerous hotels and motels to suit all pocketbooks.

DELUXE: **Château Laurier**, 1 Rideau St. K1N 8S7; Tel: 241-1414. This is a Canadian institution; it's old and gracious and the rooms have recently been refurnished. Right beside Parliament Hill. **Delta**, 361 Queen St. K1R 7S, Tel: 238-6000. It's noted for its health club facilities and its closeness to Parliament Hill. **The Westin Hotel Ottawa**. 11 Colonel By. K1N 9H4, Tel: 560-7000. This luxury hotel overlooks the Rideau Canal and is situated only minutes from Parliament Hill. *LUXURY:* **Hotel Roxborough**, 123 Metcalfe St. K1P 5L9, Tel: 237-5171. A 104-room hotel catering primarily to busines clients. **Skyline Ottawa**, 101 Lyon St. K1R 5T0, Tel: 237-3600. It has a good rooftop bar and an indoor pool. *MODERATE:* **Best Western Macies Ottawan Motor Inn**, 1274 Carling Ave. K1Z 7K8, Tel: 728-1951. This well-run hotel caters to families. **Lord Elgin**, 100 Elgin St. K1P 5K8, Tel: 235-3333. This is a well-located downtown hotel with a pleasant atmosphere. *BUDGET:* **Journey's End**, 1252 Michael St. K1J 7T1, Tel: 744-2900. Part of a reliable Canadian chain, this hotel is situated near Highway 417. **Parkway Motel**, 475 Rideau. K1N 5Z3, Tel: 232-3781.

Restaurants

As the nation's capital Ottawa boasts an extensive variety of establishments representing cuisines from all over the world. Many of the area's best restaurants are across the border in Hull, Québec.

CONTINENTAL: **Courtyard Restaurant**, 21 George (Byward Market), Tel: 238-4623. **Green Valley Restaurant**, 1107 Prince of Wales, Tel: 225-8770. **Restaurant des Beaux-Arts**, 380 Sussex (National Gallery), Tel: 563-8330. **Le Fou du Roi**, 253 St. Joseph, Hull, Tel: 819/778-0516, French. **Le Panache**, 201 Eddy, Hull, Tel: 819/777-7771. **Les Belles Gourmandes**, 22 Laval, Hull, Québec, Tel: 819/777-4211. **Maison Zorba**, 50 Montcalm, Hull, Tel: 819/778-2662, Greek. **Le Raj**, 151 Wellington, Hull, Tel: 819/777-7277, Indian. *INTERNATIONAL:* **Aux Bons Vivants**, 462 St. Joseph, Hull, Tel: 819/771-8990. **Le Jardin**, 127 York St., Ottawa, Tel: 238-1828. **Restaurant de la Promenade**, 135 promenade du Portage, Hull, Tel: 819/777-8539. **Gasthaus Switzerland**, B&B Inn, 89 Av. Darly, K1N6E6, Tel: 613/237-0335. *ITALIAN:* **La Favorita Ristorante**, 180 Preston, Tel: 233-6239. **La Gondola**, 188 Bank, Tel: 234-8244. *STEAK AND SEAFOOD:* **Hayloft Steak & Seafood House**, 200 Rideau, Tel: 232-7161. **The Place Next Door**, 320 Rideau, Tel: 232-1741. *SEAFOOD:* **Old Fish Market Restaurant**, 54 York, Tel: 563-0186.

Seasonal Events

Winterlude, a 10-day extravaganza, is held *Jan/Feb*. **Canadian Tulip Festival** in *mid-May* brings parades, music, fireworks and thousands of flowers, Tel: 562-1480. **Canada Day**, July 1 is the celebration of Canada's birthday. **Festival Ottawa** is a mid-summer performing arts festival.

Museums

Canadian Museum of Civilization, 100 Laurier St., Hull, May-mid Oct. daily, otherwise closed Mon, Tel: 819/776-7000. **Canadian Parliament Buildings**, Wellington St., daily, Tel: 996-0896. **Canadian Ski Museum**, 457A Sussex Dr., daily exc. Mon, Tel: 233-5832. **Canadian War Museum**, 330 Sussex Dr., May-Sept. daily, rest of year daily exc. Mon, Tel: 992-2774, 996-1420. **National Arts Centre**, Confederation Square, Tel: 996-5051, 755-1111. **National Aviation Museum**, Rockcliffe Airport, May-Oct 15 daily, closed Mon otherwise, Tel: 993-2010. **National Gallery of Canada**, 380 Sussex Dr., May-mid Oct. daily, otherwise closed Mon, Tel: 990-1985. **National Museum of Science and Technology**, 1867 St. Laurent Blvd., May-mid Oct. daily, otherwise closed Mon, Tel: 991-3044. **Royal Canadian Mint**, 320 Sussex Dr., summer Mon-Fri, Tel: 993-8990. **The Children's Museum**, 100 Laurier St., Hull, May-mid Oct. daily, otherwise closed Mon, Tel: 819/776-7000.

Tourist Information

Ottawa Tourism & Convention Authority, 2nd Floor, 111 Lisgar Street, Ottawa, Ontario, Canada K2P 2L7, Tel: 237-5158.

ONTARIO

ONTARIO

**GREY AND BRUCE COUNTIES
NIAGARA PENINSULA
HURONIA
MUSKOKA
CENTRAL AND
EASTERN ONTARIO
NORTHERN ONTARIO**

The name Ontario comes from an Iroquois word which is translated either as "beautiful lake" or "beautiful water." The name is appropriate given that over one-sixth of the province is covered with lakes and rivers. It is these bodies of water, as well as the pristine wilderness and sandy beaches which so often accompany them, which make Ontario an ideal destination for tourists. A good two-thirds of the province is covered by the Canadian Pre-Cambrian Shield: a massive expanse of ancient rock, deposited by glaciers, which encompasses the entire northern region of the province and extends down into Muskoka and Algonquin Park, where it thrusts down between the St. Lawrence River cities of Brockville and Kingston before relenting. The rest of southern Ontario, when not dominated by city and highway, is blanketed by farmland – rolling in the east and northwest, flat in the southwest.

The glory of the province is its provincial and national parks and lakeland resorts. And there is an abundance of both, usually in close proximity to each other and for every budget. There are over 220 Provincial Parks and numerous National Parks. Though varying in size, every park offers, at the very least, first-class hiking, while most offer excellent fishing, swimming, canoeing, boating and overnight camping. Some are heavily developed with recreation facilities, interpretive trails, and campgrounds, while others leave it up to the visitors to explore uncharted forests and lakes where moose, beavers and timber wolves that make the parks their home.

Left: Algonquin totem pole in the provincial park of the same name.

GREY AND BRUCE COUNTIES

Grey-Bruce, located in the northwestern region of southern Ontario, consists of the twin counties of Grey and Bruce and is crowned by a natural wonder, the **Bruce Peninsula**. Both counties were settled by whites in the early 19th century; magnificent, sprawling hardwood forests attracted pioneers who harvested the timber. Of all the regions in southern Ontario, the Bruce Peninsula and nearby area probably offer the best combination of unpeopled lacustrine wilderness and charming resort towns.

There are three scenic highways leading to the peninsula: west on Hwy 26 through Grey County along the Nottawasaga Bay; north through Bruce County from Point Clark along Lake Huron; and northwest from Toronto on Hwy 10 through Dufferin and Grey Counties.

SOUTHERN ONTARIO

GREY AND BRUCE COUNTIES

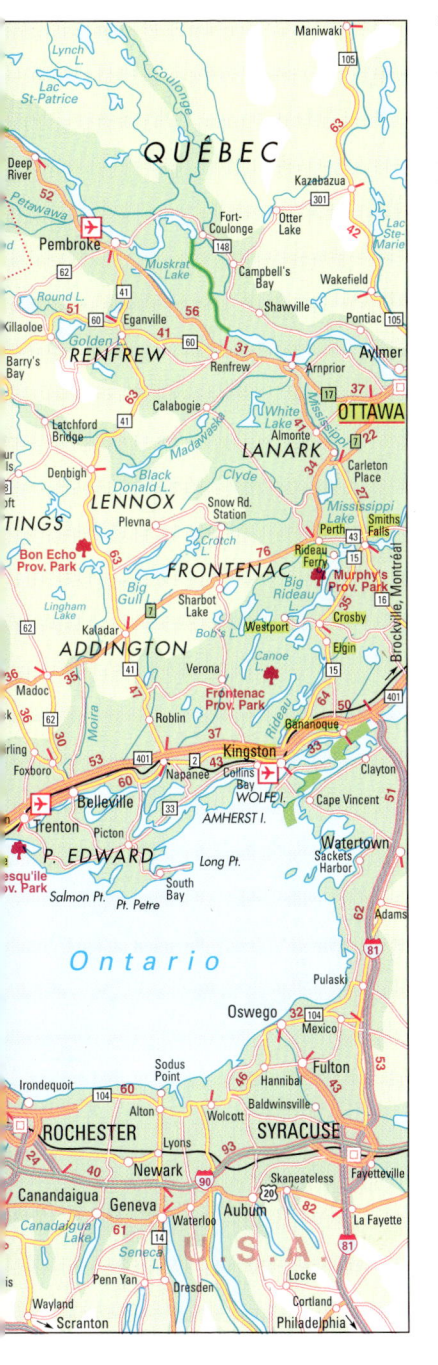

The drive from Toronto crosses through idyllic country drives with an abundance of trees, the occasional river, large statuesque barns, fresh ponds, church graveyards. Hay and pasture are the main crops, and they provide nourishment for the cows, sheep, and goats which do not show the slightest bit of interest in the human beings passing by in their automobiles. The small towns scattered throughout inland Grey-Bruce are consistently hospitable, complete with the standard Ontario fair: flea and farmers markets, music and art festivals and antique shops. **Owen Sound**, three hours from Toronto on Georgian Bay is the major center. It has several museums well worth visiting, such as the **Tom Thomson Memorial Art Gallery** featuring numerous works by the Canadian landscape painter, and the **County of Grey-Owen Sound Museum**, which covers many aspects of local history, culture and architecture.

There are a number of sights worth stopping for, however, if you're approaching the peninsula traveling west through Grey County along the Nottawasaga Bay on Hwy 26. **Craigleith Provincial Park** lies on the bay between **Collingwood** and **Thornbury**. The park provides camping facilities, nature programs, an intriguing fossil shale shoreline, hiking on the Bruce trail and, most notably, superb fishing. In the spring and fall rainbow and brown trout and splake are in abundance. The town of Thornbury, situated in the **Beaver Valley**, is 6 mi (10 km) west of the park. This charming apple-growing center, with its highly rated bed and breakfast homes and fine dining, is a good place to settle down for a day or two. A fish lock sits in Thornbury's harbor. Here, rainbow trout are tagged and measured before they travel inland up the **Beaver River** to spawn. Fish aren't the only creatures, however, who travel the river valley. **Kimberly**, a little way to south an Route 13 is the departure point for scenic, four-hour canoe trips northward to Heathcote, through a landscape well stocked in birds and wildlife. Route 13, renowned for its autumn colors, offers one of the most picturesque drives in Ontario. The **Falls**, at the village of Eugenia, is a good place to turn around at and travel back to the coast.

If approaching the peninsula from southwestern Ontario it is advisable to make your way up along the Bruce County side roads which hug the **Lake Huron** shoreline. The water along this coast is warm, shallow and clean, making the long sandy beaches ideal for families and water sports.

The area is also famous for its beautiful red sunsets. Alone the spectacle of this enormous lake – and nothing else – before you make a visit to this coastline a must. From south to north on the shore, Kincardine, Port Elgin, and Southampton, are all lovely resort towns worth stopping or staying in. **Kincardine** has a Scottish heritage, and on Saturday evenings, July through August, a pipe band marches through the downtown. And if the mighty bags aren't enough to move the stolid heart, the town boasts, in and around its impressive 19th-century buildings, a number of romantic settings: rock gardens, dance halls, lighted boardwalks, and parks with enchanting views of the harbor. **Port Elgin** is blessed to have the 1204 hectare beach side **MacGregor Point Provincial Park** just south of it to compensate for its nuclear power plant (which can also be visited). Excellent walking and biking trails allow the visitor to take in the beaver, waterfowl, and over 200 species of bird which populate the park. Private campsites, with varying degrees of modern amenities, are also available . **Southampton** offers one of the most peaceful resort beaches in Ontario – automobiles are prohibited – and, in the nearby Saugeen River, some of the province's best fishing and canoeing.

Above: The Indian painter Gelineau Fisher lives on Reiner Lake. Right: Halfway Rock Point marks the middle of the Bruce Trail.

Just east of the town, along Route 21, is the **Saugeen Indian Reserve**. In 1854, the British signed a treaty with the Saugeen and Newash Indians forcing them to surrender what is now the Bruce Peninsula and nearby area. The treaty gave the Saugeen six tracts of land, four of which remain in their control. From the road the reserve itself looks very much like any other township in the area. Turn off this road at the appropriate sign, though, and you will see a peculiar anachronism: an amphitheater, built in ancient Hellenistic style in 1979 above a Saugeen burial ground. It stands behind an active United Church with a predominantly Indian congregation, and overlooks the magnificent Saugeen River valley.

Bruce Peninsula

Bruce Peninsula lies between Georgian Bay and Lake Huron. It is the northernmost upper extension of the Niagara Escarpment which stretches 773 miles (1236 km) from Tobermory, at the northern tip of the peninsula, down to Queenston, near the Niagara Falls. Its limestone rock tells the story of the past 440 million years of geological transformation. The escarpment was originally covered by an ancient sea. When the sea retreated, some 250 million years ago, its coral reef remained, complete with fossilized sea creatures, which were transformed into limestone walls in the long period of erosion which followed. The escarpment was born when huge blocks of limestone broke off.

The landscape was further altered approximately 2 million years ago when an enormous glacier bulldozed its way through the entire region. In 1967, **Bruce Trail,** a hiking route covering virtually the entire distance of the escarpment, was officially opened. And in 1990 the United Nations designated the escarpment a "World Biosphere Reserve," acknowledging its unique geological character and the habitat it provides to innumerable species of reptiles, amphibians, mammals and birds.

BRUCE PENINSULA

The Bruce Peninsula National Park and the Fathom Five National Park, both in the northern sector, are especially worth the effort. These sites can be approached by traveling north up Hwy 6. The side roads off the highway also offer breathtaking views, secluded campsites, challenging hikes, semi-resort bays, rugged forest, and scenic drives. The best plan, if you want to see as much of the peninsula as possible, is to take one route up and the other down. And of the two the eastern route is more desirable given its proximity to the Bruce Trail and its jagged and secluded, coastline.

After passing **Wiarton** get off Hwy 6 and take Routes 9 north and 18 east to **Cape Croker.** Spectacular views of rocky cliffs and the Georgian Bay can be seen along this itinerary. After five or ten minutes a dirt road (follow the signs) leads to **Cape Croker Indian Reserve**,

Above: Freedom in the expanses of Eastern Canada. Right: The postman doesn't even ring once – rural mailboxes.

an Ojibwa tract open to the public. Although dotted with the occasional farm house, the reserve, with its dense forestation, feels decidedly isolated. A private campsite in the area provides shelter, boating and fishing facilities. Returning to 9 (be alert, the signposting is poor), a short drive north brings one to **Hope Bay**. This little bay village, surrounded by imposing cliffs, offers one of the prettiest beaches in the area and, with its little rustic cottages and trailer park, does not have the feel of a commercialized resort town. Close by, just north on Route 9, are **Greig's Caves**. Follow the signs right to **Rush Cove** after which you will have to engage in a demanding 1/2-mile. The twelve limestone caves with their mysterious grottos and secret hollows have a primordial, eerie quality about them especially when taken in during off hours. Getting back on Route 9 heading north, the drive through **Lion's Head** offers an excellent view of Isthmus Bay as well as a winding route through a heavily forested area which crosses a section of

Bruce Trail. Lion's Head is the most developed resort town on the peninsula. From here it's a short drive to the **Bruce Peninsula National Park**.

The park encompasses most of the top end of the peninsula and, just below that, a narrow section of the western shoreline south of Dorcas Bay. This fairly large tract of land includes such natural sights as limestone cliffs, clean fishing lakes, sandy beaches, mixed woodlands, and lush marshlands. Though the park is heavily visited there is plenty of room to roam in virtual isolation, always with the chance of encountering the extraordinary variety of wildlife – porcupines, lynx, wolves – which live in the area. If you come in Spring you may also spot one of the 40 species of colorful orchids that grow here.

Bruce Trail runs through the park and provides some of the province's best hiking. Cyprus Lake, west of Hwy 6, is probably the best place to head to for a combination of vigourous walk and spectacular view. Park at **Head of Trails**, the lot furthest in from the park entrance. From here take the **Horse Lake Trail** 1 km to the edge of the bluffs. Following the trail to the left, you will come across a singularly spectacular natural show, with unique rock formations, including overhanging ledges and beaches where boulders lie about like stranded whales. For another noteworthy hike, take the Dorcas Bay Rd. West (or left) off of Hwy 6 until you reach a sign pointing to Singing Sands Beach. Park as far north as possible and walk across a bridge spanning a little river. Now you are in the **Dorcas Bay Nature Reserve**. Take the left fork to an old dirt road that skirts the shoreline, with a magnificent view of the Lake Huron side of the peninsula. Be sure to bring good walking shoes or boots.

Cyprus Lake is the center of activity in the park. It offers 242 campsites, each equipped with a fireplace and table. There is no electricity, but running water and toilets are available. Motor boats are prohibited on the Lake between June 15 and Sept. 15. The town of **Tobermory** sits at the northernmost tip of the peninsula on Hwy 6. Tourists invade this invigorating resort town in the summertime, but the crowds are worth braving for the **Fathom Five National Marine Park**. The park takes in the triangular area enclosing the 19 islands which lie north of Tobermory. In the past, this passageway provided an important route for transportation and trade. The waters proved treacherous, and many a passing ship met its doom on the peninsula's sharp limestone ridges. Today the remains of at least 21 ships attract many to the park. Glass-bottomed boats provide a view of these wrecks, but the really adventurous soul will brave the cold water and strap on scuba and snorkeling gear and investigate the wrecks at close range. Underwater caves, strange rock formations, and marine life make these underwater excursions doubly enjoyable. Cruises around the islands are also available. **Flowerpot Island** – so named because of two enormous flowerpot-shaped limestone pillars – has walking trails to the flowerpots and to numerous caves.

Tobermory can also be reached from **Manitoulin Island** by taking the **Chi-Cheemaun Ferry** (From early May to mid-October). Manitoulin is one of the great (relatively) undiscovered secrets of Ontario. It is the world's largest freshwater island and offers some of the province's most picturesque coastal villages. Fishing and boating are excellent here. The island can also be reached from highways in northern Ontario.

NIAGARA PENINSULA

The peninsula, lying between **Lake Ontario** and **Lake Erie** and separated from the state of New York by the **Niagara River**, is one of the most visited and

Right: No place for romantics – the city of Niagara Falls.

probably the best known tourist regions in Canada. Only a few days should be spent in the area, as the landscape is not nearly as attractive as in other parts of Ontario. Three bridges conntect the Canadian town of **Niagara Falls** with the American town bearing the same name. **Rainbow Bridge** provides a particularly beautiful view of the falls. As for the lookout towers (Skylon, Minolta Tower) on the Canadian side, they are open round the clock.

White settlement in the region began in the 1770's in response to the American Revolution. Hundreds of Americans loyal to the British crown sought refuge in the area. While wives and children were deposited in Fort Niagara, which lay on the American side of the Niagara River, the men joined the army. In time, a fort, Butler's Barracks, went up on the Ontario side, and soon farms for refugee families were built along this western bank of the river. Settlement then extended west after an agreement was made with the local Mississauga Indians. All the main attractions in this region lie along the eastern shoreline of the Niagara River. If these attractions are all you care to see, and you're coming from Toronto, simply get on the Gardiner Expressway West at the downtown's southern base. This highway becomes the QEW and will take you all the way around Lake Ontario's semicircular western shoreline to Hwy 55, which provides a short route north to Niagara-on-the-Lake. You will be able to see the flat, pastoral landscape of the region, if you get off the QEW at **Hamilton** and onto Hwy 8 and then Route 81 both traveling east. The 81 is part of what is called the "wine and vineyard route," a path through 16 wineries and juice plants running from the western border of Niagara County to the Falls. Most of these businesses are open daily.

Other worthwhile destinations off of 81 while heading east: at the city of Grimsby take Route 12 south to **Beamer**

Memorial Conservation Area, which takes in a stretch of the Bruce Trail; further east at **Ball's Falls** take Rd. 24 south and another conservation area can be found, this one with two waterfalls at its **Twenty Mile Creek;** at the city of St. Catherines take Route 34 north to Route 87, past orchards and vineyards, all the way to **Niagara-on-the-Lake**.

With its idyllic setting on Lake Ontario, near the northern mouth of the Niagara River, and its well preserved 19th-century architecture, Niagara-on-the-Lake is one of the most delightful towns in Canada. It was the capital of Upper Canada in the 1790s, but was called Newark then. The main strip is Queen Street. An excellent attempt has been made here to recapture the (imagined?) leisure, elegance and prosperity of an earlier time. An apothecary built in 1886 has been restored. Old-style bakeries and fudge and jam shops provide tasty treats. A clock tower honors the dead of World War One. And the centerpiece of the street, an old Victorian hotel, the **Prince of Wales**, offers elegant accommodation. The *Shaw Festival,* honoring the Irish playwright George Bernard Shaw is an attraction from mid-April to the end of October. Outside of town are two interesting sights. On Hwy. 55 is a perfume factory and museum showing how the "smells" used to be produced. If you like dolls, visit the **Mahoney Doll's House Gallery** on Niagara Road. **Fort George National Historic Park** (mid-May to October), on the edge of town on the Niagara Parkway, is also worth visiting. It is a reconstruction of the twice-destroyed fort which British forces used to defend against the Americans following their revolution.

Winston Churchill once called the **Niagara Parkway** "the prettiest Sunday afternoon drive in the world." The Parkway runs south from Niagara-on-the-Lake all the way along the full length of the Niagara River to its southern estuary at **Fort Erie**.

The American state of New York is just to the east across the river. And throughout the 40-minute drive there is a

NIAGARA PENINSULA / NIAGARA FALLS

splendid view of a hilly river bank, which grows into a deep limestone chasm the closer the Falls get.

Take the parkway into **Queenston** and follow the signs to **Queenston Heights**. At the top of a towering hill is a magnificent statue of General Isaac Brock, who died while leading his troops to victory in a battle here against the Americans during the War of 1812. The monument (which can be climbed for a good look around the area) is decidedly un-Canadian, both in its grandeur and its cockiness: General Brock faces New York State across the Niagara River a top of column many feet above the ground. He appears to be taunting the Americans with his outstretched arm.

The world-famous **Niagara Falls** are next on the route. The Parkway travels right beside them and, if you follow the signs, parking is readily available. Of the American Falls and Horshoe Falls, it is the **Horseshoe** on the Canadian side that are the most spectacular. Even the most reluctant tourist can not help but be awed by the 34 million gallons of water that crash by the minute over this 54-meter (173-ft) limestone wall. But the most exhilarating way to experience the falls is to ride the Maid of the Mist Steamboat (5920 River Rd.) through the turbulent waters lying just beyond the plummeting torrents. Hooded raincoats are provided for good reason.

Fort Erie, 18 mi (29 km) south, completes the Parkway drive. The fort here, which the city is named after, hasn't so much an exciting military history as a history of inclement weather, having been levelled twice by storms. The American army also torched it once, in the year 1813. The reconstructed version, sporting a moat, a drawbridge and cannons, strikes an impressive figure especially with the drills in authentic uniforms. Inside it houses equipment from British and American armies.

Above: Wet, wet, wet – viewing the Niagara Falls by steamship. Right: Canutes prefer the lakes and rivers of Huronia.

If making your way back to Toronto take Hwy 3 west, turn right on Route 58 north until you hit Hwy 20. Turn left or west and travel the highway's scenic flat, farmland route until you are through Hamilton and back on the QEW again. One possibility is visiting one of the beaches just south of Route 3 along Lake Erie's northern coastline. **Crystal Beach**, not far west of Fort Erie, is a popular resort, and, if you have children with you, offers a large amusement park.

A word is necessary about southwestern Ontario. With apologies to those who live in and, no doubt, love this region of the province, it is not easy to recommend it as a vacation area. Encompassing 15 counties south of Grey-Bruce and west of the Niagara Peninsula, it offers neither the natural beauty, the rural charm, nor the historical interest of so many of the other regions in Ontario. And though it does certainly boast interesting attractions, its area is so great, that the driving involved would be prohibitive: Nonstop it would take ten hours to round the coastline from **Selkirk Provincial Park**, south of Hamilton, to **Point Clark**, at Bruce County's southwestern edge.

HURONIA

Huronia (or Simcoe County) takes in the area extending north to south from **Awenda Provincial Park** off Georgian Bay to the rural farmland just 36 mi (58 km) northwest of Toronto. West to east it covers the land extending from the **Nottawasaga Bay** town of **Collingwood** to **Lake Simcoe** (excluding the bottom half of the lake's eastern shoreline). Not surprisingly, both the Georgian Bay (including Nottawasaga Bay) and Lake Simcoe shorelines are the main drawing cards in the region. On a good day the Expressway 400 will take you straight north from Toronto to the city of **Barrie** in 1.5 hours. From here all the desirable lakeshore attractions can be reached in 30-45 minutes along the major highways.

If not so anxious to reach water, the agricultural territory to the west of Route

Above: Ste. Marie among the Hurons – the Jesuits used similar lathes in the 17th century.

400 offers scenic pastoral roads and charming country towns. Hwy 89 turns west off of 400, some 12.5 mi (20 km) south of Barrie and passes through two of the more engaging towns, **Cookstown**, a restored 1830's village and **Alliston**, "the Potato Capital of Ontario." About 9 mi (15 km) west of Cookstown is the **Earl Rowe Provincial Park**. With its heavily forested riverine landscape, the park offers first-rate camping, canoeing, fishing, hiking and swimming. Backtracking a few kilometers east on Hwy 89 is Route 10. It travels all the way north to **Wasaga Beach Provincial Park**. Along the way, to your left and just beyond Brentwood, which is north of Angus, are riding stables and the **New Lowell Conservation Area**, which also offers camping, canoeing, and fishing.

Wasaga Beach is, of course, the main attraction at the Wasaga Beach Provincial Park. Along with the beach front, however, the park system includes the **Nottawasaga River**, a flood plain, sand dunes, and a lagoon. The dunes in particular are of interest. Shaped by northwest winds into fragile parabolic and U-shaped figures, they are a relatively rare geological formation.

The short **Blueberry Plains Trail** provides an excellent hike through their system. The beach itself, at 9 mi (14 km), is the world's longest freshwater beach. The waterfront is a vacationer's paradise, whether for recreation or for people-watching. The park lends out sports equipment at very reasonable fees (if any at all), leaving the entire area buzzing with cyclists, boaters and volleyball players. Sunbathers – and there are many of them – be warned. This is not the beach for peaceful relaxation.

Farther north up the Nottawasaga Bay shoreline there is a series of tiny beaches which offer a greater possibility of peace and quiet. This area is dense with private residences but there are cottages and resort homes available for rental at almost any budgetary level. A narrow road hugs the shoreline – unfortunately with a row of cottages between it and the lake – which permits the water lover to sneak down to the bay and choose a beachfront to his or her liking. Some are developed with parks and food kiosks, but others are completely undeveloped, with no distractions from the awesome expanse of lake stretching to the horizon.

To the east of these tiny beaches, off the **Georgian Bay Inlet**, are the two major resort towns in the area, **Midland** and **Penetanguishene** (a hill town with gorgeous views) and . Just a five minute drive from each other, both can be reached turning east off Hwy 93 (if you're traveling north).

The town of Midland is situated on the site of one of the earliest white settlements in Canada. In 1639, French Jesuits built a self-sufficient mission community, **Sainte-Marie**, in what is now Midland, in an attempt to convert the Wendat peoples who resided in the area. They were successful for some time but the Jesuits brought, along with their European customs, European diseases which the Wendat had no inborn immunities to. The situation was further aggravated by an on-going rivalry between the Wendat and the Iroquois, who also lived in the region. In 1648, fearing an Iroquois attack, the French and a group of Christian Wendat prophylactically burnt down Sainte-Marie and retreated back to Québec.

Today in Midland an almost identical replica of this community, built from the actual plans of the original. It can be visited from late May to mid October. It is a rare to actually feel transported back to another time in a reconstructed historical site, but Sainte-Marie, with its Wendat longhouse, Catholic Church, blacksmith shop and 300-year old graveyard, succeeds marvellously in this endeavor, and offers a glimpse into the lives of these two very disparate peoples. Both towns also have a number of other historical sites worth visiting. Most noteworthy are a reconstructed Huron village at Midland's **Huronia Museum**; and Penetanguishene's **Historic Naval and Military Establishments,** which recreates, at the actual site, a 19th-century British naval base and military garrison.Both are open from May to October.

Boat cruises leave from Midland and Penetanguishene to the nearby 30,000 Georgian Bay Islands. The area's rugged scenery is breathtaking. If touring the evening cruise, in particular, should not be missed. Marinas in Midland and Penetanguishene also offer boat rides to the **Georgian Bay Islands National Park,** which consists of 59 islands and covers approximately 4.5 sq. mi (12 sq. km) of land. Like so many national and provincial parks in Ontario, it offers excellent camping, fishing and hiking, but its most characteristic features are its pristine beauty and extreme isolation. The northern islands and northern **Beausoleil Island**, which is the park's center of activity, are dominated by barren glacial rock and sturdy pine trees, while Southern Beausoleil is dense, embracing hardwood forest territory. There is no opportunity to purchase supplies or equipment of any kind at the park, so, if you do go, be sure to stock up before you leave.

As for the other shoreline in Huronia, **Lake Simcoe's** can not be given as strong a recommendation as the Georgian Bay's. For such a large lake Simcoe is frustratingly difficult to approach. Along its eastern and northwestern shorelines there are few good scenic routes. The occasional side road will take you down to the water but generally the beaches are inferior in size and comfort to the real prime beaches in the rest of Ontario. Lodges and cottages are scattered around the lake providing enjoyable overnight vacationing, but the Muskoka area, to the north, is definitely the place to go for a better touristic infrastructure.

What this part of Huronia does offer are three excellent provincial parks: **McRae** and **Mara,** which sit on Lake Simcoe, and **Bass,** which is west of the town of Orillia. All have excellent fishing – smallmouth bass, lake trout, and muskellunge being the most common species.

Orillia, with a population of 26,000, is the major agglomeration in the area. It is worth visiting if you're tiring of natural beauty or would like a taste, just a small one, of the urban. The town, with its restored and gentrified downtown, offers excellent shopping and dining, as well as frequent festivals and on-going markets. Live theater is to be had in the old (1895) opera house, and the **Stephen Leacock Museum**, a 1928 mansion built as a home by Leacock himself, affords an engaging view into the life of Canada's best known humorist.

Above: Rabbit hunt. Right: Muskoka Lake – once a region of icy glaciers, today a region for ice-cold beer.

MUSKOKA

Muskoka is one of, if not the, most popular tourist destinations in Ontario. Ontarians, themselves, are particularly fond of the region, which extends to those lakelands lying north of Huronia between Georgian Bay and Algonquin Park. From Barrie, the town of Gravenhurst, Muskoka's southernmost major center, can be reached on Hwy 11 in just over forty minutes.

Muskoka is lodge country, and if you do visit the area you should certainly try to indulge, at least for a couple of days, in this unique sort of vacationing. In 1870 a wealthy New York banker, W.H. Pratt, built a mansion on Lake Rousseau and began to charge visitors to stay overnight. Though locals thought Pratt was daft, his idea caught on and in the years that followed similar lodges cropped up in the region. Originally these resort lodges served the rich from Toronto and nearby American cities, but today they cater to people of all, or at least most, financial portfolios. Basically, the lodges serve those who enjoy the great outdoors but not so much that they wouldn't prefer a comfortable building separating them from it while they sleep. Most of the resorts, though some are more luxurious, offer only the most basic amenities, along with home-cooked style breakfasts and dinners. The rooms are clean, the decor simple, and the living slow and easy – ice tea on the veranda with a board game before a walk to the local community hall for a bingo match might make up an evening's schedule. The day, of course, would be spent at the lake, canoeing, waterskiing, or swimming, and in the winter, crosscountry skiing or skating.

The lake system is particularly ideal for vacationing because the 1600 lakes are dotted with hundreds of small islands. This geographical feature gives the lodges both a sense of intimacy and isolation as well as canoe and boat access to long (uncharted, for the visitor) stretches of water. The land itself is dominated by forest and rock. The Canadian Shield underlies the region and, though the area is rich in dark greens, the greys and browns of this billion year old rock bare themselves, crashing through the landscape, where the trees can't find enough soil to grow.

If you are driving, the best way to investigate Muskoka is by touring the three largest lake areas: **Lake Muskoka** in its central southern region, **Lake Rousseau** in the northwest, and **The Lake of Bays** in the northeast.

The Lake Muskoka route, which covers about 37 mi (60 km) begins at **Gravenhurst**, which is a typically pretty Ontario town, given a kind of elegance and instant stature by its Victorian architecture. The town acts as a dock for the *R.M.S. Segwun*, North America's last authentic steamship. Built in Scotland in 1887 and reconstructed in 1925, the ship provides a scenic cruise (May to October) of Lake Muskoka. There is plenty of room to roam on deck but the ship best serves the romantics along for the journey. There is a windowed restaurant on board, affording sweethearts an opportunity to watch the Muskoka sun set below the horizon while sharing a frosted desert. The town also offers an exciting floating barge at nearby **Gull Lake Park**, and concerts are held in the bandstand on sunday evenings in summer.

From Gravenhurst travel north on Hwy 169 to **Bala**. The small rural community is called the "Bridge Town," because, set as it is between the Mill Stream and **Bala Falls**, it boasts eight bridges. The Falls are the best feature of Bala. Though the entire area, not surprisingly, is awash with the sounds and smells of rushing water. The highway continues on through **Glen Orchard** and turn east or right on Hwy 118 to **Port Carling**. (A turn onto Route 7 north, just before Port Carling, would set you on your way on the Lake Rousseau circle tour). Sitting between Lake Muskoka and Lake Rousseau, this pretty little town offers an ideal lodge set-

MUSKOKA

ting. It was originally an Ojibwa village but white settlement forced its original occupants to leave. In the mid-1880s, however, Mohawk and Caughnawaga Indians moved into the area, and today a small Indian village, selling native handicrafts, lies along the shoreline. In the summer the town's Muskoka Festival offers first-rate theater at the Memorial Hall. And if you'd like a vigourous diversion, take Mortimer's Point Rd., which is south of the town, and find Lakeview Stables (705-765-3513). A bracing, romantic one-hour trail ride on horseback through scenic woods is available there at a rate of $15.00/hr.

From Port Carling, Hwy 118 travels southeast to Bracebridge. Along the way, just beyond **Valley Green Beach,** is a most unusual site, the **Huckleberry Rock Cut**. For a short stretch, the highway steers a course between two sheer walls of pink granite. This roofless tunnel was blasted out by man, but the deep geometric cut looks like it was carved by a steady knife-wielding hand extending down from the heavens. Bracebridge completes the circle tour of Lake Muskoka. The town is another major tourist center in the region. Sitting on the cascading Muskoka River, it is an ideal place to go for walks or cycling. A 2.5-hour boat cruise through Lake Muskoka leaves from its downtown waterfront. Or there is the amusement complex Santa's Village just 2.5 mi (4 km) west on Santa's Village Rd., offering a huge entertainment program for children.

The **Rousseau Lake circle tour** begins at Port Carling or, if you're getting off the Lake Muskoka route at Glen Orchard, at the junction of Route 7 and Hwy 118. This tour is a must because the road cuts through terrific nature offering breathtaking beauty. It is utterly free of any contrived tourist snare. Take 7 north until it becomes Hwy 632 north. At the top of this highway, just before it meets Hwy 141, you will discover **Shadow River**.

The rivers in this area are widely known for their stillness and thereby for their ability to reflect. Named for the overhanging branches mirrored in its placid waters, the Shadow River creates a magnificently tranquil environment. From the river take Hwy 141 south until you reach the Rousseau River rapids some 7 km away. You may wish to stop here for a picnic or continue through on the next spectacular stretch of road which, around **Skeleton Bay,** includes dramatic cliffs, the **Bent River,** and the bay so close it threatens to overflow into the car. At Ullswater take Route 24 south. On this route you may wish to turn left at North Shore Rd. to see the **Dee Bank Falls,** or, if you're resorting, you may wish to travel just a little farther on 24 until you see a sign which directs you to the town of **Windermere**, where one of

Above: Span of elkhorns, a prized trophy, on Lake Klotz. Right: Canoe tour on the Lake of Bays.

the areas oldest and most elegant resorts, **Windermere House,** sits. The entire tour lasts about 38 mi (60 km).

The **Lake of Bays circle tour**, at over 62 mi (100 km). is considerably longer than the other two tours. It is also farther from Huronia, requiring a 38.5-mi (61-km) trip north up Hwy 11 from Orillia and then, just above Bracebridge, another 10-mi (16-km) ride east on Hwy 117 until you reach **Baysville**. From this former logging village you can travel up either side of the Lake of Bays. Hwy 17, along the western shoreline, offers the more interesting of the two trips. The colors along this hilly stretch are particularly beautiful in the fall. After traveling 7 mi (11 km) to **Browns Brae**, be sure to get on to the Old Highway 117 for a short stretch. It brings you closer to the shoreline and also to the lovely, relatively new, **Lake of Bays Park**. A giant sturgeon is said to terrorize the swimmers in the bay here. Back on the new 117 the town of **Dorset** is no longer very far. Here stands the famous Dorset tower in **Fire Tower Park** (follow the signs). Originally used to spot fires, this enormous construction now attracts a steady stream of fearless visitors, who, wishing to take in the breathtaking panoramic scenery which surrounds it, must climb its creaking metal staircase to reach its boxed in upper deck. The trek up is a bit unnerving but well worth the effort. Dorset is also home to **Robinson's General Store**, generally, or at least locally, known as Canada's greatest general store, primarily for its wide variety of first-rate goods.

From Dorset Hwy 35 passes by, first, magnificent rock cuts at **Birkendale**, and then the robust **Marsh's Falls**, before reaching the junction of Hwys 35 and 60. Turn right and now you're just a short drive away from Algonquin Provincial Park's west gate. If you wish to complete the Lake of Bays circle tour, turn left on the 60 and then left again when you reach Route 9 south. It will take you back to Baysville. There is nothing particularly noteworthy along the way, but the drive

ALGONQUIN PARK

provides many chances to see and get close to the lake. Its cool, shallow waters are ideal for wading and splashing around in.

Algonquin Provincial Park

Algonquin, situated in Ontario's near north, is approximately a 4.5-hour drive from Toronto. The park itself is 2900 sq mi (7600 sq km) and offers some of the most satisfying wilderness vacationing in Canada. Sitting on the Canadian Shield, Algonquin is a wonderful mix of rocky shorelines, loon-filled lakes, windswept pines, lush bogs, rolling rivers, and maple-topped hills. Much of the interior is so peaceful and misty it feels as if the rest of the world has simply vanished. With the exception, of course, of the animals. The park is full of such wildlife as deer, beaver, black bears, and, in abundance, moose. In August, and this is worth noting, staff at Algonquin take visitors on expeditions in which park naturalists exchange howls with the neighborhood's timber wolves. Bird-watching and fishing are also favourite activities at the park.

There are basically two ways to take in Algonquin: either in the park's isolated interior or, more comfortably, along the 35-mi (56-km) corridor of Hwy 60, with its lodges and modern campsites. If you are at all open to roughing it, you must choose the former approach. Cars will take you a short distance in, but essentially the interior of the park can only be explored on foot or by canoe; there are innumerable challenging backpacking trails and 937 mi (1500 km) of canoe routes in Algonquin. Even during the park's busy summer months the visitor will have no difficulty finding areas of the interior which he and his companions occupy exclusively. And if you so desire, the interior does offer four campgrounds,

Above: There's no shortage of canoes to rent in Algonquin Park. Right: Passion keeps you warm – die-hard ice fisherman.

though they provide no modern amenities. Important to note: there are more than a dozen outfitting services right inside the park which rent and sell equipment as well as offer advice on how best to enjoy the area.

The Parkway corridor, along Hwy 60, offers a less challenging vacation. State-of-the-art campsites and even luxurious lodges are available with virtually immediate access to the wilderness. The trails are less demanding and the rivers and lakes therefore attract a larger crowd of people.

But a wilderness experience can still be had. For a long hike travel 9 mi (15 km) in from the park's west gate to a hiker's delight, **Mizzy Lake Trail**. The 7-mi (11-km) trail passes through numerous ponds and lakes, with plenty of good opportunities to see wildlife. A good short hike, the **Peck Lake Trail**, can be found just a short distance east on Hwy 60. This short trail circles the lake and gives the hiker a quick education in some the park's ecology.

CENTRAL AND EASTERN ONTARIO

The expanse of land lying between Toronto and Ottawa is enormous. The fastest drive from Toronto – east on the 401 Expressway and then north on Hwy 16 some 11 km east of **Brockville** – takes over five solid hours. In between the two cities, the areas most desirable for tourists lie along Lake Ontario and the St. Lawrence River, or among the **Kawartha Lakes** and, much further east, in the charming little towns that have grown around the Rideau Canal System.

The Kawarthas make up the **Trent Waterway System**, which extends from **Balsam Lake,** east of Lake Simcoe, to Rice Lake, north of the city of **Cobourg**. In 1615 the French explorer Samuel de Champlain canoed this system all the way from the Georgian Bay to Lake Ontario. Once in the Kawarthas, however, the bold adventurer had to lift his canoe out of the water and carry it to the next available lake.

KAWARTHA LAKES

Today the waterway is linked by a series of locks and canals which, though constructed to serve Ontario's 19th-century economy, now caters mainly to tourists. The Kawarthas are cottage and resort country, offering marvellous fishing, canoeing and boating. As well, the lovely rural communities in the region provide, with their museums and 19th-century architecture, relaxing and educational views back to the earlier days of the area. **Millbrook**, **Lakefield**, and **Burleigh Falls** are the towns to visit. The region is also rich in native history. Algonquin Indians lived here over a thousand years ago, and any visitor to the Kawarthas must take time out to visit the rock carvings at **Petroglyphs Provincial Park** (above Stoney Lake: from Cobourg, on the 401, take the 45 and 40 north and the 6 east). Over 900 pictographs carved by the Algonquin between 500 and 1000 years ago can be seen on the 21-meter patch of marble bedrock. It was named the **Teaching Rock** and provides a very moving testimony to this virtually defunct culture.

Another native site well worth visiting is **Serpent Mounds Provincial Park** (on Rice Lake's northern shore; from Port Hope, on the 401, take Hwy 28 north, Route 2 east, and then Route 34 south from the town of **Keene**). Over 2000 years ago the peoples of the Point Peninsula culture built a series of nine burial grounds. Today tours and interpretive trails are available for those interested in investigating these sacred sites. The largest mound is shaped like a serpent, thus inspiring the name of the park. Serpent Mounds also offers excellent camping, boating, swimming and hiking.

The trip along the western shoreline of Lake Ontario to **Brockville** is best enjoyed on Hwy 2, or the **Great Pine Ridge Rd.**, as this scenic country highway is called. Noteworthy on the initial stretch of this road is **Presqu'île Point**

Above: Cannon at Old Fort Henry in Kingston. Right: Rural idyll on the St. Lawrence, near the Thousand Islands.

THOUSAND ISLANDS

Provincial Park, south of **Brighton** on Route 66. The park, which is a small peninsula extending into **Presqu'île Bay**, has a wildlife sanctuary, an aquarium, and, in the spring and fall, excellent locations from which to watch bird migrations. Soon after this park the driver will also definitely want to take a detour on Hwy 33 south into **Prince Edward County**. This lovely peninsula in Lake Ontario offers scenic countryside, charming little towns, and three relatively unpeopled provincial park beaches.

The city of **Kingston**, which both Hwys 2 and 33 pass through, is the next noteworthy stop. Founded in 1673 for its strategic importance (it sits at the southern mouth of the St. Lawrence River), Kingston is one of Ontario's oldest and historically most important cities. Originally a naval and military community, it nowadays boasts a number of museums and sights which recapture and celebrate its past. Most notable of these is **Old Fort Henry** (junction of Hwys 2 and 15). Once the principal military stronghold of Upper Canada, the site today holds an impressive collection of 19th-century military equipment within in its imposing walls. Aside from its historical interest, Kingston also offers boat tours from its downtown harbor, fine dining, handsome limestone architecture, and an active theater community.

All along the St. Lawrence River, from Kingston east to Brockville, are the **Thousand Islands**. This is lovely boating and resorting country. **Gananoque** and **Brockville**, the two major tourist towns on the river, can be reached on Route 2 or the **Thousand Island Parkway**, as it is more commonly called. This stretch of highway is absolutely beautiful and though some of it is removed from the shoreline it is quite possible, and advisable, to dip down to the shoreline on the many side roads which snake along the river. From Brockville take the 2 or the 401 east to Hwy 16, which travels north to Ottawa.

The other option from Kingston, if you are traveling to Ottawa, is to drive up

ONTARIO

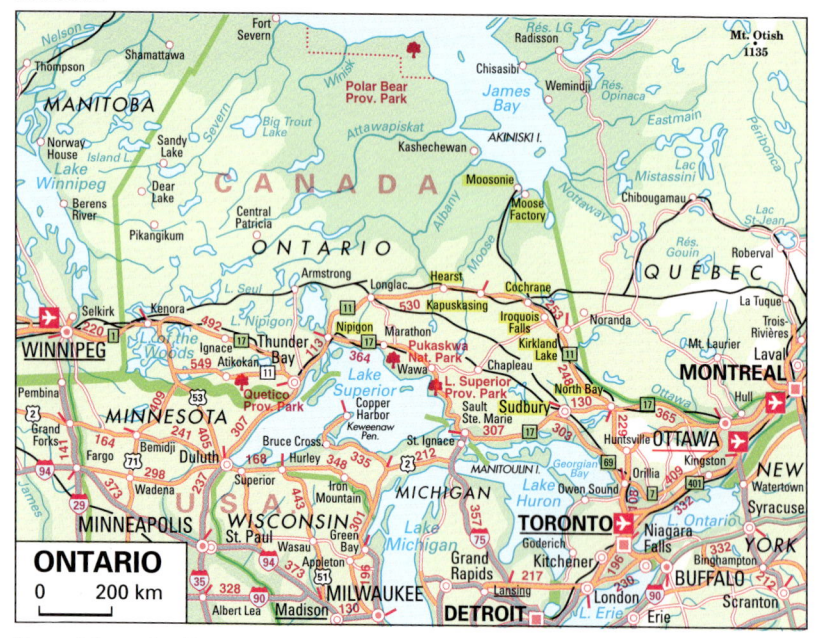

Hwys 15 north, 43 east and 16 north. This route leads through the **Rideau Canal System**. Conceived after the War of 1812, the system was to act as a military supply line between Montreal and Kingston. Hostilities never developed but the canal was ultimately completed in 1832. With its 47 locks, it is considered one of the great engineering accomplishments of the 19th century. Today it provides boaters and canoeists with safe and easy routes.

The towns along the Rideau Canal highway route are characteristic of good-old, home-grown Ontario: charming little lakeside villages with the elegant and stately character of old Canada. Suggested detours: from the village of **Crosby**, north of **Elgin**, take Hwy 42 to the city of **Westport**, one of the prettiest cities in Ontario; from **Smith Falls** take Hwy 43 south to **Perth**, also a picturesque town, with many handsome stone homes as well as an excellent Provincial Park, **Murphy's**, 7.5 mi (12 km) south on Routes 1 and 21.

NORTHERN ONTARIO

Northern Ontario has a distinctly different feel to it than the rest of the province. The towns are fewer and farther between, and, because in so many cases they are former or present mining and logging towns, they haven't the Victorian charm of other small Ontario towns. Most travelers who have gone this far, however, were not looking for scones and tea. The area provides some of the best fishing and hunting in the world, and its lakeland resorts are arguably superior to those in the south, as they are generally not as commercialized or heavily visited.

The region, which sits on the Canadian Shield, encompasses those lands which lie west of Québec and north of Muskoka, the Georgian Bay, Lakes Huron and Superior, and the State of Minnesota. In its southern portions, to the east and west of Lake Superior, the land is rich in mixed forests and in lakes and rivers. As you travel farther north, however, the land becomes less and less hospitable to

NORTHERN ONTARIO

vegetation, until only stunted trees grow in sunken marshes. Most of the northernmost area is only accessible by bush plane, train or canoe.

Northern Route

Hwy 11 comes up all the way from the city of Barrie in Huronia and extends to the town of **North Bay**. From this point there are basically two ways to see the north by car: either continue north on the 11 or travel west on Hwy 17, which is the much more scenic route. (Hwy 69 north from the town of **Victoria Bay**, located at the bottom of the Georgian Bay, provides a shorter route to the city of **Sudbury**, which has a notoriously fun science museum, especially where children are concerned.) The northern route up Hwy 11 is through mining and logging towns, and side roads lead to a variety of provincial parks.

Towns in the area, such as **Kirkland Lake** and **Iroquois Falls,** still have a radiate the atmosphere of the wild and wooly frontier, and most find interesting ways of displaying their past or present industries. The parks provide excellent camping, hiking and fishing.

The town of **Cochrane**, which is 25 mi (40 km) north of **Iroquois Falls**, is the starting point for the Polar Bear Express train ride, which operates from late June to early September. If you are in the area this is not to be missed. The train takes its passenger through thick forests, marshy bogs, crystal lakes, raging rivers and dry bush to reach its destination, the town of **Moosonie**, at the southern tip of James Bay in Canada's sub-Arctic. The town itself is not terribly engaging but from Moosonie you can take a boat ride to nearby **Shipsands Island Waterfowl Sanctuary**, or to the island town of **Moose Factory.** (A six-hour cruise around James Bay is also available). Founded by the Hudson's Bay Company in 1673, Moose Factory is one of Canada's oldest settlements. Early 19th-century architecture still survives and the **Centennial Park Museum** portrays the early development of the area. Moosonie also offers plane access to the Arctic wilderness park, **Polar Bear Provincial**. A special permit is required to visit this park, which is home to a large population of bear, moose and caribou.

From Moosonie you must either return by train to Cochrane or find a plane or water vehicle to transport you elsewhere – there are no more highways to take you further. West of Cochrane on Hwy 11 are the pulp and paper mill towns of **Kapuskasing** and **Hearst**. This long trip, 331 mi (530 km), which ends at **Nipigon**, where the northern route meets the southern, takes the traveler through forested and rocky terrain as well as past three provincial parks.

Southern Route

This southern drive extends on Hwy 17 all the way from North Bay to the western edge of the province, where Ontario meets Manitoba. If one is seeing Ontario for the first time, it is not recommended that the visitor choose this route. There are certainly many beautiful sites and much rugged wilderness to be enjoyed along the way, but it is simply too long and its desirable stopping points too similar to more accessible ones in southern Ontario for the region to be chosen for a first "getting to know you" trip to the province.

Traveling east to west along the 17, **Killarney, Lake Superior, Pukaskwa,** and **Quetico Parks,** are all magnificently preserved wilderness zones, everyone of them offering first rate sporting facilities and overnight camping possibilities always in the proximity of a lake. And again from east to west on the 17, **Lake Nipissing, Lake Nipigon,** and **The Lake of The Woods** provide first-rate lakeside resort experiences.

97

GUIDEPOST: ONTARIO

ONTARIO

How to get there
By air: Many major international carriers including KLM, Air France, Alitalia, El Al, Lufthansa, American and USAir land at **Lester B. Pearson International Airport**. Ottawa Uplands is also an international airport. Air Canada links Toronto to other Canadian cities.

By train: Via Rail links with Amtrak at Montreal, Windsor and Niagara Falls. It also provides service within the province.

By bus: Service to all parts of Ontario and beyond is provided by Eastern Canadian Greyhound Lines Ltd., Gray Coach Lines, Voyageur Colonial and others.

By car: From Michigan in the southwest the Macdonald Cartier Freeway (Hwy. 401) connects Windsor, London, Toronto and Kingston. Ontario is connected to Québec via Hwys. 401 and 417 (Québec Hwy. 40). Hwys. 17 and 11 cross northern Ontario. Hwy. 17 leads via Manitoba and Hwy. 11 via Minnesota. The Queen Elizabeth Way curves southwest from Toronto, linking it to Hamilton, Niagara Falls and New York State.

Accommodation
Ontario is a very large province. Here we will dividide the province into southern and northern Ontario and list restaurants in the same section as accommodations. Hotel rates vary greatly in Ontario. Rates will go up as you get closer to a large city and may also depend on the season.

Outdoor activities
Fishing and hunting are big attractions in Ontario. Licenses for both sports are available at **Natural Resources District offices** or can be purchased at sporting goods stores or outfitters. Fishing and hunting maps available from **Ministry of Natural Resources**, Public Service Centre, Toronto, Ontario M7A 1W3. Campers can obtain camping permits at the entrance to Ontario's 128 provincial parks. There are also four national parks in the province and a number of private campgrounds.

Tourist Information
Tourism Marketing Branch, Ministry of Tourism and Recreation, 77 Bloor Street West, Toronto, Ontario M7A 2R9, Tel: 416/965-4008 or 800/668-2746).

SOUTHERN ONTARIO
Accommodation / Restaurants
ALGONQUIN PROVINCIAL PARK: **Arowhon Pines**, Huntville, P0A 1B0, Tel: 705/633-5661. On Little Joe Lake. This deluxe resort features cottage units, a comfortable lodge with meals included. Guides are available for longer canoe trips. **Killarney Lodg**e, Hwy. 60, Algonquin Park P0A 1K0, Tel: 705/633-5551. Attractive cabins in a lakefront forest setting. The dining room in the lodge features well-prepared home cooking.

ALTON: **The Millcroft Inn**, John St., PO Box 89 L0N 1A0, Tel: 519/941-8111. This restored old knitting mill overlooks the Credit River. There's a pool, tennis courts, ice skating and first-rate food in the elegant dining room.

BANCROFT: **Best Western Sword Motor Inn**, 146 Hastings St. Hwy. 62. K0L 1C0, Tel: 613/332-2474. This 50-unit property is one of the larger complexes in the area. It faces the water and there's an indoor pool and golf nearby.

BARRIE: **Best West Royal Oak Inn**, 35 Hart Dr. L4N 5M3, Tel: 705/721-4848. 50 units including five efficiency units. Good value for moderate price. **Horseshoe Resort-The Inn at Horseshoe**, RR1, Box 10, L4M 4YB, Tel: 705/835-2790. 100 units and extensive recreational facilities including 3 pools (one indoor), tennis, golf, ski tows and trails, riding. Many rooms have fireplaces and whirlpool baths. Dining room, restaurant and coffee shop. **Relax Inn Barrie**, 55 Hart Dr., L4N 5M3, Tel: 705/734-9500. Indoor pool in this 100 unit moTel:

BRACEBRIDGE: **Tamwood Lodge**, RR1, P0B 1C0, Tel: 705/645-5172. This deluxe resort on the shores of Lake Muskoka is a rustic complex of lodge and cottages built of logs. There's an indoor pool for rainy days. Fine dining room. **Patterson-Kaye Lodge**, RR 1, P1L 1W8, Tel: 705/645-4169. Lodge rooms and one to three bedroom cottages. Friendly, informal beach resort on Lake Muskoka. 12 cottages with fireplaces. Full range of recreational facilities including ski and snowmobile trails. Dining room serves home cooking.

CAMBRIDGE: **Days Inn Cambridge**, 650 Hespeier Rd. N1R 6J8, Tel: 519/622-1070. 120 units with pools and restaurant.

CHATHAM: **Best Western Wheels Inn**, 615 Richmond St. N7M 5K8, Tel: 519/351-1100. Family resort motor inn with extensive recreation facilities. Two pools, one indoor-outdoor.

ELORA: **The Elora Mill Country Inn & Restaurant**, 77 Mill St. W. N0B 1S0, Tel: 519/846-5356. Dramatically located over a waterfall of the Grand River. Popular dining room in historic country inn.

GODERICH: **Benmiller Inn**, RR4, N7A 3Y1, Tel: 519/525-2191. Two mills on the banks of Sharpe's Creek have been extensively restored. Indoor pool. Fine dining room.

HALIBURTON: **Domain of Killien**, PO Box 810, Tel: 705/457-1100. Historic 13 unit lodge with lodge or cabin accommodations. Elegant atmosphere and dining room, sports facilities.

GUIDEPOST: ONTARIO

Sir Sam's Inn, Hwy. 118, Eagle Lake K0M 1M0, Tel: 705/754-2188. A lovely old mansion with an excellent restaurant. No children.
HAMILTON: **Royal Connaught Hotel**, 112 King Street L8N 1A8, Tel: 905/546-8111. This is the city's grand old hotel with all facilities. **Walper Terrace Hotel**, 1 King Street N2G 1A1, Tel: 905/745-4321. The grand old Walper has 115 newly renovated rooms. **Valhalla Inn**, King Street N2G 3W9, Tel: 905/744-4141. A popular stop-off enroute to the Stratford Festival. Indoor pool and famous brunch.
NIAGARA FALLS: **The Brock Hotel at Maple Leaf Resort**, 5685 Falls Ave. L2E 6W7, Tel: 905/374-4444. A popular falls resort with golf and dining room. **Days Inn**, 6361 Buchanan Ave. L2G 3V9, Tel: 905/357-7377 or 800/263-7073. Many of the 200 rooms have spectacular views of the falls. Suites have heart-shaped jacuzzis and fireplaces. **Michael's Inn**, 5599 River Rd. L2E 3H3, Tel: 905/354-2727. Overlooks Niagara Gorge and Rainbow Bridge. Indoor pool and popular pub. **Ramada Renaissance Fallsview**, 6455 Buchanan Ave. L2G 3V9, Tel: 905/357-5200. Just 500 yards from the brink of the falls. Indoor pool in a tropical garden setting.
NIAGARA-ON-THE-LAKE: **Prince of Wales**, 6 Picton St. L0S 1J0, Tel: 905/468-3246. An old hotel that has been renovated and expanded with great charm. Indoor pool and fine dining room. **Oban Inn**, 160 Front St. L0S 1J0, Tel: 905/468-2165. A gracious 19th century home turned into a most comfortable inn overlooking Lake Ontario and the Niagara River. **Queen's Landing**, 155 Byron St. L0S 1J0, Tel: 905/ 468-2195. The town's newest and largest hotel seems like it has been here forever. Indoor pool and fine dining room.
RIDEAU FERRY: **Hotel Kenney**, K0G 1H0, Tel: 613/359-5500. On Whitefish Lake. There's a view of the locks from the dining room. **Rideau Ferry Inn**, K0G 1W0, Tel: 613/267-2152. On Big Rideau Lake. Boat rentals, guides are available for fishing.
STRATFORD: **The Raj**, 123 Church St. N5A 3H1, Tel: 519/271-7129. An elegant bed-and- breakfast inn. Filled with Victorian and East Indian antiques. **The Jester Arms**, 107 Ontario St. N5A 3H1, Tel: 519/271-1121. A 13-room inn with a lively pub. **Victorian Inn**, 10 Romeo St. N. N5A 5M7, Tel: 519/271-4650. Just a block from the Festival Theatre. Indoor pool.
TOBERMORY: **Tobermory Lodge**, Lodge Rd. N0H 2R0, Tel: 519/596-2224. Overlooking Tobermory Harbor, lodge rooms or semi-detached chalets.
WASAGA BEACH: **Hotel Waldhorn**, Mosley and 32nd Sts. L0L 2P0, Tel: 705/429-4111. Just a short stroll from the world's largest freshwater beach and next to a popular beer garden.

NORTHERN ONTARIO
Accommodation / Restaurants

Many communities in Northern Ontario can only promise clean, no frills accommodations. Camping is popular in the North Country.
BURK'S FALLS: **Pickerel Lake Lodge**, Pickerel Lake Rd. P0A 1C0, Tel: 705/382-2025. Hunting and fishing packages in cottages with fireplaces.
CALLANDER: **Sunset Cove Lodge**, Sunset Cove Rd. P0H 1H0, Tel: 705/752-2820. German cooking and a large sandy beach.
COCHRANE: **Northern Lites Motel**, Hwy. 11 P0L 1C0, Tel: 705/272-4281. Popular stop-over for those who are heading up north on the Polar Bear Express.
EAGLE RIVER: **Lindmeier's North Shore Lodge**, Hwy. 594. P0V 1S0, Tel: 807/755-2441. Fly-in to Eagle Lake. Main lodge and 18 cabins. Dining room plus complete outdoor program.
FRENCH RIVER: **Chaudière Lodge**, Box 383, North Bay P1B 8H5, Tel: 705/763-2220. Reachable by plane or boat only. 13 cottages on the French River.
KAPUSKASING: **Rufus Lake Rainbow Lodge**, Fergus Rd. P5N 2Y5, Tel: 705/337-1299. 20 cottages on a natural beach.
MATTAWA: **Breton's Motel**, Hwy. 17 P0H 1V0, Tel: 705/744-5536. 13 rooms and a dining room open 24 hours a day – convenient for travelers on the Trans-Canada Highway.
NORTH BAY: **Sunset Park Motel**, 641 Lakeshore Dr. P1A 2E9, Tel: 705/647-7357. On a secluded beach on Lake Nipissing.
SAULT STE. MARIE: **Algoma's Water Tower Inn**, 360 Great Northern Rd.P6A 5N3, Tel: 705/949-8111. 150 rooms with indoor pool and fireplaces in rooms.
SIOUX NARROWS: **Rod and Reel**, Hwy. 71 P0X 1N0, Tel: 807/226-5240. Ten cottages overlooking a beach on the Lake of Woods.
SUDBURY: **Peter Piper Inn**, 151 Larch St. P3E 1C3, Tel: 705/673-7801. Some of the 45 rooms have private saunas.
TEMAGAMI: **Scandia Inn**, Hwy. 11 P0H 2H0, Tel: 705/569-3644. 12 rooms on James Lake with meeting facilities.
THUNDER BAY: **Prince Arthur**, 17 N. Cumberland St. P7A 4K8, Tel: 807/345-5411. Renovated 1911 railway hotel with a view of Thunder Bay's harbor. Fine restaurant attached.
WAWA: **The Wawa Motor Hotel**, 100 Mission Rd. P0S 1K0, Tel: 705/856-2278. 70 rooms plus 17 cottages. Indoor pool and sauna. Popular restaurant.

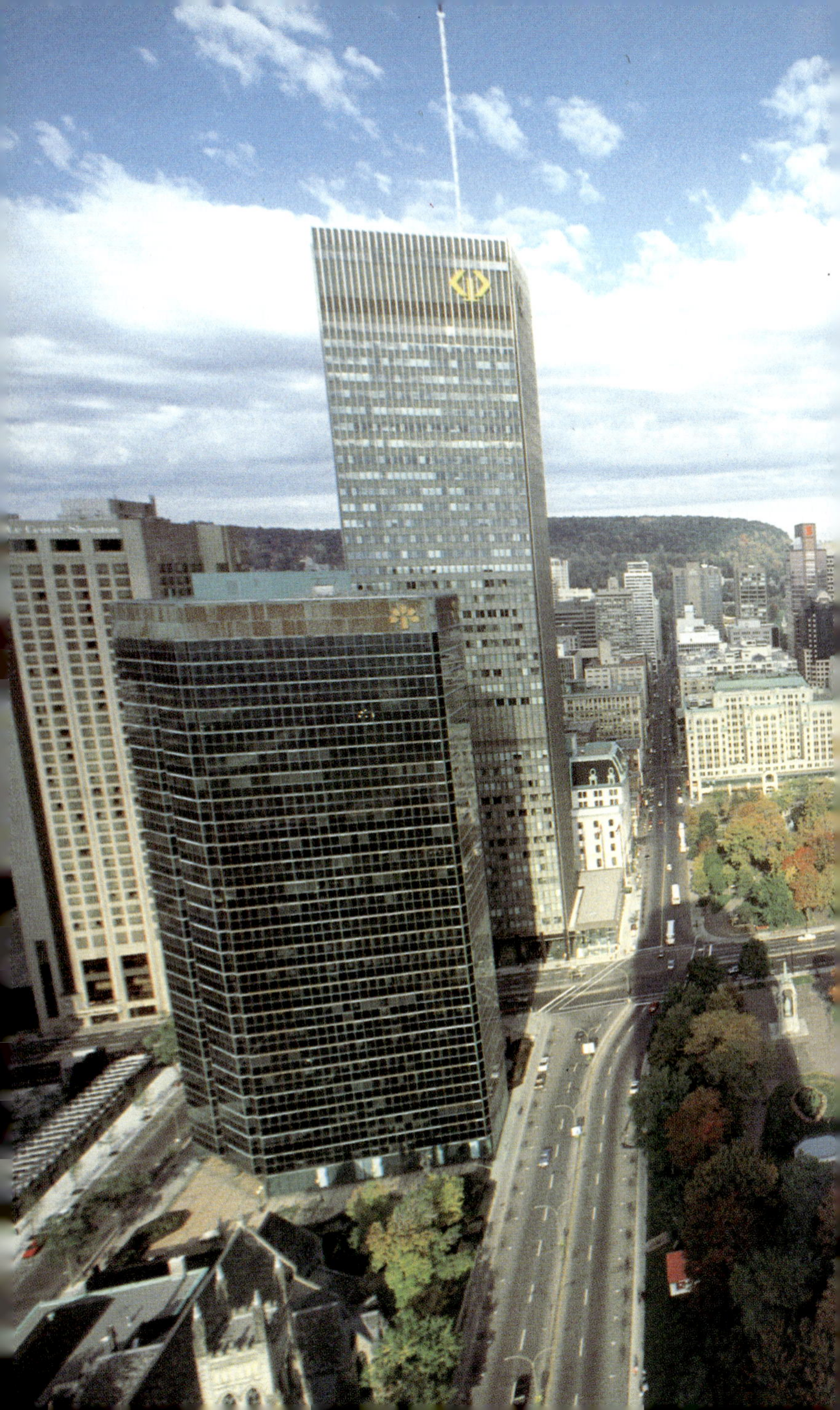

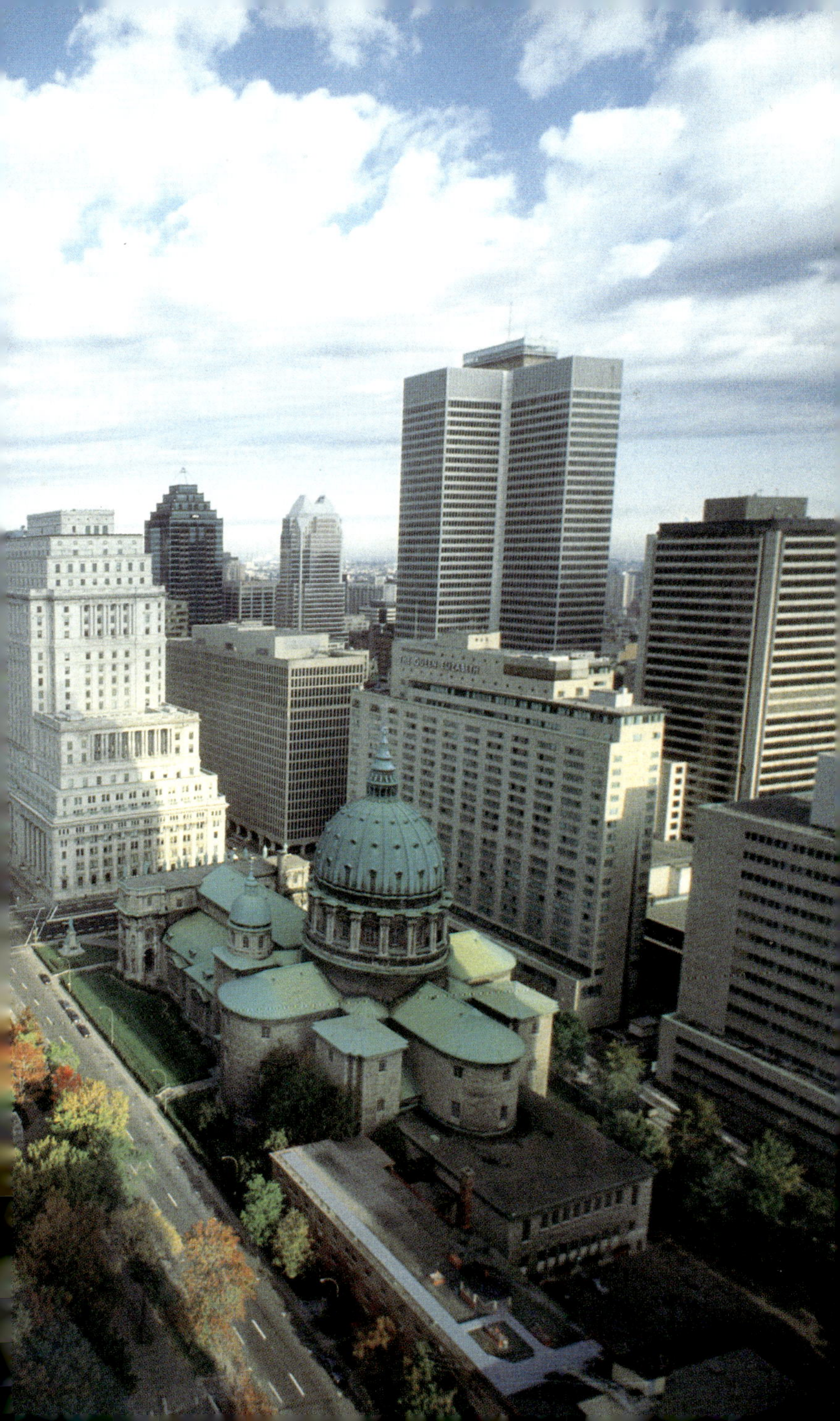

MONTRÉAL

1 Palais des Congrès
2 Banque de Montréal
3 Centre de Commerce Mondial

MONTRÉAL

**VIEUX MONTRÉAL
DOWNTOWN
ARTS AND ENTERTAINMENT
SQUARE MILE
PARKS**

Montréal and its suburbs sprawl all over the largest island in the St. Lawrence River. The Greater Montréal area is home to over 3 million people, almost half of the province's entire population. Its strategic location at the center of Canada's major waterway trade route made it the richest city in Canada within a few years of its founding in 1642. After the union of Upper (Ontario) and Lower (Québec) Canada in 1840, Montréal became the new country's first capital.

Already Canada's major inland port, the city solidified its position as the country's major center of commerce and transportation in 1873 with the founding of the Canadian Pacific Railway Company. By 1885, with Canada linked together by railroad from the East Coast to the West, Montréal became its industrial heartland. For the next 50 years, it led the country's growth and by the beginning of the 20th century, with a population of 370,000, it was Canada's largest and wealthiest city. Today, Canada's wealth is much more evenly distributed across the country. The West has boomed and Ontario has pulled ahead of Québec as the motor of the country's economy.

Preceding pages: Montréal – View from the Chateau Champlain over the Cathedral of Marie-Reine-du-Monde and Dominion Square.

However, Montréal is still widely considered to be the city with the highest quality of life. The city skyline has undergone major changes in the past 30 years, and in the past five years intensive commercial development has transformed the downtown core.

Before the arrival of the Europeans, Montréal Island was an Indian settlement. Just south of the city, across the St. Lawrence, is the Mohawk reserve of Kahnawake and not too much further away is the Mohawk reserve of Khanesetake. Both made international headlines in the summer of 1990 for their standoff with the Sûreté du Québec police force and the federal and provincial governments over land disputes and Native rights. (While the compromise to resolve this situation was less than each party would have liked, the Mohawks' plight received international attention and was instrumental in Native Canadians across the country being represented in the constitutional amendments proposed by the 1992 Charlottetown Accord.)

One third of Montréalers speak English as their first language, making it the fourth largest English-speaking city in Canada. It is also the largest French-speaking city outside of France. It is this mix of culture that gives the city its unique flair, it is why people move here.

103

VIEUX MONTRÉAL / VIEUX PORT

Other cultures too have settled here: Jews, Italians, Blacks, Chinese, Japanese, Vietnamese, Portuguese, Greeks, Argentinians, Chileans, Haitians, Jamaicans, Lebanese and Latvians are just some of *les autres*. Aside from bringing their cultural traditions, religious customs and trade ties with them, these communities have enriched Montréal with their respective gastronomic specialties, which accounts these days for the city's well-established reputation as a paradise for the connoisseur.

VIEUX MONTREAL

Perhaps the best place to begin is where Montréal itself began, in the **Vieux Montréal** and **Vieux Port** area, down by the St. Lawrence River. A visit there is a bit of time travel back to the city's origins. In 1642, it was founded by the French and named **Ville Marie**. The fur trade was doing well, and the natives had been conveniently orced off the land by that time.

The area is best toured by *calèche* (horse-drawn carriages) or on foot. Many buildings from the l7th to the l9th centuries have been preserved or restored and are open to the public. The century-spanning complexity of the city is visible when standing on **Quai Victoria**. One looks west across cobblestoned streets and centuries-old gray stone buildings set against the backdrop of Montréal's modern skyline juxtaposed with majestic cross-lit Mont Royal, where Oratoire St-Joseph's dome is the most visible landmark. One can also look east across the river to Île-Ste-Hélène and Île-Notre-Dame, where vestiges of Expo '67 and La Ronde's gigantic rollercoaster stand cheek by jowl.

The waterfront area of the Vieux Port has undergone a dramatic revitalization in recent years, with great care taken to preserve the best parts of the past. The

Above: French Empire style – the 1878 Town Hall. Right: Marché Bonsecours is since 1965 the seat of the city administration.

VIEUX MONTRÉAL / VIEUX PORT

harborside and rue de la Commune, which form the eastern boundary of Vieux Montréal, is literally the city's birthplace and its greatest tourist attraction. Extending south to rue McGill, north to rue Berri, and west to rue St-Antoine, this 100-acre site roughly corresponds to the original walled city's perimeters.

Repositories of Montréal's past include the **Pointe-à-Caillière Musée d'Archéologie et d'Histoire de Montréal**, near Place Royale, the site of the city's first European settlement. This unusual building incorporates portions of the 1643 fortifications and pillars built around ruins dating from Montréal's first Catholic cemetery. The Museum specializes in Montréal's early history, emphasizing the city's role as a cultural and commercial crossroads in its permanent and special exhibitions.

East of **Place Jacques Cartier** opposite the **Hôtel de Ville** (City Hall), is the **Château Ramezay**. Built in 1705, it is one of the few remaining fieldstone buildings from the French days, and is now a museum furnished in 18th-century style. First the headquarters of Claude de Ramezay, Montréal's eleventh governor, the Château was later occupied (in all senses of the word including military) by Benjamin Franklin, Benedict Arnold, General Richard Montgomery and John Carroll when it was taken over by the Continental Army in 1775 during the ill-fated American occupation of the city. In the immediate vicinity is **Marché Bonsecours**, with its silver dome. It was constructed in the mid-19th century, and has served many purposes: the Canadian Parliament met here in 1849, it was Montréal's City Hall until 1863, then a vegetable market. The city administration had offices here, and it also serves as a cultural information center, exhibition and convention hall. Right in the proximity (at the end of rue Bonsecours) stands the oldest religious building extant in the city, the chapel **Notre-Dame-de-Bonsecours**, where sailors once came to make votive gifts to the **Madonna**.

Both **Notre-Dame Basilica** and the Vieux Séminaire face **Place d'Armes**, one of Vieux Montréal's two principal squares. At its center stands the 10-foot-high (3 m) **statue** of Paul de Chomedey, Sieur de Maisonneuve, Montréal's founder. In 1644, with a handful of men, he successfully countered an attack by 200 Iroquois braves. This monument also pays tribute to Jeanne Mance, who established Montréal's first hospital, and Charles LeMoyne, whose sons went on to found New Orleans and Mobile, Alabama.

The **Vieux Séminaire de St-Sulpice** (1685) is one of Montréal's oldest buildings with an old wooden clock (1710) and for more than 300 years the residence and headquarters of the Sulpician monks who purchased the Island of Montréal from the Sieur de Maisonneuve and from the Societé de Notre-Dame de Montréal. This order administered the legal and religious life of Montréal.

The Vieux Séminaire is not open to the public, but the magnificent Notre-Dame Basilica, one of the largest examples of the Gothic Revival style in North America can be visited.

Just a short stroll east from Place d'Armes along rue Notre-Dame is **Place Jacques Cartier**, the "heart" of this area. Once one of the city's busiest open-air markets, it faces the **Vauquelin fountain** of Montréal's ornate **City Hall** (where in 1967, French president Charles de Gaulle shouted his famous "Vive le Québec libre"). Today it is a people place nonpareil, still the site of open-air flower and craft stalls, sidewalk cafés and bars and the fair-weather home of artists, artisans, street musicians, jugglers and more. Its 1808 **Nelson Column,** the first monument in the world to honor the British victor of the Battle of Trafalgar, has been the occasional target of more than one generation of Francophones.

Above: Focus of city life is the Place Jacques Cartier with its cafés and street musicians.

During summer months, concerts take place under the Big Top tent at adjacent **Quai Jacques Cartier**, which is where Québec's own internationally renowned **Cirque du Soleil** sets up when it comes to town. Place Jacques Cartier opens directly onto Montréal's **Vieux Port,** with its cycling paths, picnic areas, pedalboats, food and souvenir kiosks and open-air theater. Among its major attractions are the **Images du Futur** and **Expotec** high-tech exhibitions, which feature a different theme every year. Housed in Hangars No. 8 and 9 respectively, both appeal to children of all ages. Expotec is also the location of the year-round 7-storey high IMAX Super Cinema.

Just across the River, a subway stop away, is one of the most picturesque ways to explore the early origins of Canadian history. Even the location of the **David M. Stewart Museum** on Île-Ste-Hélène is a history lesson: the museum is housed in the Old Fort, built between 1820-1824 on the orders of the Duke of Wellington as a stronghold against a possible invasion by the American military. Established in l955 under the aegis of the Lake St-Louis Historical Society, the museum is renowned for its permanent collections highlighting Canada's early colonial heritage from the time of French, British and European settlers' arrival in the New World to the mid-l8th century. The museum itself and many of its collections, including rare firearms, rare documents and ancient maps, are all a bequest of a Montréal philanthropist, the late David M. Stewart, who was an amateur military historian and collector. Other permanent exhibits feature highlights of Canada's maritime history, the Amerindians role in the fur trade, and exploits by Christopher Columbus, Amerigo Vespucci, John Cabot, Jacques Cartier and Samuel de Champlain.

Its interior, with rich late-19th-century ornamentation and stained-glass windows depicting the history of Montréal, is particularly splendid. Concerts and recitals are held here throughout the year.

The fare and atmosphere at the museum's *Le Festin du Gouverneur* restaurant are a recreation of an l8th-century banquet, complete with balladeers and comedy skits. Mock battles by the *Compagnie Franche de la Marine* and bagpipe concerts by the 78th Fraser Highlanders are held on the parade grounds in summer.

Perfect Family Fare

Île-Ste-Hélène offers visitors other options: all equally popular family pastimes. Its wooded, rolling park is perfect for picnic outings and the large public pool is open to all, free of charge. The island is also home to one **La Ronde Amusement Park,** which opened during the Expo '67. It boasts the second highest roller coaster in the world, waterslides, Ferris wheels, boat rides, an international circus, a reconstructed Québec village and more. Open only weekends in May and early June, daily mid-June to Labor Day, La Ronde also allows access to the **Aquarium de Montréal**, complete with penguin tank, exhibits of tropical and freshwater fish and summertime seal show.

Adjacent to Île-Ste-Hélène is **Île-Notre-Dame**, a man-made island identifiable by the futuristic spires of the Casino de Montréal, formerly the French Pavilion at the Expo '67. It was opened in 1993, and is run by the Québec government. Formula l racing fans gather annually every June for the **Grand Prix Molson du Canada**, the only North American race on the world's top racing car circuit. The **Circuit Gilles Villeneuve** attracts a great international crowd. From Île Sainte-Hélène, the prize-winning apartment project *Habitat'97* is a short distance away on foot over the Pont du Havre. It represents a successful attempt at overcoming monotonous, modern building styles.

DOWNTOWN MONTRÉAL

The boundaries of the city's central business district and downtown core have unofficially been extended north to the uppermost streets of Vieux Montréal in recent years. There is a historical precedent for this: rue St-Jacques or St. James Street as it was known at the turn-of-the-century. Once famed as the "Wall Street of Canada," it has somewhat regained its former stature with the opening of Montréal's award-winning **Centre de Commerce Mondial** (World Trade Centre) in l992. Occupying several city blocks, this massive complex incorporates a winter-garden, office, retail and restaurant facilities and the **Hotel Intercontinental-Montréal** in a mix of restored landmark buildings and new structures designed to complement the former's architectural styles. This has helped to revitalize Vieux Montréal's original vocation as a center of commerce, though business never en-

ARTS AND ENTERTAINMENT

tirely left the area. Canada's oldest bank, the **Bank of Montréal**, founded in 1817 has been headquartered on Place d'Armes since 1840 in a neoclassical edifice modelled after Rome's Pantheon.

Square Victoria, a pleasant landscaped tribute to Queen Victoria, whose statue adorns it, is home to the **Bourse de Montréal** (Montréal Stock Exchange) and **Bell Canada-Banque Nationale** complex, both of which form the extreme southeastern end of Montréal's **Ville Souterraine** (Underground City). Something of a misnomer, as much of it is at street level, this is the ten miles of weather-protected arcade comprising ten shopping concourses with over 1400 shops, seven hotels, more than twelve commercial buildings, residential highrises, hundreds of restaurants, bars and cafés, 30 cinemas, two train stations and several Metro stations linking much of the downtown area by underground passage – a blessing considering the severity of Montréal winters.

Just five minutes north of Square Victoria and next to Chinatown, the **Palais de Congrès** (Montréal Convention Center), **Complexe Guy Fabreau** and **Complexe Desjardins**, with its multilevel **La Place** galleria and 600-room deluxe **Hotel Le Méridien,** are all part of this network.

But no trip to the downtown area would be complete without visiting the carriage trade department store **Ogilvy**, a few blocks south on rue Ste-Catherine. Despite being significantly revamped recently, it still retains the wonderful cranberry-glass chandeliers, sweeping staircase and noon-hour ritual of kilted bagpiper marching through the store as it did when it first opened as a linen shop in 1866, serving English, Scottish and Irish matrons of the day.

First established in 1837 in Québec City as Henderson, Holt and Renfrew Furriers, Montréal's **Holt Renfrew** (at Sherbrooke Ouest and Montagne) was

Above: "La foule illuminée," by Raymond Massou, in front of the Banque Nationale.
Right: Wedding in Marie-Reine-du-Monde.

the first to introduce haute couture fashions to Montréalers and, like La Baie once was, has always been famous for its fur salon. Four generations of British royalty, including Queen Elizabeth II, who received a custom-designed Labrador mink coat from Holt's as a wedding gift, have worn its furs.

ARTS AND ENTERTAINMENT

Montréal's downtown is also the center of its arts and cultural attractions, with most of the major institutions located between rue Atwater to the extreme southwest and rue St-Denis to the extreme northeast, rue Sherbrooke in the west and boulevard René-Lévesque in the east.

One might argue about the significance of the **Montréal Forum** as a cultural institution, but it is home to the *Canadiens* hockey team, which has won more Stanley Cups than any other team in the league. East of the Forum is the area's tonies residence, **Le Centre Canadien d'Architecture**, the only museum in the world dedicated soley to this discipline. It is the brainchild of Phyllis Lambert of the Montréal Bronfman family, known internationally for their Seagram enterprise and as shareholders in Dupont and Time-Warner, among other blue-chip multinational firms. Ms. Lambert, who designed the **Saidye Bronfman Centre for the Arts** as a homage to her mentor, Mies van der Rohe, invested considerable personal fortune in making the CCA come true. Two austere-looking wings designed by Montréal architect Peter Rose flank the splendidly restored Victorian mansion known as the Shaughnessy House, which Lambert had rescued from the wrecker's ball some years ago. This museum houses extensive collections of architectural paraphenelia of every description – all of it of historical and social importance. It also has a library that is the envy of many academic institutions, open to architectural scholars by special permission. The CCA regularly hosts award-winning architectural exhibitions and lectures; its beautiful, acoustically-perfect

FESTIVALS

Théâtre Paul Desmarais is the site of special concerts and symposia.

Another architectural marvel is the **Cathédrale Marie-Reine-du-Monde**, further north of blvd. René Levésque and kitty-corner from **Square Dorchester**, itself originally a Catholic cemetery. The pet project of Bishop Ignace Bourget, the cathedral was built in 1894 and is a one-third-scale replica of St. Peter's in Rome. It is a wonderfully ornate reminder to English Montréal that the Church of Rome long ruled what was then Canada's largest city.

Not far from the cathedral is **Place des Arts**, Montréal's foremost flagship to the performing and visual arts. The **Complexe Desjardins** is home to Les Grands Ballets Canadiens, L'Orchestre Symphonique de Montréal, L'Opéra de Montréal, Le Festival Mondial du Film, Le Festival International de Jazz, Le Festival de Théâtre des Amériques and Le Festival International de Danse, among other local companies and events with stellar international reputations. It is also the main venue for traveling productions of such hit Broadway musicals as *Phantom of the Opera* and *Jesus Christ, Superstar*, as well as such home-grown Québecois blockbusters as Luc Plamondon's *Starmania*.

Now part of this massive complex is the **Musée d'Art Contemporain,** relocated from its Expo '67 site in a much bigger building designed as a showcase inside and out for the museum's massive permanent collection of work by contemporary Québec artists. It also mounts special exhibitions featuring major artists and movements from the international arts scene. Its 350-seat performance space is used for theater, dance, lectures and concerts – many of them part of the annual festival events but featuring presentations on a much more intimate scale than Place des Arts' big halls allow. Place des Arts and its surrounding streets turn into one big block party the first two weeks of July, when the **Montréal Jazz Festival** takes over the town. Every inch of space indoors and out, you'll find musicians jamming and the crowd moving to the beat of Montréal's biggest annual bash. Well over 1.5 million people attend its 500-plus free concerts.

Rivalling this musical free-for-all is the late July-early August **Festival Juste Pour Rire** (Just for Laughs), the world's largest comedy festival, which happens just a few blocks east of Place des Arts. Comedy headquarters is rue St-Denis, with the Gala nights featuring the world's comedy elite taking place at **Théâtre St-Denis**. The Festival is really two festivals that overlap – French comedians from here and abroad get top billing opening week, with English-speaking comedians following a few nights later. Like the Jazzfest, the action spills onto the streets, with rue St-Denis below rue Sherbrooke closed to traffic much of the time.

It figures, then, that Montréal would be home to the world's only museum of humor – the **Musée Juste Pour Rire** on rue St-Laurent, a couple of blocks west of the Just for Laughs Festival. Founded and run by the Just for Laughs team and open year-round, this fun-house has harmless pranks and comedy classics on the bill.

THE SQUARE MILE

Downtown Montréal's other major attractions are all within blocks of one another on rue Sherbrooke, in what is still called Montréal's **Square Mile**, where the English, Scottish, and Irish social and business elite of the Victorian and Edwardian eras built their estates and spawned family dynasties. Some of these magnificent homes are still standing, though most along this stretch of Sherbrooke are now public institutions, pri-

Right: The first two weeks of July see a flare-up of jazz fever.

SQUARE MILE

vate clubs, high-class boutiques, art galleries, university quarters and embassies.

Facing the Roddick Gates of **McGill University**, itself a bequest of fur trader James McGill who owned most of the land in this area at one time, is the **McCord Museum of Canadian History**, housed in the original Strathcona Hall and originally founded by avid collector and Canadian nationalist David McCord, who left his vast collection of Canadiana and Native artifacts to the city he so loved. It presides over the **Notman Archives** and presents world-class exhibitions from its own permanent collections, as well as special touring exhibitions from across Canada that highlight the many cultures from which present-day Canadians sprang. It is considered one of the prettiest public institutions in Montréal, sensitively and beautifully restored and expanded as part of the re-gilding of great Montréal "monuments" for the city's 350th anniversary.

Some blocks south, the **Musée des beaux-arts de Montréal**, Canada's oldest art institution, now straddles two sides of Sherbrooke. The 1912 **Benaiah Gibb Pavilion** was designed by Montréal's foremost Edwardian architects, the Brothers Maxwell. Across the street is the **Jean-Noël Desmarais Pavilion**, which opened in late 1991 and was designed by former Montréaler Moshe Safdie, whose name is becoming synonymous with many of Canada's most recent public edifices, at least from Vancouver to Québec City. It has hosted and mounted many of the splashiest international exhibitions that North America has seen in the past ten years – to wit, *Age of The Metropolis* and *Picasso: A Meeting in Montréal* – which attracted record crowds for months on end. But it is also renowned for its scholarly research and presentation of exhibitions highlighting past and present Montréal and Québec artists working in a multitude of disciplines – among them, Betty Goodwin and the late Paul-Emile Borduas, both of whom are revered in international contemporary art circles.

One way to explore the Square Mile's rich heritage is to take **Héritage Montréal's** self-guided walking tour along Sherbrooke of 19 historic sites stretching from McGill University and the McCord Museum at rue University on the east side to the Sulpician Seminary and the Mother House of Dawson College at rue Atwater on the west side.

All of the public institutions mentioned above are part of this circuit, which on a sunny day might take as little as an hour to stroll by, or longer if you venture inside them, as most are open to the public. Many of them are lasting monuments to an age when Montréal's society was ruled largely by the McGills, McTavishes, McConnells, Drummonds, Holts, Ogilvies, Cantlies, McDougalls, Macdonalds, Strathconas, Birks, McIntyres, Rosses, and other Scots, English and Irish families who arrived in Canada with little possessions but fierce courage. In the process they shaped not only Montréal's destiny but the entire country's. From the late 1800s until World War Two, 70 percent of Canada's wealth was concentrated in the hands of some 25,000 Montréalers living and working in the Square Mile.

PARKS

When Jacques Cartier arrived in 1535, he was led by Iroquois living in the palisaded village of Hochelaga to the summit of Mont Royal, he planted a wooden cross, thanking God for his safe journey and claimed the land for France. The Sieur de Maisonneuve did likewise in 1643, as thanks for the divine intervention that had spared the fledgling colony of Ville-Marie from that year's devastating floods. By 1850, much of the mountain's western slope had been turned into cemeteries where the city's Catholic and Protestant faithful were buried. Today's neon-lit 115-foot (35 m) iron cross on Mont Royal, visible from 50 miles (80 km) away, was erected in 1924 by the St-Jean-Baptiste Society. A tribute to de Maisonneuve's gesture of faith, it proclaims to all Québec's deeply Catholic roots. Until the city stepped in to expropriate the mountain and its surrounding area, private estates built by 19th-century Montréalers began to overtake its sloped terraces on the Westmount and Outremont sides, with the downtown gradually rising up its east side. Les Amis de la Montagne and city officials now keep a close watch on developments here and nix those that don't conform to the spirit of celebrated Central Park landscape architect Frederick Law Olmsted's decree that it be kept as natural as possible.

Parc Mont Royal, which rises 766 ft (233 m) over the city, is still largely as Olmsted designed it: an urban sanctuary for recreation, seclusion and contemplation. Much of it is dense forest, where small animals and birds make their homes. The **Grand Chalet**, a seigneurial-style hall built at its center in 1931, offers refreshments and respite and is often used for the city's special events, as well as charity balls and other socials. The chalet's terrace overlooking the city below affords a panoramic view of the St. Lawrence and even Vermont's Green Mountains in the distance. Just 15 minutes west of the chalet lies **Lac-aux-Castors** (Beaver Lake), where toddlers wade and children sail their toy boats under the watchful eyes of sunning parents. In winter, it's crowded with skaters, who are joined on the mountain by cross-country skiers and snowshoers taking advantage of the hills and trails along this "mountain".

On the southern edge of the park is the **Oratoire St-Joseph**, dedicated to the patron saint of Canada, but in reality a memorial to brother André of Saint-Croix, who healed miraculously. He was

Right: La Ronde, amusement park on the Île-Ste-Hélène.

BOTANICAL GARDEN / BIODOME

only beatified by the Church. The Oratoire is a place of pilgrimage for André is buried here. Nearby is the **Musée Historique Canadien**, a wax museum with historic figures and scenes. Nearby are the grounds of the **University of Montréal**. To the south of the Mont Royal is the district of **Westmount** (metro station: Atwater), whose park was designed in 1966 by Mies van der Rohe.

Montréal's other great oasis is its **Jardin Botanique de Montréal** built during the Great Depression as a public works project, the brainchild of then mayor Camille Houde, one of French Montréal's greatest heros and certainly one of the city's most astute politicians. The third largest in the world, it rivals Parc Mont Royal as the city's most popular public green space. It is often featured in the wedding albums of successive generations of Montréalers of every ethnic persuasion and every social class!

Star attractions are the **Japanese Tea Ceremony Pavilion** and the **Dream Lake Friendship Garden** – the latter designed and built by the PR of China as a 350th birthday gift to Montréal.

One of its most novel attractions is the **Montréal Insectarium**, housing more than 250,000 live and dead insects from 100 countries. It was joined recently by the **Montréal Biodome**, which opened in 1992 and quickly became the city's top man-made attraction: a vast environmental museum on the site of the former Olympic Velodrome features four climate controlled ecosystems – the Laurentian forest, the St. Lawrence marine environment, the polar world and the tropical forest, along with their indigenous flora, fauna and many native animals.

In the nearby **Parc Olympique** is the impressive **Stade Olympique**, which was originally built for the 1976 Summer Olympics, but is now home to the **Montréal Expos** baseball team during the spring and summer months, as well the venue for megarock shows. And yes, the Stadium's observation deck offers a spectacular view of Montréal and the St-Lawrence River beyond.

GUIDEPOST: MONTRÉAL

MONTRÉAL
Area code: 514

Access / Local Transportation

By air: **Mirabel Airport**, Mirabel; Tel: 476-3010. 65 kilometers (40 miles) northwest of Montréal, charters and flights arriving from other than the North American continent. **Dorval Airport**, Dorval; Tel: 633-3105. On the Island of Montréal, 25 minutes west of downtown, flights from within Canada and the United States.

By bus: Autocar Connoisseur/Gray Line, Tel: 934-1222, leaves every 30 minutes from Dorval for downtown Montréal, with stops at major hotels and the **Terminus Voyageur** bus station at Metro Berri-UQAM. Autobus Aero Plus bus service from Mirabel takes about an hour to downtown Montréal's **Gare Centrale** train station and Metro Place Bonaventure behind La Reine Elizabeth HoTel: (Autobus Aero Plus also operates a shuttle service between the two airports). Inter-Québec, inter-provincial and American passenger bus lines operate out of the **Terminus Voyageur**, 505 blvd. de Maisonneuve; Tel: 842-2281.

By citibus and Metro (subway): Clean, safe and efficient, the Société de transport de la Communauté de Montréal's bus and subway system takes you almost anywhere on the island and connects with public bus and commuter train lines serving the Greater Montréal area. Passengers can transfer between the bus and Metro at no extra charge (get a transfer slip at initial boarding point). Five Metro lines connect 65 stations and run from 5:30 am to 1 am daily (except for the Blue Line, which stops at 11 pm). Exact change is required for buses. Free bus schedules and Metro maps are available at each station.

By taxi: Metered cabs and limousines serve both airports. The average fare to downtown Montréal from Mirabel is $55 Cdn. and from Dorval, $23 Cdn.

By car: Car rentals are generally expensive, though package deals and weekend rates are available. Most companies charge for mileage. **Avis**, Tel: 866-7906; **Budget**, Tel: 866-7675; **Hertz**, Tel: 842-8537; **Tilden**, Tel: 878-2771 and **Thrifty**, Tel: 636-5567 have kiosks at the airports and downtown outlets.

Visitors arriving by car from elsewhere in Canada enter Montréal by Autoroute 20 from the east or Autoroute 40 from the west (via the Trans-Canada Highway).

Three major expressways linking the American border states to Montréal are Interstate 87 from New York and Interstate 87 or 91 from Vermont. Keep in mind that the Montréal street grid is actually oriented on a northeast-southwest axis but no one follows that in giving directions to drivers or sightseers on foot. The general rule is to base your sense of direction on the two major arteries bisecting the city: rue Sherbrooke, which runs north-south, and blvd. St-Laurent, which runs east-west.

By train: VIA Rail Canada, Tel: 871-1331, from elsewhere in Québec and Canada and AmTrak, Tel: 1-800/872-7245, from the United States arrive at **Gare Centrale,** 935 rue de la Gauchetière Ouest.

Accommodation

LUXURY: **Hotel Intercontinental-Montréal**, 360 rue St-Antoine Ouest H2Y 3X4; Tel: 987-9900. **Le Meridien**, 4 Complexe Desjardins H5B 1E5; Tel: 285-1450. **Place Bonaventure**, Box 1000, 900 rue de la Gauchetière Ouest H3A 1G1; Tel: 397-2233. **Bonaventure Hilton**, 1 Place Bonaventure H5A 1E4; Tel: 878-2332. **La Reine Elizabeth**, 900 blvd. René Lévesque Ouest H3B 4A5; Tel: 861-3511. **Ritz-Carlton Kempinski**, 1228 rue Sherbrooke Ouest H3G 1H6; Tel: 842-4212. **Le Quatre Saisons**, 1050 rue Sherbrooke Ouest H3A 2R6; Tel: 284-1110. **Hotel Vogue**, 1425 rue de la Montagne H3G 1Z3; Tel: 285-5555. **Château Champlain**, 1 Place du Canada H3B 4C9; Tel: 878-9000. **Le Centre Sheraton**, 1201 blvd. René Lévesque Ouest H3B 2L7; Tel: 878-2000. **Delta Montréal**, 450 rue Sherbrooke Ouest H3A 2T4; Tel: 286-1986. **Le Radisson Gouverneurs Montréal**, 777 rue University H3C 2Z7; Tel: 879-1370. **Hotel de la Montagne**, 1430 rue de la Montagne H3G 1Z5; Tel: 288-5656.

MODERATE: **Château Versailles**, 1659 rue Sherbrooke Ouest H3H 1E3 and **La Tour Versailles**, 1808 rue Sherbrooke Ouest H3H 1E5; Tel: 933-3611. **Holiday Inn Crowne Plaza-Metro Centre**, 505 rue Sherbrooke Est H2L 1K2; Tel: 842-8581. **Holiday Inn Crowne Plaza**, 420 rue Sherbrooke Ouest H3A 1B4; Tel: 842-6111. **Holiday Inn Sinomonde**, 96 rue St-Urbain and 99 ave. Viger Ouest H2Z 1E9; Tel: 878-9888. **Howard Johnson Plaza Hotel**, 475 rue Sherbrooke Ouest H3A 2L9; Tel: 842-3961. **La Citadelle**, 410 rue Sherbrooke Ouest H3A 1B3; Tel: 844-8851. **Cantlie Sherbrooke**, 1110 rue Sherbrooke Ouest H3A 1G9; Tel: 842-2000.

BUDGET: **Journey's End Hotel,** 3440 avenue du Parc H2X 2H5; Tel: 849-1413.

Restaurants / Cafés

LUXURY: **Les Halles**, 1450 rue Crescent H3G 2B6; Tel: 844-2328, French. **L'Ile de France**, 801 rue de Maisonneuve Ouest H3A 3E5; Tel: 849-6631, French. **Bocca d'Oro**, 1448 rue St-Mathieu H3H 2H9; Tel: 933-8414, Italian. **Katsura**, 2170 ave. de la Montagne H3G 1Z2; 849-1172, Japanese. **L'Orchidée de Chine**, 2017 rue Peel H3A 1T6; Tel: 287-1878, Szechuan. **Milos**, 5357 avenue du Parc H2V 4G9; Tel. 272-3522/5242, Greek, seafood. **Le Latini**, 1130 rue Jeanne Mance H2Z 1L7; Tel: 861-3166. **Gibby's Steakhouse**, 298 Place d'Youville H2Y 2B6; Tel: 282-1837.

GUIDEPOST: MONTRÉAL

MODERATE: **Le Caveau**, 2063 rue Victoria H3A 2A3; Tel: 844-l624, French. **Chez La Mère Michel**, 1209 rue Guy H3H 2K5; Tel: 934-0473, French. **Baci**, 2095 avenue McGill College H3A 3E8; Tel: 288-790l, Italian. **Chao Phraya**, 2067 rue Stanley H3A 1R7; Tel: l-5l4-288-2155, Thai. **Faros**, 362 avenue Fairmount H2V 2G4; Tel: 270-8437, Greek, seafood. **Le Chrysanthème**, 1208 rue Crescent H3G 2A9; Tel: 397-l408, Szechuan. **Cajun House**, 1219 rue Mackay H3G 2H5; Tel: 87l-3898, Creole. **Chez Pauze**, l657 rue Ste-Catherine Ouest H3H lL9; Tel: 932-6ll8, seafood. **Moishe's Steakhouse**, 3961 St-Laurent H2W lY4; Tel: 845-1696/9545. **La Pâtisserie Belge**, 3485 avenue du Parc H2X 2H6; Tel: 845-1245. **La Brioche Lyonnaise,** 1593 rue St-Denis H2X 3K3; Tel: 842-7017. *INEXPENSIVE:* **Café Mozart**, 2090 rue de la Montagne H3G lZ7; Tel: 849-l482. **Golden Curry**, 5210 blvd. St-Laurent H2T lSl; Tel: 270-2561, Indian. **Schwartz's Montréal Hebrew Delicatessen**, 3895 St-Laurent; Tel: 842-4813. **Avocado Café**, 5l42 blvd. St-Laurent H2T lR8; Tel: 271-3234, great hamburgers. **La Desserte**, 5258 blvd. St-Laurent H2T 1Sl; Tel: 272-5797. French pastries. **Brulerie St-Denis**, 4967 St-Denis H2W 2M4; Tel: 286-9158, French pastries.

Nightlife
Pub Sir Winston Churchill, l459 rue Crescent H3G 2B2;Tel: 288-06l6. **Hard Rock Café**, 1458 rue Crescent H3G 2B6; Tel: 987-1420. **Peel Pub**, ll07 rue Ste-Catherine Ouest H3B lH8; 844-6769. **Old Dublin Pub**, 12l9-A rue de l'Université H3B 3A7; Tel: 86l-4448. **Comedyworks**, 1238 rue Bishop H3G 2E3; Tel: 398-966l. **Spectrum de Montréal**, 318 rue Ste-Catherine Ouest H2X 1A4, Tel: 861-5851. **Bar L'Opéra**, 3523 blvd. St-Laurent H2X 2T6; Tel: 284-7793. **Crocodile Discothèque**, 4236 blvd. St-Laurent H2W lZ3; Tel: 848-0044. **Le Loft**, l405 Blvd. St-Laurent H3B 3K3; Tel: 28l-8058. **Woodstock Pool Room**, 378l blvd. St-Laurent H2W lX8; Tel: 982-095l. **Café Opium**, 4725 rue St-Denis H2G 2L5; Tel: 844-8709. **Les Foufounes Electriques**, 87 rue Ste-Catherine Est H2X lK5; Tel: 845-5684. **L'Air du Temps Jazz**, 191 rue St-Paul Ouest; Tel: 842-2003. **Sherlocks**, 1010 rue Ste-Catherine Ouest, H3B 3R5, Tel: 878-0888.

Museums / Culture
Musée Gilles Villeneuve, 510 rue Frontenac, Berthierville J0K 1A0; Tel: 836-2714. **Pointe-à-Caillière Musée d'archéologie et d'histoire de Montréal**, 350 Place Royale H2Y 3Y5; daily exc. Mon; Tel: 872-9150. **David M. Stewart Museum**, daily exc. Tues; Tel: 86l-670l and **Le Festin du Gouverneur**, Tel: 879-ll4l, 20 chemin Tour, Ile-Ste-Hélène H3C 4G6. **Centre Canadien d'Architecture**, 1920 rue Baile H3H 2S6; Tel: 939-7000. **Musée d'Art Contemporain**, 185 rue Ste-Catherine Ouest H2X lZ8; Tel: 847-6226. **Musée Juste Pour Rire**, 2111 blvd. St-Laurent H2X 2T5; Tel: 845-4000. **Musée du Château Ramezay**, 280 rue Notre-Dame est, June 15-Sept 15 daily, rest of year daily exc. Mon, Tel: 861-3708. **McCord Museum of Canadian History**, 690 rue Sherbrooke Ouest H3A 1E9; Tel: 398-7100. **Musée des beaux-arts de Montréal**: Benaiah Gibb Pavilion, 1379 rue Sherbrooke Ouest, daily exc. Mon; Tel: 285-1600. **Jean-Noël Desmarais Pavilion**, 1380 rue Sherbrooke Ouest H3G 2T9; Tel: 285-1600. **Héritage Montréal**, 1181 rue de la Montagne H3G lZ2; Tel: 875-2985.

Theater / Dance / Music / Festivals
Théâtre St-Denis, 1594 rue St-Denis H2X 3K2; Tel: 849-42ll. **Centaur Théâtre**, 453 rue St-Francois-Xavier H2Y 2Tl; Tel: 288-3l6l. **Les Grands Ballets Canadiens**, 4816 rue Rivard H2J 2N6; Tel: 849-8681. **L'Orchestre Symphonique de Montréal**, 85 rue Ste-Catherine Ouest H2X 3P4; Tel: 842-3402. **L'Opéra de Montréal**, 260 blvd. de Maisonneuve Ouest H2X 1Y9; Tel: 985-2222. **Le Festival Mondial du Film**, 1455 blvd. de Maisonneuve Est H3G 1M8; Tel: 848-3883, in Aug. **Festival International de Jazz de Montréal Inc.**, 318 rue Ste-Catherine Ouest H2X 2H1; Tel: 523-3378, June/July. **Festival de Nouvelle Danse**, 4060 blvd. St-Laurent H2W 1Y9; Tel: 287-1423. **Festival Juste Pour Rire**, 2101 blvd. St-Laurent H2X 2T5; Tel: 845-3155.

Botanical Gardens / Parks
Parc Mont Royal, Tel: 844-4928. **Jardin Botanique de Montréal**, 4101 rue Sherbrooke Est H1X 2B2; Tel: 872-1400. **Montréal Insectarium**, 4581 rue Sherbrooke Est; Tel: 872-8753. **Montréal Biodome**, 4777 avenue Pierre-de-Coubertin; daily; Tel: 868-3000. **La Ronde Amusement Park**, Ile-Ste.-Hélène, June-Labor Day daily; May weekends; Tel: 872-6222. **Aquarium de Montréal**, Parc des Iles, Ile-Ste-Hélène, Tel: 872-4656.

Tourist Information
Year-round **Centre Infotouriste**, 1001 Square Dorchester H3B 4V4; Tel: 873-2015. Here, the **Réservation Québec**, Tel: 878-1000 makes one-stop bookings of accommodations throughout the province. It also gives information on hospitality services for visitors with restricted physical ability; alternatively, contact Tourisme Québec's official representative direct: **Keroul**, Box 100, Succursale M, 4545 Ave. Pierre-de-Coubertin, Montréal H1V 3R2, Tel: 252-3104. Seasonal information (mid-June-Labor Day): **Vieux Montréal Infotouriste** kiosk, Pl. Jacques Cartier, 174 rue Notre Dame Est. *By mail:* **Greater Montréal Convention and Tourism Bureau**, Les Cours Mont Royal, 1555 rue Peel, Ste. 600 H3A 1X6; Tel: 844-5400.

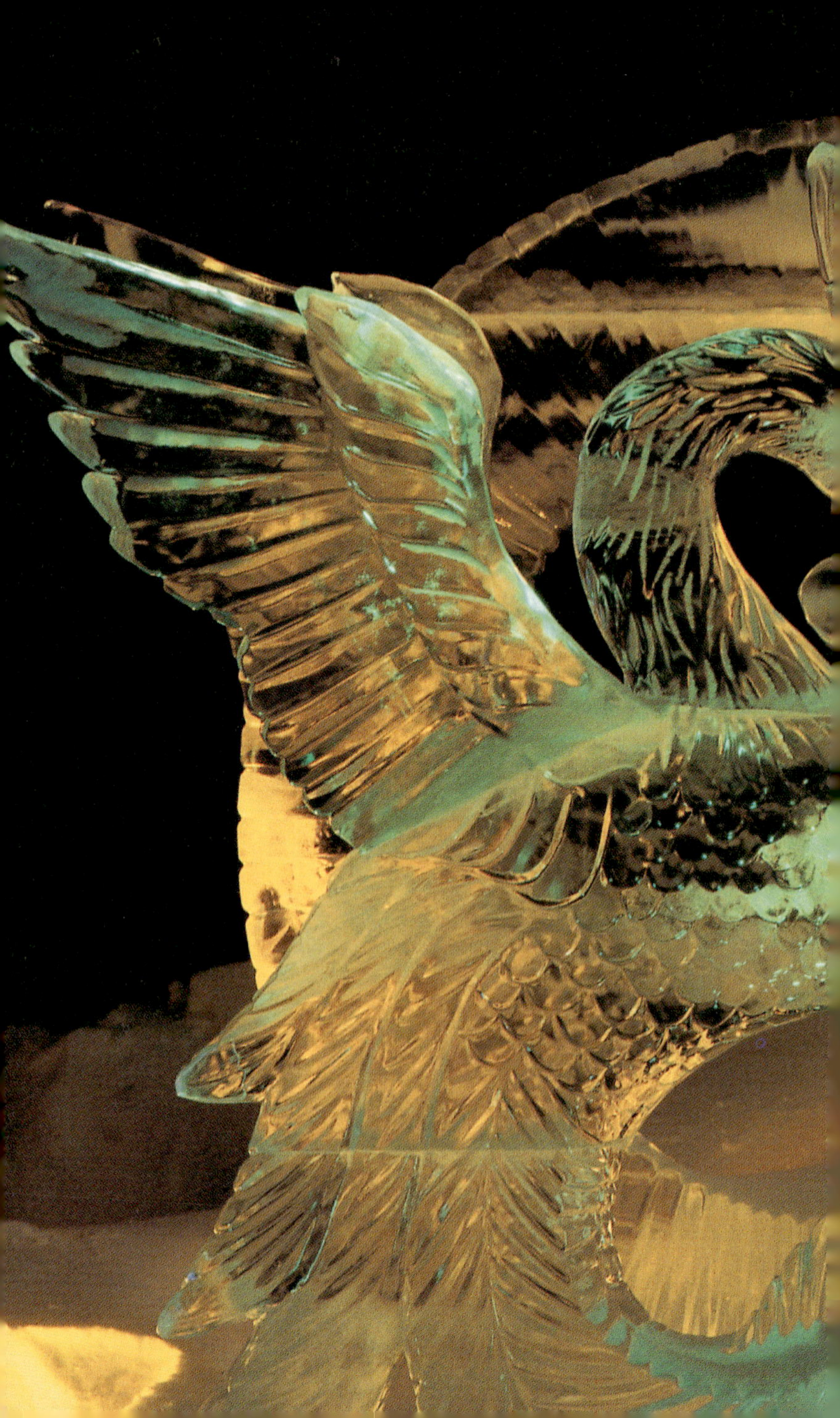

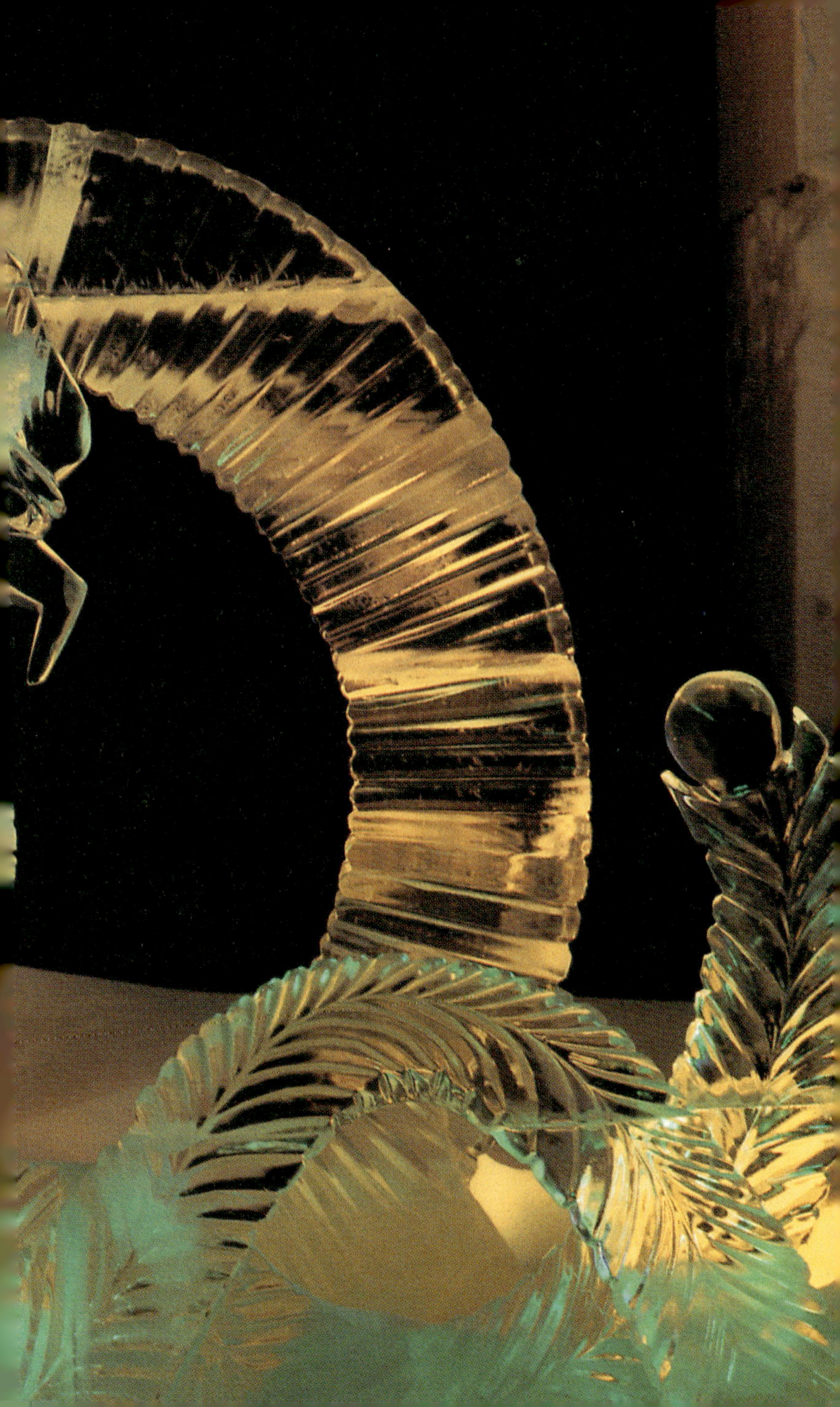

QUÉBEC CITY

QUÉBEC CITY

HAUTE VILLE
BASSE VILLE
ENTERTAINMENT
WINTER ACTIVITIES
EXCURSIONS

"Québec," a derivation of the Algonquin tribe's "Kebec" means "where the river narrows," and this great walled city (the only one north of Mexico) and its port was justly considered one of the major gateways to the continent for at least 300 years. It is also the only North American city to be designated a World Heritage Site by UNESCO, joining the ranks of other such internationally-acclaimed cities as Rome and Jerusalem. Vieux Québec (Old Québec), the world-famous historic area of Québec City, was originally divided into two distinct towns – the Haute Ville (Upper Town) and the Basse Ville (Lower Town), separated by a 350-foot cliff, Cap Diamant.

Before the British "conquest" of 1759, the Haute Ville was home to the then French colony's governors, priests, missionaries and army commanders while merchants, tradesmen, fur trappers, fishermen and laborers lived and worked in the riverfront Basse Ville. Today, the two towns are connected by several streets, 28 stone staircases (great to descend but challenging to ascend) and the Funicular. This outdoor "elevator" transports people easily up and down the cliff

Preceding pages: Ice sculpture in the street of Québec. Left: Students from all over America frolic for ten days at Carnival.

and affords a bird's-eye view of the Basse Ville and pastoral Île-d'Orleans in the St. Lawrence River.

Today, Québec's oldest municipality, home to 165,000 people, still somewhat resembles a French provincial town, given that the majority of its residents are of *vielle souche* stock. Indeed, more than 95 percent of the Greater Québec area's 645,000 population are Francophones. The British poet Matthew Arnold summed up the quality of life in Québec succinctly when he wrote: "I would rather be a poor priest in Québec than a rich hog merchant in Chicago."

In spite of a British presence throughout long periods of the past four centuries, Québec City has never relinquished its vocation as an important crucible of French-Canadian culture. Originally the center of New France's intellectual and religious life, its Séminaire de Québec, established in 1663 by the French bishop François de Montmorency Laval, was Canada's first university. Now incorporated into the Université de Laval, the Catholic institution has educated many of Québec and Canada's foremost politicians – former prime minister Brian Mulroney being just one of its more "recent" graduates. It was also where, from 1615-1639, the Catholic missionary orders of the Franciscan monks, Jesuit

FESTIVALS

priests, Ursuline and Augustine nuns first established outposts in New France. Still standing is the **Cathédrale Notre-Dame-de-Québec** built in 1678, the oldest cathedral in North America north of Mexico, which once ruled a diocese that stretched as far south as New Orleans. Québec City is also home to some of the province's leading theater companies, including **Théâtre Repère** and **la Caserne**, the brainchilds of celebrated international darling-cum-wunderkind Québecois Robert Lepage, whose multidisciplinary, multilingual creations have won him international acclaim and avid fans everywhere.

Just as Montréal, Québec City is festival- and museum-mad, especially since tourism is one of its top industries. The city's two major summertime blow-outs are the late June / early July **Nuits Internationales de Jazz et Blues de Québec** and the mid-July **Festival d'Eté Interna-**

Above: Canadian winter sport – boat races on the St. Lawrence River.

tional de Québec, now in its 26th year. It showcases the talents of more than 1000 French-speaking performers – singers, dancers, clowns, musicians, magicians, unicyclists, and the like – from 20 countries around the world. **Les Médiévales de Québec**, an annual mid-August event, celebrates the Middle Ages, with some references to the Renaissance period. Over five days, the non-stop pageantry of parades, jousting tournaments, firework displays and street performances by medieval-costumed jugglers, acrobats, musicians and dancers turn Vieux Québec into a carnavalesque tableau night and day. Best of all is the non-stop feasting on medieval fare al fresco and in the city's finest restaurants, with a $250-per person medieval banquet in the vaults of **Restaurant Le Cavour** the pinnacle of this event. Despite deep-freeze temperatures and chilling winds, the streets are as thronged in winter as they are in summer, when the 10-day annual **Bonhomme Carnaval d'Hiver** (Québec Winter Carnival) takes over the city. Now in its 35th

QUEBEC CITY

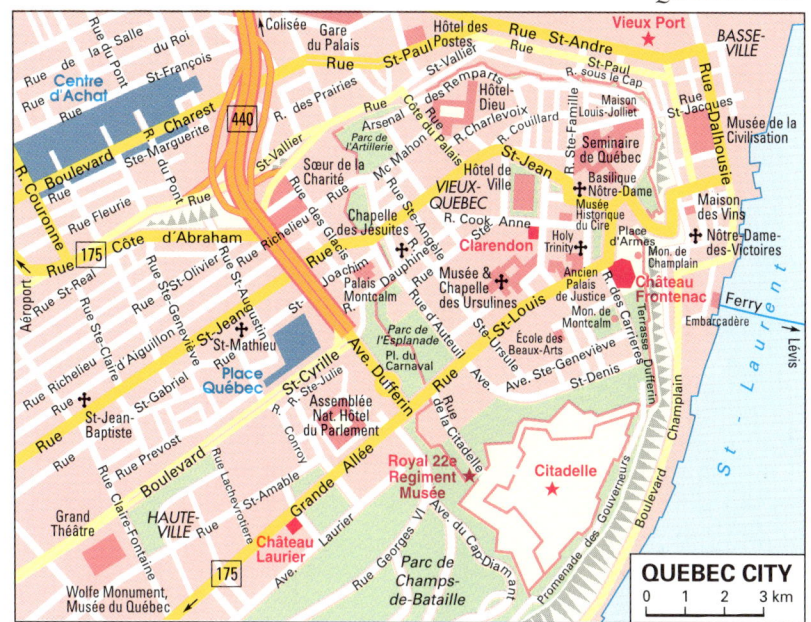

year, it attracts more than 1.5 million people annually.

For many, it is their first introduction to *la belle province* and French Québec. Fabulous ice palaces and ice sculptures, winter sports of every kind, parades led by its mascot, *Bonhomme* – a giant scarfed and toqued snowman – plenty of food, drink and people make February in the frozen north one of the hottest places to be.

HAUTE VILLE

The more famous of Vieux Québec's two areas is the walled **Haute Ville** established in 1620 by Samuel de Champlain as Fort St-Louis. But the Basse Ville, which he first founded in l608, was the site of New France's first permanent settlement and quickly became its commercial center.

Gentry and clergy originally lived there, moving some years later to the newer fortified Haute Ville at the summit of Cap Diamant out of range, they thought, of England's Royal Navy guns. From 1663 to 1759, when the English general Wolfe defeated the French under Montcalm, the population of New France grew and the fur trade, the mainstay of commerce, prospered. From this base, French explorers traveled as far south as the Gulf of Mexico and as far west as the Rockies, claiming these vast territories for France and bestowing French names on more than 4000 places throughout North America.

Fearing that the French might try to recapture their city, the British extended the walled city's perimeters. A tour will take you to the original bastions, towers and gates of the old fortifications. The ancient cannons still point at the St. Lawrence River.

In 1832, construction of the massive star-shaped **Citadelle** which still dominates **Cap Diamant**, was completed. They were right to be concerned, though the enemy was not ultimately the French, but rather the American army in 1775 and again in 1812. Both attempts failed.

121

HAUTE VILLE

As it does today, Québec City has always played a prominent role in Canada's national agenda throughout its history and that regardless of who, ultimately, ruled it under whatever flag. The Constitution Act of 1791 made it the national capital of Lower Canada, a role it retained until the 1840 Act of Union conferred this status on Montréal. In 1867, through the British North America Act formally designating Québec, Ontario, New Brunswick and Nova Scotia as provinces in the "new" country of Canada, Québec City became the provincial capital and the last political bastion of French culture on North American soil. What it gained in political terms, it lost, however, in economic terms, as the center of Eastern Canada's commerce shifted to Montréal and later Toronto.

Above: Street in the Old Town of Québec City. Right: The "Compagnie franche de la marine" remembers the English occupation in 1759.

Plains of Abraham

Given that Vieux Québec, both Haute and Basse Villes, lies within a one-square-mile (2.5 sq.-km) radius, and most of its streets are narrow cobblestoned alleys, the best way to explore the city is on foot or by calèche. Most definitely, the first place to begin the Québec City discovery tour is at the **Plains of Abraham**, which so define Canada's past and present.

Tranquil as the **Parc de Champs-de-Bataille** (Battlefields Park) surroundings may be today, it is the site of that famous Wolfe/Montcalm skirmish that delivered New France into England's hands. The rest, as they say, is history – commemorated through plaques, monuments, artillery pieces, Martello towers (now interpretation centers of the Park's 400-year history) spread over 250 acres of woodlands and gardens. Contrary to popular myth, Québec was not "conquered" in the truest sense. The 20-minute battle was but one military victory in a larger war between France and England for control of this part of the New World. Under the 1763 Treaty of Paris peace settlement, France ceded French Canada once and for all to British rule. "Je me souviens" on the Québec license plates is a stern admonition to the rest of Canada and the world that French Québec will never forget or forgive the humiliation suffered on a windswept plain over 200 years ago. Montcalm and Wolfe are captured in wax at the **Musée Historique de Cire** on rue Ste-Anne; and the **Musée des Ursulines** on rue Donacona is the final resting place of General Montcalm's mortal remains. The attached cloister **Monastre des Ursulines** was founded in 1639 and was used as a school for young French and native girls.

Near the **Wolfe Monument** in Battlefield Park is the recently expanded **Musée du Québec**. It is now comprised of two of Québec City's well-known landmarks: the original building, renamed the **Gérard-Morisset Pavilion** in honor of a former director and Québec art pioneer; and the **Baillairgé Pavilion**, the former Québec Prison, designed by one of the province's foremost architects, Charles Baillairgé. Two highlights specifically recall the prison's history: the former prison tower features a two-storey permanent installation by Montréal artist David Moore and an original cell block has been preserved. The skylit Great Hall now connects these two buildings. Here, exhibitions, performances, music, conferences, shows and movies are part of the year-round cultural activities. Since it first opened in 1933, the Musée du Québec has been the showcase for four centuries of art by Québec artists, promoting the careers of some of the most famous "Canadian" artists – Clarence Gagnon, Alfred Pellan, Jean-Paul Riopelle, Jean-Paul Lemieux and Paul-Emile Borduas, among others. Its permanent collection comprises nearly 15,000 works of art dating from the 17th century to the present.

Nearby and not to be missed is the 172-year-old **Citadelle**, which earned Québec City its nickname, "Gibralter of America" from Sir Winston Churchill during a wartime conference here in the 1940s. From the 17th to the 19th centuries, the city played an instrumental role in defending all of northeastern America.

This massive fortress took 30 years to build, comprises 25 buildings and is still an army stronghold – for the Royal 22e Van Doos Regiment. Among its attractions are the Governor-General's residence, officers' mess, the 1863 Cap Diamant redoubt and the **Royal 22nd Regiment Museum** located in a 1750 powderhouse. The daily ritual of cannon fire, the tattoo and changing of the guard are among the more pleasant reminders of military life in Vieux Québec.

Panoramic Promenade

What hasn't changed in four centuries is the breathtaking view of the mighty **St. Lawrence River**, whether seen from the

Citadelle – atop the city's highest point or anywhere else along Cap Diamant. Three equally popular vantage points are the **Earl Grey Terrace** and the **Dufferin Terrace** along with the famous **Promenade des Gouverneurs** boardwalk overlooking the cliff from Battlefields Park to **Champlain's Monument** in **Place d'Armes.**

In its path is Canada's best-known hotel **Château Frontenac**. The flagship of the Canadian Pacific Hotel chain, this green-turreted "castle" with its sloping copper roof was built in 1893 on the site of New France's one-time military headquarters, the 1620 Château St-Louis, which was later replaced in 1784 by the Château Haldimand. Named after the Comte de Frontenac, who governed the French colony from 1672-1698, it is still one of the world's preeminent luxury hotels. During the past century, it has welcomed numerous heads of state. It was designed by New York architect Bruce Price, one of the most celebrated practitioners of the château-style popular during the era. Notable among its public rooms is the 700-seat ballroom, inspired by Versailles' Hall of Mirrors. (Price's signature also marks the city's **Gare du Palais** train station and Montréal's equally magnificent Gare Windsor train station.)

Nearby **Place d'Armes**, the town's most central square, has long been the place for public parades and military events and is identifiable by the 19th-century government buildings lining its perimeter. The majestic 1887 **Ancien Palais de Justice**, which replaced the earlier 1650 courthouse nearby, stands on land originally occupied by the church and convent of the Recollet missionary founded by Franciscan monks, the first order of priests to arrive in New France in 1615. Today, a Gothic fountain in the square's center is a memorial to their holy mission.

Above: Live like the Count of Frontenac in the famous hotel château. Right: In the Rue du Trésor, you can have your portrait done.

Not far from Place d'Armes is **rue du Trésor**, a picturesque alley known far and wide as an open-air "gallery" where Québec City artists and artisans sell their wares. Perfect for browsing, visitors can pick up arts and crafts for considerably less than they cost elsewhere. On-the-spot family portraits are a highlight.

Right in the heart of this area is the **Holy Trinity Anglican Cathedral** on rue des Jardins, established in 1804 as the first Anglican cathedral outside of the British Isles. The present cathedral was built by order of King George III, on the site of the original 1681 church and monastery owned by the Recollet fathers who had made it available to Anglicans for their church services when Québec later came under British rule. Holy Trinity still observes the royal edict that the north balcony be set aside for the exclusive use of members of the British Royal Family and their representatives.

A short stroll away, along the broad elegant boulevard named **Grande Allée** that is the city's main artery, sits the l8th-century **Assemblée Nationale Hôtel du Parlement** (National Assembly Parliament) buildings, the seat of Québec's provincial government. Open to the public, with guided tours in English and French, the Hôtel du Parlement buildings were designed by Québec architect Etienne Tache in the late l7th-century Baroque style of Louis XIV and erected between 1877-1884. Four wings are set in a square around an interior courtyard. Statues in front pay tribute to founding fathers Jacques Cartier, Samuel de Champlain, governor Comte de Frontenac and valiant generals Wolfe and Montcalm.

Facing it is the venerable **Château Laurier** hotel. Smaller in scale than the city's more modern hotel towers, it is a charmingly comfortable and affordable. The Grande Allée is often referred to as Québec City's "Champs Elysées" because of the great trees, majestic public buildings and monuments, and proliferation of cafés, bistros, clubs and restaurants. It leads to **Place Montcalm** and the **Montcalm Monument**.

BASSE VILLE

Place d'Armes is the natural departure point for the city's Basse Ville, a must not only for serious antique collectors (on rue St-Paul) but also for some of the most colorful and intriguing shops, boutiques, outdoor cafés, historic sites and street musicians, jugglers and clowns that Québec City has in abundance. To get there quickly, take the **Escalier Casse-Cou** – literally, breakneck staircase – near Place d'Armes to descend from the cliff-top walled city into the riverside Lower Town area. An equally quick alternative is to take the **Funicular** from the **Dufferin Terrace**, which stops in the Basse Ville inside **Maison Louis-Jolliet**, built in 1683 for its namesake, who discovered the Mississippi River in 1672. He lived here until his death in 1700. From this point, contemporary "discoverers" can easily explore the Basse Ville and neighboring **Vieux Port.**

Two of the area's attractions are also the oldest districts in North America: **Place Royale** and **Quartier Petit Champlain.** Even today, these areas still reflect their 1608 origins as the first permanent settlement in New France. Vestiges of military and trade activities of that period can be found everywhere. Originally called Place du Marché, it became Place Royale in 1686 when the colonists erected a bust of Sun King Louis XIV.

Église Notre-Dame-des-Victoires on the south side of Place Royale is the oldest church in Québec. Built in 1688 on the site of Champlain's first residence, it takes its name from two French victories against the British, one in 1690 and one in 1711. Somewhat ironically, given its name, the church was destroyed by shellfire in 1759 during the "conquest" and has been rebuilt twice since then. Highlights of this holy edifice are: the altar in the shape of a castle; the scale model of Le Brèze – the boat that brought the Mar-

Above: Lovingly restored – the Lower City's Place Royale, dating from 1686, with a bust of Louis XIV.

quis de Tracy and soldiers of the Carignan Regiment to New France in 1664; the chapel dedicated to Ste-Geneviève, the guardian saint of Paris; and the excellent copies of paintings by such masters as Van Dyck, Van Loo and Boyermans. Also in Place Royale – and some might say the devil's work – is the **Maison des Vins**, housed in the 1869 warehouse designed by architect Claude Baillif, who also designed Jolliet's residence. This is a wine connoisseur's paradise – more than 1000 kinds of rare and vintage wines stored in its climate-controlled vaults and ranging in price from $10 to $1000 can be bought by the public from this history-steeped branch of the Société des Alcools du Québec.

Nearby Quartier Petit Champlain has boutiques, restaurants, and arts and crafts galleries galore, most housed in beautifully restored l7th-century surroundings. Characteristic of the bon vivant attitude which infects resident and vacationing revellers, this quartier is lively night and day. The action even spills out onto the streets during the spring and summer months. Just steps from the bottom of Escalier Casse-Cou is yet another of Québec City's finest Québecois restaurants, featuring traditional dishes and nouvelle versions of provincial delicacies. **Le Marie Clarisse** is housed in one of the ancient buildings lining the square. The restaurant's wooden-beamed ceiling, stone walls, sea-blue color scheme and big fireplace make it particularly attractive during cool weather or as a respite from the sun. It is a favorite haunt of Québecois because of its wine cellar.

Before heading back up to the Haute Ville**,** make time for the **Musée de la Civilisation**, located in the **Vieux Port** (Old Port) area, near Place Royale. Open only five years, the museum has garnered international praise for its comprehensive exhibitions on Québec history, French-Canadian culture, and the culture and people of the whole world.

Also in this area is the huge **Agora Vieux-Port** 5800-seat amphitheater, located between the river and Customs building. The setting for outdoor classical and contemporary music concerts, plays, variety shows, folkloric dance recitals and other types of entertainment for both adults and children, it is a mecca for residents and visitors alike and a wonderful respite for the footsore explorer.

ENTERTAINMENT

Though on a much smaller scale, Québec City like Montréal, has a lively nightlife scene that thrives year-round. During fair-weather months, much of the activity spills out onto the streets of the Haute and Basse Villes. When colder weather sets in, (and it can get very cold in these parts) the city's bars and restaurants, theaters, concert halls and sports arenas become the favorite meeting places for residents and visitors alike.

The **Orchestre Symphonique de Québec** is Canada's oldest orchestra, well-known in international music circles and with a devoted following in its home town. It is based at the **Grand Théâtre de Québec**, where the **Opera de Québec**, **Trident Théâtre** and **Danse-Partout** companies also perform. Two other venues attract international performers, as well as present a year-round roster of concerts, theater, variety show and dance productions by local and visiting artists from elsewhere in Canada, the United States and abroad.

The **Palais Montcalm**, a recently renovated 1100-seat concert hall, also has a gallery run by the city, showcasing contemporary art and an exhibition center, showing thematic exhibitions about the city's history.

The historic **Théâtre Capitole** has just re-opened after extensive renovation and restoration that transformed it into an architectural jewel inside and out, as well as a state-of-the-art performance space.

WINTER ACTIVITIES

Just as in Montréal, the other great Québec City pastime – or, more accurately, passion – is hockey. The **Québec Nordiques** face off against their archrivals from Montréal and other teams in the North American National Hockey League at the **Colisée de Québec**. And make no mistake about it: Québec Nordiques fans take the game seriously and consider their team's standings a matter of civic pride. When young hockey superstar Eric Lindros turned down their team for his first draft into the league, it was considered an affront against Québec City, and worse yet, against Francophone Québec, occupying front-page headlines and talk-show telephone lines for days on end. But it didn't stop there. Some months later when Lindros first played in the province after signing with another NHL team, he was loudly booed by the partisan crowd. So come prepared to cheer for the home team – or else!

Above: Once hotly contested, today a place for relaxation – square in front of the citadel.

WINTER ACTIVITIES

Aside from its favorite spectator sport, Québec City is also one of the prime destinations for downhill and cross-country skiers who come from around the world to ski at Mont Tremblant or Mont Ste-Anne and Stoneham, which have some of the finest skiing in North America and certainly rival the Eastern Townships (L'Estrie) ski resorts in popularity. The Greater Québec City area boasts five downhill ski centers, with a total of 120 runs for daytime skiing and 66 lit runs for nighttime skiing; it also has 22 ski centers specializing in cross-country skiing, with 278 groomed trails spread over some 660 sq. mi (1,636 sq. km) featuring heated shelters along the way.

The *Centre d'information de l'Office du Tourisme et des Congrès de la Communauté urbaine de Québec*, *Tourisme Québec* kiosk and the *Regroupement des stations de ski de fond* can provide visitors with full details about resorts close to the city for day trips or overnight stays.

EXCURSIONS

The first excursion around Québec that comes to mined are the **Chûtes Montmorency** 6 mi (10 km) to the north. The area around the 269-ft (84 m) waterfall has many hiking trails. 22 mi (35 km) northeast of town, then, is the monastery colony of **Ste-Anne-de Beaupré**, with a monastery church of the same name, an edifice built in 1923 in neo-Romanesque style, and which attracts many pilgrims.

The **Île d'Orléans** is a 22-mile-long (35 km) and 6-mile-wide (9 km) island in the St. Lawrence River. It's accessible over Hwy. 138. In 1759, General Wolfe tried to take Québec from here. The steel suspension bridge connecting the island with the mainland was built in 1935. The villages on the island are picturesque, many have 18th-century churches on display.

QUÉBEC CITY
Area code 418

Access / Local Transportation
By air: **Québec City Airport**, route de l'Aeroport, Ste-Foy, 12 miles (19 km) from downtown. It is served by national, regional and commuter airlines such as Air Canada and Air Alliance, Tel. 692-0770, Canadian International Airlines, Air Atlantic, Canadian Regional Airlines, Tel. 692-0912, and Northwest Airlink, Tel. 877-6984, serving Northern Québec. International or American visitors first fly to Montréal, where they can catch a connecting flight to Québec City.

By taxi: Metered cabs and limousines serve the airport, with Maple Leaf Sightseeing Tours one of the companies providing limousine service. Taxis are the cheaper alternative: about $23 Cdn for the up-to 30-minute trip, depending upon traffic and destination in Vieux Québec. On average, limousines will cost double this amount.

By car: **Hertz**, Tel. 871-1571 and **Tilden**, Tel. 871-1224, have kiosks at the airport, as well as downtown outlets. The trip to or from downtown Québec City will take about 30 minutes by car, possibly 45 minutes during rush hours. To drive downtown from the airport, take Route 540 to Route 175 (blvd. Laurier) that becomes blvd. Grande Allée, which continues into Vieux Québec.

By bus: Operated by Autobus Dupont, Maple Leaf Sightseeing Tours, Tel. 649-9226, operates a daily shuttle bus service regularly to and from the airport, stopping at major hotels in downtown Québec and other hotels en route by request. Orleans Express Coach Lines links Québec with the rest of the province and Intercar Cote-Nord links Québec with some of the North Shore communities. Both operate from the downtown **Voyageur Gare Centrale d'Autobus** bus station, 225 blvd. Charest Est, Tel. 524-4692.

By citibus: City busses will take you almost anywhere in the Greater Québec area. Daily pass or individual tickets (exact change). Get a transfer slip upon boarding so that bus route changes can be made at no extra charge. Free bus schedules and route maps from: Centre d'information de l'Office du Tourisme and Maison du Tourisme de Québec, and at the CTCUQ's customer service kiosk, Complexe Jacques-Cartier, 325 rue du Roi; Tel. 627-2511.

By train: VIA Rail Canada, Tel. 692-3940, from elsewhere in Québec and the Atlantic provinces arrives at the **Gare du Palais** train station downtown on 450 rue de la Gare-du-Palais.

Haute Ville Accommodation
LUXURY: **Château Frontenac**, 1, rue de Carrières, G1R 4P5, Tel. 692-3861. **Hôtel Clarendon**, 57 rue Ste-Anne, G1R 3X4, Tel. 692-2480. *MODERATE:* **Château Laurier**, 695 rue Grande Allée Est, G1R 2K4; Tel. 522-8108. **Hôtel L'Ermitage**, 60 rue Ste-Ursule, G1R 4E6; Tel. 694-0968. *BUDGET:* **La Maison Demers B&B**, 68 rue Ste-Ursule G1R 4E6; Tel. 692-2487.

Museums
HAUTE VILLE: **Séminaire de Québec** and **Musée du Séminaire**, 9 rue de l'Université; Tel. 692-2843. **Musée Historique de Cire**, 22 rue Ste-Anne; Tel. 692-2289. **Musée et Chapelle des Ursulines**, 12 rue Donnacona; Tel. 694-0694. **Musée du Québec**, 1 avenue Wolfe-Montcalm; daily; Tel. 643-2150. **Royal 22e Regiment Museum**, Box 6020, Succursale Haute Ville, 1 Côte de la Citadelle; Changing of the guard mid June-Laber Day daily at 10am; Tel. 648-3563.

BASSE VILLE: **Musée de la Civilisation**, Box 155, Station B, 85 rue Dalhousie; June-Laber Day daily, rest of year Mon closed; Tel. 643-2158.

Theater / Music
HAUTE VILLE: **Théâtre Repère** and **La Caserne**, 939 rue Salaberry; Tel. 648-1455. **Trident Théâtre**, 269 blvd. René-Lévesque Est; Tel. 643-8131. **Grand Théâtre de Québec**, 269 St-Cyrille E; Tel. 643-8131. **Théâtre Capitole**, 972 rue St-Jean; Tel. 694-4444. **Opéra de Québec**, 269 blvd. Réne-Lévesque Est; Tel. 643-8131. **Orchestre Symphonique de Québec**, 269 blvd. René-Lévesque Est; Tel. 643-8131.

Sightseeing
HAUTE VILLE: **La Citadelle**, Cap Diamant, Succursale Haute Ville, G1R 4V7; Tel. 648-3563. **Québec Nordiques** and the **Colisée de Québec**, 2205 avenue du Colisée, Parc de l'Exposition; Tel. 529-8441 NORDTEL or 523-3333. **Québec Sightseeing Tour** skibus service, 1576 rue des Hôtels, Ste-Foy; Tel. 653-9722.

BASSE VILLE: **Agora Vieux-Port**, Edifice du Havre,120 rue Dalhousie; Tel. 418/692-4540. Basilica of Ste-Anne-de-Beaupré, 22 miles (35 km) northeast on Hwy. 138, Tel: 418/827-3781.

Festivals
Les Nuits Internationales de Jazz et Blues de Québec, 60 rue D'Auteuil; Tel. 692-247l. **Festival d'Eté International de Québec**, Box 24, Station B,160 rue St-Paul G1K 7A1; Tel. l-418/692-4540. **Carnaval de Québec**, Inc, 290 rue Joly, Tel: 626-3716, Feb. **International Summer Festival**, Old Town, 160 rue St. Paul, Tel: 692-4540, July. **Les Mediévales de Québec**, Box 37060, 2 Place Québec G1R 5P5; Tel. 640-1993.

Tourist Information
Centre d'information de l'Office du Tourisme et des Congrès de la Communauté urbaine de Québec:, 60 rue d'Auteuil G1R 4C4; Tel. 692-247l or 652-2882. **Maison du Tourisme de Québec**, 12 rue Ste-Anne, Place d'Armes G1R 3X2; Tel. 643-2280, 800/366-7777.

QUÉBEC PROVINCE

QUÉBEC PROVINCE

L'ESTRIE
LES LAURENTIDES
ALONG THE ST. LAWRENCE

Canada's largest province is also its most distinct. Throughout its history, Québec's language, culture and social systems have been derived from the political, social and religious customs and traditions of Roman Catholic France rather than Anglo-Protestant England, like the rest of Canada. French is the mother tongue for over 83 percent of the population; outside of the Greater Montréal area, about 93 percent of its inhabitants are Francophones (French-speaking by birth). However, about one Québecois in four also speaks English as well as French. Some 800,000 Québecois are Anglophones (English-speaking by birth), many descendants of families which settled in Québec over the past four centuries.

90 percent of Québec lies within the Canadian Shield, an ancient rocky plateau dotted with some 71,000 sq. miles (183,890 sq. km) of fresh-water lakes and rivers. Below the shield lies the St. Lawrence lowlands, where over 75 percent of Québec's 6.89 million people live. This means that the bulk of Québec's 643,820 sq. miles (1,667,493 sq. km) are largely uninhabited and unexplored.

Left: Focus of the Canadian flag – an autumn leaf of the sugar maple.

Québec has four very distinct seasons. Summer is mercurial – it can be very hot and sunny one day, followed the next by cold, rainy and windy weather. Regardless, life is lived mostly outdoors during the summer months and at a frenetic pace, as people try to cram as much activity as possible into these three short months. Winter can begin as early as November, when the first snowfall is a fairly common occurrence – a boon to skiers – and lasts really until mid-March with at times extreme cold spells in January and February.

Discovering Québec

For those interested in history, Québec is a treasure trove of more than 400 years of historical, architectural, cultural and social landmarks just waiting to be explored. From the top of Mont Royal to the Plains of Abraham, from the majestic St. Lawrence River to James Bay, there is no other place in North America where the Old World is still as omnipresent as the New. The vibrant life of Québec City and Montréal have already been described in the previous chapter. Those looking for a more relaxed vacation and traces of traditional Québec life need only venture outside these two cities into the surrounding countryside or vacation

L'ESTRIE / LAURENTIDES

in any one of the province's many tourist regions. It is here that nature-lovers, back-pack types, sportsmen and women, day-trippers and resort-seekers will find an endless variety of breathtaking vistas and natural attractions, man-made curiosities, sightseeing activities, historical landmarks, folkloric festivities, and humble to luxury accommodations to choose from. About two-thirds of the province are suitable only to the most hardened outdoors types, as it has hardly been charted by any living being except Canadian fauna and the black fly. Two of Québec's most popular tourist destinations near Montréal are l'Estrie (the EasternTownships) and Les Laurentides (the Laurentians).

The other two favorites are Charlevoix and Gaspésie, which are east of Québec city, and where the wilderness is a still accessible and enjoyable to average human.

L'ESTRIE

L'Estrie – or the Eastern Townships as it was known before Bill 101 – is the southeast region of Québec between Montréal and the borders of Vermont and New York states. Its northern Appalachian hills were first home to the Abenaki tribe, long before "the country club set" built their summer homes and stables here. While the Abenaki have long departed, their presence remains in the

L'ESTRIE

In the past two decades, l'Estrie's many farm communities and summer estates have been joined by many all-season resorts. Wintertime attracts thousands of skiers to its downhill ski centers and cross-country trails. Early spring sees the sugar shacks overflowing with tourists sampling the traditional Québecois fare laced with the area's maple syrup bounty. Because of its southerly location, l'Estrie is also notable for its spring skiing.

Officially, the gateway to l'Estrie begins at **Granby**, about 50 miles (80 kilometers) southeast of Montréal. Home to the **Jardin Zoologique de Granby** (Granby Zoo), it has more than 1000 animals from 200 species. Now celebrating its 40th anniversary, the Zoo is recognized by The International Union for the Conservation of Nature. Among its attractions are two rare snow leopards, part of an international program to save this endangered species, native to northeast Asia. The Zoo also has an amusement park, souvenir shops, play and picnic grounds. Granby is also reputed as the Townships' gastronomic capital. Every October, the **Festival Gastronomique** attracts more than 10,000 gastronomes. "Gastronomic passport" in hand, they make the circuit of Granby restaurants, inns, and hotels, sampling the latest culinary creations. Granby also hosts a national song festival every fall and the town is notable for its many European fountains, including a 3200-year old Greek fountain on blvd. Leclerc and a Roman fountain in **Parc Pelletier**.

In addition to its fame as a gourmet's paradise, Granby and neighbor towns offer some of the finest traditional Québecois cuisine, called *la fine cuisine estrienne*. Specialties include mixed game meat pies such as *cipaille* and sweet, salty dishes combining ham and maple syrup. Maple syrup – on everything and in all its forms – is a mainstay of these Québecois dishes since l'Estrie

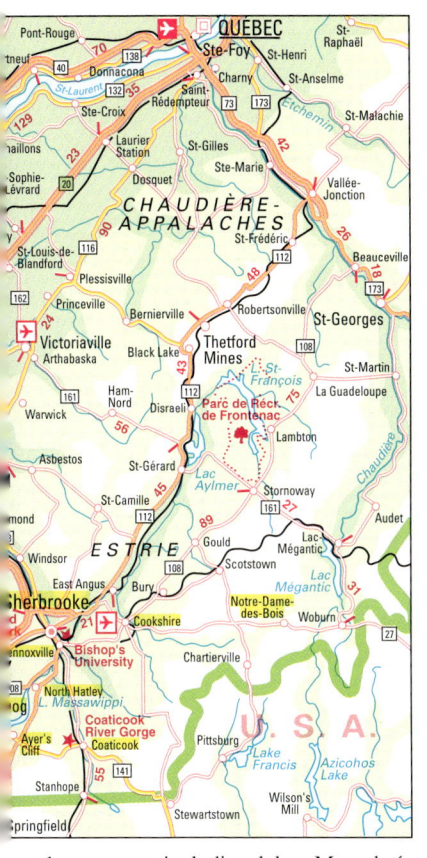

place names, including lakes Memphrémagog, Massawippi and Mégantic.

Reminiscent of New England, l'Estrie, too, has covered bridges, village greens, white church steeples and country inns dotting the landscape and lakeshores. The area did not attract a great number of Europeans until it became a major destination for loyalists fleeing the new American state in 1783. They were joined later by kin and kindred spirits who preferred life under England's rule in British North America. It was not until after 1850 that French-Canadians (as today's Québecois were then known) moved into the region in large numbers, attracted by steady employment in the then thriving railroad, lumber and asbestos-mining industries.

L'ESTRIE

is one of Québec's major maple syrup producing regions.

The combination of sunny days and cold nights every March cause the sap to run in the maple trees. Sugar shacks or *cabanes à sucre* operators tap the trees, then boil the collected sap, turning it into liquid gold. Scattered throughout l'Estrie are sugar shacks offering "sugaring off" tours of their operations, with *tire sur la neige* a special highlight. (Hot syrup is poured over cold snow to give it a taffy consistency just right for "pulling" and eating.) Many of these *cabanes* serve up traditional Québecois fare – hearty meals of ham, baked beans, and pancakes, all drowned in maple syrup.

Popular cabanes are **Erablière Robert Lauzier** in **Ayer's Cliff** and **Bolducs** in **Cookshire.** Like maple sugar, cloves, nutmeg, cinnamon, and pepper – the

Above: Rustic and traditional – collecting sap for maple syrup. Right: Anyone who travels with a snowmobile in winter needs good protection against the cold.

same spices used by the first settlers – are still favorite seasonings in l'Estrie cooking and the region's restaurants use them liberally in creating distinctive dishes. Sherbrooke's **Restaurant Au P'tit Sabot**, awarded a prize for l'Estrie's best local-style eatery, serves up Québec wild boar.

L'Estrie has become one of Québec's most popular ski centers in the past 20 years. Although it is still less crowded and commercialized than Les Laurentides, it boasts slopes on mountains that dwarf anything that area has to offer, with the exception of lofty Mont Tremblant.

The action on and off the slopes in **Bromont** (site of the 1986 World Cup) goes on night and day. Night skiing is popular here, as is the slope-side disco. The area is also well known for its cross-country skiing, with trail crossing a golf course, considered one of the finest in the area in summer. Of course Alpine and cross-country skiers, whether novices or veterans, will find plenty of challenges at

Mont Orford as well, where the ski slopes form the center of a provincial park. Nearby **Owl's Head,** favored by skiers looking for less-crowded hills, boasts l'Estrie's longest intermediate run (4 kilometers).

Popular for decades with the same diehard crowd of mostly Anglophone skiers from within Québec and elsewhere, **Mont Sutton** is one of l'Estrie's largest ski resorts, with trails that plunge and wander through pine, maple and birch trees slope-side. Sutton itself is a well-established community with craft shops, cosy eateries and bars (**La Paimpolaise** is a skier's favorite).

Another popular winter pastime is snowmobiling, especially at **Valcourt,** the birthplace of the inventor of the snowmobile Joseph-Armand Bombardier (there is a museum devoted to him) and a world center for the sport, with more than 1000 miles of paths cutting through the woods and meadows. The town holds a snowmobile festival with races and demonstrations. (For real snowmobile buffs, there is famous **Harricana**, a tough winter rallye that leaves from Québec City and leads up into the northern wilderness on a nearly 2000-mile (3000-km) track). Maps of scenic snowmobiling routes are available at l'Estrie tourist offices.

For the past 40 years, Orford's regional park has also been famous internationally for its annual arts festival. Classical music, popular classics and chamber orchestra concerts are held daily throughout the late spring and summer months. Each year, some 300 students from around the world study and perform music at the **Centre d'Arts d'Orford**. Canada's internationally-celebrated Orford String Quartet originated here and recently, **Festival Orford** has expanded to include jazz and folk music. Budding musicians rub shoulders and trade notes at master classes and in public performances with big name artists such as jazz pianist Oliver Jones and the cult-status folksinging duo of Montréalers Kate and Anna McGarrigle.

Non-history buffs will be pleasantly diverted by l'Estrie's other English summer theater, **Théâtre du Lac Brome** in **Knowlton**. Now in its 10th season, it presents a mix of Canadian and American plays every summer, as well as the occasional concert. Located behind Knowlton's popular pub of the same name, the 200-seat air-conditioned theater was a gift from **Knowlton Pub** owner Gerry Wood. Discounted theater tickets are also available, if visitors book the special bed-and-breakfast packages offered at local homes. (**The Piggery** has a similar scheme, inquire about it when making reservations.)

Knowlton itself (located at the south end of **Lac Brome**) has plenty of old and gentrified buildings with restaurants, pubs, craft shops and boutiques. Once a stage-coach stop on the Boston – Montréal run, Knowlton has preserved its history in the 1894 **Pettes Memorial Library** and nine-building **Brome County**

Historical Museum. Hiking and cycling make this town a popular year-round destination.

L'Estrie's unofficial capital is **Sherbrooke**, named in 1818 after the late Sir John Coape Sherbrooke, one of Canada's governor-generals. The city was founded by Loyalists in the 1790s. The region's most significant cultural center, Sherbrooke boasts many art galleries, including the **Musée des Beaux-Arts de Sherbrooke**, the **Musée des Sciences naturelles du Séminaire** (one of the oldest in the province) and the historic **Domaine Howard**, which is the headquarters of the Townships' historic society and conducts city tours from June to September.

The **Université de Sherbrooke's** arts center also offers a full range of year-round cultural activities, primarily in French but some in English. Sherbrooke is also renowned for its floral finery, with local greenhouses producing some 50,000 flowers yearly. Some 15,000 of these plants "adorn" the park near Sherbrooke's Renaissance-style courthouse; another 25,000 are planted along the city's main street, rue King Ouest.

The resort town of **Magog**, which celebrated its centenary in 1988, is a once-sleepy village on the tip of Lac Memphrémagog that has grown into a four-season destination. Two sandy beaches, great bed-and-breakfast spots, hotels and restaurants, boating, sailing, ferry rides, bird-watching, sail-boarding, aerobics, horseback riding and snowmobiling are just some of the activities offered. (Mont Orford and Owl's Head ski resorts are close by.) Magog's night-life scene is lively, with bars, cafés, bistros and great restaurants to suit every taste and pocketbook. Magog's **rue Principale** also has boutiques, art galleries and craft shops featuring local artisans' work. The town's "downtown" section makes for a

Above: Catamarans and sailboats for captains of all ages. Right: Abbey of St-Benoît in the spring.

pleasant stroll through streets lined with century-old homes and churches – some of which have been converted into storefronts, galleries and theaters.**Théâtre Le Vieux Clocher** presents summer pop and rock concerts, as well as French plays. In mid-July, Magog turns into the headquarters of **La Traversée Internationale du Lac Memphrémagog**, a seven-day "swimathon" across the lake, with activities for all ages. Visitors are welcome to participate. Special activities include an underwater treasure hunt, water skiing and sky-diving shows, as well as foot races.

A highlight of the Lac Memphrémagog trip is the **Abbaye St-Benoît-du-Lac**, with its bell tower rising above the trees like a sentinel. A favorite retreat for some of Québec's best-known politicians, the abbey is set on a wooded peninsula. It was built in 1912 by the Benedictines and is still home to some 60 monks, famous for producing all their own food. Apples and apple cider from their orchards and three of their cheeses (Ermite, St-Benoît and ricotta) are sold to the public. Also open to the public are the Gregorian masses held daily.

During the summer months, budget-conscious travelers can find pleasant and affordable accommodation at Bishop's University residences in Lennoxville. Meal service is also available at the student snack bar or the main cafeteria. There's also an excellent sports complex, with an Olympic-sized indoor swimming pool and outdoor tennis courts that visitors can use on a per diem basis. Bishop's University is situated on lovely grounds, with a river cutting through the campus and its golf course. Much of the architecture is reminiscent of stately New England campuses. Be sure to visit the University's 134-year-old chapel, officially a heritage building, which in May 1989 was the site of a commemorative ceremony presided over by Prince Philip, the Duke of Edinburgh. Also look for the butternut tree – an endangered species in l'Estrie – which he personally planted to mark the establishment of a 141-hectares

LENNOXVILLE

tree and bird sanctuary on the university grounds.

The arts play an important role in North Hatley and nearby **Lennoxville**. As well as the annual July antiques and folk art show, concerts, exhibitions, and poetry readings are held around town monthly. North Hatley is also an antiques treasure-trove, with some 16 stores in its vicinity; neighboring Lennoxville has more.

Both towns are major theater centers for Anglophone townies and visitors. With three decades behind it Québec's oldest professional English summer theater, **The Piggery Theatre**, is the grande dame of the region. Housed in a former pig barn in North Hatley, The Piggery has presented numerous premieres of Canadian and American plays that have achieved instant-hit status and gone on to play major theaters across Canada.

Above: Fish for dinner tonight. Right: Bromont, in the l'Estrie, has great golf courses.

There's an attractive little restaurant and bar on-site, picnic grounds, and also an art gallery.

The Piggery also hosts a popular arts and crafts exhibition each August, featuring the work of township artists and artisans.

Not to be outdone is Lennoxville's **Centennial Theatre** and **Consolidated-Bathurst Theatre** at **Bishop's University**. From September through June, Centennial Theatre presents a lineup of international, Canadian and Québecois jazz, classical and rock concerts, as well as films, dance, mime and children's theatre. Jazz greats Gary Burton, Carla Bley and Larry Coryell have played here, as have such classical artists as the Amsterdam Guitar Trio and The Allegri String Quartet – all to SRO- crowds.

Bishop University's Consolidated Bathurst Theatre, the sometime site of the annual Québec University Drama Festival, presents student productions of works by Canadian and international playwrights which are open to the public. This university town is one of the last bastions of Anglo-Québeckers in l'Estrie.

Another socio-cultural pastime that these two towns share – and one which eases the crossing Québec's "language barriers" – is micro-breweries in North Hatley and Lennoxville. North Hatley is home to **The Pilsen**, Québec's first micro-brewery, which gives group tours by reservation.

This local brew is also on tap at **The Pilsen Pub**, which has great pub food, loads of atmosphere and a convivial crowd year-round. Not to be outdone, Lennoxville also has a micro-brewery – attached to the very popular **Golden Lion Pub** – favorite haunt of Bishop's professors and students and the local watering-hole of town residents. Wine connoisseurs might prefer doing the **Dunham Winery Trail**, a tour of the thriving wineries just outside this town of century-old Victorian mansions. Vineyards open to visitors, where wine sampling is a favored activity, picnic fare is offered and wines are sold to the public include **Domaine des côtes Ardoise** and **Vignoble de l'Orpailleur.**

Lennoxville's other public historic site is the **Uplands Museum Park,** which is located in an 1862 Georgian-style house on four wooded acres in the center of town. It was built by English emigré John Paddon, who is also credited with bringing oil-lamp street lighting to this idyllic town.

The Museum is a source of civic pride and a treasure-trove of l'Estrie history, with over 300 years of local lore represented. Exhibitions change periodically and range from a retrospective on the **Wabanaki** tribe, a chronicle of the life of l9th-century inventor, gentleman-of-leisure and Lennoxville mayor Arthur Speid, the history of the Uplands' estate and l'Estrie archeology.

Following the end of the American Civil War in 1866, wealthy Southerners built their summer estates around **Lac Massawippi**, to which they retreated annually. These spacious homes have long been converted into first-class inns. **Manoir Hovey**, for example, a private estate built in 1899, has elegantly furnished rooms, many featuring four-posters and fireplaces. Its dining room is renowned throughout North America. They are the favored haunts of generations of northeastern Americans and Montréal's Anglophone social set, who discovered the area in the early l900s and have been holidaying there ever since. The area provides an excellent base for excursions in l'Estrie.

Theater and festivals of every kind abound, with the August **Festival du Lait** in **Coaticook** a reminder of the area's role as one of Québec's most productive dairy regions. (A fashion show in which bovine beauties model the latest in agricultural haute couture. must be seen to be believed.) Coaticook is more justly famous for the **Coaticook River Gorge**. Threaded with hiking trails, it is spanned by the longest suspended bridge in Ca-

LAC MÉGANTIC

nada; its observation tower offers a spectacular view of the countryside. A perennial roadside attraction every autumn is the breathtaking spectacle of mile upon mile of flaming foliage, which draws sightseers by the thousands. Area inns and restaurants are always jammed at this time of year, so it's wise to book ahead if planning an overnight stay.

Lac Mégantic

Another attractive area in l'Estrie is around **Lac Mégantic**, 65 miles (105 km) east of Sherbrooke. Centuries ago populated by Abanaki Indians only, it is nowadays particularly enjoyed by hunters and fishermen as in wintertime by cross-country skiers. Downhill skiers will have to make a 35-minute drive to the excellent resort area of Sugar Loaf in Vermont, USA.

Above: Round barns are typical of the West Brome region. Right: El Dorado for skiers – the Laurentides.

Nearby **Mont Mégantic's Observatory** in **Notre-Dame-Des-Bois** offers a cosmic experience for amateur stargazers and serious astronomers. Located in a particularly wild, beautiful and mountainous part of l'Estrie, the Observatory is at the summit of the region's second highest mountain (3515 feet, 1098 m), whose northern face records record annual snowfalls (9.75 m). A joint venture by the Université de Montréal and Université Laval, the Observatory has a powerful telescope that allows resident scientists to observe celestial bodies that the human eye could never detect. An information center at the mountain's base is open to amateur stargazers, who can also attend the evening "celestial sweep" sessions.

LES LAURENTIDES

Home to some of North America's best-known ski resorts, **Les Laurentides** (the Laurentians) begin just 35 miles (56 km) north of Montréal. Its mountain

LAURENTIDES / TERREBONNE

range is ancient, dating to the Pre-Cambrian era of 600 million years ago. Though relatively low, these rocky hills still provide excellent downhill skiing. A few peaks are above 2500 feet (760 m), with world-famous **Mont Tremblant** at 3150 feet (960 m), the tallest. It stands about 90 miles (150 km) north of Montréal, has 300 trails, most with night lighting. The Nature Park surrounding the Mont Tremblant extends over a 1235 sq. mi (3200 sq. km) area, which can be hiked through ontwo well-attended trails.

Les Laurentides actually consist of two major regions, Les Basses Laurentides (Lower Laurentians) and Les Hautes Laurentides (Upper Laurentians). **Les Basses Laurentides** is the birthplace of Les Laurentides. The province is rich in landmarks from the heyday of the *seigneurs* from the 17th to the 19th centuries, local administrators, who were given large tracts of land. While many of these properties have been absorbed into modern towns and cities, leaving virtually no trace, two of the most famous still exist within 20 minutes of Montréal: the **Seigneurie de Terrebonne** on Île-des-Moulins and the **Seigneurie du Lac-des-Deux-Montagnes.**

Terrebonne, just to the north of Montréal, was established in 1673 when Governor Frontenac gave it to Sieur André Daulier and was maintained by a succession of *seigneurs* until 1832. It was then bought by Joseph Masson, the first French-Canadian millionaire. He and his family were the last *seigneurs* de Terrebonne, their "reign" ending in 1883. The **Vieux Terrebonne** of today provides a bona fide glimpse of the past, since the *seigneurie*'s mansions, manors and buildings were all carefully restored. A particular highlight is the **Manoir Masson**, built in 1848 by the *seigneuresse* Sophie Raymond-Masson one year after her husband's death.

Administered by the Corporation de l'Ile-des-Moulins, this historical and cultural site faithfully reconstructs the seigneurial era. The past is present in the **Centre d'interpretation historique de**

141

ST-EUSTACHE / OKA CALVARY

Terrebonne museum that houses the large collection of artifacts from the life and times of Joseph Masson and his family; while the **Île-des-Moulins** art gallery presents exhibitions of works by contemporary local artists. There is also a year-round theater presenting English and French plays, as well as musical matinees and outdoor summer shows – some historical, some modern. Most of these activities are free.

St-Eustache in the south of Montréal, is a must for history buffs, for it was there that one of the most significant and tragic scenes in Canadian history unfolded: the Rebellion of l837. Since the British Conquest of 1759, French Canadians had been confined to pre-existing territories while the new townships were given exclusively to the English. This insult was compounded by the government's decision to tax all imported products from England, which made them prohibitively expensive. The end result was that in 1834, the French-Canadian Patriot Party succeeded the British Party locally. Lower Canada, as it was then known, became rife with tension between French and English. French resistance locally to the British government reached an all-time high. By December l837, the rumors of rebellion resulted in the British sending 2000 English soldiers led by General Colborne to put down the "army" of North Shore patriots by surrounding the village of St-Eustache. Local hero Jean-Olivier Chenier and his 200 patriotes took refuge in the local church, which Colborne's cannons bombed and set afire. Chenier and many of his comrades were killed during the battle; most of the town's houses and buildings dating from the seigneurial days were looted and burned down by Colborne's soldiers. Traces of the cannon balls fired by the English army canons are still visible on the façade of St-Eustache's church. Today, it is where the **Orchestre Symphonique de Montréal** has recorded all of its internationally award-winning albums.

Many period buildings on the town's side-streets are also open to the public. **St-Eustache's Arts and Cultural Services** offers guided tours for visitors. A good place to indulge the stomach is the **Pâtisserie Grande-Côte**, St-Eustache's most famous bakery. Top this fare off with one of the many varieties of honey produced and sold at **Mielerie Deschamps**. Behind-the-scene tours of both are given daily, free admission.

The other important reminder of Québec's seigneurial past, **La Seigneurie du Lac-des-Deux-Montagnes** (to the southwest of St-Eustache), was granted to the Sulpician priests in 1717. Already the *seigneurs* of the entire island of Montréal used this base to establish an Amerindian mission. Between l740-l742, the Sulpicians erected the **Oka Calvary**. Three of the seven chapels are still maintained and every September 14 since then, Amerindians and villagers have celebrated the **Feast of the Holy Cross**. Since 1870, they have been joined by thousands of Québecois who make an annual pilgrimage here, participating in the half-hour ceremony and walking up to the Calvary's summit, where there is a magnificient view of the **Lac-des-Deux-Montagnes**.

The Sulpicians' seigneurial manor, erected between 1802-1808 in the village of **Ste-Scholastique**, was used as part of the set for the celebrated film, *Kamouraska*, starring Geneviève Bujold and based on the novel by Prix Goncourt-winner Anne Hébert (one of French Québec's most renowned contemporary authors and France's most covetted literary prize). The director was the late Claude Jutra, who earned international acclaim during his career.

Right: Bicycle tour in the nature preserve of Mont Tremblant (3,139 feet / 960 m).

In 1887, the Sulpicians gave some 350 hectares near the Oka Calvary to the Trappist monks who had arrived in New France in 1880 from the Bellefontaine Abbey in France. They turned this land into one of the most beautiful domains in Québec. By 1890, the Trappists had built their **Abbaye cistercienne d'Oka**, today one of the oldest monasteries in North America. The Trappists, who are still known to this day for their cheese, founded the Oka School of Agriculture. It was awarded the title of "university faculty" in 1908, which it retained until it closed in 1960. Today, the Abbaye is renowned as a prayer retreat, where visitors can also tour the modest miller's home in which the Trappists first settled. Their gardens, chapel and gift shop are also open to the public. Close by is the **Ferme avicole d'Oka**, one of Québec's largest poultry farms founded by by the Trappists. It offers tours of the breeding grounds for more exotic pheasant, partridge, and guinea hen's as well as the more prosaic barnyard variety of fowl.

Oka is equally famous for **Parc Paul Sauve**, just 20 miles from Montréal. It is a playground for Montréalers, with camping, picnicking, cycling, sailboarding and swimming as favorite summer activities.

Les Hautes Laurentides

Founded in 1830 on the banks of the Rivière du Nord, **St-Jérôme** rivals St-Eustache in Québec's historic folklore. Today it is a thriving economic center and cultural hub. In 1868, thanks to pastor Antoine Labelle who was determined to open "northern" Québec to French Canadians, St-Jérôme adopted a vital role in the development of **Les Hautes Laurentides**. Between 1868 and 1890, he founded 20 parish towns, an impressive feat, and he convinced the government of the need to finance the "P'tit Train du Nord" railway line. **Boulevard Labelle**, the **Municipality of Labelle**, the **Papineau-Labelle** wildlife reserve, the statue of Curé Labelle in **Parc Antoine-Labelle** facing St-Jérôme cathedral are just some of the region's tributes to this great visionary.

These "landmarks" and St-Jérôme's long **promenade**, alongside the Rivière du Nord from rue De Martigny bridge to rue St-Joseph bridge, are highlights of the town's many historic sites. Descriptive plaques along the boardwalk explain the significance of past events which took place here. Similarly, the **Centre d'exposition du Vieux-Palais**, features permanent exhibitions and thematic exhibitions – most centering on the area's history and scenic splendors. **St-Jérôme's old court house** also presents shows, conferences and animation activities for children, as well as concerts. Walking tours and thematic exhibitions are also part of St-Jérôme's other great attraction: the **Parc régional de la Rivière du Nord**. Created as a nature retreat, paths throughout the park lead to the spectacular **Wilson Falls**. Rain or shine, the **Pavillon Marie-Victorin** is open daily.

The establishment of the P'tit Train du Nord made it possible to easily transport settlers and cargo to the Hautes Laurentides region. More importantly, in terms of today's booming tourism industry, it opened the region up to skiing. By the turn of the century, trainloads of skiers replaced settlers and cargo as the railway's major trade, and Les Hautes Laurentides became famous internationally as the Number One North American ski center – a position which it still holds today. It is also Canada's best developed resort area, renowned for world-class accommodation, services and activities.

By the late l920s, the Canadian National Railway (and later even the rival Canadian Pacific) were ferrying skiers into the area by the bushel. A few prominent and intrepid Montréalers staked their claim to prime lakefront property deep in Les Hautes Laurentides' wilder-

Above: Away from the lifts, skiers enjoy nature pur. Right: Autumn in Ste-Marguerite.

ness, where they built private ski lodges. Weekend trips to the ski hills around **St-Sauveur** later extended as far as **Ste-Agathe-des-Monts**. Accessible only by train until the 1930s, they became year-round family retreats after the highway was built. By the 1950s, their vocation as the clans' summertime gathering places was solidly entrenched – paralleling the widespread "cottage country" movement then developing throughout Les Hautes Laurentides. Many of these families, three generations later, still maintain their land in much the same state as it was at the turn of the century. Their magnificently unspoiled wilderness retreats represent both a passing era and a cherished legacy.

These private reserves in the midst of what is now a widespread tourist boom threatening to overtake much of the region, represent that other most Canadian experience: the summer cottage vacation, when extended family members congregate annually. Most lodgings are simple, rustic hideaways so well integrated into the surrounding landscape that they are barely visible from the shoreline.

Their concern for tradition and conservation is shared by many of the townspeople from **Morin Heights** to **Mont Tremblant**, whose Chambers of Commerce must reconcile the need to maintain the world-class stature and exclusivity of these resort destinations with the need for year-round economic prosperity.

At the moment, commercial development seems to be winning, with St-Sauveur-des-Monts the prime example of the pros and cons of the present boom.

St-Sauveur-des-Monts (Exit 60 of the Autoroute) is really the starting point of the vacation resort areas of Les Hautes Laurentides, which extend as far north as Mont Tremblant. It dominates the mountainous area in which the resorts, villages, hotels and inns of neighboring **St-Sauveur**, **Ste-Marguerite-Station**, **Morin Heights**, **Val Morin**, **Val David** and **Piedmont** appear like a crazy quilt to first-time visitors.

The center of Montréal's closest vacationland attracts tourists year-round. In the summer, holidaymakers take to its golf courses (two of the more pleasant are 18-hole links at **Ste-Adèle** and **Mont Gabriel**), campgrounds at **Val David**, **Lacs Claude** and **Lafontaine** and their beaches; in the fall and winter, they come for foliage and alpine (downhill) as well as nordic (cross-country) skiing. It has grown so quickly during the past l0 years that regular visitors who once camped on its outskirts barely recognize their former haunt.

But townspeople and cottagers alike are split on just how much more development this area can take before the boom becomes a glut, with all the downside spinoffs this implies. And important voices are joining the opposition: the Citizen's Committee, the Environment Québec, architect Roger Taillibert (who designed the Olympic Stadium of Montréal), and even the archdeacon of St. Francis of the Birds Anglican church. The sleepy Laurentian village of 4000 residents in the 1970s that didn't even have a traffic light has become a year-round resort town attracting as many as 30,000 cottagers and visitors on weekends alone. **Rue Principale** now has a plethora of brochetteries and sushi bars, in addition to the quaint French restaurants that first attracted gourmets to the area. In the summer, this main street is so overwhelmed by cars and tourists that it is now referred to as "Crescent Street North."

While it is true that the gleaming white spires of **Eglise St-Sauveur** still manage to dominate rue Principale, St-Francis of the Birds has not been so fortunate. Built in 1951, this rustic landmark built of logs is no longer a secluded retreat. Once "neighbor" to a forest dotted with simple chalets, today its backyard cedar grove confronts a massive hotel complex. Rock music intrudes from the nearby water park – likened by critics to a massive, Disneyland-clone that attracts up to 5000 people a day. "Classique de Surf," "Mr. Beach Bum" contests and "Miss Hawaiian Tropic" pageants attract a different type of tourist than the generations of Montréalers who've long populated the area with their quiet country getaways.

But aside from being one of the Laurentians most popular tourist centers with all the amenities and all the kitsch, St-Sauveur-des-Monts is famous for the **Red Birds Ski Club**, which was founded in l928 on Hill 70 – the central part of **Mont St-Sauveur**. Like the Red Birds themselves, Hill 70's name was closely linked to McGill University and the World-War-One exploits of soldiers who fought under Sir Arthur Currie, McGill's principal and the first Canadian in military history to command the Canadian Corps. He and his men took back the original Hill 70 in Lens, France, from the Germans in 1917. Hill 70 was dedicated in l933 to the memory of Currie and Red Bird family members who died in France. The bronze plaque commemorating the occasion, originally displayed on a great boulder mid-way up the hill, now occupies a place of honor over the fireplace of Mont St-Sauveur's **Base Pavilion Bar** overlooking the ski slopes.

The Red Birds established their loghouse headquarters at the base of Hill 70. Their mentor was Herman "Jackrabbit" Smith Johannsen, who virtually pioneered cross-country skiing in Canada from 1918 onward. Under his strenuous training regimen, the Red Birds attained a proficiency which led to their selection as Canada's representatives at two Olympic skiing events: Lake Placid in the year 1932 and Garmisch in the Bavarian Alps in 1936.

As for Johannsen, between 1932-1935, he opened up the famous **Maple Leaf Trail** linking **Shawbridge** (Prevost) to

Right: The broad slopes of Mont Tremblant are ideal for snow-boarders.

Mont Tremblant. Before his death at the age of 111 in 1987, he personally participated in expanding Les Laurentides' network of cross-country ski trails that today cover some 600 miles (1000 km). Inducted into the **Temple de la renommée du ski des Laurentides** (Laurentian Hall of Ski Fame) in 1982 at the age of 107, he continues to be celebrated by lovers of the sport. Every winter more than 1700 skiers ages 4 to 80 take part in the 100-mi (160-km) **Canadian Ski Marathon** in tribute to its founding patron.

As a contrast, classical concerts are held in the Église St-Sauveur every Tuesday evening during July and August. Craft shops, hand-made jewelry stores and fashion boutiques up and down rue Principale vie the café terrasses and many restaurants for visitors' attention. **La Voute Boutique** usually wins out. Located in a former bank, it is the fashion spot for such international labels as Byblos and coordinates in cotton, knits, suede, leather and sequin-styled dresses, sweaters, pants, jackets and suits – all newly arrived from France, Italy and Spain. Montréal's own internationally recognized designer lines are also available here. La Voute also stages regular fashion shows at nearby restaurants, attracting fashion lovers ages 20 to 65.

The main attraction at the $7-million **Mont Sauveur Aquatic Park** and tourist center just outside the town (take Exits 58 or 60) is the $1.7-million man-made "Colorado" rafting river, which follows the natural contours of the steep hills, making this water amusement park the non plus ultra of Laurentian diversions. For a nine-minute eternity, thrill-seekers tough it out in rafts that shoot through, over, and under this man-made whitewater ride.

Nearby **Morin Heights** offers plenty of diversions for the sunworshipper or snow-seeker. One of its most famous attractions isn't open to the public: André Perry's state-of-the-art recording studio which regularly plays host to such rock and pop legendaries as David Bowie, Sting, Chicago, The Bee Gees and others.

Snowboarding is the latest spin on an old sport at **Ski Morin Heights.** Snowboarding demands the skills and dexterity of surfing, riding a skateboard down a hill and windsurfing plus fearlessness – which generally translates into young skiers for whom risk-taking is seen as an integral part of any sport. Carefully supervised by Ski Morin Heights instructors, snowboarders must also pass a test by the center's ski patrol and ensure that their equipment meets Québec's sports safety standards.

A family-owned operation, Ski Morin Heights bills itself as " a real family ski center." While it doesn't have overnight accommodation, it does have a giant chalet and a wide variety of hospitality services and sports-related facilities. Eateries include the **Après-Vous Pub** and cafeteria, a 300-seat restaurant, **La Croissanterie** and the **Mardi Gras Pub**.

Besides the usual health and fitness features, from squash to jacuzzis, there are full services for skiers including a special ski school for children with instructors disguised as Disney characters, which fits well into the commercial landscape at least.

An equally busy town with an active nightlife is **Ste-Adèle,** full of Québec craft shops, boutiques and restaurants. Being out in the country doesn't mean giving up such Big City pursuits as first-run movies, either. Ste-Adèle's **Cinema Pine** features the same films making their Montréal debut. Residents and tourists are equally enamored of the giant artificial ice slides that attract adventurous hordes to the **Supersplash Aquatic Park** daily from mid-December to the end of April.

During the summer, these same daredevils dive into the latest thrill-inducing aquatic sport: Super Splash water slides, which find them cascading down the mountain-side with 360-degree spins into huge wave pools.

Above: For après-ski, St-Sauveur-des-Monts has a thing or two to offer.

Just a few miles north of Ste-Adèle on **Route 117** is the award-winning **Village de Seraphin**. This faithful reconstruction of small *habitant* homes, a grand country house, general store and church recaptures the simple lifestyle of the settlers who arrived in the 1840s. A special highlight is the train tour through the woods.

Mont-Rolland is also a favorite destination for intermediate and advanced skiers, who take to the hills at its **Station touristique de Mont Gabriel** also offers superb skiing, primarily for intermediate and advanced skiers. Beside the usual outdoor activities, Mont Rolland has a summer theater, where comedy, musicals, children's theater, even circus acts, are presented. The town is also famous for its **Bourbon Street Bar**, based in the Hotel La Louisiane. Montréal-based bands and solo acts appear here year-round. If adventure outings appeal, then head for the town's **Velidelta au Mont Christie** base to try deltaplaning, definitely not for the faint of heart. Similar to hang-gliding, deltaplaning frees modern-day Daedaluses to conquer the skies. Free-flying training, flight simulation, flight manoeuvres, speed and turns and a pilot's license will transform the most earth-bound into sky-high soarers within a day.

Equally adventurous is whitewater rafting on the **Rivière Rouge**. The Rouge cuts across rugged Laurentian mountains, through rapids, canyons and alongside beaches. Companies specializing in whitewater rafting are on-site at the trip's departure point near **Calumet** (Route 148 past Calumet to the chemin de la Rivière-Rouge).

Nearby **Ste-Marguerite-du-Lac-Masson** is also a popular but tamer water-sport destination, with beautiful beaches to sun, swim or sail from. In winter, naturally, it attracts scores of cross-country skiers who ply its hills and dales. Skating on the lake is an equally popular winter pastime. The town's **Service des Loisirs** is the place to visit for details about special festival events, schedules and locations. The town also boasts a bistro with a wine cellar of some 20,000 bottles, many of them vintage. Since 1987, the award-winning **Bistro de Champlain** has attracted oenophiles near and far to its wine-tasting sessions.

Val David, to the north, boasts the **Village du Père-Noël** (Santa Claus Village) and a rendezvous point for mountain climbers, ice scalers, dogsledders, hikers and summer or winter campers. The town is also an artists' enclave. Many of their ateliers are open to the public and most of their work is for sale. Check out **Atelier Bernard Chaudron Inc.** for hand-shaped and hammered lead-free pewter objets d'art.

Overlooking **Lac des Sables** is **Ste-Agathe-des-Monts**, a lively resort area and a popular ski center. The favorite summer sport is sailing, but skin-diving is one of the local specialties. Equipment rentals, scuba diving lessons and guides are available through the **Centre de plongée sous-marine** and the **Mont Tremblant Montagne Sport Shop**, which also offer offer mountain-climbing lessons and expert guides

Mid-January through mid-March, Lac des Sables is also the site of a major sports competitions, tournaments and live entertainment, **L'hiver en Nord.** Sightseers can also visit **Village du Mont-Castor**, a recreation of a turn-of-the-century Québecois village, featuring over 100 homes built in the traditional fashion of full-length logs set *pièce sur pièce* (one upon the other).

The **Crystal Villa** boutique, a thriving fashion emporium filled with clothes for men, women and children is also an architectural landmark: Originally a house, whose exterior was made of grey concrete with bits of glass and mirror set into its surface, it is one of only three or four surviving examples of a once-popular Québec style. Owner Lilianne Bru-

HAUTES LAURENTIDES

neau restored it carefully and added balconies, flowers and a garden outside while tastefully outfitting the interior

North of Ste-Agathe lies Québec's best-known ski resort, the **Mont Tremblant Lodge,** now part of **Station Touristique de Mont Tremblant**. Just 90 minutes from Montréal, this lodge is the region's northernmost resort that is still easily accessible year-round. The crowning glory of Les Hautes Laurentides, it overlooks nine-mile **Lac Tremblant.** It has the longest vertical drop (2131 feet or 650 meters) in Eastern Canada, with a wide variety of ski trails for beginners to seasoned skiers.

Mont Tremblant is also famous for car racing, which, considering the hairpin turns of these country roads winding around mountains, dipping into valleys and slicing through peaceful burgs, is not so strange. Today, the Formula 2000 **Jim Russell Championships** of the Canadian Car Championships take place on weekends from June through October.

Mont Tremblant lies in **Parc du Mont Tremblant,** which was created in 1894. Its mountain and hundreds of square miles of wilderness was once called *manitonga soutana* by the Algonquin tribe who once lived here. Meaning "mountain of the spirits," this immense wildlife sanctuary has more than 500 lakes, 230 species of birds and animals (including moose, bear, deer and beaver). Seasonal activities include moose hunting (with a permit), cross-country skiing, snowshoeing, snowmobiling, camping and canoeing.

ALONG THE ST. LAWRENCE

The most natural areas to explore from Québec City are Charlevoix and Gaspésie, which basically lie north and south respectively of the St. Lawrence River to the east of town. If coming in from Montréal, however, you should stop at **Trois-Rivières,** which is right between the two

Above: Canada's oldest wooden church was founded in Tadoussac around 1600.

cities on the left bank of the river, to stroll about the old town which is near the river. Trois-Rivières dates back to 1634 when it was a fort built to defend fur-trading interests. Nowadays the main industry is making newsprint from the vast forests to the north of town.

Charlevoix, commonly referred to as the Switzerland of Québec, begins to the east of Québec City along the old **Chemin du Roy**, now Route 138. The road follows the coast, providing ample opportunities to gaze over the water from prodigiously high cliffs. The first great natural sight, however, is the **Chûtes de Montmorency**, a 273-foot (84-m) waterfall, which is as impressive in summer as in winter when climbing up its frozen shape becomes a wild attraction. When you reach **Saint-Tite-des-Caps**, you will be in Charlevoix. The best way to visit the region is in relaxed fashion. Sights are seldom very far off, they simply appear as one drives along.

Tadoussac, an old trading post dating back to the year 1600, is situated on the confluence of Saguenay River, which at this point is more like a fjord. The river is deep and owing to the backing up of salt water from the ocean this particular area is the gathering point of several species of whales from July to October. In winter, when the river freezes over, anglers set up little huts on the ice to fish in the traditional way. It's quite a sight. Nearby **Le Désert** consists of several surprising sand dunes that are used for sand skiing competitions.

The Québec traveler faces two options here. One is to continue up the coast through Escoumins, Sept-Îles, and Havre-St.-Pierre. Again it is nature that dominates but not only.

From **Baie Comeau** a road leads inland toward Manicouagan on the river by the same name. The local power company offers tours of its two gigantic hydroelectric dams on the Manicouagan and Outardes rivers. And from Havre-St-Pierre boats take visitors to the bizarre rock formations of the **Mingan Archipelago**.

GASPE PENINSULA

The other option from Tadoussac is to drive along the Saguenay River up to **Lac St-Jean**. This area is the heart of Québec Province, where separatism and tradition burn on as if 400 years of history never took place. There are wild carnival celebrations in **Chicoutimi** (known as the "Queen of the North"), and swimming competitions on the lake. It's the realm of cunning trappers and muscular timbermen, and in spite of a fair amount of tourism, it remains quite unspoilt.

The **Gaspé Peninsula** (or Gaspésie), a long, tongue-shaped strip of land stretching eastward from Québec City on the other bank of the St. Lawrence River, is one of the most popular tourist attractions of the Province, especially during the summer months. Its main attraction is Mother Nature. The northern coast features mighty cliffs eaten away into dramatic formations by the sea, the southern coast on the Baie des Chaleurs is more gentle but no less beautiful. The inland is rugged and mountainous. The Chic-Choc and Notre-Dame ranges are home to herds of caribou, moose and even the black bear.

Nearly 850 square miles of inland Gaspé have been allotted to conservation programs. The **Gaspé National Park** is in the forest-covered Chic-Choc Mountains and includes **Mont Jacques-Cartier**, the highest mountain in Gaspésie, which stands at 4159 feet (1268 m). There are also quite a number of *réserves fauniques*, that is, animal reservations. **Matane**, **Dunière**, **Chic-Choc** and **Baldwin** are all situated around the national park.

The **Réserve Faunique de la Petite Cascapédia** and **de Port Daniel** are to the south. And of course hikers and campers are well provided for, as in most Canadian national parks.

The bulk of the population of Gaspésie is concentrated along the coast. They live

Above: On Mont-St-Pierre in the Gaspésie.
Right: Rocher Percé, 1416 feet / 433 m long and 288 feet / 88 m high, seen from Mont Ste-Anne.

GASPÉ / ROCHER PERCÉ

in little picturesque villages that cling to the rocks, each with at least one (often outsized) church. Their main economic source is fishing and its peripheral industries, and of course tourism, so the infrastructure is basically good. Gaspé gastronomy, by the way, has an excellent reputation.

Most visitors starting out from Québec City, begin a tour of Gaspé by the northern coast. One possible access is by taking the ferry from Escoumines in the Charlevoix region to Matane or Trois Pistoles. The view of the St. Lawrence, which at this point looks more like the sea, is breathtaking. Note the old wooden bridge in **Grande Vallée**. When you reach **Rivière-au-Renard**, you will be at the edge of **Forillon National Park**, which is small but quite varied, with dense forests, fields, and fascinating rock formations along the coast. The **Baie de Gaspé** offers some excellent opportunities to scuba divers.

Gaspé is the main city on the peninsula, a small town actually with a population of barely 18,000. It was the first North American landing point of Jacques Cartier (in 1534), but the wooden cross he put up to mark the event, the **Croix de Gaspé**, has been rebuilt of stone. Cartier is also the main subject at the **Musée de Gaspé**, which also features some of the more standard Canadian topics, such as life of the old colonists and so on. Another landmark of Gaspé is the **Cathedral**, which is made of wood.

South of Gaspé comes **Percé**, reputed to have the most dramatic coastline of all the peninsula. It lies on a green spit of land that has been carved away at by the sea.

The most renowned local landmark is the **Rocher Percé**, literally "pierced rock," a giant slab of limestone just off the coast. It can be waded to at low tide. Flocks of gulls and gannets use it as a landing, and its sinuous walls echo to their eerie shrieks. **Île Bonaventure**, which lies some miles off the coast, constitutes the largest sea bird sanctuary in North America.

GUIDEPOST: QUÉBEC PROVINCE / L'ESTRIE

QUÉBEC PROVINCE

Access / Transportation

By air: **Mirabel Airport**, Mirabel J7N lEl, Tel. l-514/476-30l0, 65 km (40 mi) northwest of Montréal. Charters and international flights from abroad (other than North America). **Dorval Airport**, Dorval, Tel. l-5l4/633-3l05. On the Island of Montréal 22.5 km (14 mi) west of downtown. For flights from within Canada and the United States. Canada's two major airlines fly daily from most major cities across North America. American Airlines, Delta Airlines, Continental Airlines all fly directly into Dorval; other international airlines have connecting flights to Dorval through American and Canadian passenger airlines.
By train and bus: See Guideposts Montréal, p. 115. **Car Rentals**: See Guideposts Montréal.

Driving in Québec

The legal driving age in Québec is l6 but drivers must be 2l-years-old to rent a car, have a valid driver's license and a credit card. Remember to always drive on the right-hand side of the road, facing oncoming traffic on the left. Québeckers drive at the speed limit and are notorious for changing lanes without signalling. Montréal's autoroutes require defensive driving skills, especially at entrance and exit ramps. Signage is minimal and often in French only. Road maps and city street directories are available at tourism offices, most gas stations bookstores and newsstands. It is illegal in Québec to turn right on a red light, unless a directional signal indicates otherwise. It is mandatory to stop at least five metres away from a school bus when it is stopped or parked with its lights flashing. Québec drivers rarely yield to pedestrians, even at crosswalks. Look both ways before crossing any street on foot and proceed with caution. Wearing a seatbelt is mandatory in Québec; helmets are mandatory when riding a moped or motorcycle. Parking signs: A red circle will indicate that parking is prohibited during certain hours/days. A green circle with the same information plus "30 M" means that you can park for a maximum of 30 minutes during business hours. In some parts of towns and cities you cannot park unless you are a resident and have a permit.

Official Public Holidays

January l: New Year's Day. *March/April*: Good Friday, Easter Sunday. *May:* Fête de Dollard/Victoria Day, the third Monday of the month. *June 24:* Fête Nationale (St-Jean-Baptiste Day, Québec's national holiday. *July l5-August l:* Annual Construction Holiday (two-week annual vacation period taken by most Québeckers – a good time to visit Montréal and Québec). *September:* Labor Day, the first Monday of the month. *October:* Thanksgiving, the second Monday of the month. *December 25 and 26:* Christmas Day and Boxing Day.

Tourist Information

In Montréal: **Centre Infotouriste,** l00l Square Dorchester, Montréal H3B 4V4; Tel. l-514/873-2015. **Tourisme Québec** year-round regional offices: Bromont, Granby, Lac-Brome, Lac-Mégantic, La Patrie, Magog, Mansonville, Sherbrooke, Sutton and Thetford Mines. Seasonal tourist offices (June 1-Labor Day): Asbestos, Ayer's Cliff, Black Lake, Coaticook, Cowansville, Danville, North Hatley, Notre-Dame-des-Bois, Richmond, St-Denis-de-Brompton, Stanstead.

L'ESTRIE (Eastern Townships)

Access / Local Transportation

By car: From Montréal: take Autoroute 10 East; from Vermont: U.S. Highway 91 (becomes Autoroute 55 at Rock Island border crossing); from New Hampshire: U.S. Highway 3 (becomes Autoroute 141 to Coaticook or Autoroute 257 to La Patrie); from Maine: U.S. Highway 27 (leads to Autoroute 212 to Notre-Dame-des-Bois, La Patrie and Cookshire to Autoroute 161 to Lac-Mégantic).
By bus: Buses depart almost hourly from the **Terminus Voyageur**, 505 blvd. de Maisonneuve E., Montréal; Tel. 1-514/842-2281. Some are express; others stop en route to Granby, Lac-Mégantic, Magog, Sherbrooke and Thetford Mines.

Accommodation

LUXURY: **Auberge Hatley**, Box 330, North Hatley J0B 2C0; Tel. 1-819/842-245l. **Manoir Hovey**, 575 chemin Hovey, North Hatley J0B 2C0; Tel. l-8l9/842-242l. **Auberge Ripplecove Inn**, 700 chemin Ripplecove, Ayer's Cliff J0B lC0; Tel. 1-8l9/838-4296. **Auberge Estrimont**, Box 98, 44 avenue de l'Auberge, Magog, Orford JlX 3W7; Tel. 1-8l9/843-l6l6. **Centre de Santé Eastman**, 875 chemin des Diligences, Eastman J0E lP0; Tel. l-5l4/297-3009. **Le Château Bromont Resort Spa**, 90 rue Stanstead, Bromont J0E lL0; Tel. l-5l4/866-6840. *MODERATE:* **O'Berge du Village**, 26l rue Merry S., Magog JlX 3L2; Tel. 1-819/843-6566. **La Paimpolaise**, 357 rue Maple, Sutton J0E lL0; Tel. l-5l4/538-32l3. **Auberge Schweizer**, 357 rue Schweizer, Sutton J0E 2K0; l-5l4/538-2l29. **Auberge de L'Aurore**, 5l chemin de l'Observatoire, Mont Mégantic J0B 2E0; Tel. l-8l9/888-27l5.
BUDGET: **Bishop's University**, rue College, Lennoxville JlM lZ7; 1-8l9/822-9600.

Museums / Theaters / Festivals

Musée des beaux-arts de Sherbrooke, l74 rue Palais, Sherbrooke; Tel. 1-8l9/82l-2ll5. **Musée Joseph-Armand Bombardier**, l00l avenue Joseph-Armand Bombardier, Valcourt; Tel. l-5l4/532-2258. **Centre d'Arts Orford**, 3l65 chemin du Parc, Route l4l N., Magog; Tel. 1-8l9/843-398l. **Uplands Museum Park**, 50 rue Park, Lennoxville; Tel. 1-8l9/564-0409. **Brome County Historical Museum**,130 Lakeside, Knowlton; Tel. l-5l4/243-6782. **The Piggery Theatre**,

GUIDEPOST: LES LAURENTIDES

Box 390, chemin Simard, North Hatley; Tel. 1-819/842-2431. **Centennial Theatre, Consolidated Bathurst Theatre**, Bishop's University, rue du College, Lennoxville; Tel. 1-819/822-9600. **Théâtre Lac Brome**, Box 1177, Knowlton; Tel. 1-514/243-0361. **Théâtre Le Vieux Clocher**, 64 rue Merry, Magog; Tel. 1-819/847-0470. **Festival du Lait de Coaticook**, Coaticook; Tel. 1-819/849-6010. **Festival Gastronomique de Granby**, 650 rue Principale, Granby; Tel. 1-514/378-7272.

Sightseeing
Abbaye St-Benoit-du-Lac, St-Benoit-du-Lac; Tel. 1-819/843-4080. **Jardin zoologique de Granby**, 347 Bourget, Granby; Tel. 1-514/372-9113. **Mont Mégantic Observatory**, Notre-Dame-des-Bois; Tel. 1-819/888-2822.

Tourist Information
L'Association Touristique de l'Estrie, 25 rue du Bocage, Sherbrooke J1L 2J4; Tel. 1-819/566-7404.

LES LAURENTIDES
Access / Local Transportation
By car: from Montréal: take the six-lane Autoroute 15 or the scenic secondary road, Route 117. Don't travel there on weekends, to avoid bumper-to-bumper traffic. **By bus**: Daily buses depart from the **Terminus Voyageur**, 505 blvd. de Maisonneuve E., Montréal; Tel. 1-514/842-2281. **Limocar Laurentides**, 4117 Lavoisier, Boisbriand; Tel. 1-514-435-8899, departs regularly for Ste-Adèle, Ville d'Esterel, Ste-Agathe-des-Monts, St-Jovite and Mont Tremblant. Service to **Les Hautes Laurentides** departs from the bus terminal at the Metro Henri-Bourassa station in north Montréal, stopping at Ste-Thérèse and St-Jérôme en route.

Accommodation
LUXURY: **Manoir St-Sauveur**, 246 chemin du Lac Millette, St-Sauveur J0R 1R3; Tel. 514/227-1811. **Auberge St-Denis**, 61 rue St-Denis, St-Sauveur J0R 1R4; Tel. 1-514/227-4602. **L'Eau à la Bouche**, 3003 blvd. Ste-Adèle, Route 117, Ste-Adèle J0R 1L0; Tel. 1-514/229-2991. **Le Chantecler**, Box 1048, Ste-Adèle J0R 1L0; Tel. 1-514/229-3555. **Auberge Mont Gabriel**, Station Touristique de Mont Gabriel, Autoroute 15, exit 64, Mont Rolland J0R 1G0; Tel. 1-514/861-2852. **Ville d'Esterel**, blvd. Fridolin Simard, Esterel J0T 1E0; Tel. 1-514/228-2571. **Auberge du Lac des Sables**, 230 St-Venant, Ste-Agathe J8C 2Z7; Tel. 1-819/326-3944. **Auberge Cuttle's Tremblant Club**, chemin Lac Tremblant Nord, Mont Tremblant J0T 1Z0; Tel. 1-819/425-2731. **Mont Tremblant Lodge Ski Resort**, Station Touristique de Mont Tremblant, 3005 chemin Principale, Mont Tremblant J0T 1Z0; Tel. 1-819/425-8711.

MODERATE: **Auberge Chez Girard**, 18 rue Principale ouest, Ste-Agathe J8C 1A3; Tel. 1-819/326-0922. *BUDGET*: **Auberge Swiss Inn**, 796 route St-Adolphe, Morin Heights J0R 1H0; Tel. 1-514/229-3547. **Manoir d'Ivry**, 3800 chemin Renaud, Ste-Agathe-Nord, J8C 2Z8; Tel. 1-819/326-3564.

Sightseeing / Culture
LES BASSES LAURENTIDES: **Seigneurie du Lac-des-Deux-Montagnes,**, Exit 640 W., Route 148, St-Scholastique. **Abbaye cistercienne d'Oka**, 1600 chemin d'Oka; Tel. 1-514/479-8361. **Parc Paul Sauve**, Box 1200, 2020 chemin d'Oka; Tel. 1-514/479-8337. **St-Eustache Arts and Cultural Services**, 235 rue St-Eustache, St-Eustache; Tel. 1-514/472-4440 ext. 420.
LES HAUTES LAURENTIDES: **Centre d'exposition du Vieux-Palais**, 185 rue du Palais, St-Jérome; Tel. 1-514/432-7171. **Temple de la renommée du ski des Laurentides**, 220 chemin Baulne, Piedmont; Tel. 1-514/227-2886. **Village de Séraphin**, Mont de Séraphin, Ste-Adèle; Tel. 1-514/229-4777. **Théâtre de Mont Rolland**, 2525 chemin de la Rivière, Mont Rolland; Tel. 1-514/229-5171.

Camping / Parks / Sports
LES HAUTES LAURENTIDES: Camping Ste-Agathe, 50 St-Joseph, Route 329, Ste-Agathe-des-Monts; Tel. 1-819/326-5577. **Parc régional de la Rivière-du-Nord**, 1051 blvd. Industriel, St-Jérome; 1-514/431-1676. **Mont Sauveur Aquatic Park**, 350 rue St-Denis, St-Sauveur; Tel. 1-514/871-0101. **Super Splash Aquatic Park**, 1791 blvd. Ste-Adèle; Tel. 1-514/229-2925. **Aventures en eau vive**, Tel. 1-819/242-6084 and **Nouveau Monde**, Tel. 1-514/939-7447, R.R. No. 2, chemin Rivière Rouge, Calumet. **Alouette Tourboat**, Box 250, Ste-Agathe-des-Monts J8C 3A3; 1-819/326-3656. **Centre de plongée sous-marine**, 124 rue Principale, Ste-Agathe-des-Monts J8C 1K1; 1-819/326-4464. **Fédération québécoise de la montagne**, Box 1000, Succursale M, 4545 rue Pierre-du-Coubertin, Montréal H1W 3R2; Tel. 1-514/252-3004. **Parc du Mont Tremblant**, Box 129, St-Faustain J0T 2G0; Tel. 1-819/688-2281.

Tourist Information
Tourisme Québec year-round regional offices: Carillon, L'Anonciation, Mont Laurier, Mont Tremblant, St-Antoine, St-Eustache, St-Sauveur-des-Monts, St-Jovite, Ste-Adèle, Ste-Agathe-des-Monts. Seasonal tourist offices (mid-June to Labor Day): Labelle, Lachute, Morin Heights, Notre-Dame-du-Laus, Piedmont, St-Adolphe-de-Howard, Val David. Skiing and lodging reservations, tour guides or outfitters: **Maison du Tourisme des Laurentides**, 14142 rue de Lachapelle, R.R.1, St-Jérome J7Z 5T4; Tel. 1-514/436-8532. Hunting or fishing permits: **Ministère du Loisir, de la Chasse et de la Pêche**, Box 22,000, Québec G1K 7X2. **Station Touristique de Mont Gabriel**, Autoroute 15, exit 64, Mont Rolland; Tel. 1-514/861-2852. **L'hiver en Nord**, Information Touristique de Ste-Agathe, 190 rue Principale, Ste-Agathe J8C 1K3; Tel. 1-819/326-0457.

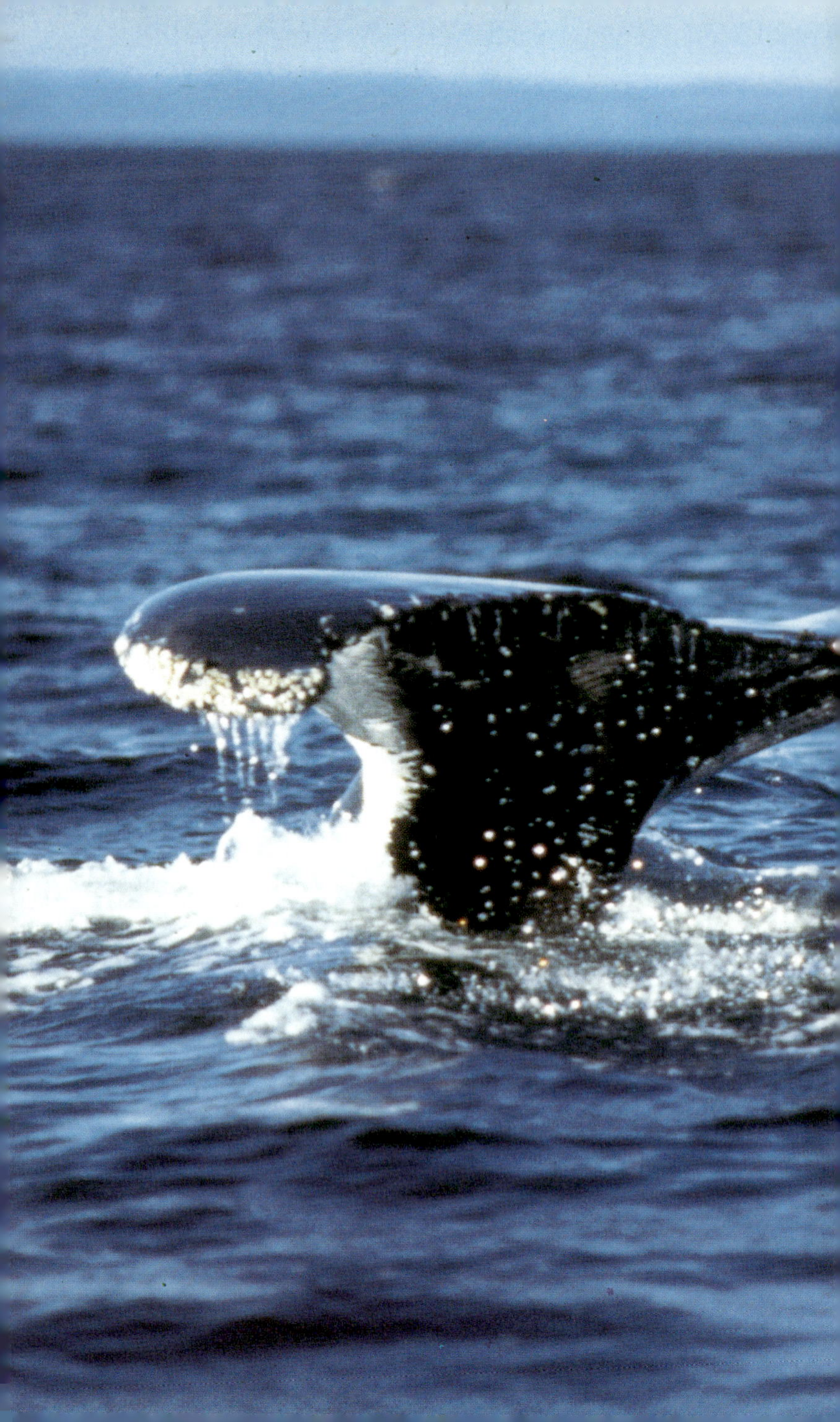

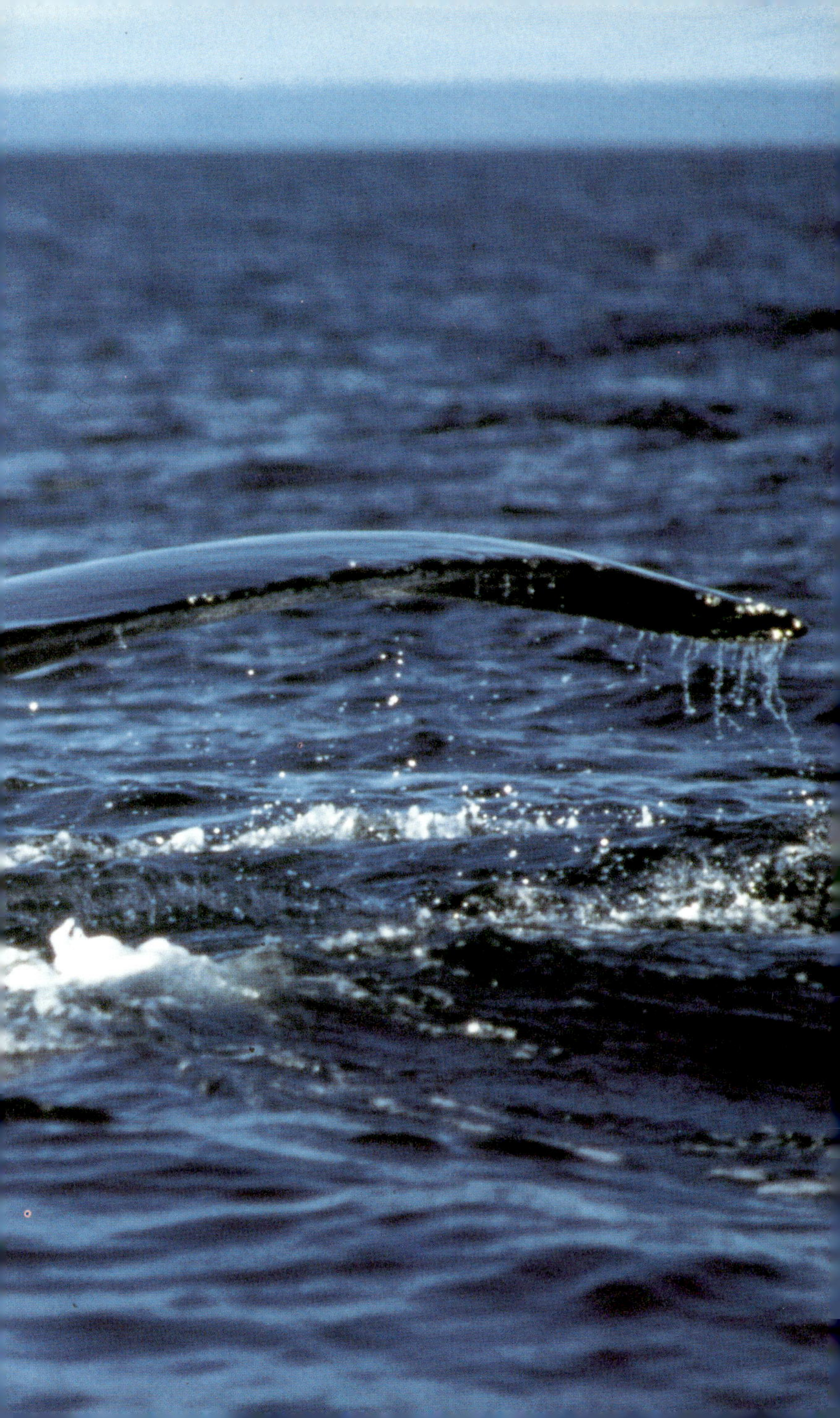

NEW BRUNSWICK

SAINT JOHN RIVER VALLEY

NEW BRUNSWICK

SAINT JOHN RIVER VALLEY
FUNDY TIDAL COAST
MIRAMICHI BASIN
THE ACADIAN COAST
RESTIGOUCHE UPLANDS

The Maritime Province of New Brunswick is, like Quebec, multicultural and multilingual. The French settled here in 1604 calling it Acadia, and in spite of rather heavy-handed British rule after 1784, they maintained their influence, but by no means alone: the mixture of Micmacs, Malecites, Loyalists and Acadians, Scots, Irish, Danish and Germans have given New Brunswick a fascinating cultural heritage. Ancient Indian sites are being excavated in the province. Even early French settlements have to be archeologically studied. During the Expulsion of the 1770s many an Acadian family left their home with outside baking ovens and chimneys intact, and such artifacts as pottery brought over from the Acadian's native southwestern France, can still be seen today. When the early British colonizers came a few years later to exploit the salmon fishery, they left their own set of distinctive artifacts.

For the sake of convenience, this culturally varied area can easily be divided up into six touring areas: the Saint John River Valley, Fundy Tidal Coast, Southeast Shores, Miramichi Basin, Acadian Coast and Restigouche Uplands.

Preceding pages: Humpbacks, right whales, and other baleen whales frolic off the coast. Left: Evening on Grand Lake.

SAINT JOHN RIVER VALLEY

Often referred to as the Rhine of North America, the Saint John River is a brilliant blue waterway wending a broad course for more than 450 miles (724 km) through expansive green vistas, luscious forests and rolling farmlands. The three major tourist areas along the way, Madawaska, Upper Saint John River Valley and Lower Saint John River Valley, are tempting for travelers on the Trans-Canada Highway who have time to make exploratory sidetrips along the route. Along the river the influence of original Indian inhabitants combines with that of a long line of settlers beginning with the United Empire Loyalists. Just over the border from Quebec, in the self-styled **Republic of Madawaska**, the town of **Saint Jacques** offers **Les Jardins de la République Provincial Park**. This campground and recreational park includes a swimming pool, tennis courts, nature trails, an amphitheater, an adventure playground, an **Automobile Museum** and **Botanical Gardens**. Nearby, **Mont Farlagne** hill is popular with skiers of the area. In the 1800s, the residents of this settlement at the junction of both the Saint John and Madawaska rivers grew weary of being pawns in border quarrels between Canada and the

159

NEW BRUNSWICK

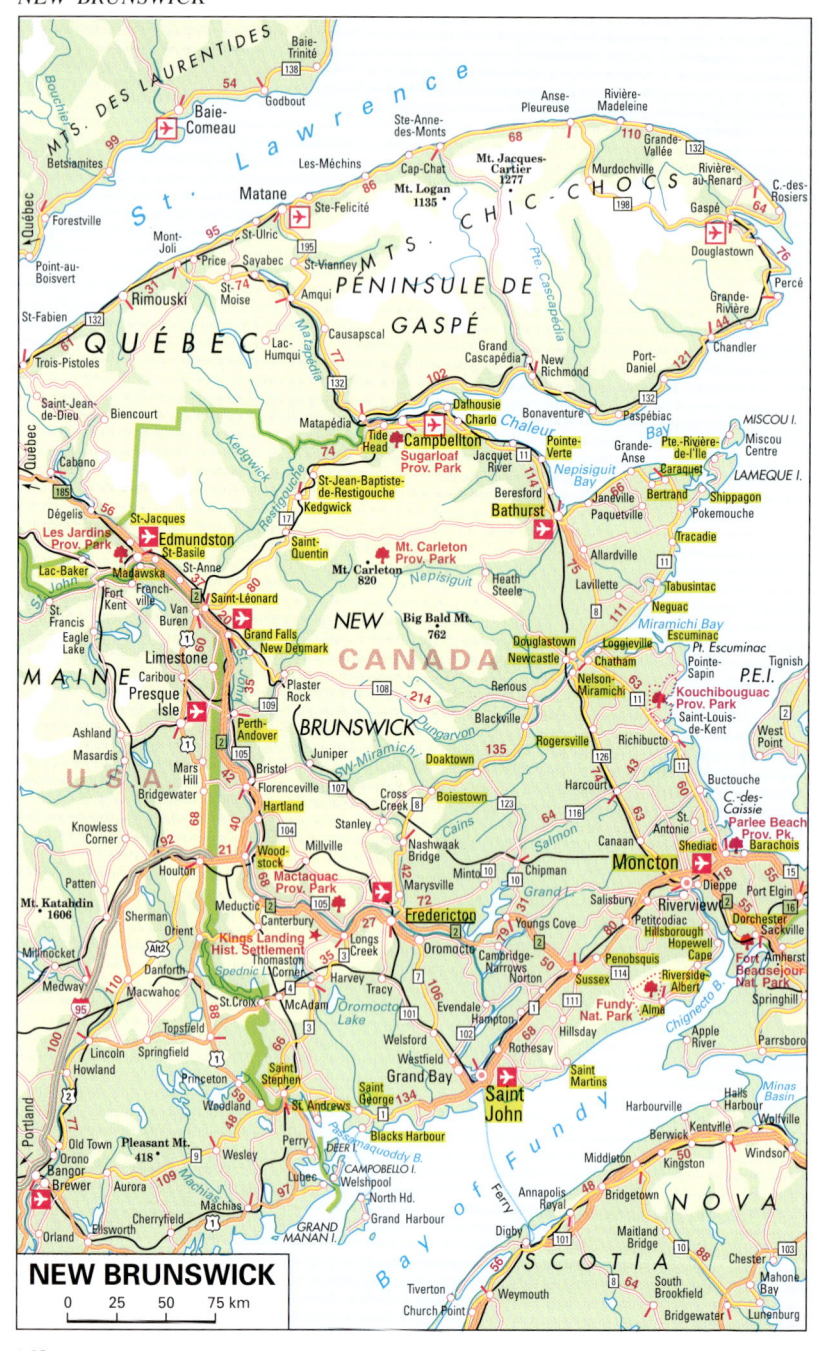

United States. In a burst of patriotic fervor they declared themselves a republic, naming Edmundston their capital and flew their own flag sporting an eagle and stars.

Edmundston, with a population just under 12,000, is lively and French (the locals are known as the *Brayons*). The **Madawaska Museum** features local history and culture; the church of **Notre Dame des Sept Douleurs** should be seen for its superb works by Canadian artist Claude Roussel. Tours of the local pulp mill (the area is an important pulp and paper center) and maple sugar facilities can be arranged. The local environment beckons too, for example down Route 120 to **Lac Baker**, with good trout fishing. There is also a beach for those who enjoy swimming, sailing, waterskiing, boardsailing and boating.

Just off the Trans-Canada Highway is "the cradle of Madawaska," the town of **Saint Basile**. Its museum houses an antique collection, a genealogy library and a replica of a 1786 chapel. Adjoining is a typical old country cemetery with tombstones dating back to 1785. Downriver at **Rivière Verte**, the shortest covered bridge in the province crosses the Quisibis River. In **Saint Leonard** the internationally known Madawaska weavers create fine woven items for a wide range of customers, from plain folk to royalty.

At **Grand Falls/Grand Sault** the Saint John River hurtles down a dramatic 75 feet (23 m), creating one of the largest cataracts east of the Niagara Falls. Power plants here generate electricity for the entire province. Thousands of visitors flock to enjoy the natural spectacle: there are stairs providing access to the mile-long (1.5-km) gorge, with walking trails to various vantage points. Grand Falls was once an important military post and a museum displays pioneer and early Victorian artifacts. In summer, the town pays tribute to its most important agricultural crop with a potato festival.

Route 108 leads east to **New Denmark**, the largest Danish colony in North America. June 19th there is Founders Day, celebrated with song and dance, traditional food and costumes. South to **Perth Andover** and the Saint John River, there are spectacular views along the Trans-Canada route and the more leisurely Route 105 paralleling it on the east bank of the river. At **Four Falls** there is a truly international golf course, where you might even hook your ball straight out of the country – into Maine, USA – on the first fairway. **Hartland**, at one of the many junctions of the two highways downriver, boasts the longest covered bridge in the world. It crosses the St. John River. The frequently photographed structure, built in 1899, stretches a full 1,282 feet (391 m. Hartland and its environs are known for the cultivation of poptatoes.

A star attraction of the Upper Saint John Valley is **Kings Landing Historical Settlement**, just off the Trans-Canada Highway near Woodstock. It offers substantial insight into what life was like during Loyalist times in New Brunswick from 1783 to 1900. Dining at the Kings Head Inn from a menu of the 1800s, watching saw and grist mills in operation, taking a look at a blacksmith shop, a one-room schoolhouse, an 1830s wooden boat, brings the past to life, especially when enacted by the more than 100 "residents" who go about their daily tasks in the village's 60 buildings. The obligatory horse-and-buggies (or carts actually) take visitors on tours.

Another focal point is **Mactaquac Provincial Park** along Route 105, with well-tended campsites, beaches, marinas, a championship 18-hole golf course and nature trails. Heading south to Fredericton and the Lower Saint John River Valley, the Trans-Canada Highway crosses a rich agricultural area. The river is particularly wide at this point, and has been dammed near Mactaquac. An interesting stop is a federal fish hatchery using waste heat from the generating station upriver to raise salmon for stocking provincial rivers and streams. Visitors are welcome to tour this unique facility.

Fredericton, a town of just under 45,000, named in honor of King George III's second son has maintained its old-fashioned charm. It was once an important military center, and this is evoked at the **Officers Square** and **Compound** by the marching feet and shouted commands still heard at the colorful changing of the guard, which takes place daily in summer. Fredericton is famed for pewterware and tapestries. More than 100 tapestries hang in public buildings – of special interest are the ones depicting Fredericton's history at the picturesque City Hall. The **Beaverbrook Art Gallery**, sponsored by newspaper magnate Lord William Beaverbrook (1879-1964) who spent his youth in New Brunswick, has a good collection of paintings including works of William Turner and Salvador Dali.

FUNDY TIDAL COAST

Route 7 south leads to St. John and to the **Fundy Tidal Coast**, where the tides are the highest in the world. 100 billion tons of briny water rise along this coast twice a day when the tide comes in. At the eastern edge of the bay the tide has been recorded at 48.6 feet (15 m), which is about as high as a four-story building. Terrific bird watching, whale-watching, recondite coves, spectacular seascapes are the lures of the Fundy Coast especially when the tide is out. The four "saintly" towns along this coast are popular tourist spots, quaint, stately, traditional in their architecture.

Route 1 leads westwards to **St. George** and **St. Stephan**. A must is a visit to **St. Andrews**, which sits at the end of a peninsula jutting out into **Passamaquoddy Bay**. It is the departure point for whale-watching boats, and has good lobster.

Above: Walkways protect nature in Fundy Park. Right: Hopewell Cape – Erosion from the huge tides.

Ferries from Letete and Blacks Harbour on the other side of the Bay go to **Deer**, **Campobello** and **Grand Manan** islands. The latter has exciting nature, with breathtaking cliffs, beaches and birds. The fact that people here live from fishing is obvious when visiting the pretty villages, where lobster pounds are stacked high in the harbors and smoke houses seem to puff away non-stop.

Saint John, near the junction of Routes 7 and 1, on the estuary of the Saint John River, was incorporated in 1783. It is a community of more than 78,000, with a delightful blend of 19th-century buildings and trendy boutiques, restaurants and lively night spots. The **New Brunswick Museum** hosts decorative art objects, as well as human and natural history of New Brunswick. The protected harbor was first discovered by explorer Champlain on St. John's Day in 1604, but it only became a large settlement after Loyalists fleeing the USA landed here in 1783. The *Loyalist Days* held in mid-July reenact this period.

The tides of Fundy Bay create a strange phenomenon in the river at Saint John: the **Reversing Falls Rapids**, caused by the sea pushing upstream. Interesting side trips from Saint John on Highway 1 east toward the Southeast Shores include **Sussex** in Kings County, the "covered bridge capital" of Atlantic Canada, with a total of 17 of the picturesque structures. Sussex is the site of an annual hot air balloon festival and fall fair. Route 1 ends here; Route 2 leads east to **Penobsquis** and Route 114, also known as **Tidal Trail**, along the southeast coast with the Moncton - Hopewell Cape - Fundy National Park stations.

Southeast Shores

There are two dramatic coastlines in this region: the rock formations along the rugged south coast of the Bay of Fundy, presenting sharp contrast to the warm sandy salt-water beaches and wind-swept dunes of the eastern shores of the Northumberland Strait. Each coast has a national park: **Fundy National Park** is a rugged area spread about the town of Alma 44 miles (70 km) from Route 2. The tides change every 6 1/4 hours, making for an impressive experience. The **Flower Pot Rocks**, strange formations resulting from years of tidal movement, is the most interesting sight in the park. Kouchibouguac National Park is about 100 miles (160 km) north of Moncton.

Moncton, a city of more than 55,000, is accessible directly via Route 2, or by a detour through the Fundy National Park. Route 114 leads through pleasant fishing towns such as **Riverside-Albert** and **Hillsborough**. Moncton has made a comfortable blend of its French and English heritage. For a summary glimpse into the past of this almost 250-year-old community, try the **Moncton Museum** or the **Acadian Museum and Art Gallery**, situated on the campus of the Université de Moncton, the only francophone university in the province. From Moncton, Highway 106 leads south to **Dorchester**, where **Bell Inn**, built in 1811, is believed to be the oldest stone building in the province. Route 935 circles Dorchester Cape where a huge colony of sandpipers can be seen on the pebbled beach around July 20. The **Tantramar Marshes** also atract a wide variety of birds.

The region is known for two other natural phenomena. The first, in Moncton itself, is a 6-foot (2-m) **tidal bore**, when the sea comes rushing upriver during the tide. To the northwest of the city is **Magnetic Hill**, which gives the optical impression that cars can ride uphill without using their engine. From Moncton, Route 15 heads straight to the beach and to **Shediac**, lobster capital of the world, which has an annual lobster festival. **Parlee Beach Provincial Park** has one of the finest beaches in the province. Following the shoreline north on Route 15, the road steers through the delightful small towns to **Kouchibouguac National Park**, one of the main destinations of the Southeast Shores. The name is a Micmac Indian word meaning "river of the long tides." The park, with 92 square miles (235 sq. km) of forests, salt marshes, sensational beaches and winter ski trails, lies about 62 miles (100 km) north of Moncton.

South of Moncton, on the main route 114, is **Hopewell Cape** and Shepody Bay. The coastline here has been sculpted into free-standing rocks by the tides and waves. The National Park of **Fort Beauséjour** lies about 37 miles (60 km) southeast of Moncton. French settlers established a base here in the 17th century. In 1755, the British took over the fort, whose only visible remains are the earthworks. People come here, however, for the delightful view of the bay.

MIRAMICHI BASIN

In the center of the province, with only a bit of seashore, lies tranquil **Miramichi Basin**, the remote heart of New Brunswick, a paradise for sportsmen, famous for fishing (Atlantic salmon in particular), canoeing and hunting. The name, believed to be the oldest place name in Eastern Canada, allgedly goes back at least to the 16th century. Scottish and Irish settlers have left a legacy of lumber camp and shanty town ballads, as well as ghost stories. At **Rogersville**, on Route 126, Trappist monks built a monastery in 1904, and there is a monument honoring the original Acadian settlers. Other historical in the region such as **Escuminac, Loggieville, Chatham, Newcastle, Douglastown, Nelson-Miramichi** and **Doaktown** are all of historical interest. **Doaktown's museum** pays tribute to the "King of Game Fish", the Atlantic salmon, portraying the past, present and future of the salmon and its struggle to survive. At **Boiestown**, the geographical

Right: In Acadian Historical Village in Bertrand.

center of New Brunswick, the **Central New Brunswick Woodmen's Museum** chronicles the history of the old time lumber camps. The local industry nowadays is wood and paper, but Chatham was once known for its shipbuilding.

THE ACADIAN COAST

Extending north along the Straits of Northumberland and west around the Baie des Chaleurs, the **Acadian Peninsula** juts boldly out into the sea. Fishing is the mainstay, but agriculture and peat moss harvesting are also important.

The southern doorway to the Acadian Peninsula is the fishing village of **Neguac**, proud of the fact that more people with the surname Savoie live here than anywhere else in the world (suggesting a one-time large migration from southeastern France). Neguac has a bird sanctuary, local artists and artisans, and good windsurfing. Its most lively moment is in May at the opening of the lobster season. All along routes 8 and 11, major highways crossing the area, small towns like **Tabusintac**, **Tracadie**, (Indian for "ideal place to camp") and **Shippagan**, pay tribute to Acadia with museums and historic buildings. The **Shippagan Marine Centre**, offers a marine museum and restaurant besides the research laboratories.

Winding along the coast to **Miscou Island**, the road passes through such charming places as **Cap Bateau**, **Petite-Rivière de l'Île**, **Ste-Marie-Ste-Raphael** and the wildlife park of **Le Paradis des Animaux**. **Miscou Island**, reached by a toll-free ferry, is a remote and sparsely populated island ringed with great beaches. The lighthouse on the tip, in operation since 1856, serves as a major navigational beacon for ships looking for the entrance to the Baie des Chaleurs. A star of the Acadian Coast of the Baie des Chaleurs is the **Acadian Historical Village** on Route 11 just beyond **Bertrand**. The story of the Acadian deportation in 1755, and the determination to survive is recreated in authentic detail; the village evokes well the daily life of a community

RESTIGOUCHE UPLANDS

in the 19th century. Its 40 houses are used to demonstrate traditional handicrafts, and the "Acadians" who inhabit the village are dressed in their traditional garb.

Bathurst, located at the mouth of the Nepisiguit River (another Micmac name, meaning "tumultous river") is the region's only main city, with a population of just under 15,000. This important industrial center boasts the largest zinc mines in the world; tour information is available at tourist information centers. Nearby **Tetagouche**, **Grand** and **Pabineau** falls are sights to see, with picnic facilities nearby. Beaches, parks and nature preserves are features of **Bathurst**; further on at **Pointe-Verte** is a lake where one can fish or go scuba diving.

RESTIGOUCHE UPLANDS

Jacques Cartier, who reached this area in 1534, considered the bay the most

Above: Museum-like education with a "Victorian" teacher.

beautiful one in the entire Gulf of St. Lawrence and gave it the name **Baie des Chaleurs**, Bay of Warmth. Route 11 and later Route 17 both cross the region. Restigouche River, with five main branches and countless flowing streams is famed worldwide for its salmon (one weighing 72 lbs was caught here!). Route 134 follows the bay to **Charlo** which has a museum of local curiosity and a fish hatchery, besides scenic water falls.

Just east of **Dalhousie** and **Campbellton** is one of the longest sand bars in the world, **Eel River Bar**, with sea water on one side and fresh water on the other. It is a popular area for boardsailing and boating. Pretty **Dalhousie** is an important center of the wood industry. The **Restigouche Museum** documents pioneer days and the development of fishing and farming.

Campbellton, population 9,000 plus, is the only city in this area, and it's where sportsfishermen from all over the world come to test their skills. Nearby at **Atholville**, **Sugarloaf Provincial Park** with its 929-feet (283-m) mountain offers camping, tennis, hiking, and in winter skiing and skating. The only Alpine slide in Atlantic Canada is a highlight of the park. A chairlift takes travelers to the top. **Tide Head**, at the junction of routes 134 and 17, is called the "Fiddlehead Capital of the World," fiddleheads being in this case the tender tips of young ferns. Route 17 now continues inland for nearly 150 miles (240 km) through forests of birch, ash and fir to the Saint John River Valley, joining up with the Trans-Canada Highway at **Saint-Leonard.** Along the way, **Oliver's Historical Museum** at **Saint-John Baptiste-de-Restigouche** details the birth of the region, and at **Kedgwick** the **Heritage Lumber Camp** contains replicas explaining the forest heritage.

At **Saint-Quentin**, known for its maple woods, there is fine hunting and fishing. **Mount Carleton Provincial Park**. named after the mountain, can be investigated either on foot or in a canoe.

GUIDEPOST: NEW BRUNSWICK

NEW BRUNSWICK
(Telephone area code: 506.)
Accommodation
EDMUNDSTON: *MODERATE:* **Auberge Wandlyn Inn**, 919 Canada Rd. Tel: 735-5525. **Journey's End Motel**, 5 Bateman Ave. Tel: 739-8361. *BUDGET:* **Beaulieu Tourist Room**, 255 Power Rd. Tel: 735-5781. **Praga Hotel**, 127 Victoria St. Tel: 735-5567.

GRAND FALLS/GRAND-SAULT: *MODERATE:* **Hilltop Motel**, 131 Madawaska Rd. Tel: 473-2684. *BUDGET*: **Old Farm House**, RR #1, Tel: 473-1573.

PERTH-ANDOVER: *BUDGET:* **Valley View Motel**, RR #4, Tel: 273-2785.

FREDERICTON: *LUXURY:* **Lord Beaverbrook Hotel**, 659 Queen St. Tel: 455-3371. *MODERATE:* **Fredericton Inn**, 1315 Regent St. Tel: 455-1430. **Silverwood Motel**, RR #6, Tel: 458-8676. *BUDGET:* **Back Porch Bed & Breakfast**, 266 Northumberland, Tel: 454-6875. **The Manger Inn**, 263 Saunders St. Tel: 454-3410.

ST. STEPHEN: *LUXURY:* **Loon Bay Lodge**, Tel: 466-1240. *MODERATE:* **Fundy Line Motel**, 198 King St. Tel: 466-2130. *BUDGET:* **Scoodic Motel**, Bay Rd. Tel: 466- 1540.

ST. ANDREWS: *LUXURY:* **Algonquin Hotel**, Tel: 529-8823. *MODERATE:* **Blue Moon Motel**, 310 Mowat Dr. Tel: 529-3245. *BUDGET:* **Puff Inn Bed & Breakfast**, 38 Ernest St. Tel: 529-4191.

ST. MARTINS: *MODERATE:* **Quaco Inn**, Tel: 833-4772. *BUDGET:* **Homestead Bed & Breakfast**, Tel: 833-4768.

SAINT JOHN: *LUXURY:* **Delta Brunswick Hotel**, 39 King St. Tel: 648-1981. *MODERATE:* **Fundy Line Motel**, 532 Rothesay Ave. Tel: 633-7333.*BUDGET:* **Anchor Light Motel**, 1989 Manawagonish Rd. Tel: 672- 9972.

GRAND MANAN ISLAND: *MODERATE:* **Compass Rose**, North Head, Tel: 662-8580. *BUDGET:* **Grand Harbour Inn**, Grand Harbour, Tel: 662-8681.

MONCTON: *LUXURY:* **Hotel Beausejour**, 750 Main St. Tel: 854-4344. *MODERATE:* **Moncton Motor Inn**, 1905 Main St. Tel: 382-2587. *BUDGET:* **Garner's Bed & Breakfast**, 8 Roseberry St. Tel: 386-1885.

SHEDIAC: *MODERATE:* **Chez François**, 93 Main St. Tel: 532-4233. *BUDGET:* **Auberge Seaside Haven Inn**, 75 Clader St. Tel: 532-9025.

DOAKTOWN: *MODERATE:* **Homestead Inn Bed & Breakfast**, RR #2, Tel: 365-7912.

BATHURST: *MODERATE:* **Danny's Inn**, St. Peter Ave. West, Tel: 546-6621. *BUDGET:* **Harbour Inn Bed & Breakfast**, 262 Main St. Tel: 546-4757.

CAMPBELLTON: *MODERATE:* **Auberge Caspian Inn**, 26 Duke St. Tel: 753-7606. *BUDGET:* **Sanfar Cottages**, Restigouche Dr. Tel: 753-4287.

Museums
(Call for hours.)
Madawaska Museum, 195 Hebert Blvd., Edmundston, Tel: 739-7254. **Kings Landing Historical Settlement**, 21 miles (34 km) west of Fredericton on Trans Canada Hwy., June-early Oct. daily, Tel: 363-5805. **Beaverbrook Art Gallery**, 703 Queen St. Fredericton, daily, Tel: 458-8545. **New Brunswick Museum**, 277 Douglas Ave., Saint John, daily exc. Mon, Tel: 658-1842. **Miramichi Atlantic Salmon Museum**, Main St., Doaktown, Tel: 365- 7787. **Central New Brunswick Woodmen's Museum**, 1 mile (1.6 km) east of Boiestown on Route 8, Tel: 369-7214. **Marine Center**, Route 113, Shippagan, Tel: 336-4771. **Acadian Village**, Route 11, 6 miles (10 km) west of Caraquet, Tel: 727-3467. **Penny Annie's Museum**, Route 11, Charlo, Tel: 684-3130. **Restigouche Regional Museum**, 437 George St., Dalhousie, Tel: 684-4685. **Oliver's Historical Museum**, Saint-Jean-Baptiste-de-Restigouche, Tel: 284-2444. **Kedgewick Heritage Lumber Camp**, Route 17, Kedgewick, Tel: 284- 3138.

Parks
Fundy National Park, Superintendent, PO Box 40, Alma, EOA, Tel: 887-6000. **Fort Beauséjour National Historic Site**, 37 mi (60 km) east of Moncton on Hwy 2, Exit 550, Aulac, EOA3CO, Tel: 536-0720.

Transportation
There are several toll-free ferries on the lower reaches of the Saint John River and Kennebecasis River. Other free ferries operate between Letete and Deer Island and during summer between Lameque and Miscou islands. There are toll ferries between New Brunswick and Prince Edward Island, Nova Scotia or Quebec. Within the province ferries operate from Blacks Harbour to Grand Manan and Deer Island to Campobello (the latter in summer only).

Tourist Information
Tourism New Brunswick maintains tourist information centers at major entry points: Edmundston, Woodstock, St. Stephen, Aulac, Campobello and Campbellton. Information: **Tourism New Brunswick**, P.O. Box 12345, Fredericton, N. B. Canada E3B 5C3, Tel. 1-800-561-0123, 453-2964 (from Canada and the U.S.A.) and Tel. 1-800-442-4442 (from within New Brunswick).

167

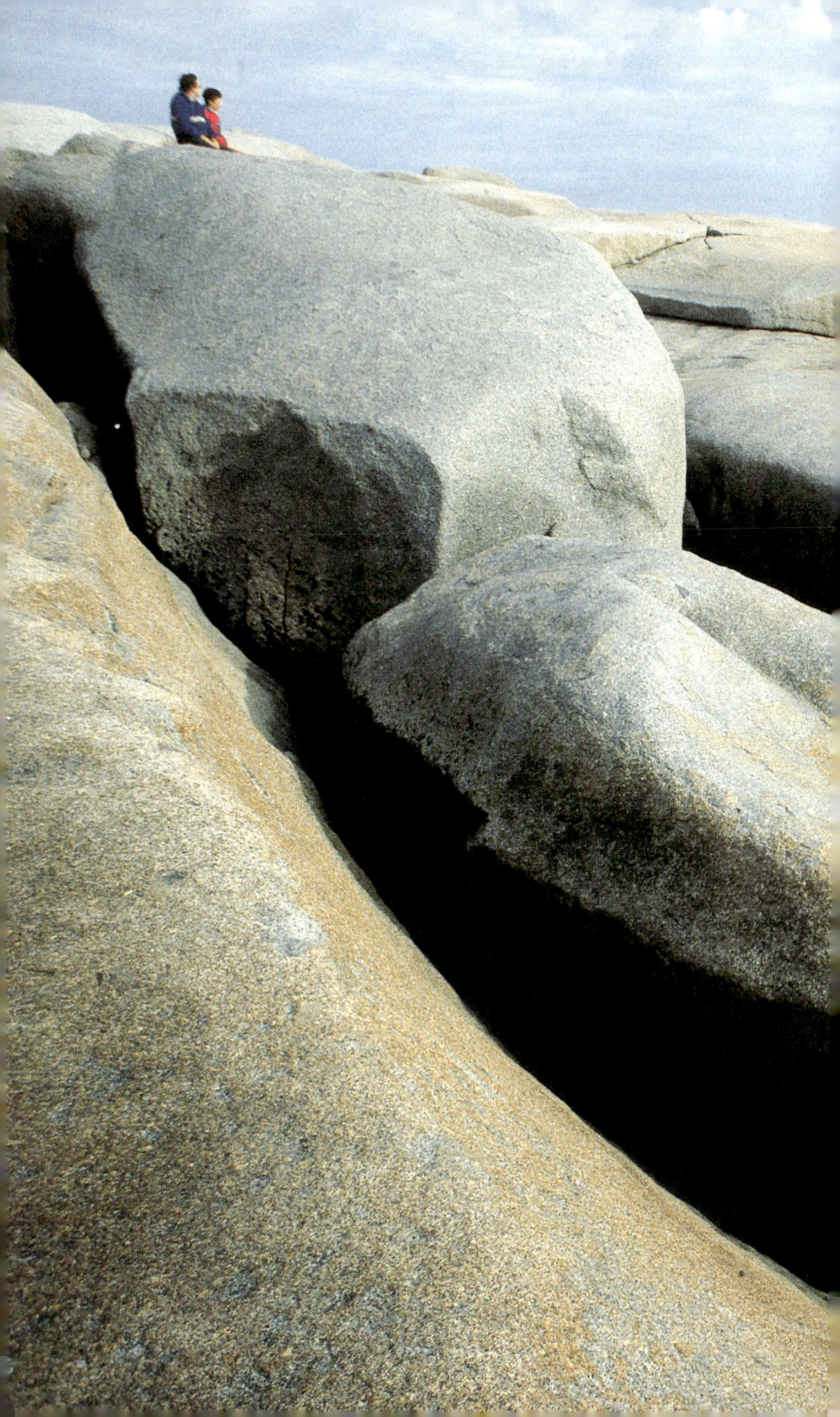

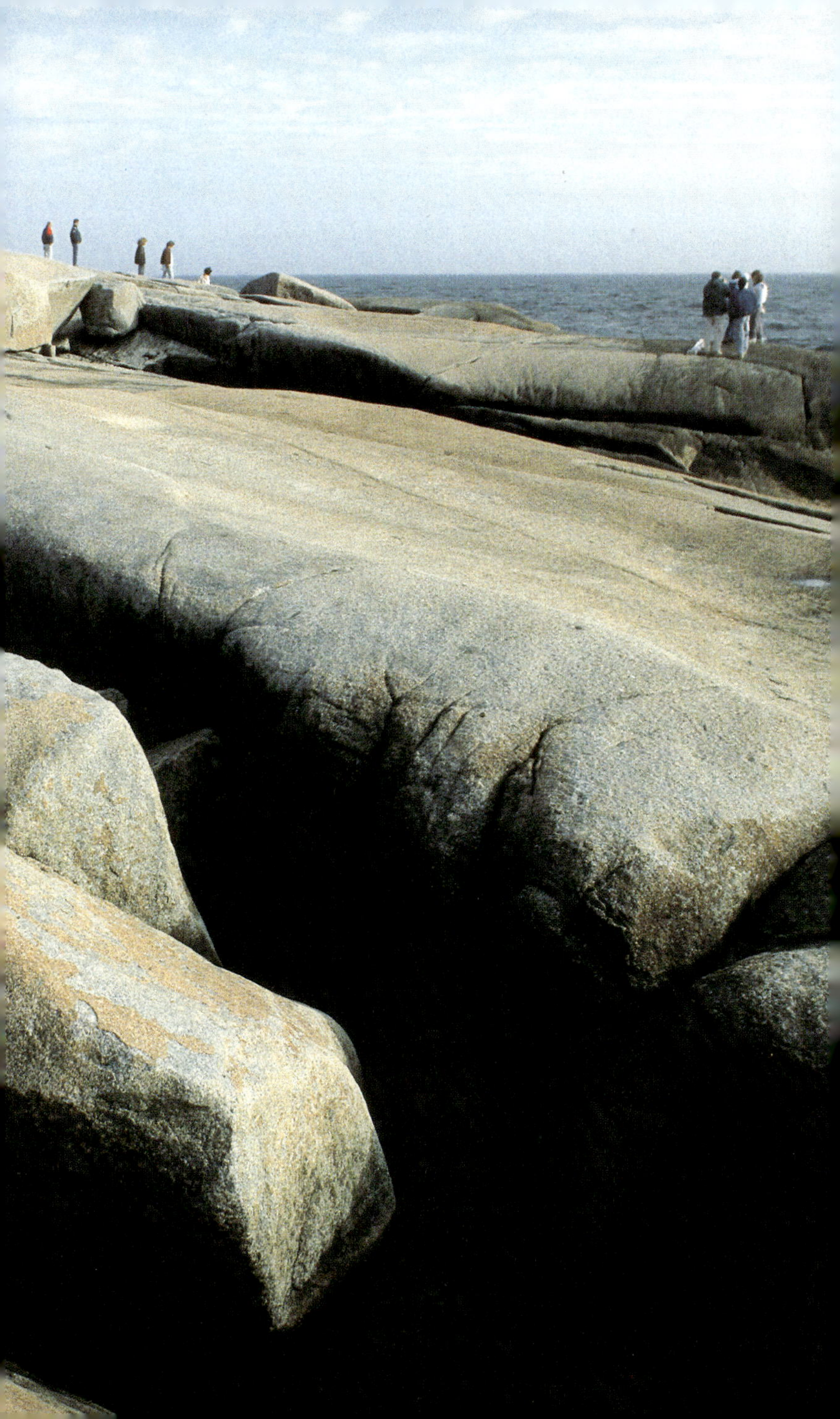

NOVA SCOTIA

NOVA SCOTIA

LIGHTHOUSE TRAIL
EVANGELINE TRAIL
GLOOSCAP TRAIL
SUNRISE TRAIL
CABOT TRAIL
CAPE BRETON
MARINE DRIVE

The Maritime Province of Nova Scotia is small, 21,245 square miles (55,024 square kilometers) with a population of less than 900,000. It is composed of a peninsula attached to southeastern Canada by the isthmus of Chignecto and extends to the Atlantic Ocean between the Bay of Fundy and Northumberland Strait. Its northern section is the island of Cape Breton, which is joined to mainland Nova Scotia by a causeway over the Strait of Canso. The land is varied, green and fertile in the south, rocky and barren on the northeastern edge of Cape Breton.

The French established their first New World colony here in 1604, and founded the "Habitation Port Royal" (today Annapolis Royal) a year later. The English king, James I, was unwilling to accept the French presence, but nothing ever came of his plans to create a purely British New Scotland, whence the name Nova Scotia. Scotsmen did in fact settle the area in the early 17th century, but it was not until 1713, when the French ceded their North American territories to the British after the Seven Years' War, that Nova Scotia became officially British.

Preceding pages: Rocky coast near Halifax. Left: The bagpiper in Peggy's Cove hearkens back to the Scottish settlers of 1621.

At one time Nova Scotia was the center of Acadia, and to this day French influence and a certain sense of "Acadianism," if you will, remains.

What makes Nova Scotia particularly attractive is its combination of sea and land, and the climate which is unusually mild for Canada, thanks to the sea. Nine trails for driving have been worked out that offer ways to experience the beauty of the scenery and the variety of cultures.

LIGHTHOUSE AND EVANGELINE TRAILS

The **Lighthouse Trail** beckons landlubbers and sealovers alike with its picturesque lighthouses, beaches, coves, and small fishing ports. It skirts the southwestern coast of the province, from Yarmouth to Halifax. It illustrates well the sometimes harsh realities of life as a seafarer, with tales of hidden treasures, shipwrecks, rum runners, pirate raids, war, in short everything that keeps children wide-eyed, and tends to fascinate adults as well.

Cape Sable Island has several communities of interest, besides being Nova Scotia's southernmost extension. At the **Archelaus Smith Museum** in Centreville you can find out more about marine life on and below the surface. Other mu-

NOVA SCOTIA

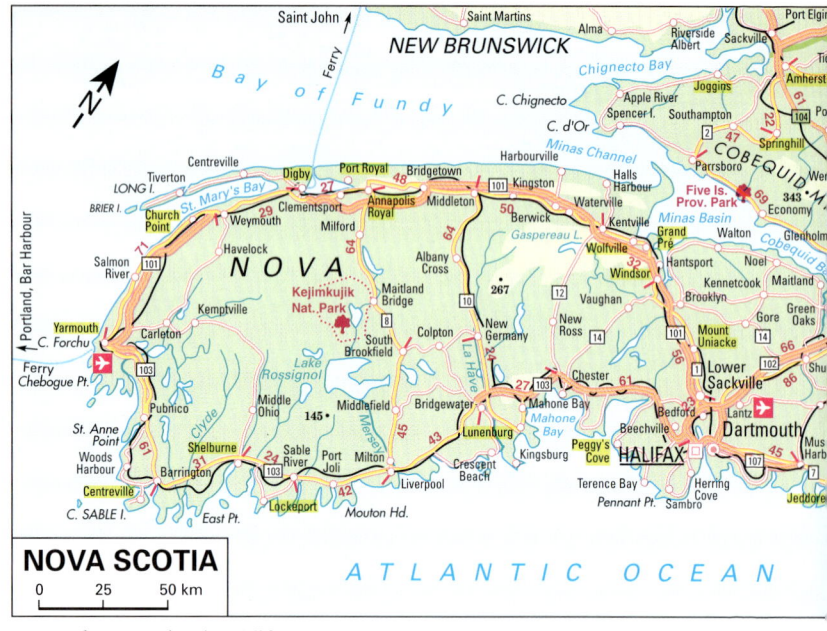

seums documenting local life are in Shelburne and in Lockeport, but not to be missed is the **Fisheries Museum of the Atlantic** in Lunenburg, which offers tours aboard two fishing ships.

Picturesque **Peggy's Cove** is Canada's most visited fishing village. Although the lighthouse is no longer operating, it is used by the Canadian post office during the summer months. The post office has its own stamp cancellation, an image of the lighthouse.

Continuing along the route toward Halifax, the road proceeds along the heavily wooded coast, with glimpses of scenic fishing villages with their nets and lobster pots along the way.

The **Evangeline Trail**, which curves across southern Nova Scotia from Yarmouth to Halifax, connects some of the oldest and most significant places in Canada's European history. It was named after the heroine of H. W. Longfellow's 1847 poem *Evangeline*, which poignantly describes the plight of the French Acadians during the Expulsion of 1755. Several points along the way, notably the historic site of Grand Pré, bring back to life that tragic episode. Today's Acadians live mainly along St. Mary's Bay in an area aptly named the French Shore, while the fertile Annapolis Valley was planted with apple orchards and strawberry fields by New Englanders who had fled from revolutionary America.

Yarmouth, settled in 1761, is the province's largest seaport west of Halifax. It provides ferry service to the United States. The coast here is rugged and there are some 50 marked historic sites in the vicinity. **Cape Fourchu**, with its historic lighthouse built in 1840, was named by Samuel de Champlain who discovered it in 1604. The trail northward leads through numerous communities that subsist on fishing, lumbering and farming. The village of **Church Point**, or Pointe de l'Eglise, may have only 318 inhabitants but it also has the tallest and largest wooden church in North America, **St. Mary's**, built in 1903-05 in the form of a cross. The church is part of the bilingual Université de Sainte-Anne, the only (partly) Francophone university in the province. The *Festival Acadien de Clare*, the oldest Acadian celebration in the Atlantic Provinces, is held here the second week in July, along with other Acadian festivals along the shore. The **Municipality of Clare** is home to Nova Scotia's largest Acadian population.

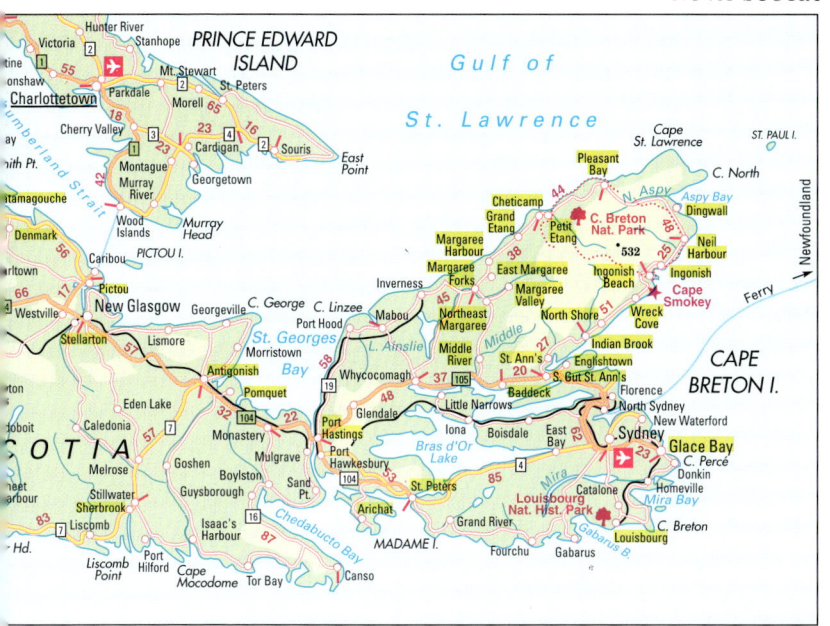

Digby overlooks the broad Annapolis Basin and is an important shipping point. The **MV Princess of Acadia**, operated by Marine Atlantic, makes three trips daily across the Bay of Fundy between Digby and Saint John, New Brunswick. A highlight of the trail is **Kejimkujik National Park**, a 143-square-mile (370-sq-km) wilderness preserve on Route 8, known as **Kejimkujik Scenic Drive**. It is 72 miles (115 km) long. **Port Royal**. **Fort Anne Historical Site** at **Annapolis Royal** preserves Canada's oldest historical fort while **Port Royal National Historic Site** commemorates the earliest European settlement in North America north of Florida. **Wolfville**, settled in the 1760s by New England planters, is the home of Acadia University. Highland Avenue leads up to Wolfville Ridge and **Stile Park** with a panoramic view of the gentle Gaspereau Valley. The trail leaves the Bay of Fundy to turn inland and head toward **Grand Pré** with its National Historic Site. The bronze on front of the church represents the pining Evangeline of the Longfellow poem. **Windsor**, the gateway leading out of the Annapolis Valley, is located exactly midway between the North Pole and the Equator. The trail continues across the province to **Mount Uniacke** and the provincial museum of **Uniacke House**.

GLOOSCAP TRAIL

Glooscap was a mighty warrior who ruled the Micmacs of Nova Scotia long before the white man arrived on his land. According to legend his magic controlled the huge Fundy tides. He lived in perfect harmony with his animal friends until one day he became angry when Beaver

GLOOSCAP TRAIL / SUNRISE TRAIL

taunted his people. In a fury he flung out five clumps of mud, which rose out of the sea to become the **Five Islands**. At the same time he scattered the semiprecious jewels that rockhounds from around the world come searching for. The trail named after Glooscap makes its way from the New Brunswick border along Bay of Fundy shores for 221 miles (355 km). There are well-tended hiking paths, pretty waterfalls, and tidal bores that make rivers run backwards, as well as **Five Islands Provincial Park** and one of Canada's richest coal seams displayed partly at the **Miner's Museum** in **Springhill**. The trail goes from the **Fort Edward National Historic Site** near **Windsor** and wanders to **Truro** for tidal bore viewing, to Five Islands Park, down to **Cape d'Or Lighthouse** and past the fossil cliffs at **Joggins** to Amherst. At low tide visitors can walk way out onto the **Minas Basin** on the sea bed, or dig for clams along the water line. Amethyst, agate, jasper and onyx, or fossils are some of the treasures found along the cliffs.

SUNRISE TRAIL

This coastal route skirts the warm waters of the Northumberland Strait where long sandy beaches mark the way through surf and sand and old Scottish settlements. Here the Nova Scotian Scottish Connection is celebrated with the sounds of bagpipes, drum and highland fiddle. The lobster fishers bringing in their always livens up the wharfs, while inland there are hiking trails and old mills where flour is still ground the old-fashioned way. From **Amherst** the trail stretches to the **Canso Causeway** and **Cape Breton Island**, passing the **Cumberland County Museum** (Amherst), the **Sunrise Trail Museum** (Tatamagouche), the **Balmoral Grist Mill** (Balmoral Hills), the **Sutherland Steam Mill** (Denmark), and the **Pictou Country Historical Mu-**

Above: Most-photographed harbor in Canada – Peggy's Cove.

seum (in Pictou, birthplace of Nova Scotia, where the annual *Pictou Lobster Carnival* has been held since 1934), through **Arisaig Park** and the university town of **Antigonish**, another Micmac word, this one with the neat meaning "the place where branches were broken off" (by bears gathering beechnuts).

Next comes the tiny village of **Pomquet**, settled in 1761 by Acadians from St. Malo, Brittany, birthplace of explorer Jacques Cartier. **Pomquet Beach Park** features supervised swimming and a picnic area.

CABOT TRAIL

Nova Scotia's Cabot Trail is as adventurous as its namesake and alive with the Scottish, French and Micmac Indian heritage of the land. It leads along the northern tip of Cape Breton Island and is probably one of the most beautiful drives in North America. Wild and rugged, it was named for sailor and navigator John Cabot, who explored these shores in the pay of England's Henry VII.

Beginning and ending at Baddeck on the quiet reaches of Bras d'Or Lake on the southeastern coast of Cape Breton Island, the trail loops north around the highlands at the top of the island and around a sprinkling of old French settlements on the west coast before heading inland east to Baddeck again. It wends its way over 1000-ft-high (300-m) headlands, through cozy coastal fishing ports and simple villages, where Scottish and French accents make intriguing music for the traveler's ear.

The main attraction in **Baddeck** is the **Alexander Graham Bell National Historic Site**, overlooking the waters of the Bras d'Or. Bell did more than just invent the telephone. He dabbled in engineering, developing a hydrofoil that is displayed in the museum, and even found a system to teach the deaf. The site honors his wide range of achievements in grand style. At St. Ann's, 12 miles (18 km) north of Baddeck, the **Gaelic College of Celtic Arts and Crafts** is the only institution of its kind in North America. The college preserves Nova Scotia's Scottish heritage by offering instruction in Gaelic language, song and customs. In the **Great Hall of the Clans**, the tartans hang proud and bright and in **Giant MacAskill Pioneer's Museum** repose relics of the Scottish settlers who chose St. Ann's natural harbor because a fearful gale blew them into haven there.

To the north, birds like the greater shearwater, Leach's petrel, the red phalarope and the puffin hover overhead as the trail leads through tiny places like **Indian Brook**, **North Shore**, **Skir Dhu** and **French River** to **Wreck Cove**, whose jagged coastline tells its tale as honestly as its name.

Soon the road begins to climb **Cape Smokey**, a 1,200-foot (375-m) ascent along breathless hairpin turns leading to Ingonish. The cape is a high promontory; its crown of white mist gives its name.

Ingonish sits between North Bay and South Bay, with rugged **Middle Head Peninsula** separating the two and with spectacular views of both the Ingonish coastline and the surrounding highlands. It is one of the oldest settlements on the Atlantic seaboard; Portuguese fishermen wintered here as early as 1521 and the name is believed to have Portuguese origins.

Ingonish Beach is headquarters for **Cape Breton Highland National Park**, a great tableland lying between the Atlantic Ocean and the Gulf of St. Lawrence, rising precipitously from sea level to a height of 1,750 feet (546 m). At this point the trail begins to outline the park high above the water. Inland the park is crisscrossed with hiking trails. Fox, coyote, mink, bobcats, moose and white-tailed deer sometimes show themselves to visitors, and the elusive lynx hides out here in its last Nova Scotia stronghold.

The trail continues past **Neil Harbour**, a quaint fishing village where wharfs are piled high with lobster traps and fishermen sell fish and lobster directly from their boats. The sands of **Dingwall**, another fishing village along the way, are great for clam digging, and the two lighthouses, one on each side of the sandbar, make for a pretty picture. The base of **Sugar Loaf Mountain** near **Cabot Landing** is the site of a yearly reenactment every June of the landing of John Cabot and his son Sebastian.

The northernmost point of the Cabot Trail is **Cape North** that has a community museum relating the history of the area.

Then the trail leads up out of **Sunrise Valley**, along spectacular gorges, toward **North Mountain** 1,460 feet (445 m). Lookouts along the way have been well chosen especially that on the summit of

Above: Neil Harbour, idyllic fishing village in the northeast of Cape Breton. Right: He made a rich haul.

Big Intervale and of **North Aspy River**, which flows north into Aspy Bay. The trail then descends the slopes of North Mountain to **Pleasant Bay**. Until 1927 the town could only be reached by water or by a narrow footpath over the mountains that encircle it. Three rivers empty into the bay, and though there is some farming, fishing is the livelihood of the locals, who are mostly of Scottish and English descent. The village is surrounded by the largest sugar maple stand in Atlantic Canada, with 300-year-old trees.

Heading south from Pleasant Bay to the Cheticamp River, a fine salmon stream, the trail winds through a landscape of deep valleys and lofty peaks, crossing **French Mountain**, which stands at 1,492 feet (455 m).

Another entrance to Cape Breton Highlands National Park lies between **Petit Étang** and **Cheticamp**. At Petit Étang ("little pond") begins the four-hour **Acadian Trail** leading to the top of the Highlands with a panoramic view of the area. The people of Petit Étang and Cheticamp are descendants of those Acadians expelled from mainland Nova Scotia by the British in 1755. **Les Trois Pignons** in Cheticamp is the Acadian fishing village's information and genealogical center with exhibits of local artists.

The trail leaves the Highlands and continues through **Grand Etang** ("big pond") to the **Margaree Valley**, where field and forest are dotted with salmon pools.

The **Salmon Museum** in **Northeast Margaree** is dedicated to the history of the river and its denizen. The **Museum of Cape Breton Heritage**, displaying local history and handicrafts, is also located here. From Margaree Harbor on the coast the river goes east off the Cabot Trail onto a local road through **East Margaree, Margaree Forks, Margaree Center** and **Margaree Valley**, small places famous for large spring and fall salmon runs. The trail from Northeast Margaree crosses the Middle River to reach the little villages of **Upper Middle River**, **Middle River** and **Lower Middle River**. The Cabot Trail then joins the Trans-Canada Highway 105 back to Baddeck.

THREE CAPE BRETON TRAILS

Three older trails explore more of Cape Breton island. The **Marconi Trail** is a rugged coastal road from Glace Bay to **Louisbourg** on the island's eastern shore.

At trail's end is the **Fortress of Louisbourg**, a step back in time to the glorious days of colonial France. It was once the protector of a large fishing port and an obvious insult to the British, who razed it in 1760. Canada's largest historical reconstruction, the fort takes a full day to tour.

At Glace Bay, the **Marconi National Historic Site** marks the location of Marconi's first transatlantic wireless broadcast in 1902. Another place of interest is the **Miners Museum** at Quarry Point, where former miners give tours through a real coal mine.

Above: Fort Louisbourg, lovingly restored, was once a French fortress on the Atlantic.

The **Fleur-de-lys Trail** has a strong French-Acadian flavor. Some of the oldest and most atmospheric fishing ports in North America are here on **Isle Madame**, a 400-year-old Acadian enclave. **Arichat**, with its commanding view of the ocean, is a perfect example, though its erstwhile prosperity has dwindled considerably. The **Lenoir Museum** is one of the attractions. **St. Peters**, on the "mainland" gave its name to an important canal that was begun in 1854 to connect Bras d'Or Lake to the Atlantic. The village also has two museums, one honoring the Canadian marine photographer William MacAskill, the other the life and times of the French explorer Nicolas Denis.

The **Ceilidh Trail** along both St. George's Bay and the Northumberland Strait meets the Cabot Trail at Margaree Forks. Ceilidh is Gallic for partying and true to its name, it is lively: almost everyone along this trail seems to either play the fiddle or is proficient at Scottish step dancing. The **Mabou Highlands** offer rugged coastal cliffs, and fine beaches.

MARINE DRIVE

This famous highway skirts the edge of the sea along the capes and beaches, marshes, estuaries and headlands along the Atlantic. Fine salmon and trout fishing is to be found in the rivers and streams heading inland.

Fisherman's Life Museum at **Jeddore** reveals the homespun life of a turn-of-the-century fisherman. **Musquodoboit Harbour**, besides being a sight in itself, also has an interesting Railway Museum with a good collection of old cars and railroad paraphenalia. At **Sherbrooke Village** things are pretty much the same as they were back in 1870, minus the excitement of a gold rush. The guides in period costumes do a fine job recreating the atmosphere of these bygonedays as they introduce visitors to the restored houses.

GUIDEPOST: NOVA SCOTIA

NOVA SCOTIA
(Telephone area code: 902)

Accommodation

EVANGELINE TRAIL
YARMOUTH: *LUXURY:* **Rodd Grand Hotel**, 417 Main St. Tel: 1-800-565-RODD. *MODERATE:* **Journey's End Motel**, 96 Starrs Rd. Tel: 742-1119. *BUDGET:* **Clementine's B & B**, 21 Clements St. Tel: 742-0079.
DIGBY: *LUXURY:* **Pines Resort Hotel**, Shore Rd. Tel: 245-2511. *MODERATE:* **Admiral Digby Inn**, French Shore Rd. Tel: 245-2531 or 1-800-465-6262. *BUDGET:* **Thistle Down Inn**, 98 Montague Row, Tel: 245-4490.
ANNAPOLIS ROYAL: *MODERATE:* **Bread and Roses Country Inn**, 82 Victoria St. Tel: 532-5727. *BUDGET:* **The Poplars B & B**, 124 Victoria St. Tel: 532-7936.
WOLFVILLE: **Blomidon Inn**, 127 Main St. Tel: 542-2291.

GLOOSCAP TRAIL
AMHERST: *MODERATE:* **National B&B Homestead**, Hwy 104 Exit 3 Tel: 667-5513. **Pied Piper Motel**, Upper Nappan RR6 Tel: 66703891.
TRURO: *MODERATE:* **Keddy's Motor Inn**, 437 Prince St. Tel: 895-1651. *BUDGET:* **Nestle Inn B&B**, 67 Duke St. Tel: 893-7509.

SUNRISE TRAIL
PICTOU: *MODERATE:* **Braeside Inn**, 80 Front St., Tel: 486-4288. *BUDGET:* **Willow House Inn**, 3 Willow St. Tel: 485-5740.

CABOT TRAIL
BADDECK: *MODERATE:* **Telegraph House**, Chebucto St., Tel: 295-9988. *BUDGET:* **The Point B&B**, 4 Twining St., Tel: 295-3368.
INGONISH: *LUXURY:* **Keltic Lodge**, Ingonish Beach, Tel: 285-2880. *MODERATE:* **The Island Inn**, Ingonish Beach, Tel: 285-2404.

CAPE BRETON TRAILS
LOUISBOURG: *MODERATE:* **Louisbourg Motel**, 1225 Main St., Tel: 733-2844. *BUDGET:* **The Manse B&B**, 17 Strathcona St., Tel: 733-3155.

LIGHTHOUSE TRAIL
PEGGY'S COVE VICINITY: *MODERATE:* **Clifty Cove Motel**, Indian Harbor Route 333, 1.6 mi (2.5 km) northwest of Peggy's Cove.
Seabright Bed & Breakfast, Hwy 103 Exit 5, Route 333 to Seabright, Tel: 823-2987.

Museums / Historic Sites
Grand Pré National Historic Site, Acadian Village, May 15-Oct 15, 9 a.m.-6 p.m., grounds all year. **Fort Anne National Historical Site**, Annapolis Royal, May 15-Oct 15 daily, rest of year Mon-Fri, 10 p.m.-5 a.m. **Port Royal National Historic Site**, Port Royal, May 15-Oct 15, 9 a.m.-6 p.m. **Uniacke House**, Mount Uniacke, May 15-Oct 31, Mon-Sat 9:30 a.m.-5:30 p.m.; Sun 1-5:30 p.m. **Miner's Museum**, Springhill, June 1-30, 10 a.m -5 p.m.; July 1-Aug 31, 9 a.m.-8 p.m.; Sept 1-Oct 14, 10 a.m.-4 p.m. **Cumberland County Museum**, 150 Church St. Amherst, Mar 1-June 1, Tue-Sat 10 a.m.-4 p.m.; June 1-Labor Day, Mon-Sat 9 a.m.-5 p.m. Sun 2- 5 p.m.; Labor Day-Dec 1, Tue-Sat 10 a.m.-4 p.m. Sun 2-5 p.m.; Dec 1-Mar 1, Wed-Sat 10 a.m.-4 p.m. **Sunrise Trail Museum**, Main St. Tatamagouche, daily in summer, weekends only early June and late Sept. **Balmoral Grist Mill**, Balmoral Mill, May 15-Oct 15, Mon-Sat 9:30 a.m.-5:30 p.m. Sun 1-5:30 p.m. **Sutherland Steam Mill**, Denmark, May 15-Oct 15, Mon-Sat 9:30 a.m.-5:30 p.m., Sun 1-5:30 p.m. **Mining Museum and Library**, Stallerton, June 15-Sept 15, 10 a.m.-2 p.m. **Alexander Graham Bell National Historic Park**, Baddeck, July 1-Sept 30, 9 a.m.-9 p.m., rest of year 9 a.m.-5 p.m. **Great Hall of the Clans**, South Gut St. Ann's, May 15-Oct 15, 8:30 a.m.-4:30 p.m.; July-Aug 4:30-8 p.m. **Giant MacAskill Pioneer's Museum**, Englishtown, May 20-Oct 14, 9 a.m.-6 p.m. **Les Trois Pignons**, Cheticamp, May-Oct Mon-Fri 9 a.m.-5 p.m.; July-Aug daily 9 a.m.-8 p.m. **Fortress of Louisbourg National Historic Site**, Louisbourg, June 1-Sept 30, 9:30 a.m.-5 p.m.; July 1-Aug 31, 9 a.m.-6 p.m., outdoor walking tours rest of year. **Marconi National Historic Site**, Glace Bay, mid-June-Labor Day daily 10 a.m.-6 p.m. **Miners Museum**, Glace Bay, June 7-Sept , 10 a.m.-6 p.m.; Sept-June Mon-Fri 9 a.m.-4 p.m. **Fisherman's Life Museum**, Jeddore, May 15-Oct 15, Mon-Sat 9:30 a.m.-5:30 p.m. Sun 1-5 p.m. **Sherbrooke Village**, Sherbrooke Hill, May 15-Oct 15, 9:30 a.m.-5:30 p.m.

Tourist Information
Tourism Nova Scotia, PO Box 130, Halifax, Tel: 424-4248.
AMHERST: Highway 104 just past the New Brunswick border on the right. Mid- June-Mid Sept 8 a.m.-9 p.m.; remainder of year 8:30 a.m.-4:30 p.m.
ANNAPOLIS ROYAL: At Annapolis Tidal Power Project, Route 1, Evangeline Trail. May 15-Oct 15, 9 a.m.-5 pm.; July-August 9 a.m.-8 p.m.
ANTIGONISH: Off Highway 104, Exit 32 going east. June 1-Sept 30, 9 a.m.-5 p.m.; July-Aug 8 a.m.-8 p.m. **DIGBY**: Shore Road en route from ferry terminal. May 15-Oct 15, 9 a.m.-5 p.m.; July-August 9 a.m.-8 p.m. **PICTOU**: Off rotary at town limits. July-August 8 a.m.-10 p.m.; May 15-June 30 and Sept 1-Oct 15, 9 a.m.-5 p.m.
PORT HASTINGS: On right after crossing causeway to Cape Breton. July-Aug 9 a.m.-9 p.m.; May 15-June 30 and Sept 1-Oct 15, 9 a.m.-5 p.m.
YARMOUTH: 228 Main St., up the hill from the Marine Atlantic Terminal. Open July-August 8:30 a.m.-8:30 p.m.; May 15-June 30 and Sept 1- Oct 15, 9 a.m.-5 p.m.

HALIFAX

HALIFAX

Although Halifax is the capital of Nova Scotia and the cultural, commercial and industrial center of all the Atlantic Provinces, it does not exude a brusque bigcity atmosphere. Instead, the salty tang of the sea permeates the city with a dreamy, leisurely quality, without it being in the least way sleepy. Halifax, whose population is about 320,000, lies on a rugged rocky bootshaped peninsula jutting out into the Atlantic Ocean. It is still a growing city, but it has not forgotten its relationship to the past. A cosmopolitan outlook is well balanced by respect for tradition, the older values of another day. The result is a vital and dynamic atmosphere combined with a pleasant nostalgic feeling for the seafaring days. For Halifax is first and foremost a port city and has been in Fact since its founding in 1749.

Halifax's rocky peninsula provides the area with two harbors, the outer harbor, which offers extensive berthing facilities, and the inner Bedford Basin, deep enough for the world's largest ships. Halifax has a twin city, Dartmouth, Nova Scotia's second largest city. It was incorporated in 1961 when it increased its area tenfold by absorbing surrounding suburbs. It faces Halifax across the deep basin which provides sailing and boating for the close communities of Halifax, Dartmouth, and a third, the town of Bedford.

Haligonian History

Halifax was founded by the British to establish their strength in the North Atlantic and the many old stone and wooden buildings, highly valued as re-

Left: Student as a "Guard of the 78 Highlanders" in front of the citadel in Halifax.

minders of the past, provide a picturesque contrast to today's modern office towers. The striking skyline on the edge of the waters of Halifax harbor looms protectively over the historic properties along the waterfront, providing a fine example of the Haligonian blend of old and new.

The history of Halifax began much earlier than its founding in 1749. Long before the white man came, Micmac Indians used the harbor for fishing, hunting, and as a point of departure for war expeditions. In 1605 Samuel de Champlain found the harbor but it was not until 1648 that the French, coming to colonize a New France, established the fishing center of Chebucto there. The Micmacs got along well with the French while doing their best to discourage colonial British fishermen who sailed up from Nantucket to help themselves to the rich harvest in the sea. When the British forces came to challenge French claim to the land, they accused the French of setting the Indians against them. In spite of what support the Indians might have provided, mainland Nova Scotia was lost to the French in 1713, and when the French constructed Fort Louisbourg on Cape Breton Island, Colonel Edward Cornwallis countered by founding Halifax.

For many years the city was merely a military garrison until British sovereignty was established over the whole of Canada in 1763. Halifax then became a keystone in the defense strategy of the western world, an important station on the Atlantic seaboard for the British army and navy. The city thrived both during American Revolution, when thousands of British Loyalists fled to Nova Scotia from New England, and again during the War of 1812. Queen Victoria's father, Prince Edward, was instrumental in fortifying Halifax with a mighty tower, leading it to boast the strongest defenses outside of Europe. The port was an British army and navy base until both defense and dockyard were taken over by the Canadian government. During World War One and World War Two Halifax's strategic position on the Atlantic seaboard made it Canada's largest and most important naval base. Halifax was never attacked, never beseiged, but nevertheless late in World War One, in December of 1917, the city suffered a traumatic maritime disaster. A Belgian relief ship, the *Imo*, collided in the harbor with the French ship *Mont Blanc* carrying a full cargo of munitions, creating the largest man-made explosion before the nuclear age. More than 2000 people were killed and almost all of the north end of Halifax was destroyed. Windows as far as 50 miles away shattered as all 3000 tons of the *Mont Blanc* were blasted into bits and sent far and wide: one of her cannon barrels landed three and a half miles away and her anchor shank, weighing more than half a ton, flew two miles in the opposite direction. The shock wave was felt on Cape Breton Island 270 miles away. Now on every December 6th at 9am there is a service by the Memorial Bells at Fort Needham, close to where the *Mont Blanc* exploded. There is an exhibit on what is simply called "The Explosion" at the Maritime Museum of the Atlantic on Lower Water Street.

The heart of Halifax

The **Harbor**, as could be expected, is at the very heart of city life, and it is the place to begin a tour of Halifax. Catching a commented tour on the *Haligonian III* is the best way of getting a "fish eye" view of the piers, the dockyards and the skyline of Halifax. The waterfront, a warm, vibrant place, offers visitors the opportunity to stroll along the piers, visit museums, take a walking tour and shop at the **Historic Properties on the Harbor** at Upper Water and Hollis Streets. The old wood and stone buildings at Historic Properties have been restored, and evoke

Above: Lighthouse on George's Island in front of the skyline in Halifax. Right: The "Bluenose II," under full sail.

HISTORIC PROPERTIES

the bygone days when hard cartwheels rattled over the cobblestones and the cries of the harbormaster echoed over the water. Harbor tours and boat trips are offered daily, including seasonal sailings aboard the famous *Bluenose II*, a schooner that is both the pride of Haligonians and the "sailing ambassador" of Nova Scotia. It was built in 1961 in Lunenburg where the original *Bluenose* still berths today. The old schooner, which dominated international fishing competitions in the 1920s and 1930s, is depicted on the Canadian dime. When not available for public sailings, the ship is present at festivals throughout Nova Scotia.

From the Harbor there are fishing charters and a regular ferry service between Halifax and Dartmouth. The Dartmouth waterfront has boardwalks leading from the Dartmouth Ferry Terminal, providing visitors with excellent views of McNabs Island, Georges Island and the two bridges, the A. Murray MacKay and the Angus L. MacDonald, which span the harbor and link Halifax and Dartmouth.

Dartmouth has the oldest saltwater ferry system in North America: the first harbor ferry, beginning service in 1752, was a large rowboat with a sail. Today the ferry ride across the scenic harbor from the Dartmouth waterfront can be had for only 50 cents.

The **Maritime Museum of the Atlantic** at the Harbor records Halifax's long romance with the sea. It serves to certain extent as the hub of the waterfront and gives major insight into the history and workings of seafaring life. It has exhibits on the navy on sailing days, on shipwrecks and lifesaving, the age of steam, and the restored chandlery of William Robertson and Son as well as an extensive collection of sailing memorabilia. The lens used in the Sambro lighthouse from 1906 to 1967 is impressive seen at close range, as are colorful ship's figureheads and scale models of vessels. There are relics of the tragic sinking of the Titanic, lost off the Grand Banks of Newfoundland in 1912. Many of the dead were brought to Halifax; some of those

HISTORIC PROPERTIES

who could be identified were taken home for burial but 155 bodies that could not are buried in **Fairview**, a suburb of Halifax.

Moored behind the museum during the summer months is *HMCS Sackville*, a restored flower-class corvette used on North Atlantic convoys during World War Two. The ship has been restored as a memorial to the courage of all who served in Canada's navy. Visitors are encouraged to examine every nook and cranny as well as to view a multimedia presentation graphically narrated by a veteran of the Battle of the Atlantic, which is in the interpretation center immediately adjacent to the ship. Also berthed at the wharf behind the museum is the *CSS Acadia*, a hydrographic vessel that was a pioneer in charting the waters of the North Atlantic.

Province House, seat of government and Canada's oldest provincial legislative building, was built between 1811 and

Above: Donated by Prince Edward – the Bell Tower, landmark of the city.

1819. Charles Dickens, on a visit to Halifax, concisely described it as "a gem of Georgian architecture."

Governing the port of Halifax has always been done in style. Neo-Gothic **Old City Hall**, built in 1890, 50 years after Halifax was incorporated as a city, welcomes visitors not only to stroll through its portals, but to actually meet with the mayor during an informal afternoon tea every weekday during July and August from 3:30pm to 4:30pm. The mayor's arrival is heralded by the Halifax Town Crier. This old tradition of publicly calling attention to important local events has been going on ever since the port was first established.

City Hall is at one end of **Grand Parade**, a park-like square which, as its name suggests, was originally used for parades. At the other end is **St. Paul's**, the first Anglican church in Canada and the oldest church in Halifax (1750). Lodged above the door in the north wall (inside a porch that was added later) is a piece of the ammunition ship *Mont Blanc*, blasted into the wall from the explosion two miles away. Another result of the explosion is the mysterious silhouette of a human head in the third upstairs window along Argyle Street. Legend has it that at the time, the minister was blown through the window. Far less ephemeral are the memorial tables and gravestones of celebrated Nova Scotia pioneers.

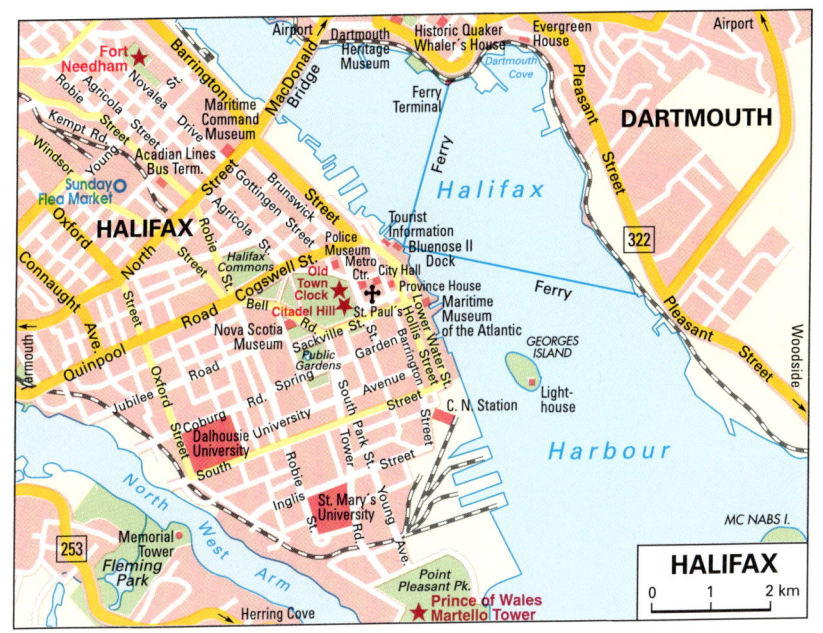

Metro Centre, with the large modern **World Trade & Convention Center** is adjacent. The Metro Centre, a world-caliber meeting site, seats 10,000 people for live concerts, indoor sports (it is the home of the Halifax Citadels hockey team), and Halifax's reknowned Nova Scotia International Tatoo. The convention center is easily spotted by its huge weathervane depicting the famous *Bluenose*. It houses a hall of fame devoted to sports in Nova Scotia, with photos, clippings, trophies, medals and other paraphernalia. There is also a library and theater on the expansive premises.

The recently restored **Old Town Clock** at the base of Citadel Hill looks toward the harbor down George Street through Grand Parade. Regarded as a symbol of Halifax, the landmark has recently been restored to its original 1803 appearance, when it was presented to the town by Prince Edward, son of George III. He was military commander-in-chief at the Halifax garrison from 1784 until 1800 and had a special liking for round buildings.

Another such structure born of his particular preference was **St. George's Anglican Church** on Brunswick Street, which dates to about 1800. Prince Edward's other round contribution can be found in Point Pleasant Park at the "tip" of Halifax, so to speak. The **Martello Tower** was borrowed from Corsica, its thick walls almost immune to 18th-century artillery. A fairly small number of soldiers could hold out for quite a while against a stronger enemy. This defensive system became fashionable throughout much of eastern Canada. The function and history of the Martello Tower is extensively described inside.

CITADEL HILL

Citadel Hill

Ever since the city was founded in 1749, **Citadel Hill** and its star-shaped fortress have served not only a defensive purpose. During clipper ship days the signal masts atop the hill were used to tell merchants their ships had arrived in harbor. The current fortress at **Citadel National Historic Park** is the fourth such structure there. Built between 1828 and 1856 by British soldiers, it is a regal reminder of the modern city's historic foundations. There's a daily reminder as well, when soldiers fire the **Noon Day Cannon** from the ramparts, keeping alive a century-old tradition. Exhibitions depict the evolution of the fortress, and there are guided tours and a sight and sound show. Often college students portraying members of the 78th Highlanders and the Royal Artillery. For a while, the city used leftover cannons to mark street corners. The last remaining one is at Barrington and Bishop Streets. For military buffs, the **Army Museum** in the Cavalier Building at the Citadel has an extensive collection of military memorabilia.

The **Old Burying Ground** on Barrington Street at the foot of Spring Garden Road received its first grave the day after Cornwallis arrived to found the city. Back then it marked the far southern boundary of the pioneer settlement. The site was recently restored and there is an interpretation center to help visitors ramble through Halifax's past and learn the history of this first "common" burial ground in the city. The oldest stone is from 1754, and marks the grave of the man who ran the first ferry across Halifax Harbor, John Conner.

The **Nova Scotia Museum** on Summer Street contains comprehensive displays of both social and natural history of the province. The museum also features temporary displays from international traveling exhibits, and there is an exten-

Above: Loading a historic cannon on the citadel. Right: The region's coastal fishermen still work as their ancestors did.

sive collection of Micmac Indian artifacts. Sometimes public activities such as local historic architecture tours, Nova Scotia birdwatching expéditions, and even an occasional clam dig, are offered.

The **Brewery Centre** is indeed in an old brewery and houses shops and restaurants (and offices). It is also the site of a weekend produce and crafts market open Friday and Saturday from 7am and selling various handicrafts, jams, breads and fresh vegetables.

A 17-acre English country garden lies behind the wrought-iron gates of **Halifax Public Gardens**. Begun in 1866, the Gardens, the oldest formal gardens in North America, are a collection of Victorian rockeries, flowing brooks, sundials, fountains, flowerbeds, weeping willows and subtropical plants enjoyed by the resident ducks, swans and pigeons as well as the public. Sunday afternoons there is a musical performance in the bandstand, built to commemorate Queen Victoria's Golden Jubilee in 1887. **Halifax Commons**, Canada's oldest park, is filled with locals enjoying their cricket matches, lawn bowling and soccer. This popular playground, a large grassy expanse stretching to the west and northwest of Citadel Hill, originally was set aside as a pasture for cattle belonging to citizens. **Fort Needham**, on the site of an old fortification, is a memorial park overlooking the north end of the city, the section most devastated by the Halifax Explosion of 1917. A handsome bell tower has been erected on the crest of the hill and is illuminated at night. Continuing northeastward, one cames to the **Police Museum** on Gottingen Street, which has a comprehensive exhibition of photos and artifacts relating to the over 150-year-old Halifax Police Department.

Beyond the center

Historic **Fort McNab** on McNabs Island, lying at the outer extremity of Halifax Harbor, was established in late 1880. From the first decade of Halifax's settlement on, it played a major role in protecting the British naval station at Halifax. Designed to mount breechloading guns, it was significantly more powerful than the older forts, and formed a defense system unique to the North American continent at that time.

York Redoubt National Historic Site is a 200-year-old fortification situated on a high bluff overlooking the entrance to Halifax Harbor about 6 miles (11 km) from the center. Established in 1793 at the outbreak of war between Britain and France, it was a key element in the defense of Halifax Harbor during the second half of the 19th century as well. It features a collection of rifles, mounted muzzle-loading guns, a photo display, and an excellent view of the harbor.

Dartmouth, which can be accessed by ferry or by car over the MacDonald bridge, has its share of museums. The **Dartmouth Heritage Museum** displays highlights of that city's history, as well as

DARTMOUTH / CULTURAL SCENE

an art gallery with changing exhibits. The **Quaker Whaler's House**, built around 1785 goes back to the days when whalers from Nantucket Island (Massachusetts) used to stop in Halifax. The **Evergreen Historic House** is a fine example of a large restored Victorian home. It contains the Dartmouth Heritage Museum collection of Victorian furniture.

The Cultural Scene

Festivals and fanfare go on most of the year in Halifax, from lobster races to town crier contests. Halifax celebrates its birthday in summer (July 24 is Natal Day) with various activites, fireworks, and a concert on Citadel Hill. And there are more than 20 fine commercial art galleries in the city offering works of well-known local artists as well as others. The **Art Gallery of Nova Scotia** is a provincial agency for the collection, preservation and exhibition of works of art as well as for art education. The gallery houses provincial collections of fine arts, and organizes and displays traveling exhibits. The **Dalhousie Art Gallery** at Dalhousie University exhibits Canadian drawings and Canadian, American and European paintings, sculpture, prints, archeology and graphics year round. The new **Nova Scotia Centre for Craft and Design** houses the offices, craft gallery and studio facilities of the Production Crafts Section, Cultural Affairs Division of the Nova Scotia Department of Tourism and Culture. Created for the development, exhibition and promotion of Nova Scotia crafts, the center offers information on art and crafts throughout the province in addition to organizing exhibitions. Finally, the city's nightlife includes cabarets presenting popular artists, theatrical offerings, concerts both popular and classical, cinemas and many pubs, some with live music. The city also has no dearth of restaurants, whereby no visitor should fail to try the local seafood.

Above: Halifax has an active culture scene all year round.

GUIDEPOST: HALIFAX

HALIFAX
(Telephone area code: 902.)

Accommodation
LUXURY: **Château Halifax**, 1990 Barrington St., Tel: 425-6700. **Citadel Inn Halifax**, 1960 Brunswick St., Tel: 422-1391. **Delta Barrington**, 1875 Barrington St., Tel: 429-7410. **Halifax Hilton**, 1181 Hollis St., Tel: 423-7231. **Halliburton House Inn**, 5184 Morris St., Tel: 4223-2324. **Halifax Sheraton**, 1919 Upper Water St., Tel: 421-1700. *MODERATE:* **Bicentennial Motel**, 4 Melrose Ave., Tel: 443-9341. **Bluenose**, 636 Bedford Hwy., Tel: 443-3171. **Chebucto Inn**, 6151 Lady Hammond Rd., Tel: 453-4330. **Country Hospitality Inn & Suites**, 1 Yorkshire Ave., Tel: 465-4000. **King Edward Inn**, 2400 Agricola St., Tel: 422-3266. **Sea King Motel**, 560 Bedford Hwy., Tel: 443-0303. **Travellers Motel**, 773 Bedford Hwy., Tel: 835-3394. **Waverley Inn**, 1266 Barrington St., Tel: 423-9356. *BUDGET:* **Fountain View Guest House**, 2138 Robie St., Tel: 422-4169. **Gerrard Hotel**, 1234 Barrington St., Tel: 423-8614. **Heritage House Inn**, 1253 Barrington St., Tel:.423-4435. **Prince's Lodge Motel**, 554 Bedford Hwy., Tel: 443-0348.

Restaurants
CHINESE: **Alfredo, Weinstein and Ho**, 1739 Grafton St., Tel: 421-1977, Italian, Chinese, Jewish; **China Town**, 3375 Bedford Hwy.; **Great Wall**, 1649 Bedford Row; **King Wah**, 6430 Quinpool Rd.; **Oriental Restaurant**, 5361 Inglis St. *CONTINENTAL / EUROPEAN:* **Le Bistro**, 1333 South Park St.; **La Bohème**, 1541 Birmingham St.; **The Hungry Hungarian**, 5215 Blowers St. *GREEK:* **Athens**, 1558 Barrington St.; **Old Man Morias**, 1150 Barrington St. *INDIAN:* **Chicken Tandoor**, 1264 Barrington St. *ITALIAN:* **Da Maurizio Dining Room**, Brewery Complex; **The Gondola**, 5175 South St.; **Papa Gino's**, Sackville at Granville St. *JAPANESE:* **Suisha Gardens**, 1505 Barrington St. *NORTH AMERICAN:* **Mother Tucker's Food Experience**, 1668 Lower Water St.; **Mrs. Murphy's Kitchen**, 5670 Spring Garden Rd. *SEAFOOD AND STEAK:* **Clipper Bar and Grill**, Historic Properties; **Clipper Cay**, Historic Properties; **Daily Catch**, 2590 Agricola St.; **Five Fishermen**, 1740 Argyle St.; **Nemo's**, 1865 Hollis St. *VEGETARIAN:* **King Spring Roll**, 1284 Barrington St. (also Vietnamese); **Satisfaction Feast**, 1581 Grafton St.; **The Vegetarian Delight**, Queen St.

Museums
Army Museum/Halifax Citadel, June 1-14, 9 a.m.-5 p.m., June 15-Labor Day, 9a.m.-6 p.m., Labor Day-Nov. 30, 9 a.m.-5p.m. **Art Gallery of Nova Scotia**, 1741 Hollis, Tues-Sat 10 a.m.-9 p.m., Sun noon-5:30 p.m., Tel: 424-7542. **Dalhousie Art Gallery**, 6010 University, Tel: 424-7542, Tue-Fri 11 a.m.-5 p.m., Sat-Sun 1-5 p.m., closed Mon. **Dartmouth Heritage Museum**, 100 Wyse Rd. Dartmouth, June 1-Labor Day Mon-Fri 9 a.m.-9 p.m., Sat 9 a.m.-6 p.m., Sun 2-5 p.m., Sept-May Mon-Sat 1-5 p.m. Sun 2-5 p.m., Tel: 464-2300. **Evergreen House**, 26 Newcastle St. Dartmouth, July-Aug 10 a.m.-6 p.m. **Halifax Citadel National Historic Site**, Citadel Hill, June 15-Labor Day 9 a.m.-6 p.m., remainder of year 9 a.m.-5 p.m., Tel: 426-5080. **Halifax Police Museum**, 1975 Gottingen St., 8:30 a.m.-4:30 p.m. by appt. only. **Historic Quaker Whaler's House**, 57-59 Ochterloney St. July-Aug 9:30 a.m.-5:30 p.m. Tel: 464-2300. **Maritime Museum of the Atlantic**, Lower Water St., May 15-Oct 15, Mon-Sat 9:30 a.m.-5:30 p.m. (to 8 p.m.Tue), Sun 1-5:30 p.m., Oct 16-May 14 Tue-Sat 9:30 a.m.-8 p.m., Sun 1-5 p.m.; Tel: 424-7490, CSS Acadia open summer only. **Nova Scotia Centre for Craft and Design**, 1683 Barrington St., 8:30 a.m.-4:30 p.m. weekdays. **Nova Scotia Museum**, 1747 Summer St., June 15-Oct 15, Mon-Sat 9:30 a.m.-5:30 p.m. (Wed to 8 p.m.), Sun 1-5:30 p.m., Nov 1-May 14 Tue- Sat 9:30 a.m.-5 p.m. (Wed to 8 p.m.), Sun 1-5 p.m., closed Mon, Tel: 429-4610. **Nova Scotia Sport Heritage Centre**, 1800 Argyle St., weekdays 9 a.m.-4 p.m., Sat-Sun 10 a.m.-2 p.m. **Old Burying Ground**, Barrington St., June-Sept 9 a.m.-5 p.m. **Prince of Wales Martello Tower**, Point Pleasant Park, June 15-Labor Day 10 a.m.-6 p.m., Tel: 426-5080. **Province House**, Hollis St., Mid-June-Mid Sept Mon-Fri 9 a.m.-6 p.m., Sat, Sun, holidays 9 a.m.-5 p.m., mid-Sept-mid-June Mon-Fri 8:30 a.m.-4:30 p.m., except holidays, Tel: 424-8967. **York Redoubt National Historic Site**, off Purcells Cove Rd. on Rte 253, June 15-Labor Day 10 a.m.-6 p.m., Tel: 426-5080

Markets
In addition to the Farmers Market at the Brewery Centre, Tel: 492-4043, there is the Halifax Forum Sunday Flea Market, Windsor Street, 10 a.m. to 2 p.m., and another at West End Mall Sundays from 10 a.m. to 2 p.m.

Transportation
A good way to see the city is to take a **Gray Line of Halifax** tour, 6040 Almon St., Tel: 454-9321. **Cabana Tours**, PO Box 8683, Station A, Tel: 423-6066. **Murphy's on the Water**, ferry tours (2 hrs) for sightseeing, May to Oct, from Murphy's Pier, Tel: 420-1015

Tourist Information
City Hall, Duke and Barrington Streets, Tel: 421-8736; at **Halifax Airport**, Air Canada, Tel: 429-7111. **Nova Scotia Tourism and Culture,** Historic Properties, Tel: 424-4247; **Check In Nova Scotia**, South Park Street, Sackville (seasonal), Tel: 425-5781. There is an **"Info to Go"** van on the outskirts of the city. **Help Line** for crises and emergencies: Tel: 421-1188.

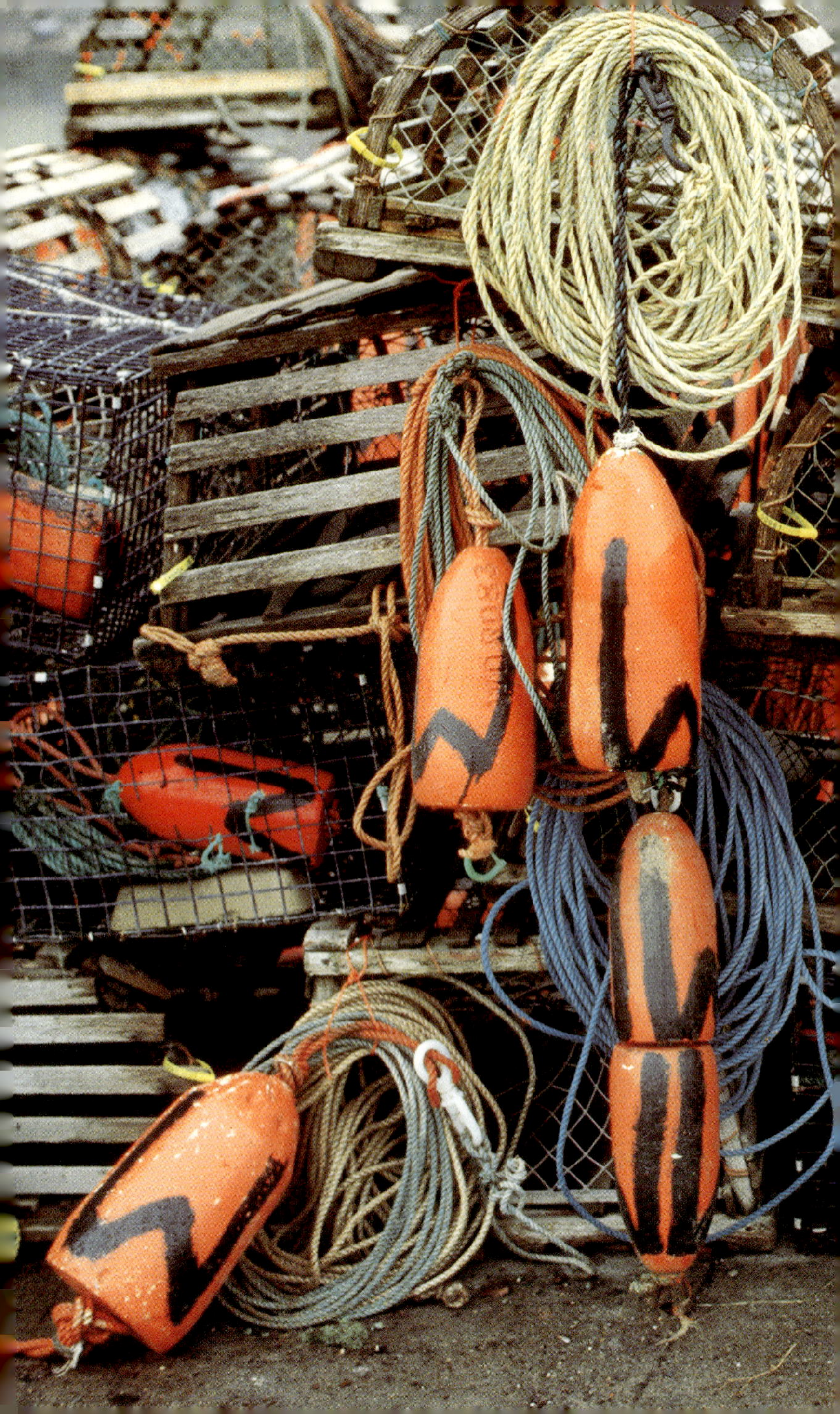

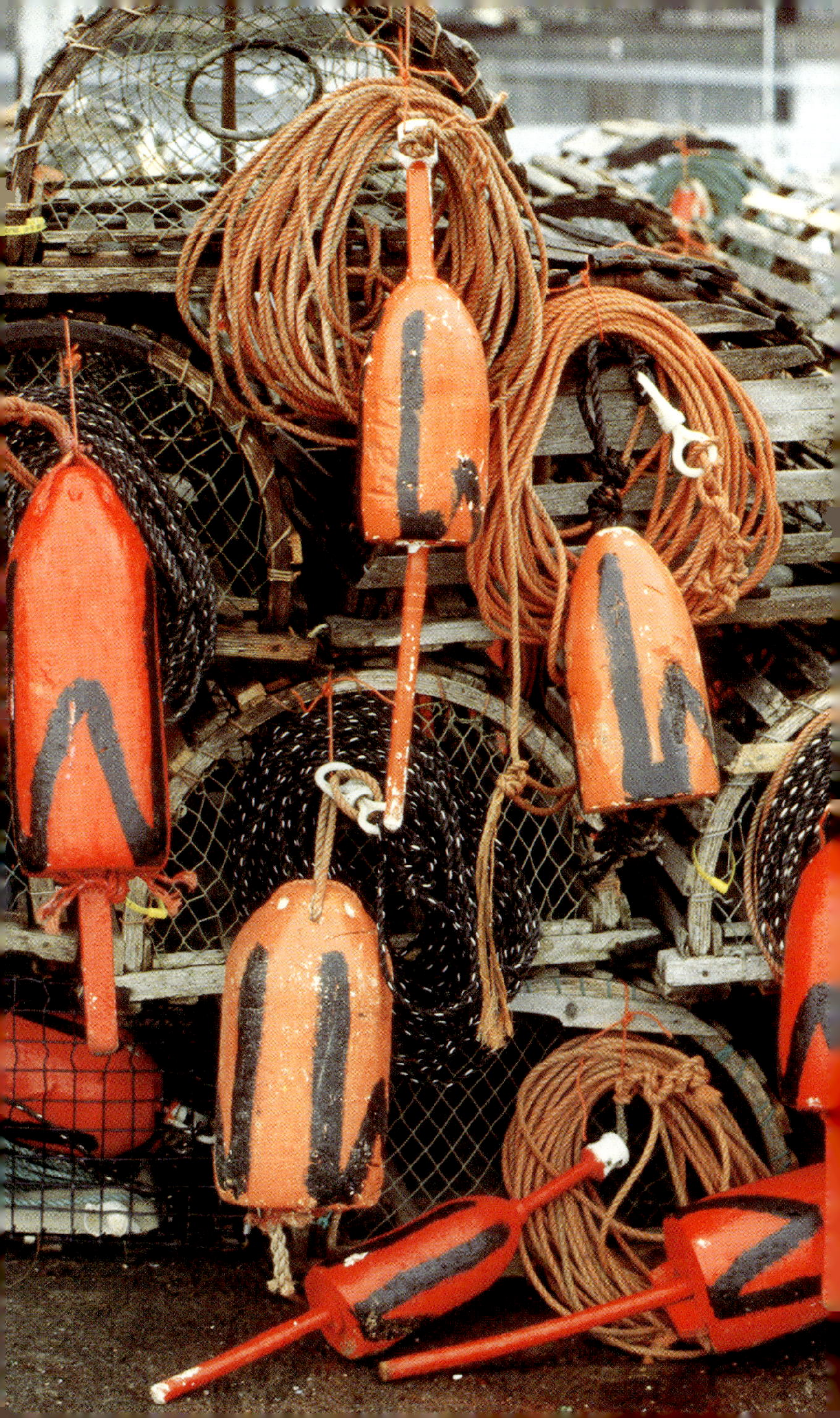

PRINCE EDWARD ISLAND

PRINCE EDWARD ISLAND

PRINCE COUNTY
QUEENS COUNTY
KINGS BYWAY

Prince Edward Island, usually referred to simply as PEI, is the smallest Canadian province. Its 2184 sq. miles (5525 sq. km) make it even smaller than some of Canada's National Parks, but it also means that the province can be toured within about five days. The island, vaguely in the shape of a crescent, lies in the Gulf of St. Lawrence. It is separated from the northern coasts of the Maritime Provinces of New Brunswick and Nova Scotia by the narrow Northumberland Strait. Two ferries cross the Strait year round: from the port of Cape Tormentine in New Brunswick and from Caribou in Nova Scotia to Wood Islands, PEI.

PEI is a well-known haven of peace and tranquillity for those seeking a place to truly "get away from it all." The islanders are warm, hospitable and very relaxed. Nature too seems to possess this tranquil quality, with expansive rolling hills where rich green and reddish farmland offer a harmonious patchwork of color. Dotting this mellifluous landscape are little villages where the pace of life has remained oblivious of the internal combustion engine and the microchip. In the recondite ports along the capricious coastline one might still find some old salts who, plied with the right lubrication, can spin a yarn longer than the Canadian border.

Preceding pages: Buoys help fisherman to locate their lobster-pots. Left: Evening at sea.

From Cradle to Cradle

The island's early inhabitants were the Micmac Indians, who welcomed its fertile soil and the abundance of fish in the surrounding and inland waters. They called this new home *abegweit*, meaning "land cradled by waters," and they lived here relatively undisturbed until the 16th century. In 1534 the French explorer Jacques Cartier first set foot on the island, but it took a while though before French settlers began arriving, their ranks swollen by Acadians from Nova Scotia, who had been expelled by the British in 1755.

Three years later, however, the British also lay claim to the "land cradled by waters," which the French explorer Champlain had called *St-Jean*, and repeated their expulsion procedures. They founded Charlottetown as their capital in 1763, naming it after the wife of the British king George III. Their arrival also opened the floodgates to settlers who came mostly from Scotland and Ireland. In 1799 the island, now a separate province, was renamed for Prince Edward, the Duke of Kent, the father of Queen Victoria.

LADY SLIPPER DRIVE

In a rather quiet fashion, the islanders maintained a sense of independence throughout much of the 19th century, especially whenever the term union was mentioned, be that with the other Maritime provinces or the rest of Canada. And it is because of this that the great conference in 1864 that led to the confederation of Canada was held in Charlottetown, which is why PEI is referred to as the "Cradle of the Confederation." PEI itself only joined nine years later.

Like their Micmac predecessors, today's islanders draw quite a livelihood from agriculture and fishing. While many fruits (raspberries, blueberries, strawberries), vegetables and grains grow well in PEI's iron-rich soil, potatoes are by far its number one cash crop. 150,000 acres are devoted to the spud, which was first cultivated here in 1771. The island's abundant annual potato yield accounts for most of Canada's potato exports, as well

Above: At ebb tide, there's always something to discover on the beach at Brackley Bay.

as more than 90% of the country's domestic seed potatoes. Tourism annually adds around $70 million dollars to PEI's economy, and is heaviest from May to October. Each PEI's counties, Prince, Queen and King, has a well-marked drive enabling visitors to quickly grasp the major sights. They are respectively – and from west to east – Lady Slipper Drive, Blue Heron Drive and Kings Byway.

PRINCE COUNTY

Lady Slipper Drive, named after a wild orchid, steers a 180-mile (290-km) course along the coast of western and northwestern PEI. It begins at the West Point Lighthouse, a century-old wooden beacon that was operated manually until full automation in 1963. The lighthouse, which stands on the island's westernmost tip on the grounds of Cedar Dunes Provincial Park, today includes a museum, handicraft outlet, dining room and guest rooms. 76 lighthouses once operated along PEI's coast, but only 16 still serve

PRINCE EDWARD ISLAND

their original purpose of steering vessels through the local shipping lanes and warning of the nearby shoreline.

Lady Slipper Drive passes by the monument to French explorer Jacques Cartier located in **Jacques Cartier Provincial Park** near the Kildare Capes. These windswept red sandstone cliffs battered by tides, especially impressed Cartier. The town of **Alberton** is known for its *fox houses*, great manors built from the proceeds of the now-defunct silver fox pelt industry. The Drive then forks: To the north it leads to **Green Provincial Park**, where the **Yeo House** (built in 1864 and named after a shipping magnate) is now a museum devoted to the old shipbuilding industry an PEI. Then comes **Malpeque Bay**, renowned throughout North America for its oysters. These mollusks are cultivated and farmed in the sheltered bays and coves along this section of PEI's coast. Another local marine bounty is Irish moss, a seaweed used in the emulsifying trade. Horses are still used in the harvesting process.

The southern route leads to the so-called Région Evangéline. French Acadiens settled the towns and villages around Egmont Bay in the early 1700s, and French remains the dominant language to this day. When the British expelled the Acadians from the island in 1758, many families hid in the woods to wait for more propitious times, thus salvaging an oasis of Francophone culture. 3 miles (5 km) west of **Mont-Carmel** on Cape Egmont is the home of the **Acadian Pioneer Village**, a re-creation of an early Acadian settlement (1800-1820) with pretty houses in bright colors that could be spotted from the sea by their fisherman owners. The town also has the only restaurant on PEI – Étoile de Mer – serving authentic Acadian dishes. Every Labor Day weekend, Acadian handicrafts, livestock and farm produce are exhibited in **Abram-Village** during Le Festival Acadien. A few miles farther, in the village of **Miscouche**, is the **Acadien Museum**, which has ancestral portraits of Acadian families from the last century among its array of artifacts .

QUEENS COUNTY

Lady Slipper Drive joins **Blue Heron Drive** in Queens County just east of **Summerside**. It follows the island's north central coast to Malpagne, the place with eastern Canada's most beautiful gardens (**Malpagne Garden**) passing through Prince Edward Island National Park before heading down to the southern shore. Just before entering the park from the western side, the road goes through the town of **New London**, birthplace of Lucy Maud Montgomery. Born in 1874, she grew up in a tiny, green-trimmed white cottage that is now a museum filled with Montgomery memorabilia including her wedding dress and original editions of her books. One of Prince Edward Island's top year-round attractions is **Green Gables House**, situated in the national park near the Cavendish entrance. This special abode plays a leading role in

Above: Sunset over St. Dunstan's Basilica, Charlottetown.

the novel *Anne of Green Gables*, written by Montgomery. Published in 1908, this romantic novel set in PEI has become a bestseller, especially among teenagers the world round. It has been adapted for screen and stage and is performed regularly during the summer at the Charlottetown Festival. Real "Anne buffs" can follow a tour that covers some of the sites from the book, and ends at Montgomery's grave in the **Cavendish cemetery**.

The finest beaches are located within the boundaries of **Prince Edward Island National Park** along the island's north coast. Two of the most popular are Cavendish and Brackley, while the beaches of Rustico Island and Dalvay are more deserted. Dunes shaped by swirling winds rise as high as 65 feet and are the dominant feature of the terrain at **Blooming Point**. Stanhope Beach is one of Canada's preferred areas for surfing.

Bathed by the warm currents of the Gulf of St. Lawrence, beaches are just one of many reasons why this is among Canada's favorite national parks. Its large tract of wetlands is home to many different species of wild geese including Canada geese, mallards, teal, ring-necked ducks and American black ducks. Bird watchers head for Brackley Marsh where it is possible to observe great blue herons, terns and perhaps even a rare piping plover, one of several endangered species in the park. Free guided events such as beachcombing and bird-watching along with evening presentations are offered throughout the year.

Charlottetown

Urbane rather than urban, PEI's largest "metropolis" is the small and tidy provincial capital of **Charlottetown** (population 15,000). Although the smallest of all provincial capitals, it played a major role in Canadian history, hosting the conference that resulted in Canadian nationhood. The building where the historic meeting of the Fathers of Confederation took place, **Province House**, is a three-story Georgian-style structure completed in 1847. The articles that officially formed a united Canadian nation in 1867 were signed in the high-ceilinged "Confederation Chamber."

The preservation ethic is strongly adhered to on PEI, and this is especially evident along Charlottetown's side streets where numerous wooden houses fin gingerbread style remain intact. In **Victoria Park** adjacent to Charlottetown harbor are several stately 19th-century structures including Government House, a white colonial building erected in 1834, and the Victorian mansion known as Beaconsfield, built in 1877 and which today houses the historical exhibits of the **PEI Museum & Heritage Foundation**. Also situated in the park facing the harbor are remnants of Fort Edward, constructed in 1805 as part of a series of fortifications to safeguard the harbor.

The most impressive of the city's contemporary buildings is the **Confederation Centre of the Arts**. Completed in 1964 as a national memorial to the Fathers of Confederation, it functions as the capital's cultural hub. The Centre houses a 1100-seat theater plus a library, art gallery with more than 1500 works and a collection of Canadian crafts. It hosts the annual **Charlottetown** Festival held from late June through mid September. Thousands flock yearly from all across Canada to the Centre theater during festival time to see performances of *Anne of Green Gables* and other Canadian musicals. The harness races held at Charlottetown **Driving Park** are another popular summer pastime. One of Canada's premier rural fairs, **Old Home Week**, takes place here in August.

After leaving Charlottetown, Blue Heron Drive winds around a peninsula south of the Capital, passing the small town of Rocky Point. Nearby is **Fort Amherst / Port-La-Joye National Historic Park**, the place where 300 French colonists came ashore in 1720 and established Port La Joie – the first white, non-Indian settlement on the island.

The British, who drove the French out in 1758, built Fort Amherst on the same spot. Only the earthworks remain visible today, and a small museum on the site explains the significance of the historical events that occurred here through an interpretive slide show and other exhibits. Nearby, a reconstructed 16th-century Micmac village illustrates how the Indians lived before the Europeans. On display are birchbark wigwams and canoes.

Moving further along down to PEI's south-central coast, the drive provides some excellent vantage points from which to observe the striking red sandstone seascapes. At the tiny fishing port of **Victoria-by-the-Sea**, the historic Victoria Playhouse stages live theater performances during the summer. This is also a good place to hunt for antiques and handicrafts or go for a sail out of Victoria harbor in an old rigged schooner.

KINGS BYWAY DRIVE

KINGS BYWAY DRIVE

Kings Byway Drive (ca 238 miles/380 km) travels around eastern Prince Edward Island is ringed by , which passes through several villages whose appearance and way of life has changed little since the turn of the century.There are also wildlife sanctuaries on this part of the island and farm homes where many families choose to spend a week or two as paying guests.

In **Orwell** on the southeast coast you should visit **Orwell Historic Village**, which dates to the late 19th century. It is today operated by the PEI Museum and Heritage Foundation. Here crops and livestock are raised and tended much as they were a century ago, while the village's shingled buildings, constructed between 1864 and 1896 still stand on their original sites.

Above: Brightly colored and shingled – picturesque farmhouses on Prince Edward Island.

Summer is festival time at Orwell, as lively *ceilidhs* – Scottish folk music fests – are scheduled weekly. Two special celebrations also take place every summer: the **Strawberry Social** in Mid July and the **Scottish Festival and Highland Games** in late Autust. At the former guests gulp down heaping portions of ice cream and strawberries and join in games and dances. The Scottish Festival recreates games played by their ancestors such as hammer throwing, tossing the caber (similar to a telephone pole) and putting the stone.

Further along the southeast coast is **Lord Selkirk Provincial Park**, marking the spot where three ships carrying 800 Scottish Highlanders from the Isle of Skye touched land in 1803 after an arduous voyage across the Atlantic. **St. John's Presbyterian Church** in the nearby village of Belfast was built by these Scottish settlers in 1823. A short detour here down a side road leads to the island's oldest lighthouse at **Point Prim**, which has been helping guide ships into Charlottetown Harbor since 1846.

Heading up toward the far eastern tip of the island (site of another attractive lighthouse), Kings Byway Drive passes by Murray Harbour inlet. The **Log Cabin Museum** in the port town of Murray Harbour contains 200-year-old antiques and relics that provides further insight into the 19th-century lifestyle on PEI.

The **Northumberland Mill and Museum** near the village of **Murray River** contains an authentic water-powered grist mill. Murray River's Handcraft Co Op Association shop has a fine selection of island crafts, while at Murray Harbour North there is a large seal colony visible from the Seal Cove Campground. And a little further beyond **Souris**, is a fisheries museum in Basin Head illustrating the means and the life associated with that local industry. A final excursion should be made along the beaches here, whose white sands "sings" when walked on.

PRINCE EDWARD ISLAND
(Area code 902)
Access / Local Transportation
By air: There are direct flights to Charlottetown daily from Montréal, Toronto and Halifax with Canadian Airlines International. Air Canada flies daily (one-stop) from Ottawa and Toronto as well as Boston and New York.

By ferry: Car ferries connecting Prince Edward Island and mainland Canada depart regularly from Cape Tormentine, New Brunswick to Borden, Prince Edward Island and from Caribou, Nova Scotia to Wood Islands, Prince Edward Island.

By bus: There is service by double-decker buses around Charlottetown as well as to the north shore. Island Transit Co-operative offers service between Charlottetown and Tignish and also from Charlottetown to Souris and to New Glasgow, Nova Scotia.

Sightseeing / Parks / Museums
Green Provincial Park, Lady Slipper Drive, northwestern Prince Edward Island, Prince County; within the park is **Yeo House**, a shipbuilding museum. **Acadian Pioneer Village**, Lady Slipper Drive, Mont-Carmel, Prince County. **Acadien Museum**, Lady Slipper Drive, Miscouche, Prince County. **Prince Edward Island National Park**, Blue Heron Drive, Queen's County, north central coast. **Lucy Maud Montgomery Museum**, New London, Queen's County; birthplace of the author of the famous book (esp. among teenagers) *Anne of Green Gables*. **Green Gables Farmhouse**, within the National Park, near Cavendish entrance. **Orwell Corner Historic Village**, King's Byway Drive, Eastern Prince Edward Island. Here, a summer festival takes place with Scottish folk music and dancing. **Lord Selkirk Provincial Park**, southeast coast. **Log Cabin Museum**, King's Byway, Murray Harbour. **Northumberland Mill and Museum**, Murray River. **Fisheries Museum**, Basin Head, near Souris.

Tourist Information
Visitor Service Division, Tourism PEJ, West Royalty Industrial Park, Charlottetown, C1E 1BO, Tel: 368-4444 or 1-800/463-4PEJ.
Prince Edward Island N. P., Director, Dept. of Canadian Heritage, 2 Palmer's Lane Charlottetown, PEJ, C1A 7V6, Tel: 566-7050.

CHARLOTTETOWN
Accommodation
LUXURY: **Charlottetown Hotel**, Box 159, Charlottetown, PEI C1A 7K4, Tel: 1-800/565-1430. Indoor tropical pool. **Kirkwood Motor Hotel**, 455 University Avenue, Charlottetown, PEI C1A 4N8, Tel: 892-4206. Two restaurants, heated indoor pool. **Prince Edward Hotel and Convention Center**, 18 Queen Street, Charlottetown, PEI C1A 8B9, Tel: 566-2282. Restaurant, lounge, saunas, indoor pool. **Rodd's Royalty Inn and Conference Center**, Box 2499, Charlottetown, PEI C1A 7K7, Tel: 1-800/565-1430. *MODERATE:* **Holiday Island Motor Lodge**, 307-309 University Avenue, Charlottetown, PEI C1A 4M5, Tel: 892-4141. Overnight and housekeeping units. *BUDGET:* **Court Bed & Breakfast**, 68 Hutchinson Court, Charlottetown, PEI C1A 8H7, Tel: 894-5871. Full breakfast included. **Sherwood Motel**, Rte. 15, Brackley Point Road, R.R. 1, Winsloe, PEI C0A 2H0, Tel: 892-1622.

Sightseeing / Culture
Victoria Park, adjacent to Charlottetown harbor, with the **PEI Museum and Heritage Foundation** and Fort Edward. **Province House**, Richmond St., where the historic meeting of the Fathers of Confederation took place, July-mid Oct. daily, rest of year Mon-Fri, Tel: 566-7626. **Confederation Centre of the Arts**, Confederation Plaza and Grafton St., with theater, library and art gallery. Museum Tues-Sat, Sun afternoons, Tel: 628-1864.

SUMMERSIDE
Accommodation
LUXURY: **Garden of the Gulf Motel/Quality Inn**, 618 Water Street East, Summerside, PEI C1N 2V5, Tel: 436-2295. 9 hole golf course, beach and outdoor pool. *MODERATE:* **Glade Motor Inn & Cottages**, Rte. 1A, Box 1387, Summerside, PEI C1N 4K2, Tel: 436-5564. Horseback riding, nature trails, outdoor pool. **Macquarrie's Lighthouse Motel**, 802 Water Street, Summerside, PEI C1N 4J6, Tel: 436-2992. Adjacent to golf, beaches and shopping. **Silver Fox Inn**, 61 Granville Street, Summerside, PEI C1N 2Z3, Tel: 436-4033. *BUDGET:* **Cairns' Motel**, 721 Water Street East, Summerside, PEI C1N 4J2, Tel: 436-5841. Golf, riding academy.

CAVENDISH
Accommodation
MODERATE: **Bay Vista Motor Inn**, Breadalbane, RR1, PEI C0A 1E0, Tel: 963-2225 (mid-June to mid September only). Lounge, pool. **Cavendish Maples Cottages**, Green Gables P.O., Cavendish, PEI C0A 1N0, Tel: 963-2244 (late May to late September), two and one bedroom cottages. **Anne Shirley Motel and Cabins**, Cavendish, PEI C0A 1N0, Tel: 963-2224 (June 1-September 25). Beach, fishing, golf nearby. *BUDGET:* **Marco Polo Inn**, Box 9, Hunter River, PEI C0A 1N0, Tel: 963-2352 (June 27-September 7). Two heated pools. **Shining Waters Lode & Cottages**, Cavendish, PEI C0A 1N0, Tel: 963-2251 (May 1-October 15), heated pool.

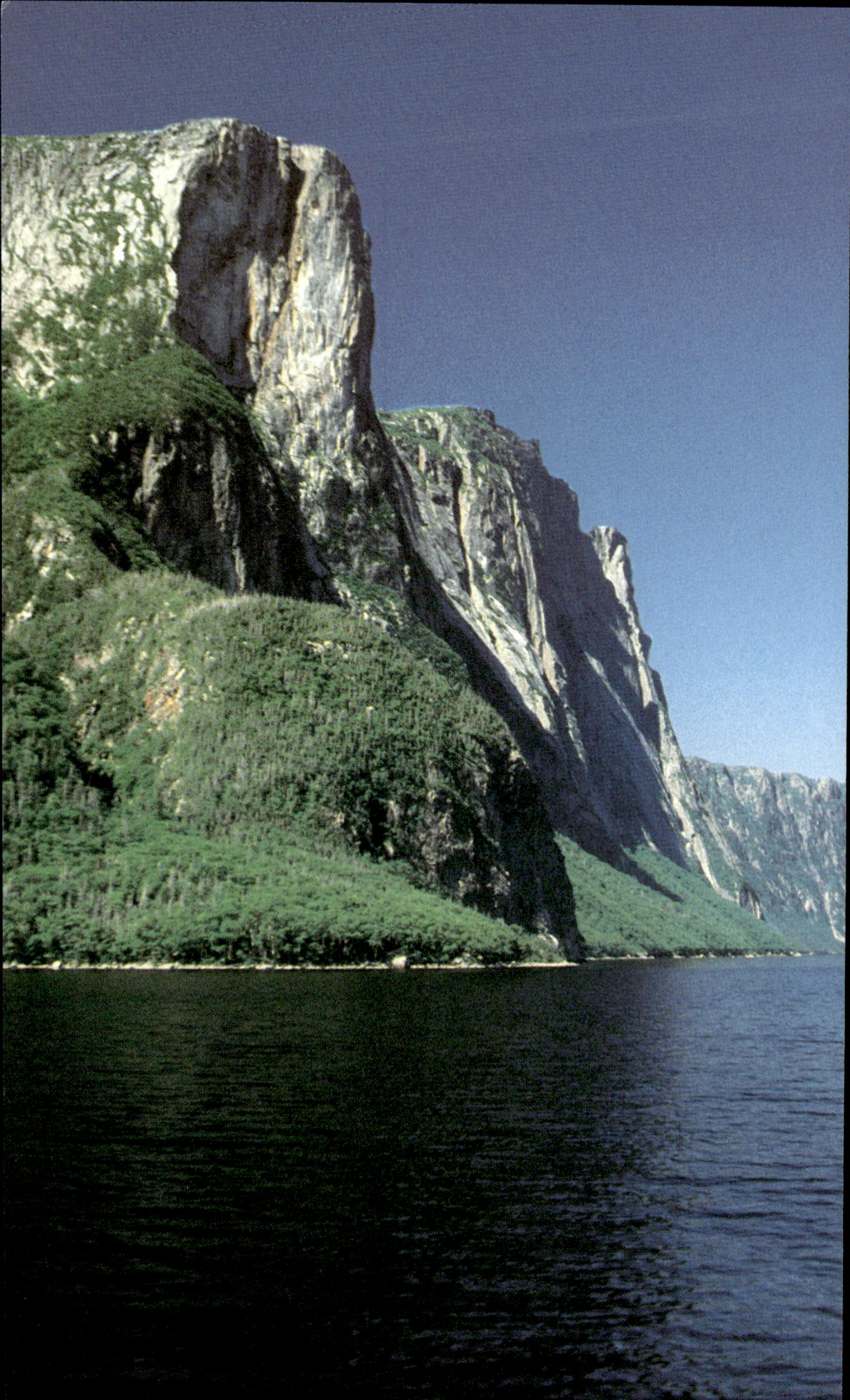

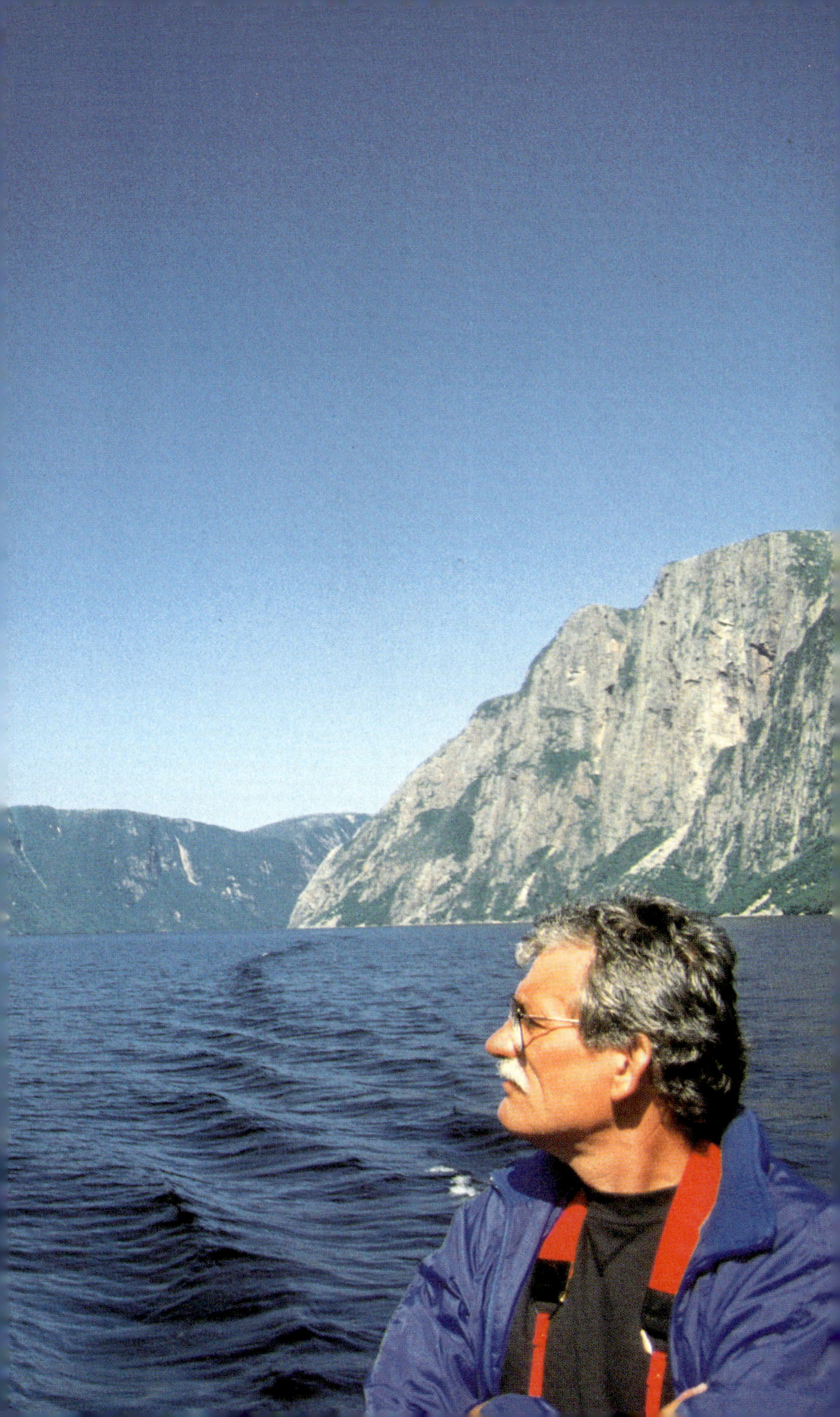

NEWFOUNDLAND

NEWFOUNDLAND AND LABRADOR

ST. JOHN'S
TRAVELING NEWFOUNDLAND
TRAVELING LABRADOR

The province of Newfoundland and Labrador (typically referred to solely as Newfoundland) did not become a part of Canada until almost halfway through the 20th century. This youngest of all the nation's provinces was a colony of Great Britain for 250 years prior to uniting with the Canadian Federation in 1949.

Geographically speaking, Newfoundland and Labrador together encompass an area greater in size than every state in the U.S. except Alaska, Texas and California. Located between the Gulf of St. Lawrence and the Atlantic Ocean, Newfoundland is a breathtaking, ruggedly beautiful island of jagged mountains, wooded river valleys and windswept tundra. Few people live in the forbidding interior. Much of the population is concentrated in a few cities and towns, and the rest spread among the hundreds of small "outport" villages situated around the small bays and inlets dotting the coast.

More than one-fifth of the population lives in St. John's, the provincial capital, which is located on a peninsula extending from Newfoundland's southeast coast. Corner Brook in far western Newfoundland is the second largest city, followed in size by the towns of Gander and Grand Falls.

Largely uninhabited except for a sprinkling isolated coastal cities, Labrador is located at the far eastern edge of the Canadian mainland. Jacques Cartier called it "cain's land," certainly a fitting description for an explorer in search of the Promised Land, perhaps. Separated from Newfoundland by the narrow Strait of Belle Isle, it is bordered by the province of Québec to the west and south and the Atlantic Ocean on its east coast.

While Labrador has mountains with altitudes up to 5500 feet (1800 m) and some imposingly steep and high cliffs along the coast, much of its interior is a vast plateau of barren, treeless tundra. Extending as far north as the Arctic, this denuded landscape has been worn away over the centuries by the relentless grinding of retreating glaciers. It's precisely this kind of wild landscape that makes it most attractive to outdoors types.

The inhabitants of both Newfoundland and Labrador have relied on fishing since the 1500s as a major source of income. The ocean off Newfoundland's east coast is home to the world's most extensive fish breeding grounds. Known as the *Grand Banks of Newfoundland*, it extends some 300 miles into the Atlantic

---

Preceding pages: Western Brook Pond in Gros Morne National Park (Newfoundland). Left: Lichen, moss and heather characterize the tundra of Labrador.

NEWFOUNDLAND / LABRADOR

NEWFOUNDLAND / LABRADOR

and supplies fishermen with huge daily catches of cod and herring There also is an extensive concentration of lakes and rivers that makes up approximately 10 percent of Newfoundland and Labrador's territory.

Since the turn on the century, forestry and mining have become vital contributors to the local economy, outpacing fishing in importance and providing the interior regions of the province with some sustainable income. However, unemployment continues to run high as Newfoundland and Labrador is the poorest of all Canadian provinces. It is hoped that the discovery of oil in the Continental Shelf off the Newfoundland coast may give a significant boost to the province's future economic prospects.

The most homogeneous of all Canadian provinces, approximately 98 percent of Newfoundland's population of nearly 600,000 was born here and almost everyone's mother tongue is English. The only exceptions to this rule are the small pockets of French speaking Acadians and Québecois and the few scattered communities of native Inuit.

As a result of both physical and cultural isolation from the rest of Canada, assimilation with their fellow Canadians has been minimal and, in some respects, Newfoundlanders seem to still be living in a separate nation. They speak a language of strange-sounding dialects laced with foreign phrases and idioms and tinged with the accents of their British and Irish ancestors. Some of the customs and traditions still practiced in the local villages were handed down by the early settlers from Ireland and the west English country towns of Cornwall, Devon and Dorset.

Probably due to their noticeable differences from the rest of the population, Canadians from the other provinces often like to poke fun at the oddball "Newfies," making them the butt of a range of jokes, snide comments and derogatory refer-

ST. JOHN'S

ences. However, most Newfoundlanders realize that this constant ribbing is the price they must pay for maintaining the distinctive regional identity that sets them apart.

ST. JOHN'S

St. John's is the capital of Newfondland and has long been the province's dominant commercial and political force. It stands on the eastern edge of Avalon Peninsula. It is in fact one of North America's oldest cities; explorer John Cabot named the harbor St. John's and proclaimed the island to be the "new found land" upon his arrival here in 1497, on June 24, which is St. John's day.

Cabot, who later went on to explore the Canadian mainland, set sail from Corn-

Above: Park ranger with his Newfoundland at Cape Spear, the most easterly point in North America. Right: The business center of St. John's, overshadowed by the Basilica of St. John the Baptist.

wall in western England, and many of the earliest settlers who followed Cabot here were colonists from England and Ireland and other parts of the British Isles.

St. John's rapidly grew into a sizeable town during the early 16th century and by 1534, when French explorer Jacques Cartier stopped here, it had become a leading trade and commercial center. Deriving wealth and status from its strategic location and burgeoning fishing industry, for more than 200 years St. John's was fought over by several European powers including Britain, France, Portugal, Spain and Holland. Added to this cauldron of contending forces were frequent raids on the city by bands of marauding pirates. It remained at the center of bloody sieges and sea battles between these various warring factions until well into the 18th century.

Of all the forces vying for control of St. John's, France and England were the chief rivals and combatants. It was not until 1762 that the British decisively recaptured the city from the French by defeating them in Europe in the Seven Years' War. From then on St. John's would be firmly under British rule.

After three major fires destroyed much of the city during the 1800s, St. John's had plenty of practice rebuilding itself from the ashes. Today, memories of its earliest days can be conjured up along **Water Street**, which remains the city's hub of commerce even after 400 years. Here much hustle and bustle is centered around the shopping complex of **Murray Premises**, a restored merchant house of the early 19th-century. Besides the shops and restaurants the **Newfoundland Museum** holds a permanent exhibition of local maritime history here covering everything from naval war to oceanography and the economy of the sea.

Several buildings in the city are tied directly to the city's British heritage. On King's Bridge Road is **Commissariat House**, a restored 1830 Georgian structure where the Assistant British Commissary general once resided. The Commissariat and the nearby **Church of St. Thomas** dating from 1836 are two of the only buildings to escape the fires that wiped out much of the city.

Two churches that have both been designated National Historic Sites stand adjacent to one another in the downtown area. The **Basilica of St. John the Baptist** on Military Road is built in the shape of a cross and features a ceiling intricately decorated with gold leaf, and a valuable collection of statues. Construction and furnishing of this majestic church took 50 years, from 1842 to 1892. On nearby Church Hill, the mid-19th-century **Anglican Cathedral of St. John the Baptist** is regarded as a prime example of ecclesiastical Gothic architecture found in North America.

There is no more important historical site in St. John's than the **Signal Hill National Historic Park**. Situated on a high cliff, it provides panoramic views of the city, harbor and coastline. Due to its strategic location, as early as the 1500s Signal Hill was used as a lookout to warn of the approach of enemy ships. It was

ST. JOHN'S / AVALON PENINSULA

here in 1762 that the final battle in the Seven Years' War between the British and French took place. But Signal Hill is also the place where the famed inventor Gugliemo Marconi received the first transatlantic signal sent by wireless telegraph on December 12, 1901. **Cabot Tower**, erected here between 1898 and 1900 to commemorate the 400th anniversary of the arrival of explorer John Cabot, served as a wireless station until 1960.

At the Signal Hill Interpretation Center, Newfoundland's military history is explained through an audio-visual program and a series of exhibits. Adjacent to the Interpretation Center is **Gibbet Hill**, an infamous spot where long ago bodies of hanged criminals dangled in public view as a grim deterrent to other aspiring criminals.

One of the prettiest parts of St. John's, the little fishing community of **Quidi Vici**, lies to the north of Signal Hill on the shores of a pictouresque inlet. It, too, was once upon a time a stronghold, and the **Battery** (originally built by the French) overlooking the village has been restored. Quidi Vici Lake is the site of the annual St. John's Regatta.

Avalon Peninsula

Just seven miles south of St. John's on Route 10 is **Cape Spear National Historic Park**, site of Newfoundland's oldest existing lighthouse (still manned by a person!) and the place marking the most easterly point on the North American continent. Known as the 1835 Lighthouse, it has been restored and turned into a museum depicting the life of a lighthouse keeper during the 1840s.

Continuing further south along the peninsula's coast to the town of Bay Bulls,

Right: The Cabot Tower of 1897 commemorates the 400th anniversary of the island's discovery.

from mid-June to mid-September you can take a guided boat tour to three islands contained within the **Witless Bay Islands Ecological Reserve**. While you can't land on the islands, you get close enough to observe hundreds of thousands of kittiwakes, storm petrels, puffins and murres that come to nest here every summer. The birds can be seen close-up, and on the way to or from the islands it is possible that a group of whales may also make an appearance.

Another day trip from St. John's is a two hour drive via the Trans-Canada Highway and south along Route 100 to the historic town of **Placentia** and **Castle Hill National Historic Park**. Basque fishermen from Spain arrived at this section of the Avalon peninsula in the early 1500s, although a town was not established until French colonists settled here in 1662. They called the town Plaisance, and built fortifications at sea level and on the surrounding hills as a base from which to launch attacks on the British stronghold in St. John's during the late 17th and early 18th centuries.

The British renamed the town Placentia and built their own fort which they called **Castle Hill** after being granted control of the area in 1713 by the Treaty of Utrecht. The remains of both the French and British defenses can be toured, and there are other exhibits at the park's interpretative center.

TRAVELING NEWFOUNDLAND

The Trans-Canada Highway is Newfoundland's only major highway connecting St. John's and Port-aux-Basques, a distance of 565 miles from east coast to west coast. Running both north and south off this main road are numerous side roads leading to scenic outport villages where one can get a glimpse of the "real" Newfoundland.

Driving west along the Trans-Canada Highway, you leave the Avalon peninsula behind and soon come within range of two other delightful peninsulas – Bonavista to the north and Burin to the south.

Cape Bonavista at the tip of the **Bonavista Peninsula** is 75 miles north of the Trans-Canada Highway along Route 230, a typical provincial road that passes through one of the earliest settled areas of the province.

If you've never been to Newfoundland before, driving north toward Cape Bonavista will provide an introduction to the basic, no-frills style of life that revolves around fishing and the myriad activities associated with living at the ocean's mercy. Most of the houses along the country roads and in the villages are built in the distinctive colorful box style that has long been the abode of choice in this part of the world.

Canadian geese begin arriving at their nesting grounds here on the northern shores of the Bonavista Peninsula in early spring. They congregate in the bird sanctuary that has been established to protect them while they nest from early spring until fall in the coastal waters.

There is plenty of wildlife lurking in the woods and valleys of the peninsula, so while driving it's wise to stay alert as one never knows what kind of creature may rear its head and suddenly appear in your rear view mirror. As a matter of fact, moose and even black bear have been sighted near the road that heads toward the Cape.

Cape Bonavista is believed to be the first place John Cabot saw of the New World upon his arrival from his voyage across the Atlantic on June 24, 1497. The Cape Bonavista **lighthouse**, a sturdy structure painted in red and white, dates from 1843 and is today a museum complete with guides in period costumes.

The town of Bonavista was already an important British fishing settlement by the early 1600s. It reached its heyday by the beginning of the 1800s when it ranked as one of Newfoundland's chief commercial centers due to its successful fishery. Today down by the harbor you may still see some of the fishing shacks and drying racks that were in use prior to the development of large-scale refrigeration and the construction of storage and packing plants. In the heart of town there is an old **whipping post** where floggings used to be meted out to misbehaving villagers.

Settled almost four centuries ago, the town of **Trinity** is another historically important town located on the Bonavista Peninsula. Established in 1615 by fishermen from western England, it contains two well preserved 150-year-old churches plus several other 19th- and early-20th-century buildings. **Hiscock House** is a restored merchant house reflecting what rural life was like at the turn of the century.

The **Burin Peninsula**, shaped like a boot protruding into the Atlantic, lies in the opposite direction of the Bonavista Peninsula; it can be reached from the Trans-Canada Highway by driving south on Route 220. The road crosses a desolate, rocky landscape dotted with bogs and marshes, eventually arriving at the peninsula's largest town, **Marystown**. Still a shipbuilding center today, Marystown is where some of the trawlers that made up one of the world's largest fishing armadas were constructed in the early 1900s.

The **Grand Bank**, which is part of Newfoundland's continental shelf, lies in the Atlantic just off the Burin Peninsula. Many residents of villages situated around the southern tip of the Peninsula are fishermen who spend most of their working hours harvesting the Grand Banks, in the tradition of the French, British and Portuguese fishermen who first fished these rich waters in the 1500s.

Returning to the Trans-Canada Highway and driving westward, it is not far before you come to the entrance of **Terra Nova National Park**. Here you can camp out alongside one of the parks

Above: Lobster-pots in Salvage. Right: The picturesque coast near Twillingate.

many lakes and streams, or relax in a sheltered bay or hike through some of the dense woods in the park's interior.

Besides the popular warm weather activities of camping, picknicking and hiking, there are opportunites for more strenuous pursuits such as bicycling, canoeing and wilderness trekking. Park naturalists are on hand for guided tours and there are two outdoor theaters presenting both live performances and informative documentary films.

After leaving Terra Nova, there are several more side trips you can take between here and the west coast. One of the most intriguing is known as the **Road to the Isles**, which starts at the Notre Dame exit off the Trans-Canada Highway and heads north in the direction of Notre Dame Bay and the far northern village of **Twillingate**.

The road crosses a series of causeways connecting colorful outport villages where fresh lobster and mussels are sold. One of the favorite pastimes in this area is watching for giant icebergs that can often be seen drifting along the coast. The ice, which may be thousands of years old, may appear blue or green under the reflecting sun.

Newfoundland's other national park, **Gros Morne**, lies on the island's west coast amidst one of the most scenic regions in all of eastern Canada. Here are majestic fjords highlighting a landscape of lakes and mountains that is home to more than 200 species of birds as well as herds of woodland caribou. Anyone who likes to camp or hike is especially well provided for here, with more than 150 camping sites and hiking trails that lead deep into the park's rugged interior.

Less adventurous hikers can take a walk on an easy trail through forests of birch and aspen to Western Brook Pond where they can join a narrated boat tour through a fjord, passing under 2000-foot (650-m) vertical cliffs with waterfalls spilling down their sides.

Two National Historic Parks – Port au Choix and L'Anse aux Meadows – are located father up Newfoundland's west

L'ANSE AUX MEADOWS

coast. The fishing village of **Port au Choix**, 50 miles north of Gros Morne on Route 430, is the site of a **burial ground** of Maritime Indians who inhabited both the Newfoundland and Labrador coasts some 5000 years ago. Thousands of years before Europeans dared venture across the Atlantic, these Indians were here living off the land and sea aided by their primitive harpoons, lances and stone-tipped darts. Many of these implements and artifacts were discovered in cemeteries uncovered during excavations at Port au Choix in 1967/68.

Another 100 miles north at the tip of Newfoundland's Great Northern Peninsula is **L'Anse aux Meadows**, the place where a band of 35 Vikings, under the leadership of the intrepid Eric the Red, are believed to have landed and settled almost 500 years before explorer John Cabot sighted his "new found land."

Above: Pre-Cambrian stones in Gros Morne National Park. Right: Small iceberg in Norman Sound in Terra Nova National Park.

Found in the 1960s by a Norwegian team of archeologists, it is the earliest European settlement so far discovered to have existed in North America. Radiocarbon dating of materials and artifacts determined that a Norse settlement was established here approximately 1000 years ago, a fact that was long doubted. Several sod houses resembling the Vikings' original dwellings have been reconstructed on the site, and many of the collected artifacts are on display in the visitor reception center.

While the route described here starts at the capital St. John's and proceeds in a westerly direction, many choose to begin a Newfoundland tour by car from the west coast and head east. Motorists arriving in their own vehicles must cross over to Newfoundland by taking the Marine Atlantic ferry from North Sydney, Nova Scotia to either Port-aux-Basques on the west coast or to Argentia (a two-hour drive from St. John's) on the Avalon Peninsula. The North Sydney – Port-aux-Basques ferry, open year round, takes 6 hours, while the North Sydney – Argentia ferry operates during the summer months only and takes 18 hours. Many visitors choose to arrive on one ferry and depart on the other.

TRAVELING LABRADOR

Of all the wilderness areas contained within the eastern Canadian provinces, Labrador is by far the most untouched and undisturbed by man. Unlike most places still left on earth, nature truly reigns supreme over a landscape shaped and eroded by massive, retreating glaciers.

With its short, cool summers and long, frigid winters, Labrador appeals to a particularly hearty breed of traveler/adventurer. (Due to the difficulty of getting from one place to another, travel to many places in Labrador often turns out to be an adventure in itself.)

Since it is near the Arctic, Labrador's weather is always unpredictable and most visitors tend to come between June and September. Freak snows have been known to occur even in late June, but temperatures by then are generally comfortable. Nature lovers traveling this far north also get the opportunity to witness the magnificent spectacle of the northern lights illuminating the night sky. Those considering traveling all the way north to Labrador should understand that roads are few and far between; the road system is currently being expanded and upgraded, but as it turns out most visitors typically come here to spend as much time away from roads and civilization as possible. The roads are more a part of local economic development than to serve the tourist trade.

While Europeans didn't arrive here until Basque whalers from Spain established a coastal community at Red Bay in the 16th century, the native Inuit and Innu peoples have lived here for thousands of years. Surviving in such a harsh and hostile climate has profoundly influenced native culture, as their lives have been shaped by both fear and respect for the natural world. Native rituals and traditions have long been closely attuned to maintaining a harmonious relationship with the environment.

Most of the 30,000 people that inhabit this gigantic territory of almost 120,000 square miles (276,000 sq.km) are concentrated in and around the towns of **Goose Bay**, **Churchill Falls** and the **Wabush/Labrador City** region as well as the fishing villages along the east coast.

After the arrival of the Basques, the coastal village of **Red Bay** rapidly grew to become one of the earliest industrial complexes and largest whaling ports in the world by the late 1500s.

Archeological teams that work here every summer have recovered large quantities of tools and various artifacts used by these early settlers. Between mid-June and the end of September, visitors to Red Bay can view the ongoing excavations and also see the laboratory

Above: Angler's dreams come true in the rivers of Labrador.

where artifacts are catalogued and restored.

Many of the first settlers came to the Labrador coast in the late 1600s and early 1700s from Newfoundland during the summer and established temporary fishing villages along the east coast. Over the centuries these eventually became permanent settlements, and many inhabitants of coastal villages such as Forteau, Pinware, Lodge Bay and Mary's Harbour, believe it or not, are descendants of these original settlers.

A good place to learn more about the history of Labrador, the land and its people is by examining the manuscripts, book collections, photographs and various exhibits at the **Labrador Heritage Museum** in Goose Bay. Goose Bay today acts as the major distribution center of goods for all of coastal Labrador and is also the site of regional government offices.

It is possible to travel on a good quality road from Goose Bay west through the interior to Labrador City via Churchill Falls.

The road provides access to hundreds of wilderness rivers and lakes that attract dedicated sports fishermen coming in pursuit of some of the finest salmon and trout found anywhere in North America.

At the town of **Churchill Falls** deep in Labrador's interior along the Churchill River, the wilderness is momentarily interrupted by an awesome manmade creation. Here one comes across the huge turbines that make up one of the world's largest hydroelectric generating power stations.

Churchill Falls is one of the few outposts of civilization in Labrador's subartic interior. Since most of Labrador is still inaccessible by road, hunters and fishermen usually seek the services of licensed government outfitters who fly guests via floatplane to camps and lodges located in prime hunting and fishing areas.

GUIDEPOST: NEWFOUNDLAND / LABRADOR

NEWFOUNDLAND

Access / Local Transportation

By air: Both Air Canada and Canadian Airlines International operate regular scheduled flights to St. John's from major cities throughout Canada and the U.S. and within Newfoundland. Regional airlines Air Atlantic and Air Nova have flights from points in Maritime and Atlantic regions of Canada.

By ferry: There is daily year round car ferry service operated by Marine Atlantic from North Sydney, Nova Scotia to Port-aux-Basques, Newfoundland (up to five crossings per day in summer); the trip takes approximately six hours. Reservations are required for all crossings and must be picked up at the ferry terminal one and a half hours before sailing.
During summer (from mid June-mid September, three days a week) there is also ferry service from North Sydney, Nova Scotia to Argentia, Newfoundland; the crossing takes 18 hours and there is room for some cars. Contact Marine Atlantic Reservations Bureau, Tel: 1-902-794-7203.

By train: Train service to Newfoundland is operated by VIA RAIL through the ferry crossings from North Sydney to Port-aux-Basques. Connections can also be made to VIA RAIL via AMTRAK train service from New York.

By bus: Most major bus lines in North America connect with Acadian Lines in Nova Scotia to the ferry in North Sydney.

By car: Newfoundland is connected from Port-aux-Basques in the west to St. John's in the east by 565 miles of the Trans-Canada Highway.

Accommodation

Newfoundland's lodging facilities range from full service hotels to motels and comfortable bed & breakfast inns. The cities of St. John's and Corner Brook offer the greatest choice. Some older properties may not have private bathrooms in all units. Most establishments accept Master Card, Visa and American Express credit cards.

Tourist Information

Tourist Commission's Main Office, New Corner St., in City Hall, Tel: 576-8106, Mon-Fri 9 a.m.-4:30 p.m.

ST. JOHN'S

Accommodation

LUXURY: **Airport Inn**, Box 9432, St. John's, NF, Tel: 1-709/753-3500. Situated near the airport five miles from downtown. **The Battery Hotel**, 100 Signal Hill, St. John's, NF A1A 1B3, Tel: 1-709/726-0040. Panoramic view, indoor swimming pool and sauna. **Hotel Newfoundland**, Cavendish Square, Box 5637, St. John's, NF A1C 5W8, Tel: 1-709/726-4980. Swimming pool, sauna and squash courts. **Holiday Inn Government Centre**, 180 Portugal Cove Road, St. John's, NF, A1B 3P9, Tel: 1-709/ 722-0506. Dining room and heated swimming pool. **Radisson Plaza Hotel**, 120 New Gower Street, St. John's, NF A1C IJ3, Tel: 1-709/739-6404. Indoor swimming pool plus meeting and banquet facilities.

MODERATE: **First City Motel**, 479 Kenmount Road, St. John's, NF, A1B 3P9, Tel: 1-709/722-5400. Basic, comfortable rooms. **Greenwood Lodge and Motel**, 53 Greenwood Crescent, Mount Pearl, St. John's, NF A1N 3J1, Tel: 1-709/364-5300. Breakfast room, lounge and picnic tables.

BUDGET: **The Olde Inn**, 157 Le Marchant Road, St. John's, NF A1C 2H4, Tel: 1-709/722-1171. Bed & breakfast.

Restaurants

LUXURY: **Newman's**, fine dining in the Radisson Plaza Hotel, Tel: 1-709/739-6404. **Cabot Club**, overlooking St. John's harbor in the Hotel Newfoundland, Tel: 1-709/726-4980.

MODERATE: **The Colony**, fresh seafood and tasty local dishes, Tel: 1-709/753-9510. **The Flake House**, delicious seafood specialties, Tel: 1-709/ 576-7518.

BUDGET: **Blue Door Café**, varied menu, Tel: 1-709/726-7822. **Captain's Cabin**, Newfoundland dishes, Tel: 1-709/726-3280.

CORNER BROOK

Accommodation

LUXURY: **Glynmill Inn**, Cobb Lane, Box 550, Corner Brook, NF A2H 6E6, Tel: 1-709/634-5181, with Steak house and lounge. **Holiday Inn**, 48 West Street, Corner Brook, NF A2H 2Z2, Tel: 1-709/634-5381, outdoor pool, wheelchair-accessible. **Mamateek Motor Inn**, TCH, Corner Brook, NF A2H 6G7, Tel: 1-709/639-8901. Fishing, hunting and skiing nearby.

LABRADOR

GOOSE BAY

Accommodation

LUXURY: **Labrador Inn**, Box 58, Station "C", Goose Bay, LB NF, Tel: 1-709/896-3351. Dining room and cocktail lounge. **Royal Inn**, 5 Royal Avenue, Happy Valley, LB NF A0P 1E0, Tel: 1-709/896-2456, Continental breakfast included.

LABRADOR CITY

Accommodation

LUXURY: **Carol Lodge**, 215 Drake Avenue, Labrador City, NF A2V 2B6, Tel: 1-709/944-3661. Alpine skiing, fishing and hunting nearby.

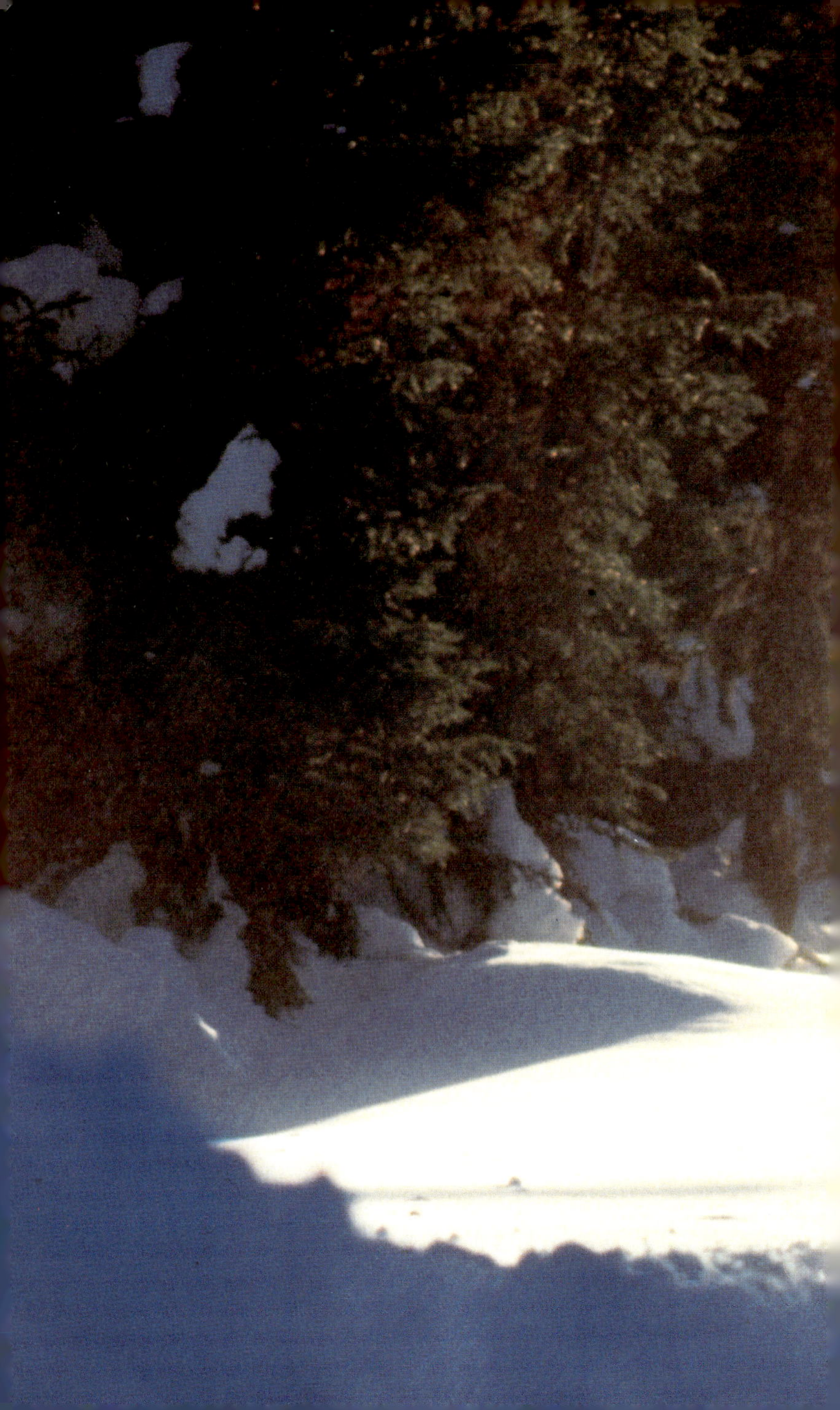

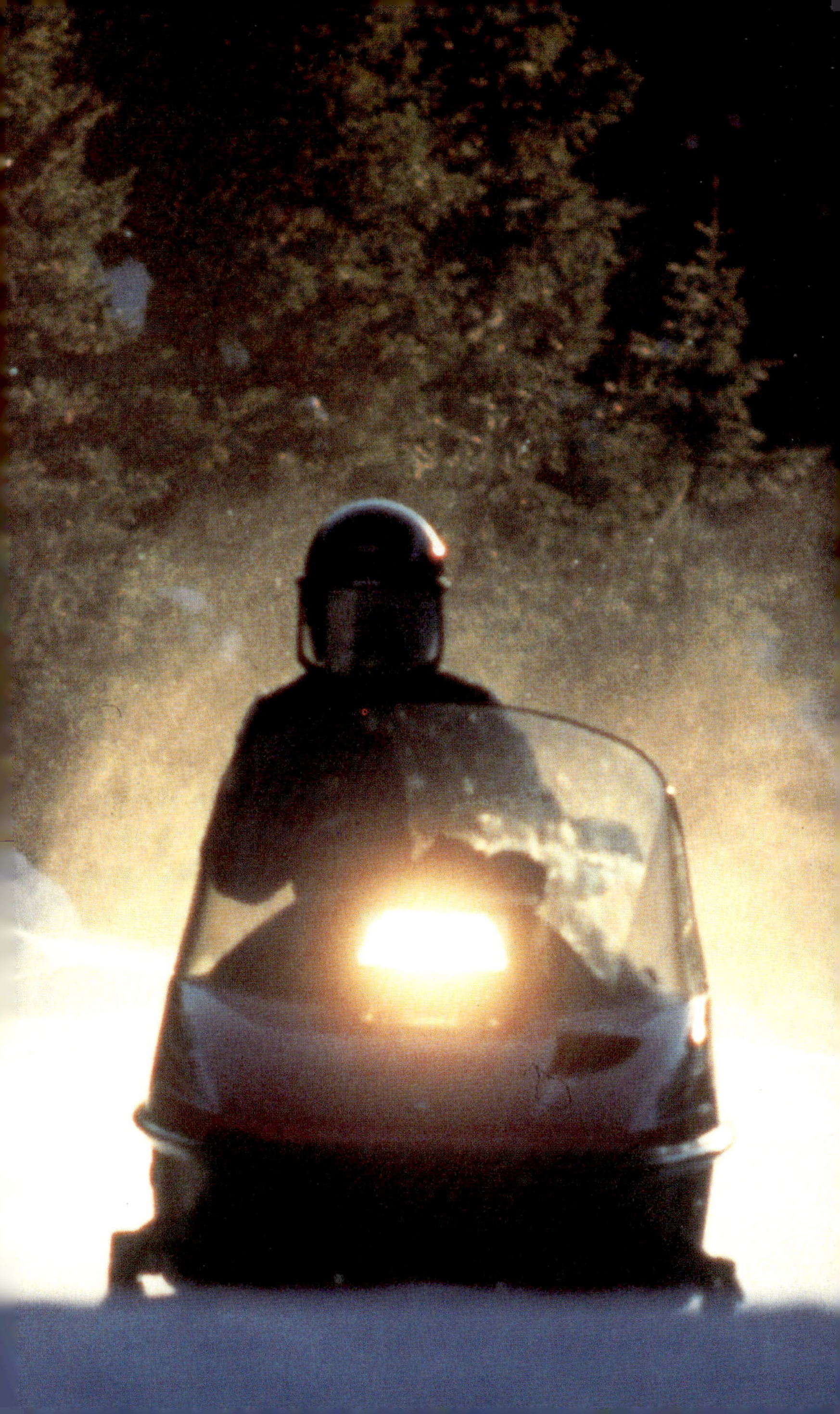

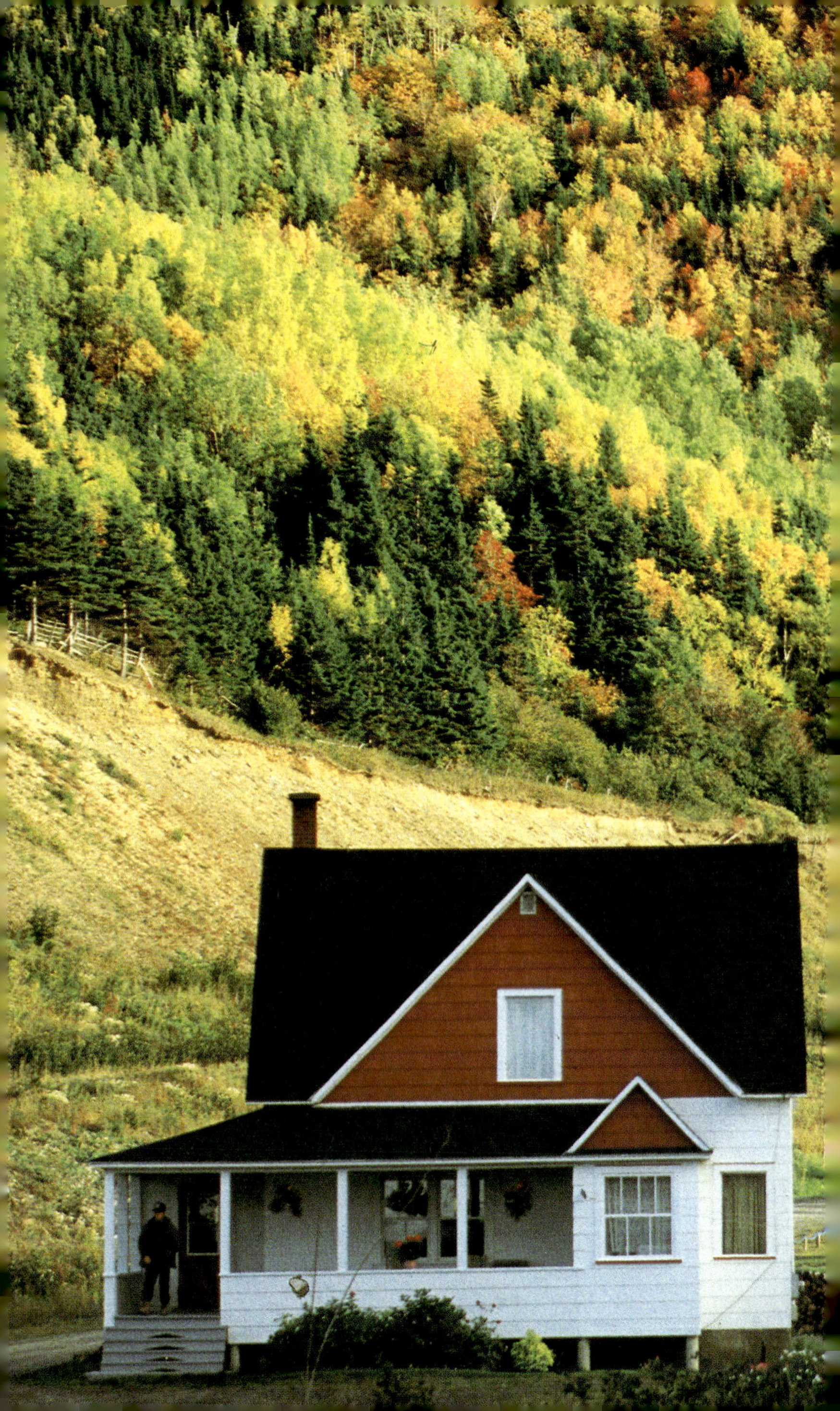

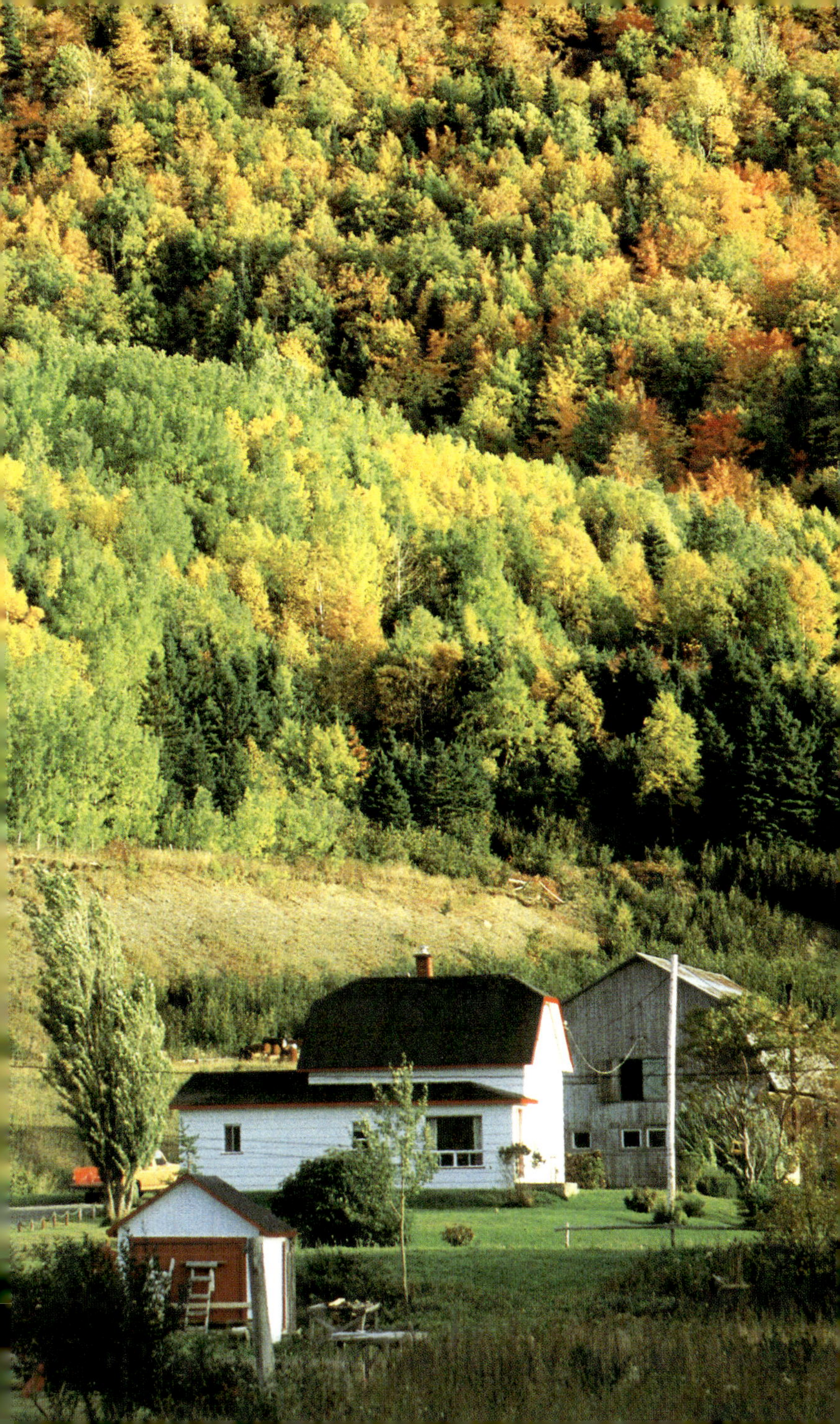

NATIONAL PARKS

Eastern Canada boasts quite a number of provincial and national parks, most of which offer a wide range of amenties such as skiing, swimming, hiking, even rock climbing, in addition to campsites and various nature programs. Animal- and birdwatching are among the main activities, so besides proper hiking equipment, it is also advisable to bring along good binoculars. The following is a selection of some of the most interesting.

Pukaskwa National Park, 735 sq miles (1880 sq km), is located in Northern Ontario along the northern shore of Lake Superior. The landscape is pure Canadian Shield: hilly terrain, rocky ridges and cliffs, and spotted with fresh-water lakes. Coastal sand dunes, sedge

Preceding pages: Snowmobile fun in the province of Québec. Autumn on the Gaspé. Above: Gannet colony on Bonaventure Island. Right: Human intervention has decimated the elk herds in the east.

meadows, wetlands, and boreal forest, are the dominant habitats. Lake Superior is cold and huge. Behaving as a small ocean does, it creates chilly, erratic weather. July and August average temperatures range between 7°C and 15°C. Wildlife includes moose, wolf, black bear, and, a rare species, woodland caribou. Pukaskwa's waters are residence to lake, white sucker, and yellow pickerel. If you visit between May and September you'll be pestered by blackflies and mosquitoes. Excellent hiking is on the Coastal Hiking Trail and on backcountry trails. The White and Pukaskwa rivers offer white water rafting.

Pointe Pelée National Park encompasses a small peninsula in southwestern Ontario which extends into Lake Erie. It is a few miles south of Leamington. Pointe Pelée's landscape is relatively young, 10,000 years old. With its sand and gravel base it has varied and heavily concentrated woodland and grassland habitats. Beaches run around the perimeter of the park, including the specta-

NATIONAL PARKS

cular wind-swept peninsula tip. The park is famous for its bird life; the variety and concentration of so many species, especially in mid-May, make Pointe Pelée one of the best birdwatching locations in North America. Over 300 species have been documented since the turn of the century. Mammals at Point Pelee include deer, raccoons, mink and weasels. Reptiles and amphibians include the northern leopard frog, six species of turtle, and a wide range of snakes. Dragonflies and monarch butterflies make for colourful insect life. Lake Erie and the park's inner marsh have many kinds of fish, such as northern pike, largemouth bass, and yellow perch. Besides the usual activities one can also visit by train.

St. Lawrence Islands National Park is Canada's smallest national park. Located among the Thousand Islands in the Ontario section of the St. Lawrence River, the park consists of 21 separate islands, made of billion-year-old Pre-Cambrian rock. Following the glacial retreat in the last Ice Age, the barren rock left behind was, over time, taken over by lichen, which soon spawned the growth of soil, moss, grass and then, finally, hardy forests. The islands have developed a number of varying microclimates, which have in turn engendered an extraordinary variety of flora and fauna. Mammals include chipmunks, squirrels, deer, fox, coyote and porcupine. Two rare animals which inhabit the park: the wild turkey and the very large and non-poisonous black rat snake. There are boats to tour the islands, and a stop (with your passport) should be made at Heart Island, USA, to visit Boldt's Castle, or find your way to the Upper Canada Village, a recreation of "ye olde Canada" off the Thousand Islands Parkway.

La Mauricie National Park is located between Québec and Montreal. The park was created in 1970 to protect the Canadian Shield landscape of lakes, forests, and the Laurentide mountains. Fish include brook and lake trout and Arctic char. La Mauricie is habitat to 180 species of bird and 40 species of mammal.

NATIONAL PARKS

Above: Bird preserve on the Gaspé. Right: Bruno goes for a swim in the area of Lac St-Jean.

Forillon National Park is located on the small northeastern tip of the Gaspé Peninsula in Québec's Appalachian Mountain country. It lies just off the Atlantic Ocean at the eastern mouth of the St. Lawrence River. This area was made a national park because of its wide variety of flora and fauna and because of the ten rock formations which dominate its majestic landscape. The cliffs, coves, and valleys of the park were carved out by glaciers and the sea over the last 600 million years. Land habitats also include forest, abandoned fields, salt meadows, salt marshes, natural prairies, sand dunes, peat bogs, watercourses, and lakes and ponds. Plants which normally do not grow close to each other do so at Forillon; for instance, low Arctic plants grow nearly side-by-side with sugar maple and yellow birch trees, an unusual combination. There are over 225 species of bird in the park; exotic specimens include the red-tailed hawk and the black-legged kittiwake. Mammals are also in abundance: moose, black bear, red fox, snowshoe hare, muskrat, and the white-tailed deer are generally friendly park residents. A special treat here is a whale-watching boat ride into the Atlantic Ocean.

Mingan Archipelago National Park consists of a series of 40 islands and islets near the town of Mingan on Québec's Côte Nord. The park is part of a unique ecological and geological region. 20,000 years ago the islands lay under water, crushed by a massive glacial accumulation of snow. When the glacier melted the land began to literally rise, but only emerged beyond the ocean surface in the past 3000 years. Today the islands continue to rise and to provide wind and water with limestone with which to carve grottoes, arches, cliffs, and, most notably, towering monoliths. Forest and maritime tundra vegetation grow around these magnificent monoliths. The archipelago is home to a wide variety of plants, most of which thrive on limestone soil. These include the livelong saxifrage, the sparrow's egg lady's slipper and the kalm's lobelia. Many species of bird migrate to the islands, including spring-to-late-summer colonies of the beautifully coloured Atlantic puffin. There are of course boat tours and special programs to elucidate local nature.

Kouchibouguac National Park is situated in New Brunswick on the northern side of Northumberland Strait. The park sits on a gently sloping maritime plain but nevertheless encompasses seven natural environments: forests, barrier islands, peatlands, estuaries, fields, salt marshes and freshwater bodies. These seven habitats are home to over 600 species of flora, including 27 species of orchid. Red spruce and balsam fir dominate the forested areas of the park. Kouchibouguac is also home to over 200 species of bird. The piping plover and the osprey are two endangered species which the park protects. Over 30 species of fish swim the park's water, while mammals such as the moose, red fox, black bear, and white-tailed deer meander the land. **Kelly's Beach**, a 16-mile (25-km) stretch of white sand on a system of barrier islands near the Northumberland Strait, is very popular.

Fundy National Park sits on the New Brunswick shore of the **Bay of Fundy**. Fundy offers imposing red cliffs, heavily treed Acadian forests, raised bogs, as well as magnificent views of the smaller Chignetco Bay (contained within the larger bay). The Bay of Fundy is famous for its daily alternation of extremely high and low tides, which results from ocean water entering such a long funnel-shaped bay. When the ocean recedes an entire ecosystem of animal, bird and insect life is exposed on the beach. Peregrine falcons, an endangered species, migrate to the park in the spring and fall and prey on many of these creatures. Porcupines, coyote, bobcat, the eastern panther, and the raccoons stake out their own domains in the park's forested areas.

Prince Edward Island National Park offers 30 sq miles (77 sq km) of (interrupted) beach along the province's northern shoreline. Aside from flat saltwater beaches, the park is distinguished by striking sand dunes, red sandstone cliffs, marsh ponds, narrow forests, and cosy little bays. The neverending, panoramic view of the Gulf of St. Lawrence is perhaps the park's most impressive feature. Its territory is too narrow to be a home to large mammals but red fox and other smaller mammals are permanent inhabitants. The blue heron rules the skies, while the park also serves as a nesting ground for the endangered piping plover and a large number of other species. The park offers modern amenities, such as showers and laundromats, which most national parks do not. If the natural beauties of the environment do not suffice, you may want to visit the Farmer's Bank in South Rustico, Canada's smallest and still functioning.

NATIONAL PARKS

Kejimkujik (abbreviated to ked-gee) **National Park** is located in southern Nova Scotia. The park is a land of lakes, rivers, bogs and forests, all situated on a relatively level terrain. The dominant region of the park is located on and around Lake Kejimkujik. The lake is speckled with islands and is fed by the snaking Mersey River. The forests are of the Acadian variety, growing coniferous red spruce and balsam fir, as well as hardwood maples, oaks, and birch. The spring's blossom of flowers is enchanting, particularly so because of its wide variety of orchids. Deer, beaver, and muskrats inhabit the forests, and the trees and skies are home to such birds as woodland warblers, woodpeckers, and the barred owl. Blandings turtle is the pride of the park, but it is not easy to find. The Kejimkujik Seaside Adjunct is a kind of footnote to the park along the coast near Port Joli in the south. The main feature here are the seals and the piping plover who nest along the shore.

Cape Breton Highlands National Park, 375 sq. miles (950 sq. km), is located in the northern region of Nova Scotia's Cape Breton Island. It border both the Atlantic Ocean and the Gulf of St. Lawrence. The highlands were originally a huge plain, which, over time, was lifted to heights of over 300 meters. Today the park's landscape is a combination of steep wooded valley, wind-swept beach, and barren tundra plateau. Estuaries and inlets ring the shoreline. Most notably, the Cabot (driving) Trail winds though much of the park's perimeter and affords spectacular views of the scenery. There are over 230 species of bird, from the bald eagle and Iceland gull, to the Arctic tern. Often seen mammals include moose, hare, and deer, while coyote, bear, fox, lynx and bobcat are occasionally spotted.

Gros Morne National Park is situated on the west coast of Newfoundland.

Above: Unspoiled nature on Cape Breton Island. Right: Don't try this at home – rendezvous with a polar bear.

NATIONAL PARKS

Almost half of the park is covered by the Long Range Mountains. The rest of the landscape boasts steep landlocked fiords, sandy beaches, and marshy lakes. Gros Morne's geological profile is of international interest because it is characterized by a rare juxtaposition of rock from the depths of the earth's mantle and of rock from the earth's crust. In certain locations there are fossil developments marking the clear separation of these widely different geological creations. Despite the rugged geography Gros Morne has nearly a thousand species of plants. Boat trips along the coast in the spring afford exciting sitings of pilot whales, harbor seals, and minke whales. Beaver, caribou, and hare dominate the woods, while cows, sheep, and horses roam freely in the more open sections of the landscape. A particularly spectacular site is Western Brook Pond, which is deeply embedded in the Long Range. And in Cow Head is a museum that describes life in Newfoundland a century ago.

Terra Nova National Park, with a surface area of 158 sq. miles (400 sq. km), is located on the northeastern shore of Newfoundland. Terra Nova's landscape is a mosaic of deep fiords, boreal forests, gloomy barrens, mossy bogs, fresh water lakes and ponds, and the windswept Appalachian mountains. There is also a magnificent coastline. To find out more about the geological growth of the park it is worth visiting the Ochre Lookout Tower which stands about 16 miles (26 km) from the northern gate. Almost 30 percent of the park is under ocean water, and in many places the shoreline's rock has been sculpted by the sea into caves and cliffs. It's worth noting that swimming off Newfoundland is for the brave, as the water temperature seldom reaches the 15°C mark. Bird and mammal life is rich in the park. Bald eagles, ospreys, the great black-backed gull, and the boreal chickadee fly Terra Nova's skies, while lynx, black bear, fox, mink, and moose roam the mainland terrain. One can spot pods of up to 50 pilot whales in **Newman's Sound**.

Auyuittuq National Park lies north of Pangnirtung on Baffin Island, already within the Arctic Circle. The park, one of the largest at 8486 sq. miles (21,470 sq. km), is dominated by the Penny Highlands, a mountain range rising 7000 feet above sea level and crowned by a 2200-square-mile ice cap. Skiing is superb here, offering the thrillseeker a virtually isolated athletic and wilderness experience. Animal life here, as in all of Baffin Island, is a little different, with the Fuggy Muskoxen, the antediluvian looking walros, the cuddly (but not necessarily friendly) polar bear. Snow conditions are best in the spring but temperatures are generally more comfortable in the summer and of course the days are a good deal longer. The park also offers excellent camping, fishing, and climbing opportunities, and, in the windy Pangnirtung Pass, some of the most spectacular hiking in Canada.

ECONOMY

ECONOMY

Looking at eastern Canada province by province, one finds quite a varied economic base. Québec and Ontario, for example, have a wealth of natural resources (hydroelectricity, forests, agriculture and metals such as nickel, zinc and gold). Ontario, Canada's most prosperous province, also has fishing and produces over half the country's manufactured goods. Of the Atlantic provinces, were fishing, tourism and agriculture play a major role, New Brunswick and Nova Scotia are in the lead. The weather of Price Edward Island has a strong influence on the local economy, which relies heavily on federal transfer payments. And Newfoundland, Canada's perennially poorest province, has had to fall back on forestry and mining to pick up the slack left by an unexplained disappearance of northern cod from its waters. No discussion of Canadian economics, however, can be conducted without constant reference to the American behemoth to the south. The United States has been both benefactor and menace to Canada. And today, in the age of NAFTA (1993) and a separate Free Trade Agreement (1989) between the two countries, America's influence is more substantial than it's ever been.

In its formative years before and after Confederation in 1867, Canada was predominately a producer of basic commodities such as fur, fish, lumber, and grain. Its economy, therefore, was largely dependent on the export of goods. This resulted in a certain development of wealth but made the new nation far too vulnerable to erratic foreign markets – particularly British and American.

In 1879 Canada's first Prime Minister, John A. Macdonald, sought to address this vulnerability by implementing what was called the National Policy. It has

Above: Thunder Bay is Canada's largest grain port. Right: Every year, Canada exports more than 600,000 tons of salmon, cod, flounder, herring and lobster.

often been put forth, usually by Canadian businessmen, that Canada lacks the stomach for risk, and even the creative imagination to develop an economy remotely approaching the vigor and diversity of that of the U.S. And the National Policy is often cited as being prototypical of this native conservatism and timidity. The policy, through a system of subsidies and tax incentives, ultimately created a wide-ranging manufacturing sector: electrical equipment, chemicals, cars, aluminum, pulp and paper, radio and home appliances were all industries which flourished in the years prior to World War Two. But because of their protected status, productive inefficiency was fostered and they failed to become fully competitive in the international marketplace.

Following World War Two, Canada's economy was greatly invigorated, largely because of its special relationship with the U.S., the winner with the fewest losses in the war. With an enormous and prosperous market to the south, Canada's natural resource industries thrived. The arrival of skilled immigrants and foreign capital into the country also increased the range and strength of the economic base. Notably, however, much of the growth in employment came from foreign-owned, usually American, manufacturers flourishing within tariff shelters. And along with this handicap, Canada was virtually a non-player in the export market for non-resource goods.

In the late 60's and early 70's, America's economy weakened. At the same time the Liberal government of Pierre Elliot Trudeau, made efforts to separate itself from the American economy: trading partnerships in Europe and Japan were cultivated and bold new domestic economic policies were implemented. Wage and price controls were imposed, a national energy program was established, foreign economic interventions were monitored, and national resource-based mega-projects were pursued.

The Trudeau government's initiatives were a mixture of successes and failures.

ECONOMY

But in the 1984 election the Canadian people saw more of the latter than the former and elected the Progressive Conservative's Brian Mulroney with a huge majority. Mulroney's economic goals and philosophy departed sharply from Trudeau's. Almost all of the Liberal's projects were dismantled and Mulroney ushered Canada into the age of free trade.

In 1988, the Mulroney Government signed a Free Trade Agreement with the United States, which went into effect in January of 1989. To put it simply, the FTA stipulates that all existing tariffs between the two countries, amounting to $131 billion a year in trade, be eliminated by 1998. To a large extent, Canada entered into the agreement out of fear of growing American protectionism – the U.S. had, in the 70's and 80's, installed such non-tariff barriers as countervailing and anti-dumping duties. But the Conservative government and Canadian business (it was often difficult to tell the difference between the two) argued that the agreement would create many new Canadian jobs, encourage American capital investment in the country, and, in general, introduce Canada to the new global economy.

At the time of writing, just four years into the FTA, it is difficult to judge the agreement's immediate success, let alone its long term repercussions. Some observers have argued that there has been an enormous job loss in Canada because of the agreement – American workers receive lower wages than Canadian and this state of affairs can, and has, induced companies to move their plants to the U.S. Others have argued that the FTA has been a boon to Canadian business – encouraging American investment. Perhaps it should be taken as some sign of the agreement's early success that the conservative government was decimated by Jean Chrétien's Liberals in the 1993 election, winning only two seats in a 292-seat parliament.

One thing is certain, though. The free trade debate in Canada has opened up a question which for most of the country's history remained (at least for the general public) a non-issue: the hard-to-define nature of the Canadian soul and its extreme vulnerability to American influences. Canada, before the FTA, was already the Western country most dominated and influenced by another, the U.S., but this new agreement, opening the country up as it does to uninhibited free market forces with a much stronger partner, seems to some to ring the death knell for Canada as we know it. Will our (subsidized) cultural industries be protected? Will our national health system be undermined? Will our worker's wages be slashed? Will existing environmental regulations by weakened?

And the signing of the North American Free Trade Agreement (NAFTA), by Canada, the U.S. and Mexico in 1993, has done nothing to ease Canadian worries. Though signed (somewhat reluctantly) by Chrétien's Liberals, the deal was constructed during the Mulroney government. By its supporters, NAFTA has been hailed as a document which will enlarge the economies of all three countries involved, while firming up a trading bloc to rival and contain those of the Europe and Asia.

The problem with the agreement, however, is that it places extraordinary powers in the hands of non-elected trading bodies which exist beyond the jurisdiction, not only of ordinary citizens, but also of the federal governments of those nations involved in the deal. This is to say that such federally instated "technical barriers" to trade as factory health regulations and environmental controls could be nullified by virtually autonomous trade bodies if they are deemed to inhibit free trade.

Right: V-8 engines are great for one's image and lousy for the environment.

ENVIRONMENT

ENVIRONMENT

In Canada's developing years, before and after the Confederation of 1867, the country's vast wilderness was seen as something to be overcome. In the 20th Century, however, as technology grew more powerful, a new myth developed: that of limitless resources. Canada's highly successful industrial life has contributed greatly to the country's relative prosperity, but it, along with excessive consumerism has in recent years placed a considerable strain on the natural environment.

Fortunately, in recent years, as with much of the Western world, an environmental consciousness has developed in Canada, largely initiated and stoked by special interest groups. Government regulations have become stricter, ecological agreements have been signed with the neighboring – and not always cooperative – United States, industry has become more active in its clean-up and regulatory efforts, and ordinary citizens have made the environment a significant political issue. In a recent poll of Canadians, about one third listed the environment as the country's top priority, while over 90 percent indicated they were at least concerned about the issue. One expert has estimated, however, it would cost each Canadian household $1400 were a substantial environmental clean-up implemented.

Travelers in the rural areas will seldom be affected by the scourge. The Great Lakes and their waterways, particularly those portions bordering major industrial centers such as Toronto and Detroit, are badly polluted, but for the most part you will encounter few problems with pollution. And those problems which do exist in non-urban centers are not areas a tourist is ever likely to want to go to or to even hear about.

Smog is the most serious problem in urban areas. In Canada East, the Windsor-Québec Corridor and the Southern Atlantic Region are the two major problem areas. In both cases, proximity to the

229

ENVIRONMENT

United States has made pollution particularly bad. The Corridor is a narrow strip, connected by highway, which extends from Québec City all the way southwest to Windsor. It runs along the north shores of the St. Lawrence River and of Lakes Ontario and Erie. A recent government brochure indicated that ozone levels are excessive about 16 days per year in Toronto and about 11 days in Montreal. Standards are relatively strict, and the only people immediately at risk are asthmatics, the elderly, and occasionally children.

As for Atlantic Canada, the Bay of Fundy region, including southern New Brunswick and parts of southwest Nova Scotia, is the major problem area. Winds carrying pollutants from America's Eastern Seaboard is the primary reason for significant pollution here. Ozone levels exceed air quality standards in Saint John, New Brunswick 3 to 4 days a year.

Above: There's room for improvement in environmental consciousness. Right: Flowering lupine in a Newfoundland spring.

With damage to the environment has of course come damage to animal life. Many species in Canada have become extinct or are currently on the endangered list. Hunting and destruction of habitat are the two main culprits. The great auk, Labrador duck and sea mink, have, for instance all been exterminated. Parks are currently engaged in strengthening dwindling populations of woods buffalo, whooping cranes, white pelicans, and sea otters.

In general, these programs have been moderately successful, but far greater financial input is needed if endangered species are to be replenished. Unfortunately, efforts to protect animal, often creates problems for native cultures. The action for baby harp seals, for instance, has seriously affected the Inuit of northern and Eastern Canada, where seal hunting has been a part of life for centuries. Recently natives have begun to organize protests, their efforts meeting with varying degrees of attention from the Canadian government.

ENVIRONMENT

Since the 1960's acid rain has been recognized as a serious problem in Canada. Caused by industrial pollutants spewed into the earth's atmosphere, this environmental menace has an enormously damaging effect on aquatic ecosystems. Damage to forest and agriculture, though not as well researched, is also a serious consequence of acid rain. Acidic deposition also poses a potentially dangerous threat to humans with the contamination that results from acid rain's exposure to the pipes providing drinking water. In the 1970's and '80's industrial emissions were reduced as a consequence of government pollution controls, and since that time some aquatic ecosystems in Canada have recovered somewhat.

The Great Lakes have been most badly effected by acid rain because of their proximity to Canadian and American industry. The federal government and the eastern provinces have recently agreed to reduce acid rain-inducing emissions by 50 percent by 1994. Unfortunately it has always been difficult to gain similar commitments from the Americans.

Hazardous wastes have also become problems in Canada. In the 1980's there were a series of incidents – a PCB spill on the Trans Canada Highway, contaminated fuels being transported from the U.S., and pulp mill pollutants causing the closure of a west coast fishery – which raised public awareness to the potential dangers of storing, disposing and transporting hazardous wastes.

Particularly troublesome has been the treatment of nuclear wastes. Nuclear fuel is currently stored at the reactor sites from which they derived, but recent government plans have called for the permanent underground storage of nuclear waste in stable rock formations in the Canadian Shield. The waste will be monitored for a (relatively) short period of time (40 years), and then simply left to, hopefully, gradually neutralize over an extended period of time. Not surprisingly no communities are unanimously enthusiastic about taking part in this program, and, as a result of this and objections which scientists have raised, no final decision has been made about how to deal with nuclear waste.

Canada's National and Provincial Parks play a vital role in protecting the natural environment outside of urban areas. In 1964 a formal basic national parks policy was developed, and in 1979 was put into law. It stipulated that the parks' natural ecological processes were not to be disrupted by interference from human beings. In recent years, *Environment Canada* has developed a program of dividing the Canadian landscape into to-be-preserved "natural regions." These regions have been chosen because of various unique biological and ecological features which they possess. To date 39 terrestrial and 29 marine regions have been identified and 21 and 2, respectively, of these designated areas have actually been formally set aside as "worthy of preservation."

ICE HOCKEY

ICE HOCKEY

Hockey originated in Canada early in the 19th Century. Its precursors were crude ice games such as shinty and hurley, played in the United Kingdom, and bandy, played in Russia and the Scandinavian countries. It is believed that immigrants from these countries mixed their games with each others' and with the native Indian games of lacrosse and baggataway. Hockey – likely from the French hoquet, meaning "shepherd's crook," – was the result. In 1875 the game, as it is known today, was first played, and in 1917 the NHL was established.

The elements of hockey are simple: twelve modestly-armored skaters, five aside, each team with a goaltender, pass a small rubber disc amongst each other with bladed sticks until they gain an

Above and right: The superiority of Canadian ice hockey is something of a national myth. It remains one of the roughest male-dominated sports there is.

agreeable opportunity to propel this "puck" into the opposing team's goal. The game places extraordinary physical and psychological demands on its players and produces a great spectacle.

Or to speak of hockey as a proud and zealous Canadian would: "It takes as much coordination, strength, guts, and smarts as any sport, but all on a foreign surface with a puck zooming around at 100 mph and someone trying to check your face into the boards."

For most of its 77 years, only six teams played in the NHL: in Canada, Toronto Maple Leafs and Montreal Canadiens, the team with the most Stanley Cups, the league's championship trophy; and in the U.S., Boston Bruins, New York Rangers, Chicago Black Hawks, and Detroit Red Wings. Despite the four American teams, the league's players were almost always Canadian. This began to change only around 1967 when the league expanded into six more American cities. In the past 25 years (there are currently 26 teams, all in North America) the addition of American, Swedish, Finnish, Czech and Russian players have made the league a truly international one.

But despite this, it has always been difficult to organize a truly international championship of hockey. Although world championships and Olympic tournaments have been played since World War Two, rules against professional participation and, later, the NHL schedule prevented the world's best from participating. In 1972, however, the "Series of the Century" was organized between Russia and Canada. The canadians found themselves, after five games, not only trailing the highly skilled Russians 3 games to one 1 (with one tie), but also with their national myth of hockey supremacy in tatters. Team Canada, however, "dug deep" and rebounded to win the last three games in Moscow, winning the series on Paul Henderson's much-celebrated goal.

ICE HOCKEY

The national myth had to be rewritten: "We might not always be the most talented, but we always have enough heart to win it in the end." Since this series Canada's best have dominated the rest of the world in competition in the Canada Cup (winning in 1976, 1984, and 1987, losing in 1980 to the Russians).

And individual Canadians remain the true giants of the game. Detroit's gritty Gordie Howe ("Mr. Hockey") dominated the NHL in the 1950's and 60's, but was so capable and durable an athlete that he played in the exacting league until the nearly incomprehensible age of 52, on an offensive line with his two sons, no less. Most NHLer's don't survive in the league beyond their early thirties. The Edmonton Oiler's and, now, the Los Angeles King's Wayne Gretzky ("The Great One") broke Howe's long-standing career points total record in just 11 seasons. This, despite Gretzky's only above-average physical abilities – his greatness lay, and still lies, rather, in his ability to "see the entire rink," to "anticipate the puck," and to imagine and execute plays that have never been attempted before. And then there is the greatest of them all, Bobby Orr ("The Golden Boy"). In the late 1960's and the 1970's, while playing for the Boston Bruins, Orr transformed the game of hockey by adding an offensive dimension to his position of defenseman. No player in the history of the game dominated the rink as Orr did. His end to end rushes transported opposing players back to the sullen, gasping futility of their early childhoods, where they chased far older children up and down stretches of frozen Canadian lake.

Hockey is indeed Canada's beloved game. The nation invented it and the nation excels at it. And Canada always has hockey to turn to if it's having trouble defining and celebrating its national soul; if it's having trouble finding common ground between its French and English halves, if it's having trouble discovering something it does better than the Americans; and if it wants to bear witness to its collective never-say-die heart of gold.

BAFFIN ISLAND

Baffin Island is located in the Arctic Archipelago, and is part of the Keewatin District of Canada's Northwest Territories. It is separated from Northern Québec by the Hudson Strait, from Greenland by the Davis Strait, and from the mainland portion of the NWT by the Foxe Basin.

Baffin Island was first settled by Inuit peoples some 1500 years ago. Today the Iglulik Inuit live in the northern section of the island, while those living in the south are generally referred to as the Inuit of South Baffin Island. These southern peoples bear considerable cultural resemblance to the Labrador Inuit.

Although Vikings likely visited Baffin after they reached Greenland in the 11th century, the first recorded contact with Europeans occurred in 1576, when the Englishman Martin Frobisher landed while searching for the Northwest Passage to China. Two more voyages, in 1576 and 1577, followed this one, but all were failures: the passage was never found, shiploads of worthless ore (thought to be gold) were carted back to England, several Inuit and two of Frobisher's men were killed in misunderstandings between the two cultures, and, on one occasion, Frobisher received an Inuit arrow in his buttocks, fitting retribution for all the trouble he had caused.

Baffin Island is an extension of the Canadian Shield, which stretches deep into the Canadian mainland. The eastern shoreline, running south to north is dominated by towering mountains, while the land to the west and south, though still covered with granite, is mainly marked by valleys and lowlands. There is very little vegetation in any part of the island, particularly in the north, and what is there is mainly grassy marshland. Few trees can withstand the icy climate. The island is also dotted by several freshwater lakes.

A trip to Baffin offers rare opportunities to view Arctic wildlife, kayak around icebergs, take a dog-sled ride, and revel in the midnight sun. But a trip to Baffin also requires a major commitment, both of financial and physical resources. Because the region is so isolated, undeveloped, and cold, it is advisable that a visitor arrange his or her trip, well ahead of time through an outfitter. Package tours, which include transportation (you need a plane to get to Baffin, and often to get around once you're there) and accommodation, usually in modest hotels, start just below $2000 (Canadian) per person and cost as much as $15.000. Travelers, unless their family's constitution benefits from a recent generational mixing with a walrus clan, should also schedule their trip for the spring or summer (April-August); January in Iqualit averages highs of -25°C and lows of -34°C, while in July, the warmest month of the year, high temperatures hover around 19°C and dip down to around 8°C. Winters in Baffin, particularly as you travel north, are also inhospitable because of the shortage of sunlight hours.

Most trips to Baffin begin in Iqaluit because the town is accessible by plane from Ottawa and Montreal, and because it offers air service to every Baffin community, with the exception of Sanikiluaq. Iqaluit is also a good place to start a trip to the region as its Information Center, Unikkaarviit, its museum, Nunatta Sunaqutangit, and the nearby (20 minutes by boat) Qaummaarviit Historic Park offer an interesting overview of the region and of the Inuit people who inhabit it. The more enticing wilderness destinations are found elsewhere.

Lake Harbour is the community closest to Iqaluit. And the lush Soper River Valley affords an engaging link between the

Right: In the snowy expanses of northern Canada, huskies defend their legendary reputation as draft animals.

two settlements. It is possible to hike through the area or to canoe and raft its white waters. The valley is located, in part, in the Katannilik Territorial Park Reserve, which is rich in wildlife.

To the west of Lake Harbour is Cape Dorset, which is well known for its art. In the 1950s the Canadian Government helped promote Inuit carving, and today Cape Dorset is the site of a thriving artistic community which includes a marvellous permanent collection of sculpture. The community is also the site of an important archeological discovery. In 1925 the remains of an ancient Inuit people who lived in the area between 1000 BC and AD 1100 was uncovered. Today it is possible to take dog-sled rides and boat trips to the site, as well as to the nearby Dewey Soper Bird Sanctuary.

Pangnirtung, to the north of Iqaluit, is probably the most picturesque community on Baffin Island. Circled by glaciated mountains and refreshed by the waters of Cumberland Sound, the town has become a well-developed tourist centre, replete with modern amenities, fishing zones, arts centres, and an historic whaling station at Kekerton, just 12 hours away by snowmobile in the spring. Just north of Pangnirtung, Auyuittuq National Park is the main attraction in the area. (see National Parks chapter)

Pond Inlet is the most frequented northern destination on Baffin Island and for good reason. This community of less than a 1000 people is blessed both with a natural shelter, in its indigenous rock and glacial formations, and with a spectacular view, in the similarly glaciated and mountainous Bylot Island which lies 25 miles north across Eclipse Sound. This combined area between the large and small islands is rich in bird life as well as marine animals, such as walrus, seals and whales. The area is particularly enchanting in the spring when massive ice blocks break from glaciers and make their shimmering way alone through open water. Summertime, meanwhile, affords the extraordinary opportunity of experiencing days with 24 hours of sunlight.

THE CREE WAY OF LIFE

In 1971, the Prime Minister of Quebec announced the development of a project to create huge amounts of hydroelectric power in the area around James Bay. The only prerequisite was the damming of all of the rivers that flowed into James Bay within this area, which measured 500,000 square kilometers; some of the rivers were to be rechannelled altogether. Experts had determined that the area was suitable for the building of a hydroelectric plant on the basis of a satellite photograph. From such a height, of course, they couldn't detect that the area was also home to people whose lives revolved around the caribou and beaver, geese and ptarmigan that lived there.

The James Bay Territory is home to some 6,000 Cree, members of an Algonquin Indian tribe called Kiristino by the Ojibwas. The French corrupted this to Cri, the English to Cree. To the Cree, a resident of Fort George is *cise-si-pi-wiyuyu*: a person from the great river. Wemindji, Eastmain and Rupert House dwellers are *wi-nipe-ku-wiyiyu-c* (coast people or salt-water-people), while people from Nemiskau, Waswanapi and Mistassini are *nu-hcmi-wiyuyu-c*, inland or bush people. The Cree themselves are variously eeyou, iyuu or ilnu, all of are different regional dialects for the word which mean simply People.

The Cree lawsuit against the James Bay Project made residents of Quebec – and, indeed, of the world – more familiar with a way of life which they'd never known existed, although it had been around for some 5,000 years. "We, the representatives of individual Cree communities which will be affected by the planned hydroelectric plant, defend ourselves actively against the damming of our rivers, as we believe that only

Right: Caribou and elk leather (clothing) is decorated with beads and porcupine quills.

beavers have the right to build dams in this country." Thus ran the argument of the chiefs of the Cree villages – each an autonomous entity – against the building of a water reservoir 1036 sq. km in area. Tried before the Canadian Supreme Court, the lawsuit was not able to prevent the project; but it did make clear what the Indians would lose, and what they have lost, after the flooding. The James Bay and Northern Quebec Agreement between the Cree and the Government of Quebec, which regulates the use of the land, expropriation and compensation, was seen by the Cree people as a compromise.

For the Cree, season are determined by the flight of the wild geese. When they fly north, it is summer, the time to fish. The currents of Sakami, near Fort George, were a major fishing-ground, where they could catch over 200 fish a day. After the river's direction was altered, it took the Cree three days to catch 50 fish. The Eastmain river bed is completely dry.

At the end of October, the geese fly south and the rivers freeze. Once, this meant that families had to move their hunting grounds to the interior; this involved, for some families, a canoe journey of up to two months. On snowshoes or in canoes, families travelled as far as 1000 miles, all the way to the coast of Labrador. Today, there's hardly an Indian left who knows how to build these canoes out of birch bark, spruce roots, cedar wood, spruce gum, and animal fat. Wooden boats came into use in the 1930s, and outboard motors began to be added around 1940. Today, trucks are an additional help, and snowmobiles have replaced the runner-less sleds. The move to winter camp today is carried out with the help of a bush plane, and takes two days at most.

Cree culture centers around hunting. Many of the traditional hunting-grounds were flooded when the dams were built, and the Cree haven't in every case been able to organize new trap-lines. New division of these lines means that there's less land available to individual hunters, and survival in the bush is therefore more difficult. In traditional communities, furthermore, no one wants to change these boundaries, which are looked on as a kind of tribal law. The tribal fathers say that the land belongs to the spirits of men who lived here long ago, as well as to the spirits of the hunters' ancestors and those of the animals whom they and their ancestors hunted. The land has a soul, and shouldn't be dealt with carelessly, arbitrarily.

The owner of a trap-line administrates the land, protecting its plants and its animals for future generations, and handing the land on to his descendants when he grows old.

Hunting-grounds are used cyclically; after two years of hunting, the land has a one-year period of rest, during which period its owner is taken into someone else's trap-line. This is the solution which will be employed today for those families who have lost their hunting-grounds to the dams.

The Cree hunt predominantly beaver, whose pelts they sell to the Hudson's Bay Company. The Agreement, furthermore, assures them exclusive rights to the pelts and the hunting of polar bears, mink, ermine, weasels, pine marten, and black bears, which have a special position in Cree religion. Sacrifices of tobacco are made before and after bear hunts, and the hunter has to dream of the bear's den. Once, many hunters had this ability; today, it lies in the hands of the shaman, who is able to take up spiritual contact with the bears. The hunter approaches the bear alone, begins a dialogue with him, and begs to be forgiven. Twigs are spread out before the mouth of the bear's cave so that the animal's blood does not touch the ground. When Crees eat bear, the meat is held in the fire so that the bear can return, with the smoke, into the bush. The skull is fastened to a special tree to appease the bear's spirit. The bear's chin area is

CREE WAY OF LIFE

sacred; it is cut out of the bear's pelt, ornamented, and used as an amulet.

Part of the respect which the Cree show to the animals they hunt is that they don't kill too many of any one species; otherwise, their luck at hunting might disappear. Something in the nature of bear and otter requires the Cree to hunt these animals with special care. Animals are hunted for food, not because someone wants a bearskin rug. Nearly 90% of the Cree's nourishment comes from the meat of the animals they hunt, whose skins they process and whose furs they sell. Since the Agreement was signed, a distinction has been made between hunting as a way of life and hunting for sport. As a result, the hunting seasons imposed on sport hunters don't apply to the Cree.

Not every Cree village still has its own shaman. There's a story about the spiritual powers of the shamans which dates from the 1960s. A tornado was heading for the village of Mistassini. Two old hunters, one of whom was known for his spiritual strength, went toward the storm. When the men had gotten as near to the storm as seemed necessary, they strewed tobacco in its path, the usual procedure in such cases, handed down from generation to generation. The tornado spared Mistassini.

With the signing of the treaty, the Cree way of life was officially recognized as a unique culture and way of life. School education was expanded for Cree children: trappers tell their legends and pass on traditional Indian healing methods; elders take the children into the bush to teach them about survival. Within the family, the "Walking Out Ceremony" for children has persevered. When they are between two and three years old, children walk out of their parents' house or tent on foot for the first time. The boys have to shoot their bow and arrow at a dead goose held up on a pole; they then go into

Above: Bernard Abraham, the vice-chief of the Ojibwas in Long Lake, Ontario. Right: Indian cemetery on a reservation near Constance Lake, Ontario.

CREE WAY OF LIFE

a tent where the tribal elders are gathered, and present them with a gift. The girls carry a small axe and a bundle of wood. Anyone who wants to continue to live in the bush in the traditional manner should also be able to do this in future. Besides the bush schools, Cree can also go to city schools, go on to university and train to be, for example, doctors and lawyers.

In some communities, chiefs are still elected in the traditional manner. The candidates stand out in the open, their faces turned to the wall. The villagers then stand behind the candidate they support. The candidate with the most people behind him becomes Chief; the next six are members of the tribal council.

The financial compensation awarded by the Agreement have changed Cree lives, and made many things simpler. Today, every family has a pick-up truck, and permanent homes are being built; teepees, called *mitchuap* in Cree (which means "the place where many people can live"), are generally used only for cooking. In winter, hunters and trappers take their Skidoos into the bush. This enables them to return to their villages frequently during the hunting season, and hardly any of them still build the traditional massive winter huts. The snowmobiles, of course, are loud and drive away the animals; furthermore, gas stations have had to be set up in the bush. However, since they enable hunters to cover great distances in a short time, they've become a permanent part of trapper culture. The roads which were built for La Grande Project have also been to the Cree's advantage: fresh vegetables and other products can now be transported even to remote areas.

Many Indians outside of Quebec have accused the Cree of selling their land. The Cree themselves see things a little differently. The reparations have allowed them to continue their traditional way of life and to preserve their cultural identity, including their language. They have not been forced onto reservations, where 70% of Canada's 400,000 other Indians and Inuit live today.

PREPARATIONS

Climate and Travel Times

The climate of eastern Canada varies somewhat, but it can be generally described as quite warm in summer to very cold in winter.

The coastal regions are tempered by the Atlantic Ocean, which can be very pleasant during a heat wave, or when the inland regions are frozen solid. The same applies to the coastal regions of the Great Lakes.

The St. Lawrence Valley, on the other hand, can become unbearably muggy in summer. Hot and humid weather is often relieved by extremely violent rain storms accompanied by thunder and lightening. The Canadian winter can be notoriously cold at times (Ottawa is on average colder than Moscow), but the cold snaps are often accompanied by clear blue skies. If traveling by car pay heed to snow storm or blizzard warnings: Getting stuck in one can be fatal.

Spring in Canada is a short but pleasant season, especially for Canadians emerging from four months of winter. Its duration cannot be determined, and the odd snow storm in late April or even beginning of May cannot be excluded. The autumn months, beginning mid-September, bring cool nights and warm sunny days.

The extraordinary colors of the Canadian forests during this period attract hordes of tourists. Snow can come as early as the end of October.

When to travel to eastern Canada depends on the aims of the traveler. Winter activities are excellent in the Laurentides north of Montréal and in L'Estrie to the southeast, for example. Mardi Gras festivities are very lively occasions, especially in Québec City and Ottawa (the Winterlude festival). During the warm season one can engage in swimming, boating, hiking in most places.

Clothing

The climate determines the size of your suitcase. A good down coat, scarfs, sweaters, wool socks, insulated boots and thick gloves will take care of the winter. Light cottons are for summer, whereby one should expect the odd cool night, especially along the coast. Expect rain, of course. Hiking boots and a comfortable pair of shoes are essential for "doing" the National and Provincial Parks and the cities respectively.

Customs

Duty-free for visitors over 16 years of age are: 50 cigars or 200 cigarettes or 2 pounds (0,9 kg) of tobacco; 40 ounces (1,1 liters) of spirits or wine, or 288 ounces (8,2 liters) of beer. Additional quantities of alcoholic beverages up to two Imperial gallons (9 liters) may be imported but will be subject to duty and taxes and a provincial fee. The legal age for importing alcoholic beverages is that of the province of entry!

Gifts up to Can$ 40,-- may be imported duty free (in addition to alcohol and tobacco). Visitors may bring in sporting outfits and other equipment for personal use by declaring them at entry. Contact an embassy or consulate for further information concerning hunting and fishing equipment. Customs prohibit the entry of revolvers, pistols and all other firearms into Canada with the exception of rifles and shotguns (other than fully automatic) for hunting purposes. The latter may be brought into Canada without special permit, but owners must provide customs with a description of their equipment and the serial numbers of firearms so all such articles may be readily cleared upon return.

Dogs and cats must have a certification stating the animal has been vaccinated against rabies for the past three years. Date of vaccination and description of

GUIDELINES

the animal must be legible. Puppies, kittens and seeing-eye dogs are exempt.

Border crossings

Citizens and permanent residents of the United States merely need a proof of citizenship when entering Canada (birth certificate or Alien Registration Card). If you are not a US citizen and are visiting the USA, you will need a passport, but not a visa. You should nevertheless check with the nearest Canadian Embassy or Consulate.

Currency

The Canadian dollar is legal tender in the country. It comes in bills of Can$ 1, 5, 10, 20, 50 and 100. Coins come in 1 c, 5 c (nickel), 10 c (dime), 25 c (quarter), and, rarely, 50 c and Can$ 1. American currency is often accepted, but the exchange rate will not be that of a bank, so it is advisable to change money as soon as possible, or arrive in the country with traveler's checks issued in Canadian currency. These are frequently accepted as payment in hotels, restaurants, shops and gas stations. Eurocheques are not even looked at! Exchange of foreign currency can be done at banks, international airports, some hotels, travel agents and tourist bureaus. Major credit cards are widely accepted, and in fact the easiest way of getting around.

Automatic banking machines are very common, and if your credit or debit card provides access to a banking network affiliated with a Canadian network you will have access to Canadian cash at any bank. Don't forget your PIN number.

Embassies and Consulates of Canada

AUSTRALIA: Canadian Consulate General, 50 Bridge Street, 8th Floor, AMP Centre, **Sydney** N.S.W. 2000, Tel: (61-2) 231-6522, Fax: (61-2) 223-4230. GREAT BRITAIN: Canadian High Commission, Canada House, Trafalgar Square, **London** SW1Y 5BJ, Tel: (71) 629-9492, Fax: (71) 321-0025. USA: The Canadian Embassy, 501 Pennsylvania Avenue N.W., **Washington D.C.** 20001, Tel: (202) 682-1740, Fax: (202) 682-7726. Canadian Consulate General, Three Copley Place, Suite 400, **Boston** MA 02116, Tel: (617) 536-1731, Fax: (617) 262-3415. Canadian Consulate General, 2 Prudential Plaza, 180 North Stetson Avenue, Suite 2400, **Chicago** IL 60601, Tel: (312) 616-1860, Fax: (312) 616-1877. Canadian Consulate General, 300 South Grand Avenue, Suite 1000, **Los Angeles** CA 90071, Tel: (213) 687-7432, Fax: (213) 620-8827. Canadian Consulate General, Exxon Building, 16th Floor, 1251 Avenue of the Americas, **New York**, NY 10020-1175, Tel: (212) 768-2400, Fax: (768-2440). Further Consulates can be found in: Atlanta GA, Buffalo NY, Cincinnati OH, Cleveland OH, Dallas TX, Detroit MI, Minneapolis MN, Pittsburgh PA, San Francisco CA, Seattle WA. NEW ZEALAND: **Wellington**, The Canadian High Commission, 61 Molesworth St., Thorndon, Wellington, Tel: (011-64-4) 473-9577, Fax: (011-64-4) 471-2082. **Auckland**, Consulate of Canada, Princes Court, 2 Princes St., Tel: (011-64-9) 309-3690, Fax: (011-64-9) 307-3111.

Health

There are no public health hazards in Canada. However, it is wise to watch out for the extreme cold, and heed smog and ozone warnings. If skiing make sure you are wearing sun glasses. In summer, especially around June, the moskitoes and above all the black fly (a tiny insect with impressive stinging power) represent a pest. A long snowy winter and warm spring make them a veritable plague. If you intend a lot of outdoor activities be equipped with a strong insect repellent.

GUIDELINES

Medical services in Canada are excellent but costly. Travel health insurance is imperative, and a credit card should be kept handy in case payment is required.

Tourist Information

The individual provinces maintain offices for public relations in many cities throughout the world. The embassies and consulates, however, all have a tourist division that can be tapped for information. (See above)

TRAVELING TO CANADA

By airplane: Eastern Canada's main international airports are in Toronto, Ottawa, Montréal and Québec City. Many other towns have airports that can be accessed by connecting flights, including Windsor (Ontario), Halifax (Nova Scotia), St. John and Fredericton (New Brunswick), Charlottetown (Prince Edward Island), St. John's (Newfoundland). Most major international carriers serve the major airports. Connections with US cities are very frequent. Toronto's Lester B. Pearson Airport is 27 km (17 mi) northwest of the city, taxi to downtown costs Can$ 40,--. Ottawa International Airport is 14 km (8 mi) south of the city, busses to downtown cost Can$ 8,--, taxis about Can$ 21,--. Montréal has two airports, Dorval and Mirabel. Busses to downtown cost Can$ 8,50 and 13,50 respectively, taxis Can$ 24,-- to 60,-- respectively. Québec City's airport is 19 km (12 mi.) from the city. Busses to downtown cost Can$ 7,50, taxis Can$ 22,--, and there is daily bus service to Montréal/Mirabel for Can$ 35,-- Halifax Airport is 42 km (28 mi.) fromthe city. Busses cost Can$ 18,-- (return), taxis Can$ 25,--.

Canada's national airline Air Canada has a more dense network of flights from abroad and within the country. For reservations and information outside Canada: **Australia**: A & W House, 8th Floor, Sydney N.S.W. 2000, Tel: (02) 232-5222. **Great Britain**, 78 Conduit St., London W1R 9TG, Tel: 081-7592636; Gresham Chambers, 45 West Nile St., Glasgow, Tel: 0345-18-1313. In the **USA** call toll-free: 1-800-776-3000; Continental Airlines represents Air Canada in the USA, with offices in many cities, including Boston, Chicago, Cleveland, Denver, Fort Lauderdale, Houston, Las Vegas, Los Angeles, New York and Washington D.C.. **New Zealand**: 1, Dingwall bldg, 87 Queen St., Auckland, Tel: 793-371. **South Africa**: P.O.Box 52701, Saxonwold 2132, Johannesburg, Tel: 888-8931. Canada's other national airline is Canadian Airlines International which has a fair number of international flights: **Australia**, 30 Clarence Street, Sydney, N.S.W.2000, Tel: 299-7843. **Great Britain**, 15 Berkeley Street, London W1X 6ND, Tel: 081-667-0666 or outside London 0345-616-767. **New Zealand**, Jetset Center, 44-48 Emily Place, Auckland, Tel: 309-0735. **USA**: CIA holds offices in numerous cities, including Boston, Los Angeles, San Francisco, Seattle. Call 1-800-426-7000 for information and reservations.

By car: There are numerous points of entry from the United States. The major ones are from Detroit into Windsor, Ontario; Hwy 75 north of Detroit to Sault Ste. Marie, Ontario; from Buffalo, New York, across the Niagara River to St.Catherines; Hwy 87 in New York State west of Lake Champlain and Hwy 89 to the east of the lake in Vermont both lead to Montreal. Interstate 91 in Vermont allows easy access to Montreal or Sherbrooke. Interstate 95 accesses Fredericton, New Brunswick.

By bus/rail: Several cities in the northern USA (Boston, New York, Albany, Buffalo, Chicago) have direct bus and rail contact to Canadian cities. Contact any AMTRAK office for rail information, or the local port authority or bus station. Busses can be a fairly inexpensive and comfortable way of traveling while seeing a great deal of landscape.

By ship: Access to Prince Edward Island and Newfoundland is by ferry only and several other coastal destinations are easier to get to by boat than by long and tedious driving. There is regular car ferry service from Portland and Bar Harbor, Maine (USA), to Yarmouth, Nova Scotia. For information on how to get around on the waters of Atlantic Canada call toll-free: for **New Brunswick**, Tel: 1-800-561-0123, within New Brunswick, Tel: 1-800-442-4442; **Newfoundland and Labrador**, Tel: 1-800-563-6353; **Nova Scotia**, in Canada, Tel: 1-800-565-0000, in Maine, Tel: 1-800-492-0643, in the rest of the USA, Tel: 1-800-341-6096; **Prince Edward Island**, Tel: 1-800-565-0267. If traveling during the summer make sure you reserve ahead of time to insure a place.

For cruises to Canada or other ferries contact either your local tourist bureau, a travel agent, or one of the provincial tourist bureaus listed in the guideposts at the end of the chapters in the book.

TRAVELING IN EASTERN CANADA

Most visitors to Canada opt for road travel, thereby taking into account a great deal of driving, as the country is big. Canada's roads are in good shape, and the network is fairly dense in the southern part of the country. All provincial capitals are connected by the Trans-Canada Highway (except Newfoundland and Prince Edward Island, of course), which enters Ontario near Winnipeg, skirts the Great Lakes and the St. Lawrence River, before crossing New Brunswick and Nova Scotia.

Foreign drivers licenses are respected for varying lengths of time depending on the province. US drivers visiting Canada can obtain a single insurance card that will be accepted as evidence of financial responsibility by police authorities. It is obtainable through the driver's own insurance company. If you don't own the vehicle you are driving you will need a letter from the owner or a copy of the rental contract.

Distances and speed zones are posted in kilometers, and the Royal Canadian Mounted Police is fairly severe about violations. Speed limits are as follows:
100 series highways   100 km/h, 62 mph
Other highways . . .   80 km/h, 50 mph
Cities and towns . . .   50 km/h, 30 mph

If a school bus is flashing amber lights it may be passed with caution. If it is stopped and flashing red lights, traffic in both directions must come to a full stop and wait until the bus proceeds. Right turn on red is allowed except in Québec. Drinking and driving is prohibited. Seatbelts are mandatory.

One of the favorite ways of getting around is in a camping vehicle. Regulations governing these are as follows: Size limit: height, 13.6 feet (4.1 m); width, 8.6 feet (2.6 m); combined maximum length of car and trailer, 68 feet (21 m). Trailers require a safety chain, a breakaway switch, pot-type flares for emergencies, license plate light, braking system for trailers with a 3300 lb (1500 kg) gross weight and towing mirrors.

Some distances:
Toronto-Winnipeg (Man.):	2085 km
Toronto-Ottawa:	399 km
Ottawa-Montréal:	200 km
Montréal-Québec City:	251 km
Montréal-Halifax:	1332 km

Another way of getting around in Canada is by bus or train. There are numerous bus companies operating very comfortable coaches at reasonable prices that get you to most areas. A selection of companies: **Acadian Lines**, 6040 Almon Street, Halifax, Nova Scotia. **Gray Coach Lines**, 580 Commissioners Street, Toronto. **S. M. T. Limited**, 300 Union

GUIDELINES

Street, St. John, New Brunswick. Voyageur Inc., 505 est, Blvd de Maisonneuve, Québec, Québec.

Excellent train service is provided by VIA Rail, Canada's railway company. The trains themselves and the service offered range from plain ferrying of passengers to actually giving them a vacation. For overnight passengers there are rooms with showers available, enjoyable lounges, and the so-called dome cars that allow passengers a 360 degree view of the landscape passing by. The *Ocean* and *Atlantic* trains between Montréal and Halifax are of this category: normal coach section (no lying) Can$ 83-139 one-way, or with room, Can$ 131-219. Prices fluctuate with the season. A Canrail Pass purchased at your country of origin is one practical way of moving around efficiently and fairly inexpensively. It costs around Can$ 349-510 (depending on season) for adults, and Can $ 460-319 for youths and senior citizens (maximum 24 years and minimum 60). It is valid for thirty days in coach class and can be used for 12 days. Another more expensive version (Can$ 654-493 and 604-463) includes 3 days with a Hertz rental car and 12 days travel in the VIA 1 class, which includes snacks, drinks and a three-course meal. VIA 1 runs along the "Corridor," from Windsor to Québec City.

Airplane travel is ideal when it comes to rapid transit throughout the huge country. Numerous small companies run local services at astonishingly low rates. Travel agents should be able to help out. Air Canada offers several flying passes using a coupon system. If intending to do a lot of travel, this could be good value. The passes must be purchased at your country of origin.

Canadian International Airways has a very dense network of flights throughout the country even to such remote places as Repulse Bay, Goose Bayand Churchill. For reservations and information: 1-800-665-1177.

Ferries

To get to Prince Edward Island you can take two different routes. **Marine Atlantic** connects Cape Tormentine, New Brunswick, with Borden (1-902-855-2030); Northumberland Ferries connects Caribou, Nova Scotia, with Woods Islands (1-800-565-0201). Both ferries run year round, but you should check in the off-season and make reservations during the high season, especially if coming by car.

Marine Atlantic also provides service from North Sydney, Nova Scotia, to Port-aux-Basques and Argentia (in summer), Newfoundland. Call 1-902-564-3418 (North Sydney), 1-709-695-2124 (Port-aux-Basques); 1-709-227-2311 (Argentia)

PRACTICAL INFORMATION

Accommodations

Canada is by no means short of places to stay for the night, and all price categories are represented. The large hotel chains have penetrated the country from end to end, and you can easily make reservations well in advance in your country of origin (Best Western, Hilton, Holiday Inn, Hyatt, Novotel, Ramada, Sheraton, TravelLodge, etc...). There are also many smaller hotels and privately run ones that offer excellent accommodation often at reasonable prices.

Along the major roads and in some of the livelier areas one finds well-tended motels offering basic accommodations. Sometimes the amenities will be a little better (you might have a swimmingpool or a mini-golf), and the price goes up accordingly. The bed-and-breakfast scene has experienced considerable growth these past years. Staying in a private home, enjoying breakfast in familial surroundings, and feeling somehow cared for is one of the most pleasant aspects of this kind of accommodation. The prices range considerably. Inexpensive are youth hostels, of course, and staying at universities during the summer breaks. The best way is to inquire with the local tourist offices. The Canadian Hostelling Association, 333 River Rd., Tower A3, Vanier City Ottawa has more information on youth hostels.

If planning to travel in touristically well-trodden regions, such as the Laurentides, make reservations ahead of time. Even in the larger cities it can be difficult to find accommodations during the high tourist season or if a convention or trade fare is taking place. Graduation time in May also means capacity crowds in the university towns.

Camping is a favorite way to go. Quite a number of campgrounds in Canada are run by the government, particularly in the National Parks. The grounds are generally well kept. Each spot is equipped with table and chairs and a place for a camp fire. Supplies, including firewood and charcoal, can usually be bought at the campsite's store or from privateers in the neighborhood. In spite of the size of the country, even campgrounds can become filled up during the high season. Therefore if looking for a place either telephone in advance or start looking early. Each province publishes a camping guide available free of charge from a branch of the local tourist office.

Automobile club

For all questions concerning driving in Canada, contact the **Canada Automobile Association**, 1775 Courwood Crescent, Ottawa, Ontario, K2C 3J2.

Auto rentals

Renting a car in Canada is fairly inexpensive when compared, say, to Europe. All major rental companies (Avis, Budget, Hertz, National, Dollar, Rent-a-Wreck and Tilden) are represented in cities and some towns.

If shopping around for good value try out the local agencies. The best way is using the Yellow Pages and the telephone. Make sure all taxes are included in the offer. One-way rentals can be expensive, so plan a round trip with the car. Another tip on how to save money, especially when it comes to motorhomes and campers, is to rent from your country of origin. For cars the driver must be at least 21 years of age. For motorhomes and campers the age limit is 25. The overwhelming majority of rental agencies will only take credit cards! Checks and even cash – surprisingly enough – are seldom if ever accepted.

Banks

Banks are generally open from 10 am to 3 pm Monday through Thursday, and from 10 am to 6 pm on Fridays. Some banks open up on Saturday mornings. Drive through tellers are common, and the majority of banks have automatic tellers that are open 24 hours for debit or credit card business.

Business hours

Stores usually stay open from 9 am to 7 pm on Mondays and Tuesdays and from 9 am to 9 pm from Wednesday to Friday, and from 9 am to 5 pm on Saturdays. Some even open on Sundays or keep longer hours in the areas where tourism is heavier.

Electricity

Canada, like the USA, runs on 110 Volts, 60-cycle AC power, with American-type plugs. Visitors from Europe should either bring an adaptor or purchase one in Canada at an electrical appliance store. Many appliances nowadays have 110-220 switches, and laptop trans-

GUIDELINES

formers automatically take 110 Volts, but it is wise to check your manual beforehand.

Embassies and Consulates

AUSTRALIA, High Commission, 50 O'Connor St., Suite 710, Ottawa, Ontario K1P 6L2, Tel: 613/236-0841, Fax: 236-4376. **BRITAIN**, High Commision, 80 Elgin St., Ottawa, Ontario K1N 6M8, Tel: 237-1090, Fax: 237-7980. **NEW ZEALAND**, Metropolitan House, 99 Bank St., Suite 727, Ottawa, Ontario K1P 6G3, Tel: 238-5991, Fax: 238-5707. **SOUTH AFRICA**, Embassy, 15 Sussex Dr., Ottawa, Ontario K1M 1M8, Tel: 744-0330, Fax: 741-1639. **USA**, Embassy, 100 Wellington St., PO Box 866, Ottawa, Ontario K1P 5T1, Tel: 238-5335, Fax: 238-8750. Consular Section, 85 Albert St., Ottawa, Ontario, Tel: 238-5335.

Emergencies

The telephone number to remember is 911, which connects you to the police, fire department, medical services, etc... If in need of a hospital or the like, dial 0 for the operator.

Post Offices

Opening hours for post ofices is generally 9 am to 6 pm, Monday through Friday, and Saturday mornings. In cities some post offices will even open on Sundays and holidays. Stamps are available in stamp machines and in some shops.

Public Holidays

The federal system governing Canada means that there are two sets of public holidays, national and provincial. Some dates are permanent, and others are arranged in such a way as to provide Canadians with a long weekend.
New Year: January 1

Good Friday and **Easter Monday**: End of March or beginning of April
Victoria Day: On the Monday closest to May 25
Canada Day: July 1
Labor Day: First Monday in September
Thanksgiving Day: Second Monday in October
Remembrance Day: November 11
Christmas Day and **Boxing Day**: December 25 and 26

In addition to these, Newfoundland and Labrador mark several other holidays:
St. Patrick's Day: Monday nearest March 17
St. George's Day: Monday nearest April 24
Discovery Day: Monday nearest June 25
Memorial Day: Beginning of July
Orangeman's Day: Monday closest to July 10

New Brunswick celebrates **New Brunswick Day** on the Monday closest to August 5. And the twin cities of Halifax and Dartmouth (Nova Scotia) celebrate **Natal Day**, their common birthday, on August 2.

Telecomunications

The system in Canada is similar to the American one. Telephone numbers have seven digits. When calling to another province or another area code, you will have to find out the area code. To get directory assistance dial 1-555-1212. Directory assistance in another area code is 1-area code-555-1212. There is a charge for this service.

Area codes for Canada East:
Southwest Ontario	514
Toronto	416
Ottawa and eastern Ontario	613
Montréal	514
Québec City	418
New Brunswick and Gaspé	506
Nova Scotia	902
Prince Edward Island	902
Newfoundland and Labrador	709

GUIDELINES

Coin-operated public telephones are readily available on the street, in supermarkets, gas stations, restaurants, but not at post offices. For local calls use quarters. For long distance calls use a credit card (dial 0 and then your number; an operator will come on the line) or one of the many available phone cards. The latter often provide cheaper service. To avoid sometimes massive surcharges in hotels, use your phone card as well. If need be you can also call and reverse the charges by dialing 1-800-465-0049, or dial 0 for the operator. Telegrams can be sent either by telephone or at the nearest office of CN/CP Telegraph company.

Time Zones

Eastern Canada has four time zones:
- Central Standard Time (CST): Far western Ontario.
- Eastern Standard Time (EST): Rest of Ontario, most of Québec and Western New Brunswick.
- Atlantic Standard Time (AST): Eastern New Brunswick, Nova Scotia, Prince Edward Island, Eastern Labrador and far eastern Québec.
- Newfoundland Standard Time (NST): Newfoundland Island
- Midnight CST is: 1 am EST, 2 am AST, and 2:30 am NST, 6 am GMT.

Daylight Saving Time (when watches are turned ahead by one hour) begins on the first Sunday in April and ends on the last Sunday in October.

Tipping

As in America tips are for the most part not included in restaurant bills. 10 to 15 percent over the sum is usual. Waitpersons are paid below minimum wage as it is expected that they will be earning from the tips, a fact to keep in mind when tipping. Cab drivers, bellboys, hairdressers, porters and the like should be tipped at the customer's discretion.

Weights and Measures

Canada operates on the metric system which can be difficult for those used to the vagaries of Anglo-saxon weighing and measuring. By the same token, computing in ones head while on what appears to be an endless drive is one way of passing time if the excitement about the landscape is letting up a little.

Metric Imperial
1 kilometer . . . . 0,62 miles
1.6 kilometers . . . . 1 mile
1 meter . . . . . . 3.28 feet (1.09 yards)
1 centimeter . . . . 0.39 inches
1 sq. kilometer . . . . . 0.386 sq. miles
1 sq. meter . . . . 10.76 sq. feet
1 hectare . . . . 2.47 acres
1 ton . . . . 1.1 tons (USA)
         0.984 tons (British)
1 kilogram . . . . 2.2 pounds
1 liter . 0.264 gallons or 2.1 pints (USA)
      0.22 gallons or 1.7 pints (British)

QUÉBEC SPECIAL

When driving through Québec you must remember you are basically in a French-speaking country. Furthermore, they also speak a 17th century French dialect interspersed with American words; referred to somewhat disparagingly as *joual*, a misformed pronunciation of the word *cheval* meaning horse. Some say Québecois is merely an old-fashioned version of French. And indeed the occurence of English words in the language to express modern items (clutch, truck), does support this view. At any rate French Canadians are proud of their heritage, their language, their dialects, and anyone who has studied French at some time will find it most enjoyable to listen to. Many Francophone Québecois do speak English, but it does bridge cultures to try your hand at the host language, and secondly road signs are often in French only. Pictograms are of course helpful, but what do you do when you see the words "priorité de vir-

247

GUIDELINES

age au clignotement du feu vert?" It means "Turn on flashing green light."

On the road

arrêt	stop
gauche	left
droite	right
nord	north
sud	south
est	east
ouest	west
sens unique	one way
cul-de-sac	dead end
rue barrée	street closed
chemin à accès limité	restricted road
stationnement	parking
entrée interdite	no entry
ligne d'arrêt	stop line
fin des voies rapides	highway ends
(prochaine) sortie	(next) exit
passage à niveau	level crossing
cédez	yield
piéton	pedestrian
interdit or prohibé	prohibited

Speaking of driving: parking signs in Québec are a challenge even for the hardened locals. Times are written in 24-hour notation. A red circle indicates that parking is prohibited during certain hours and perhaps even certain days (lun.-ven. means Monday to Friday). A green circle with the same information plus a "30 M" would mean that you can park for a maximum of 30 minutes during business hours.

Everyday language

oui/non	yes/no
s'il vous plait	please
merci	thank you
bonjour	hello
salut	hi!
bonsoir	good evening
bonne nuit	good night
au revoir	good bye
excusez-moi	excuse me
pardon	pardon me

Parlez-vous anglais?	Do you speak English
Ou est...?	Where is...?
la poste	the post office
l'arrêt d'autobus	the bus stop
la gare	the train station
l'hôpital	the hospital
la police	the police
au secours!	help!
Quel heure est-il?	What time is it?
Laissez moi tranquille!	Leave me alone!

Restaurants and hotels:

une table non-fumeurs	a non-smoking table
pour deux (trois, quatre)	for two (three, four)
une chambre (double)	a (double occupancy) room
avec douche	with a shower
Petit déjeûner	breakfast
Déjeûner	lunch
diner	dinner
casse-croûte	snack
garçon	waiter
couteau	knife
fourchette	fork
cuillère	spoon
verre	glass
l'addition	the bill
pourboire	tip
c'est service compris?	Is the service included?

AUTHORS

Eva Ambros, project editor and author of *Nelles Guide Egypt*, spent twelve years working as a guide for study tours in Egypt. She is currently living in Munich, where she works as a free-lance writer and editor. She is one of the Project Editors of *Nelles Guide Canada*.

Mary Kelly is a communication consultant, editor and writer based in Montréal, Canada. She has written extensively about the province of Québec for such interntional travel guidebook pub-

AUTHORS / PHOTOGRAPHERS

lishers as Fodors, Viking Penguin, Berlitz as well as for numerous Canadian magazines and newspapers. For the *Nelles Guide Canada* she wrote the articles about *Toronto*, *Montreal*, *Québec* and *Québec Province*.

Eleanor Morris lives as a writer and photographer in Austin, Texas. She is the author of Recommended Country Inns of the Southwest: Arizona, New Mexico And Texas. For the *Nelles Guide Canada* she wrote the articles about *History*, *New Brunswick*, *Nova Scotia*, and *Halifax*.

Valentin P. Nadezhnikov is a free-lance writer who lives and works out of a campmobile that allows him to "always be where the sun is shining." He was born of Russian parents in Calgary in 1937, studied astronomy and anthropology before devoting himself to traveling and travel writing. He is one of the Project Editors of *Nelles Guide Canada* and co-author to the articles about *Ottawa*, *Québec Province* and *Nova Scotia*.

David Ravvin is a free-lance writer living in Toronto. He has written for the theatre, TV, advertising, and journalism. For the *Nelles Guide Canada* he wrote the articles about *Geography*, and *Ontario* and the features *Nature Parks*, *Economy*, *Environment*, *Ice Hockey*, and *Baffin Island*.

J.-Martina Schneider is an editor and author of works of non-fiction. She wrote the feature *The Cree Way of Life*.

Jonathan D. Siskin is a free-lance writer living in New York. He is the author of the articles about *Prince Edward Island*, *Newfoundland* and *Labrador*.

Carla Straessle-Compton is a travel writer and editor from Toronto. She was a co-author to the article about *Toronto*.

Deborah Williams is a former newspaper reporter and editor. She has traveled for more than twenty years in the Caribbean, Canada and the U.S.A. Her work has appeared in a wide variety of books, magazines and newspapers in the United States and Canada. She also contributed chapters to the *Nelles Guides The Caribbean* and *New York*. For Nelles Guide Canada she wrote the article about *Ottawa*.

PHOTOGRAPHERS

Archiv für Kunst und Geschichte, Berlin 20, 21, 30
Bersick, Gerhard, Prof. 19, 22 l, 22 r, 29, 41, 42, 48, 81, 86, 122, 126, 166, 229, 230
Braunger, Manfred 25, 26, 44/45, 64, 69, 83, 94, 95, 150, 153, 165, 170, 174, 180, 186, 200/201, 206, 207, 211, 212, 213, 220, 231
Hayes, Danielle B. 187, 188, 198
Janicke, Volkmar E. 16, 51, 202
Kalmár, János 37, 54, 60, 78, 85, 89, 90, 226, 238, 239
Kienas, Falk 31, 68
Lange, G. 136, 182, 183, 184, 194, 225, 233, 237 l, 237 r
Ministère du Tourisme du Québec :
- **Bognar**, Tibor 105
- **Boutin**, Jocelyn 137, 139
- **Chalifour**, Benoît 134, 140
- **Désilets**, Antoine 221, 223
- **Desjardins**, Daniel 91
- **Dorval**, Didier 141
- **Dumas**, Alain 144
- **Edgar**, Robin 148
- **Gascon**, Michel 18
- **Georgi**, Henry 147
- **Gignac**, Marcel 34, 88, 214
- **Majeau**, Sylvain 15, 80, 152, 156/157, 158, 192, 216/217, 222
- **Renaud**, Marc 106, 111, 113, 143, 145
- **Zimbell**, George S. 138
Mosler, Axel 1, 8/9, 10/11, 14, 27, 32, 39, 40, 43, 57, 59, 61, 70, 74, 84, 92, 93, 104, 108, 116/117, 118, 120, 124, 125, 128, 130, 135, 163, 168/169, 176, 177, 178, 190/191, 196, 218/219, 224, 227, 232, 235
Stankiewicz, Thomas Cover, 46/47, 50, 55, 56, 72, 100/101, 109, 162
Wagner, Heike & Bernd Backcover, 12, 66, 79, 123, 209, 210.

INDEX

A

Abram-Village 195
Acadia 21-25, 159, 171
Acadian Coast 159, **164-166**
Acadian Peninsula 164, 165
Acadians 25, 26, 164, 165, 172, 173, 175, 178, 193, 195, 205
Acadian Trail 176
Alberton 195
Algonquin 19, 21, 23, 94, 119, 150, 236
Algonquin Island 52
Algonquin Provincial Park 75, 88, **92-93**
Alliston 86
American Revolution 26, 49, 82, 162, 181
Amherst 174
Anglo-Canadians 32, 36, 65, 104
Annapolis Royal 171, 173
Antigonish 175
Argentia 212
Arichat 178
Arisaig Park 174
Athabaska, Indian tribe 19
Atholville 166
Atlantic Provinces 13, 15, 28, 181
Atwood, Margaret 13
Auyuittuq National Park 225, 235
Avalon Peninsula 206, 208, 212
Awenda Provincial Park 85
Ayer's Cliff 134

B

Baddeck 175, 177
Baffin Island 18, **234-235**
Baie Comeau 151
Baie de Gaspé 153
Baie des Chaleurs 152, 164-166
Bala 89
Baldwin Animal Reserve 152
Ball's Falls 83
Barrie 86, 88, 97
Basin Head 198
Basses Laurentides 141
Bass Provincial Park 88
Bathurst 165, 166
Bay Bulls 208
Baysville 91, 92
Beamer Mem. Conserv. Area 83
Beausoleil Island 87
Beaverbrook, Lord William 162
Bedford 181
Belfast 198
Beothuk, Indian tribe 19, 20
Bertrand 165
Big Intervale 176
Birkendale 91
Blacks Harbour 163
Bloc Québécois 33, 42

Blueberry Plains Trail 86
Blue Heron Drive 194, 196, 197
Boiestown 164
Bonavista 209, 210
Bracebridge 90, 91
Bras d'Or Lake 175
Brighton 95
British 24-27, 26-32, 35, 36, 38, 40, 49, 50, 79, 82, 119, 121, 125, 126, 142, 171, 177, 181, 193, 195, 197, 206, 207, 208
British North America 26-31, 133
British North America Act 41, 43, 122
Brock, Isaac, General 84
Brockville 75, 93, 95
Bromont 135
Browns Brae 91
Bruce County 75-79
Bruce Island National Park, 79, 80
Bruce Peninsula 14, 75, **79-82**
Bruce Peninsula National Park 80, 81
Bruce Trail 79, 80, 81, 83
Burin Peninsula 210
Burleigh Falls 94
By, John, Colonel 66, 69
Bylot Island 235
Bytown 65, 66

C

Cabot, John 19, 20, 107, 175, 176, 206, 208, 209, 212
Cabot Landing 176
Caboto, Giovanni see Cabot, John
Cabot Trail 175-177, 178
Calumet 149
Campbellton 166
Campobello Island 163
Canadian Shield 13, 14, 75, 89, 92, 96, 131, 234
Canso Causeway 174
Cap Bateau 165
Cape Bonavista 209
Cape Breton 24, 171
Cape Breton Highlands National Park 175, 176, 224
Cape Breton Island 20, 174, 175, 181, 182
Cape Breton Trails 177-178
Cape Croker Indian Reserve 80
Cape Dorset 235
Cape Fourchu 172
Cape North 176
Cape Sable Island 171
Cape Smokey 175
Cape Spear Nat. Hist. Park 208
Cartier, Jacques 21, 23, 39, 107, 112, 125, 153, 166, 175, 193, 195, 203, 206

Castle Hill Nat. Hist. Park 208
Caughnawaga, Indian tribe 90
Cavendish 196
Cedar Dunes Prov. Park 194
Ceilidh Trail 178
Centre Island 52
Centreville 171
Champlain, Samuel de 21, 22, 23, 39, 65, 70, 93, 107, 121, 125, 126, 163, 172, 181, 193
Charlevoix 132, 150, 151
Charlo 166
Charlottetown 193, 197
  Beaconsfield Mansion 197
  Confederation Ctr. of the Arts 197
  Fort Edward 197
  PEI Museum and Heritage Foundation 197
Charlottetown Accord 33, 41, 42, 43, 103
Chatham 164
Chemin du Roi 151
Cheticamp 176
Chic-Choc Animal Reserve 152
Chic-Choc Mountains 152
Chicoutimi 152
Chomedey, Paul de, Sieur de Maisonneuve 105, 112
Chrétien, Jean, Prime Minister 33
Churchill Falls 213, 214
Church Point 172
Chutes de Montmorency 151
Coaticook 139, 140
Cobourg 93
Cochrane 97
Collingwood 77, 85
Columbus, Christopher 19, 107
Cookshire 134
Cookstown 86
Corner Brook 203
Cornwallis, Edward, Colonel 181
Craigleith Provincial Park 77
Cree Way of Life 236-239
Crosby 96
Crystal Beach 85
Cyprus Lake 81

D

Dalhousie 166
Dalvay 196
Dartmouth 181, 183, **187-188**
Dee Bank Falls 91
Deer Island 163
Dewey Soper Bird Sanctuary 235
Digby 173
Dingwall 176
Doaktown 164
Dorcas Bay Nature Reserve 81
Dorchester 164
Dorset 91
Douglastown 164

INDEX

Dunière Animal Reserve 152

E

Earl Rowe Provincial Park 86
Edmundston 161
Elgin 96
Elizabeth II, Queen 33
Escoumins 151
Escuminac 164
Evangeline Trail 172

F

Fathom Five National Marine Park 79, 81
Five Islands Provincial Park 174
Fleur-de-Lis Trail 178
Flowerpot Island 82
Forillon National Park 153, 222
Fort Amherst 197
Fort Bonséjour N. P. 165
Forteau 214
Fort Edward Nat.Hist. Site 174
Fort Erie 84
Fort McNab 187
Four Falls 161
Franciscans 22, 39, 119, 124
Fredericton 161, 162
French 19, 22-28, 31, 35, 38, 40, 49, 119, 121, 126, 142, 159, 171, 175, 181, 197, 206-208, 236
French Canadians 25, 28, 31, 33, 35, 36, 65, 104, 133, 142
Front de Libération du Québec (FLQ) 32
Frontenac, Governor 141
Fundy National Park 163, 223
Fundy Tidal Coast 159, **162-164**

G

Gananoque 95
Gaspé 153
  Cathedral 153
  Croix de Gaspé 153
  Musée de Gaspé 153
Gaspé National Park 152
Gaspé Peninsula 15, 21, 132, **151-153**
Gaspésie see Gaspé Peninsula
Gaulle, Charles de 32, 106
Georgian Bay 14, 77, 79, 80, 85, 86, 88, 94, 96, 97
Georgian Bay Islands National Park 87
Glace Bay 177
Glen Orchard 90
Glooscap Trail **173-174**
Goat Island 61
Goose Bay 213, 214

Granby 133
Grand Etang 177
Grand Falls 161, 203
Grand Manan Island 163
Grand Pré 172, 173
Grand Sault 161
Grande Vallée 153
Gravenhurst 88, 89
Great Lakes 13-15, 19, 31, 49, 65
Green Provincial Park 195
Grey County **75-79**
Gros Morne Nat. Park 211, 224
Gulf of St. Lawrence 166, 175, 193, 196, 203
Gull Lake Park 89

H

Halifax **181-189**
  Army Museum 186
  Citadel Hill 186-187
  Citadel Nat. Historic Park 186
  Dalhousie Art Gallery 188
  Fort Needham 182, 187
  Historic Properties on the Harbour 182
  Maritime Museum 182, 183
  Martello Tower 185
  Nova Scotia Centre for Craft and Design 188
  Nova Scotia Museum 186
  Old Burying Ground 186
  Old City Hall 184
  Police Museum 187
  Province House 184
  St. George's Anglican Church 185
  St. Pauls Anglican Church 184
Hamilton 83
Hanlan's Point Island 52
Hartland 161
Hautes Laurentides 141, **143-150**
Havre-St-Pierre 151
Hearst 97
Hillsborough 164
Hopewell Cape 163, 165
Horse Lake Trail 81
Huckleberry Rock Cut 90
Hudson Bay 13, 18, 19, 24
Hull 65, 68, 69,71
  Canadian Mus. of Civilization 71
  Chaudière-Falls 65, 71
  Children's Museum 71
  Gatineau Exhibition Centre 71
  Green Island 71
  Jacques Cartier Park 71
  Leamy Lake Ecological Park 71
  Maison du Citoyen 71
  Rideau Falls 71
  Saint-François-de-Sales 71
  Sentier de Portage 71
Huronia **85-88**, 88, 97
Hurons 20, 21, 23, 24, 49

I

Île Bonaventure 153
Île-des-Moulins 141
Île d'Orléans 129
Indians 17, **18-20**, 22, 25, 33, 35, 37, 49, 103, 159, 212, 239
Indian Wars 23-24
Ingonish 175
Inuit **17-18**, 19, 33, 35, 37, 205, 213, 230, 234, 235, 239
Inuit culture 17, 18
Iqualuit 234, 235
Irish 36, 40, 66, 110, 112, 159, 164, 193
Iroquois 19, 20, 24, 75, 87, 112
  Cayuga 20
  Mohawk 20, 23, 90, 103
  Oneida 20
  Onondaga 20, 23
  Seneca 20
  Tuscarora 20
Iroquois Falls 97
Isle Madame 178

J

Jacques Cartier Prov. Park 195
James Bay 97, 132, 236
Jardins de la République Provincial Park 159
Jeddore 178
Jesuits 22, 24, 39, 87, 119
Joggins 174

K

Kapuskasing 97
Katannilil Territorial Park Reserve 235
Kawartha Lakes 93, 94
Kedgwick 166
Keene 94
Kejimkujik National Park 173, 223
Kekerton 235
Killarney Park 97
Kimberley 77
Kincardine 78
King, Mackinzie 68
Kings Byway 194198
Kings Landing Historical Settlement 161
Kingston 75, 95, 96
Kirkland Lake 97
Kleinburg
  Kortright Centre for Conservation 61
  McMichael Gallery 61
Knowlton 135, 136
Kouchibouguac National Park 164, 222

251

INDEX

L

La Mauricie National Park 221
Labrador 13, 15, 203, **213-214**
Labrador City 213, 214
Lac Baker 161
Lac Brome 136
Lac Claude 146
Lac-des-Deux-Montagnes 142
Lac des Sables 149
Lac Lafontaine 146
Lac Massawippi 133, 139
Lac Mégantic 133, 140
Lac Memphrémagog 133, 136, 137
Lac St. Jean 152
Lac Tremblant 149
Lady Slipper Drive 194, 195
Lake Erie 14, 20, 23, 61, 82, 85
Lake Harbour 234, 235
Lake Huron 14, 23, 75, 78, 79, 96
Lake Muskoka 89, 90
Lake Nipigon 97
Lake Nipissing 97
Lake of Bays 89
Lake of Bays Circle Tour 91, 92
Lake of Bays Park 91
Lake of The Woods 97
Lake Ontario 14, 20, 51, 55, 61, 82, 83, 93, 94, 95
Lake Rice 93, 94
Lake Rousseau 88, 89, 90
Lake Simcoe 85, 86, 87, 93
Lake Superior 96
Lake Superior Park 97
Lakefield 94
L'Anse aux Meadows 20, 212
L'Anse aux Meadows National Historic Park 211
Laurentians see Les Laurentides
Laurier, Sir Wilfried 68
Le Désert 151
Lennoxville 137, 138
  Bishop's University 138
  Centennial Theatre 138
  Consolidated Bathurst Theatre 138
  Uplands Museum Park 139
Le Paradis des Animaux 165
Lesage, Jean 31
Les Laurentides 13, 132, **141-150**
L'Estrie 132, **133-140**
Les Trois Pignons 176
Letete 163
Lighthouse Trail 171
Lockeport 172
Lodge Bay 214
Loggieville 164
Lord Selkirk Provincial Park 198
Louisbourg, fortress 24, 25, 177, 181
Loyalists 49, 133, 136, 159, 161, 162, 163, 181
Lunenburg 172

M

Mabou Highlands 178
Macdonald, John A. 226
MacGregor Point Prov. Park 78
Mactaquac Provincial Park 161
Madawaska, Republic of 159
Magog 136, 137
  St.-Benoît-du-Lac 137
Manicouagan 151
Manitoulin Island 82
Maple Leaf Trail 146
Mara Provincial Park 88
Marconi National Site 177
Marconi Trail 177
Margaree 177
Marine Drive 178
Marsh's Falls 91
Mary's Harbour 214
Marystown 210
Massey, Vincent 30
Matane Animal Reserve 152
McNabs Island 183, 187
McRae Provincial Park 88
Meech Lake Accord 33, 43
Micmac, Indian tribe 19, 159, 164, 173, 175, 181, 187, 193, 197
Midland 87
Millbrook 94
Mingan Archipelago National Park 151, 222
Miramichi Basin 159, 164
Miscouche 196
Miscou Island 165
Mississauga, Indian tribe 82
Mizzy Lake Trail 93
Moncton 164
  Acadian Museum and Art Gallery 164
  Moncton Museum 164
  Université de Moncton 164
Montcalm, Louis-Joseph, General 38, 121, 122, 125
Mont Gabriel 146, 149
Mont Jacques-Cartier 152
Mont Mégantic Observatory 140
Mont Orford 135, 137
Mont-Rollant 149
Mont Ste-Anne 128
Mont St-Sauveur 145, 146
Mont Sutton 135
Mont Tremblant 128, 141, 145, 147, 150
Montgomery, Lucy Maud 196
Montgomery, Richard, General 105
Montréal 14, 15, 21, 24, 29, 32, 96, **103-115**, 132
  Aquarium de Montréal 107
  Cathédrale Marie-Reine-du-Monde 109
  Centre Canadien d'Architecture 109
  Château Ramezay 105
  City Hall 106
  Complexe Desjardins 108, 110
  Complexe Guy Fabreau 108
  David M. Stewart Museum 106
  Expotec 106
  Hôtel de Ville 105
  Images du Futur 106
  Jardin Botanique de Montréal 113
  Jean-Noel Desmarais Pavilion 111
  Marché Bonsecours 105
  McCord Museum of History 111
  McGill University 110
  Montréal Biodome 113
  Montréal Insectarium 113
  Mont Royal 105, 112
  Musée des Beaux-Arts 111
  Musée d'Art Contemporain 110
  Musée Historique Canadien 113
  Musée Juste pour Rire 110
  Notman Archives 111
  Notre-Dame Basilica 105
  Oratoire St-Joseph 105, 112
  Palais de Congrès 108
  Parc Mont Royal 112
  Place d'Armes 105
  Place des Arts 110
  Place Jacques Cartier 105, 106
  Pointe-à-Caillère Musée d'Archeologie et d'Histoire 105
  S. Bronfman Center for Arts 109
  Square Mile 110-112
  Stade Olympique 113
  Théâtre Paul Desmarais 109
  Théâtre St-Denis 110
  Vieux Montréal 104-107
  Vieux Port 104, 106
  Vieux Séminaire de St-Sulpice 105
  Ville Marie 105
  Ville Souterraine 108
Moore, Henry, sculptor 56, 59
Moose Factory 97
Moosonie 97
Morin Heights 145, 147
Mount Carleton Prov. Park 166
Mount Uniacke 173
Mulroney, Brian 42, 43, 119, 228
Murphy's Provincial Park 96
Murray Harbour 198
Muskoka 75, **88-93**, 96
Musquodoboit Harbour 178

N

National Parks 220-225
Neguac 165
Neil's Harbor 175
Nelson-Miramichi 164
Newash, Indian tribe 79
New Brunswick 15, 22, 25, 27, 28, **159-167**, 193
Newcastle 164
New Denmark 161

INDEX

Newfoundland 15, 19, 20, 28, 33, **203-213**
New France 22-24, 24, 25, 39, 121, 122, 124, 126, 127, 181
New London 196
New Lowell Conservation Area 86
Niagara Falls 15, 61, 79, 82, 84
Niagara Falls, city 82
Niagara-on-the-Lake 82, 83, 84
   Fort George Nat. Hist. Park 83
   Mahony Doll's House Gallery 83
Niagara Peninsula 83-85
Niagara River 61, 82, 83
Nipigon 97
North American Free Trade Agreement (NAFTA) 33, 228, 226
North Bay 97
North Hatley 137, 138
North Mountain 176
Northumberland Strait 164, 171, 174, 178, 193
Notre-Dame-des-Bois 140
Nottawasaga Bay 75, 77, 85, 87
Nova Scotia 15, 20, 22, 26, 28, **171-179**, 181, 193

O

Oka 143
   Abbaye Cistercienne d'Oka 143
   Ferme avicole d'Oka 143
   Parc Paul Sauve 143
Oka Calvary 142, 143
Olmsted, Frederick Law 112
Ontario, Central **93-96**
Ontario, East **93-96**
Ontario, North **96-97**
Ontario, Province 13, 14, 28, 29, 36, 49, **75-99**
Orford Regional Park 135
Orillia 88
Orwell Historic Village 198
Ottawa 65-73
   Agricultural Museum 71
   Basilica of Notre Dame 70
   Byward Market 70
   Canadian Ski Museum 70
   Central Experimental Farm 71
   Dow's Lake 71, 72
   Log Farm 71
   Major's Hill Park 69, 72
   Mile of History 69
   National Arts Centre 69
   National Gallery of Canada 70
   Nepean Point 70
   Nicholas Goal 69
   Old Commissariat 69
   Parliament Buildings 66
   Parliament Hill 66, 67, 68
   Peace Tower 69
   Rideau Canal 66, 69, 71
   Rideau Convent Chapel 70
   Royal Canadian Mint 71
   War Museum 71
Ottawa River 65, 66, 67, 68, 69, 71
Outauac, Indian tribe 65
Owen Sound 77
Owl's Head 135, 137

P

Pabineau Fall 166
Pangnirtung 235
Papineau-Labelle Wildlife Res. 143
Parc Régional de la Rivière du Nord 144
Parlee Beach Provincial Park 164
Passamaquaddy Bay 162
Peck Lake Trail 93
Peggy's Cove 172
Penetanguishene 87
Penobsquis 163
Percé 153
Perth 96
Perth Andover 161
Petite-Rivière de L'Île 165
Petit Etang 176
Petroglyphs Provincial Park 94
Pictou 175
Piedmont 145
Pinware 214
Placentia 208
Pleasant Bay 176
Point Clark 75, 85
Pointe-Verte 166
Point Pelee National Park 220
Point Prim 198
Polar Bear Provincial Park 97
Pomquet Beach Park 175
Port au Choix 212
Port au Choix Nat. Hist. Park 211
Port-aux-Basques 208, 212
Port Carling 90
Port Daniel 152
Port Elgin 78
Port-La-Joye National Park 197
Port Royal National Historic Site 22, 173
Presqu'île Point Prov. Park 95
Price Edward Island 28
Prince County 95, **194-195**
Prince Edward Island 15, **193-199**
   Blooming Point 196
   Brackley Marsh 197
   Green Gables Farmhouse 196
   Stanhope Beach 196
Prince Edward Is. N. P. 196, 223
Pukaskwa National Park 97, 220

Q

Quarry Point 177
Quaummarviit Hist. Park 234
Québec Act 26, 36, 40
Québec City 119-129, 132
   Agora Vieux-Port Amphitheater 127
   Ancien Palais de Justice 124
   Assemblée Nationale Hôtel du Parlement 125
   Baillairgé Pavilion 122
   Basse Ville 119, 126-127
   Cap Diamant 119, 121, 123
   Citadelle 121, 123
   Escalier Casse-Cou 126, 127
   Gérard-Morisset Pavilion 122
   Grand Théâtre de Québec 127
   Haute Ville 119, 121-126
   Holy Trinity Cathedral 125
   Maison Louis-Jolliet 126
   Musée de la Civilisation 127
   Musée du Québec 122
   Musée et Chapelle des Ursulines 122
   Musée Historique du Cire 122
   Notre-Dame-de-Québec 120
   Notre-Dame-des-Victoires 126
   Palais Montcalm 128
   Plains of Abraham 38, 122-123
   Quartier Petit Champlain 126, 127
   Royal 22e Regiment Museum 123
   Séminaire de Québec 119
   Théâtre Capitole 128
   Théâtre Repère 120
   Université Laval 119
   Vieux Port 126, 127
   Vieux Québec 119
Québec, Province 13, 14, 22, 26-32, 36-40, 41, 65, **131-155**
Queens County 196-197
Queenston 79, 84
Queenston Heights 84
Quetico Park 97
Quidi Vici 208

R

Ramezay, Claude de, Governor 105
Red Bay 213
Rèserve Faunique de la Petite Cascapédia 152
Restigouche Uplands 159, 166
Riverside-Albert 164
Rivière-au-Renard 153
Rivière du Nord 143
Rivière Rouge 149
Rivière Verte 161
Rocky Point 197
Rogersville 164
Rouge River 60
Rustico Island 196

S

Saguenay River 23, 151, 152
Saint Basile 161
Saint Jacques 159

INDEX

Saint John 163
Saint John Baptistede Restigouche 166
Saint John River 159, 161, 163
Saint John River Valley 159-162
Saint-Leonard 161, 166
Saint-Quentin 166
Saint-Tites-des-Caps 151
St. Andrews 162
St. Ann 175
St-Eustache 142
St. George 162
St. George's Bay 178
St-Jérôme 143, 144
St. John's 203, **206-208**, 212
  Cabot Tower 208
  Church of St. Thomas 207
  Commissariat House 207
  Gibbet Hill 208
  Newfoundland Museum 207
  Signal Hill Nat. Hist. Park 207
  St. John the Baptist, Cathedral 207
  St. John the Baptist, Basilica 207
St. Lawrence Islands Nat. Park 221
St. Lawrence Lowlands 13, 14, 15, 131
St. Lawrence River 13, 21, 22, 75, 93, 95, 103, 104, 119, 123, **150-153**
St. Mary's Bay 172
St. Peters 178
St-Sauveur 145
St-Sauveur-des-Monts 145, 146
St. Stephan 162
Ste-Adèle 146, 148
Ste-Agathe 150
Ste-Agathe-des-Monts 145, 149
Ste.-Anne-de Beaupré 128
Ste-Marguerite-du-Lac-Masson 149
Ste-Marguerite-Station 145
Ste-Marie-Ste-Raphael 165
Ste-Scholastique 142
Saugeen Indian Reserve 79
Scots 36, 40, 78, 110, 112, 159, 164, 171, 174, 175, 193, 198
Seigneurerie du Lac-des-Deux-Montagnes 141, 142
Selkirk Provincial Park 85
Sept-Îles 151
Serpent Mounds Prov. Park 94
Shawbridge 146
Shediac 164
Shelburne 172
Sherbrooke 134, 136
Sherbrooke, Sir John Coape 136
Sherbrooke Village 178
Shippagan 165
Shipsands Islands Waterfowl Sanctuary 97
Simcoe County see Huronia
Skeleton Bay 90
Skiing 128, 133, 134, 135, 140, 141, 144, 146, 147, 150

Smith Falls 96
Soper River Valley 234
Souris 198
Southampton 78
Springhill 174
Stoneham 128
Stoney Lake 94
Stratford 61
Sudbury 97
Sugarloaf Provincial Park 166
Sulpicians 39, 105, 142
Sunrise Trail 174-175
Sussex 163
Sutton 135

T

Tabusintac 165
Tadoussac 23, 151
Terra Nova Nat. Park 210, 225
Terrebonne 141
Tetagouche Fall 166
Thornbury 77
Thousand Islands 95
Tobermory 79, 82
Toronto 14, 15, **49-63**
  Art Gallery of Ontario 59
  Beaches, cottage community 55
  Cabbagetown 58
  Canada's Wonderland 61
  Canadian National Exhibition 51
  Canadian Sports Hall of Fame 51
  Casa Loma 60
  Children's Village 51
  Chinatown 57, 59
  Cinesphere 51
  CN Tower 52
  Commerce Court 54
  Downtown 52-57
  Eaton Centre 56
  First Canadian Place 54
  Fort York 51
  George M. Gardiner Museum 59
  Hockey Hall of Fame 51
  Holy Trinity Church 57
  Jane Mallet Theatre 54
  Kensington Market 58
  Marine Museum of Upper Canada 51
  Metro Toronto Zoo 60
  Nathan Phillips Square 56
  New City Hall 55, 56
  O'Keefe Centre 54
  Old City Hall 55
  Old Parsonage 57
  Ontario Science Centre 59-60
  Pantages Theatre 57
  Parliament Building 59
  Premiere Dance Theatre 52
  Queen's Quay Terminal 51, 52
  Riverdale 57
  Riverdale Farm 58

  Royal Ontario Museum 58-59
  Royal York Hotel 53
  Saltwater Circus Theater 61
  Scadding House 57
  Skate Toronto 52
  Skydome 53
  St. Lawrence Market 54
  Toronto Dominion Centre 54
  University of Toronto 58
Toronto Islands 52
Tracadie 165
Trent Waterway System 93
Trinity 210
Trois-Rivières 150, 151
Trudeau, Pierre E. 33, 41, 227, 228
Truro 174
Twillingate 211

U

Ullswater 91

V

Valcourt 135
Val David 145
Valley Green Beach 90
Val Morin 145
Victoria-by-the-Sea 198
Victoria, Queen 65, 67
Vikings 19, 20, 212, 234
Village de Seraphin 149
Village du Mont-Castor 149
Village du Père Noël 149

W

Wabanaki, Indian tribe 139
Wabush 213
Ward's Island 52
Wasaga Beach Provincial Park 86
Wendat, Indian tribe 87
Westport 96
Wiarton 80
Wilson Falls 144
Windermere 91
Windsor 173, 174
Witless Bay Islands Ecological Reserve 208
Wolfe, James, General 25, 38, 121, 122, 125
Wolfville 173
World War One 29, 30, 181
World War Two 29, 30, 38, 49, 72, 182, 184, 227
Wright's Town 65

Y

Yarmouth 172
York 49, 50
York Redoubt Nat. Hist. Site 187

Explore the World
NELLES MAPS

AVAIBLABE TITLES

Afghanistan 1 : 1 500 000
Australia 1 : 4 000 000
Bangkok - *Greater Bangkok,
Bangkok City* 1 : 75 000 / 1 : 15 000
Burma → *Myanmar*
Caribbean Islands 1 *Bermuda,
Bahamas, Greater Antilles*
1 : 2 500 000
Caribbean Islands 2 *Lesser Antilles*
1 : 2 500 000
Central America 1 : 1 750 000
Colombia - Ecuador 1 : 2 500 000
Crete - Kreta 1 : 200 000
China 1 - *Northeastern*
1 : 1 500 000
China 2 - *Northern* 1 : 1 500 000
China 3 - *Central* 1 : 1 500 000
China 4 - *Southern* 1 : 1 500 000
Dominican Republic - Haiti
1 : 600 000
Egypt 1 : 2 500 000 / 1 : 750 000
Hawaiian Islands
1 : 330 000 / 1 : 125 000
Hawaiian Islands 1 *Kauai*
1 : 125 000
Hawaiian Islands 2 *Honolulu
- Oahu* 1 : 125 000
Hawaiian Islands 3 *Maui - Molokai
- Lanai* 1 : 125 000

Hawaiian Islands 4 *Hawaii, The
Big Island* 1 : 330 000 / 1 : 125 000
Himalaya 1 : 1 500 000
Hong Kong 1 : 22 500
Indian Subcontinent 1 : 4 000 000
India 1 - *Northern* 1 : 1 500 000
India 2 - *Western* 1 : 1 500 000
India 3 - *Eastern* 1 : 1 500 000
India 4 - *Southern* 1 : 1 500 000
India 5 - *Northeastern - Bangladesh*
1 : 1 500 000
Indonesia 1 : 4 000 000
Indonesia 1 *Sumatra* 1 : 1 500 000
Indonesia 2 *Java + Nusa Tenggara*
1 : 1 500 000
Indonesia 3 *Bali* 1 : 180 000
Indonesia 4 *Kalimantan*
1 : 1 500 000
Indonesia 5 *Java + Bali* 1 : 650 000
Indonesia 6 *Sulawesi* 1 : 1 500 000
Indonesia 7 *Irian Jaya + Maluku*
1 : 1 500 000
Jakarta 1 : 22 500
Japan 1 : 1 500 000
Kenya 1 : 1 100 000
Korea 1 : 1 500 000
Malaysia 1 : 1 500 000
West Malaysia 1 : 650 000
Manila 1 : 17 500

Mexico 1 : 2 500 000
Myanmar (Burma) 1 : 1 500 000
Nepal 1 : 500 000 / 1 : 1 500 000
Trekking Map *Khumbu Himal /
Solu Khumbu* 1 : 75 000
New Zealand 1 : 1 250 000
Pakistan 1 : 1 500 000
Peru - Ecuador 1 : 2 500 000
Philippines 1 : 1 500 000
Singapore 1 : 22 500
Southeast Asia 1 : 4 000 000
Sri Lanka 1 : 450 000
Tanzania - Rwanda, Burundi
1 : 1 500 000
Thailand 1 : 1 500 000
Taiwan 1 : 400 000
Uganda 1 : 700 000
Venezuela - Guyana, Suriname,
French Guiana 1 : 2 500 000
Vietnam, Laos, Cambodia
1 : 1 500 000

FORTHCOMING

South Pacific Islands
Trekking Map *Kathmandu Valley /
Helambu, Langtang* 1 : 75 000

*Nelles Maps in european top quality!
Relief mapping, kilometer charts and tourist attractions.
Always up-to-date!*

Explore the World

NELLES GUIDES

AVAILABLE TITLES

Australia
Bali / Lombok
Berlin and Potsdam
Brittany
California
  Las Vegas, Reno, Baja California
Cambodia / Laos
Canada
  Ontario, Québec, Atlantic Provinces
Canada
  The Rockies, Pacific, Prairie, and the Territories
Caribbean
  The Greater Antilles, Bermuda, Bahamas
Caribbean
  The Lesser Antilles
China – Hong Kong
Corsica
Crete
Cyprus
Egypt
Florida
Greece – *The Mainland*
Hawai'i
Hungary
India
  Northern, Northeastern and Central India
India – *Southern India*
Indonesia
  Sumatra, Java, Bali, Lombok, Sulawesi
Ireland
Israel - *with Excursions to Jordan*
Kenya
London, England and Wales
Malaysia
Mexico
Morocco
Moscow / St Petersburg
Munich
  Excursions to Castels, Lakes & Mountains
Nepal
New York – *City and State*
New Zealand
Paris
Philippines
Portugal
Prague / Czech Republic
Provence
Rome
Scotland
South Africa
South Pacific Islands
Spain – *Pyrenees, Atlantic Coast, Central Spain*
Spain
  Mediterranean Coast, Southern Spain, Balearic Islands
Sri Lanka
Syria – Lebanon
Tanzania
Thailand
Turkey
Tuscany
U.S.A.
  The East, Midwest and South
U.S.A.
  The West, Rockies and Texas
Vietnam

FORTHCOMING

Brazil
Croatia – *Adriatic Coast*
Myanmar (Burma)
Norway

Nelles Guides – authorative, informed and informative.
Always up-to-date, extensivley illustrated, and with first-rate relief maps.
256 pages, appr. 150 color photos, appr. 25 maps